W9-BRL-157

INSIGHT GUIDES

THE NETHERLANDS

www.insightguides.com/Netherlands

⊙ Walking Eye App

Your Insight Guide now includes a free app and eBook, dedicated to your chosen destination, all included for the same great price as before. They are available to download from the free Walking Eye container app in the App Store and Google Play. Simply download the Walking Eye container app to access the eBook and app dedicated to your purchased book. The app features an up-to-date A to Z of travel tips, information on events, activities and destination highlights, as well as hotel, restaurant and bar listings. See below for more information and how to download.

MULTIPLE DESTINATIONS AVAILABLE

Now that you've bought this book you can download the accompanying destination app and eBook for free. Inside the Walking Eye container app, you'll also find a whole range of other Insight Guides destination apps and eBooks, all available for purchase.

DEDICATED SEARCH OPTIONS

Use the different sections to browse the places of interest by category or region, or simply use the 'Around me' function to find places of interest nearby. You can then save your selected restaurants, bars and activities to your Favourites or share them with friends using email, Twitter and Facebook.

FREQUENTLY UPDATED LISTINGS

Restaurants, bars and hotels change all the time. To ensure you get the most out of your guide, the app features all of our favourites, as well as the latest openings, and is updated regularly. Simply update your app when you receive a notification to access the most current listings available.

Shopping in Oman still revolves around the traditional souks that can be found in every town in the country – most famously at Mutrah in Muscat, Salalah and Nizwa, which serve as showcases of traditional Omani craftsmanship and produce ranging from antique khanjars and Bedu jewellery to halwa, rose-water and frankincense. Muscat also boasts a number of modern malls, although these are rare elsewhere in the country.

TRAVEL TIPS & DESTINATION OVERVIEWS

The app also includes a complete A to Z of handy travel tips on everything from visa regulations to local etiquette. Plus, you'll find destination overviews on shopping, sport, the arts, local events, health, activities and more.

HOW TO DOWNLOAD THE WALKING EYE

Available on purchase of this guide only.
1. Visit our website: www.insightguides.com/walkingeye
2. Download the Walking Eye container app to your smartphone (this will give you access to both the destination app and the eBook)
3. Select the scanning module in the Walking Eye container app
4. Scan the QR code on this page – you will be asked to enter a verification word from the book as proof of purchase
5. Download your free destination app* and eBook for travel information on the go

* Other destination apps and eBooks are available for purchase separately or are free with the purchase of the Insight Guide book

Contents

THE BEST OF THE NETHERLANDS: TOP ATTRACTIONS

For a small country, the Netherlands packs in a wealth of attractions, including dynamic cities, artistic treasurehouses and many places to sample the country's distinctive historic and contemporary culture.

△ **Alkmaar cheese market**. From the first Friday of April to the first Friday of September, Alkmaar's morning cheese market is a 'must visit' for foodies and traditionalists. The epitome of Dutchness. See page 162.

△ **Van Gogh Museum**. The definitive collection of the late 19th-century Dutch artist's works, housed in a grand museum in Amsterdam's Museumplein. *Sunflowers*, painted in Arles in 1889, is not to be missed. See page 147.

▽ **Anne Frankhuis**. The Amsterdam house where the Jewish Frank family hid from the Nazis during World War II is a stark reminder of the still-prevalent horrors of racism and genocide. See page 141.

△ **Flowers**. The Netherlands' most famous export is best experienced at the daily Aalsmeer flower auction or the magnificent Keukenhof Gardens, a carpet of colour from March to mid-May. See page 103.

△ **The Hague.** The home of the Netherlands parliament gives a real sense of this country's international importance, from the International Court of Justice to the Golden Age art collection at the Mauritshuis. See page 167.

△ **The Wadden Islands.** Off the coast of Friesland, these five islands — Texel (famed for its sheep), Vlieland, Terschelling, Ameland and Schiermonnikoog — are the perfect place to get away from it all. See page 295.

▷ **Hoge Veluwe National Park.** The country's largest national park is not just a great place for walking, cycling and nature-watching but it also has a fantastic Van Gogh collection at the Kröller-Müller Museum. See page 254.

◁ **Euromast.** The view from this tower in Rotterdam gives those with a head for heights a fantastic overview of the country's second city, from Europe's largest port to the tallest building in the Netherlands. See page 188.

▽ **Zuiderzee Museum.** Great for kids, this rural/coastal life museum in Enkhuizen has both indoor and outdoor attractions including 130 rebuilt and relocated original buildings and a display of regional costumes. See page 271.

△ **Jheronimus Bosch Art Center.** Exploring the work of medieval fantasy artist Hieronymus Bosch, this museum in Den Bosch is the focus of attention in 2016 to mark the 500th anniversary of his death. See page 229.

THE BEST OF THE NETHERLANDS: EDITOR'S CHOICE

Relaxed canalside living, art from the Golden Age to Van Gogh, quirky festivities, Gothic churches, and cycle routes aplenty through town and country... Here, at a glance, are our recommendations for your visit.

Amsterdam's famous canals.

UNIQUE AMSTERDAM

Canals. Amsterdam's famous canals define the city; the 'Golden Bend' is a classic stretch of imposing gables reflected in still, green water. See page 146.

Red-light district. No other city tolerates the seamy side of life in quite the same way. Amsterdammers don't shock easily! See page 153.

Indonesian cuisine. A legacy of Dutch colonialism, restaurants in Amsterdam serve what is regarded as the finest Indonesian cuisine outside Indonesia itself. See page 109.

NEMO Science Center's Roof Terrrace. In fine weather, locals and tourists can be found playing chess, drinking coffee and enjoying the views. See page 131.

Hash, Marijuana and Hemp Museum. You might not want to try it but it's worth learning about the city's cannabis culture. See page 155.

WORLD-CLASS GALLERIES

Rijksmuseum, Amsterdam. Rembrandt's *The Night Watch* is the most famous work in this superlative collection, which also includes works by Vermeer and Van Gogh. See page 148.

Kröller-Müller Museum, Gelderland. A magnificent collection of modern art – Van Gogh, Mondrian et al – in a tranquil, rural setting. See page 254.

Mauritshuis, The Hague. An outstanding gallery of Dutch and Flemish masters, including Vermeer's *Girl with a Pearl Earring*. See page 170.

Boijmans van Beuningen Museum, Rotterdam. Originally two private collections, this museum takes visitors on a grand tour of Western art. See page 189.

Frans Hals Museum, Haarlem. Housed in a beautiful 17th-century building, this is an absorbing collection by a Golden Age master portraitist. See page 160.

In Amsterdam's red light district.

'The Nightwatch' at the Rijksmuseum.

OFF THE BEATEN TRACK

Orvelte, Drenthe. A show village with a difference, filled with ordinary, working people proud to be preserving their traditional crafts and skills. See page 280.
Walcheren, Zeeland. In the southwestern corner of the country is Walcheren island – a haven of long sandy beaches and dyke-protected dunes. See page 214.
Giethoorn, Overijssel. One of the loveliest villages in the east, set in a landscape of narrow waterways and thatched cottages. See page 261.
De Biesbosch. South of Rotterdam, the Biesbosch, or Reed Forest, is a shifting landscape of wetlands and marshes explorable by bike or boat. See page 222.
De Peel. Evocative region of bogs and marshes, near Van Gogh's home village of Nuenen, now preserved as peatland nature reserves. See page 231.

De Biesbosch.

MAGNIFICENT CHURCHES

Maastricht. The imposing churches of St Servaas and St Jan – one Romanesque, the other Gothic – stand side-by-side in the centre of Maastricht. See page 242.
Groningen. The 95-metre (311-ft) spire of the Martinikerk soars above this genial university town in the far-flung north. See page 284.
Gouda. Superb 16th-century stained glass adorns the Unesco-listed Gothic church of St Jan in this well-known, pretty market town. See page 196.
Utrecht. The 14th-century Domtoren with its 465 steps dominates Utrecht, rising to an incredible 112m (368 ft) above the flat landscape. See page 201.
's-Hertogenbosch. The cathedral of St Jan in the southern town of 'Den Bosch' boasts the country's greatest Gothic architecture. See page 225.

St Jan Cathedral, 's-Hertogenbosch .

TYPICALLY DUTCH

Edam. Just north of Amsterdam, this tiny old village – where the cheese comes from – is picture-perfect enough to eat. See page 162.
Leiden A medieval centre of culture and learning: home to the Netherlands' oldest university and imbued with a classic, timeless quality. See page 175.
Utrecht. This amiable 2,000-year-old car-free town enjoys a contrast between its lively student population and its antique appearance. See page 199.
Delft. As painted by Vermeer – and, seemingly, little changed since. Nieuwe Kerk contains the burial vault of the Dutch royal family. See page 179.
Maastricht. With its French and Flemish influences, this upmarket southern city gives a different slant on what is 'typically Dutch'. See page 240.

A sunny day in Utrecht.

Indulge in a glass of jenever.

BEST DRINKING DENS

Arendsnest, Amsterdam. On the Herengracht canal, this narrow pub with wood and brass décor specialises in Dutch beer. http://www.arendsnest.nl/

Wynand Fockinck, Amsterdam. This 17th-century *proeflokaal* in the red-light district is the ultimate spot to try *jenever* or 'Dutch gin'. http://wynand-fockink.nl/en

Jopenkerk, Haarlem. Housed in a former church, this microbrewery and bar is the perfect place to sample a 15th-century beer recipe. www.jopen kerk.nl/haarlem

SS Rotterdam, Rotterdam. The poolside terrace of a former 1950s cruiseliner is an elegant spot to enjoy a summer drink. http://ssrotterdam. com/restaurants-bars/lido-terrace/

Texelse Bierbrouwerij, Texel. Apart from the beer, the main reason to visit this micro-brewery is to sit on the seaside terrace. www.texels.nl

Grand Café, Groningen. Once a church, the high-ceilinged café and courtyard in Hotel Prinsenhof, a former monastery, offer a unique experience. http://grand cafegroningen.nl/

Walking on mud flats in Wadlopen.

QUIRKY AND UNUSUAL

Elfstedentocht. An all-day ice-skating endurance race between eleven towns in the north – only staged when the rivers and canals are frozen solid. See page 291.

Wadlopen. The 'sport' of *wadlopen*, or mud-wading (a guide is essential), is a mainstay of villages on the northern Waddenzee coast. See page 293.

De Efteling. The Netherlands' biggest, best and most popular theme park, is great fun for kids of all ages. See page 232.

Carnival Towns. Places such as Den Bosch and Bergen op Zoom in the Catholic south celebrate the pre-Lenten carnival with gusto. See page 233.

Rotterdam port tours. Board a supertanker-dodging craft for a glimpse of how Europe's largest port goes about its daily business. See page 190.

Delta Park, Zeeland. Fascinating exhibition telling the story of Zeeland's 2000-year struggle with the sea, through models and boat trips. See page 209.

Efteling theme park.

TOP CYCLING ROUTES

Het Twiske, near Amsterdam. An easy escape from the city is into the quiet Waterland area of the Het Twiske park. See page 150.
Arnhem Airborne. A 27-km (17-mile) route takes in the main sights of this famous battle including the John Frost Bridge. See page 258.
Texel South. A 38-km (24-mile) route takes cyclists on an exhilarating ride through the Dunes of Texel National Park. See page 295.
Vlissingen. Starting and ending at this far-south seaside resort, a 49-km (30-mile) route covers both coast and canal. See page 216.
Overijssel. In the east of the country, Overijssel offers some great back-country rides including the hills of Salland, near Deventer. See page 264

Back country cycling.

Waterlooplein market.

CASTLES AND STATELY HOMES

Kasteel Amerongen. This fascinating 16th-century castle in the Utrecht countryside was where Kaiser Wilhelm II signed his abdication in 1918. See page 205.
Paleis Het Loo, Apeldoorn. Bequeathed to the state by Queen Wilhelmina, this is perhaps the loveliest Dutch palace (with magnificent gardens). See page 259.
Valkenburg. Atop a wooded hill near Maastricht rises this splendid, semi-ruined (thanks to the Spanish and French) 12th-century fortress. See page 238.
Paleis Noordeinde. One of three official royal palaces, Noordeinde in The Hague is the 'working' residence of King Willem-Alexander. See page 172.
Kasteel Hoensbroek. Dubbed 'the finest castle between the Maas and the Rhine', this imposing medieval fortress dominates the countryside around Heerlen. See page 237.
Kasteel Arcen. An imposing 18th-century moated château, with especially pretty formal gardens, plum on the River Maas in Limburg. See page 236.

MARKETS AND SHOPPING

Waterlooplein, Amsterdam. Amsterdam's most alluring flea market, a rambling, open-air affair that spreads over the Waterlooplein square every day bar Sunday. See page 150.
Bloemenmarkt, Amsterdam. Splendid 'floating' flower market – the stalls occupy permanently moored barges lining the Singel canal between Muntplein and Koningsplein. See page 135.
Markthal, Rotterdam. Opened in 2014, this spectacular covered market, complete with apartments, is the place to go for food shopping. See page 187.
Dordrech. This historic city's Friday and Saturday market, along with its Christmas market, have been voted the best in the country. See page 193.
De Porceleyne Fles, Delft. Although it's possible to buy genuine Delftware elsewhere, this is the last pottery left in Delft itself. See page 180.

Paleis Het Loo.

DUTCH TREATS

It conquered the sea, championed the tulip and produced Rembrandt and Mata Hari. This small country is a big hitter.

Detail of a Delft blue tile.

From great artists to controversial extreme right-wing politicians and from intrepid explorers to sex and drugs, the Netherlands is a lot more than just windmills, clogs and tulip fields.

The Netherlands has a long and varied history. Few other countries, let alone such a small one, can claim a period comparable to the 17th-century Golden Age, when Holland and its allied provinces dominated European culture and commerce. Along the way, the Dutch created many of the concepts of modern humanism, including freedom of religion and freedom of the press – concepts that remain the ideals for modern democratic society. Known for its tolerance and liberalism, in 2001 The Netherlands became the first country to legalise same-sex marriage.

In addition, the Dutch (the world's tallest race) have made their country one of the most accommodating for foreigners. Almost everyone speaks English, along with several other languages. These days, with its large immigrant population, the Netherlands is a melting pot of almost daunting proportions. Accommodation – from campsites to hotels – is abundant in every price range. The beer (Heineken, Grolsch and Amstel) is cold, the coffee is always *klaar*, or freshly brewed, and the apple pie is irresistible.

North Sea sand dunes fun.

For travellers who enjoy meeting people and absorbing different ways of life, this culturally and geographically diverse country will have an instant appeal. Many visitors tend to stop off in Amsterdam before making their way through an itinerary of other European capitals. But, just as Paris does not represent all things French, so too Amsterdam is not typical of the Netherlands, and to understand the Dutch mentality, you should explore the rural, relaxed provinces. Here, windmills are not just props in a landscape, and the Afsluitdijk is a phenomenon of human endeavour that can be explored by walking along the man-made polders. There are 16th-century castles to visit, royal woods to wander, and romantic windswept dunes to stroll. Outside the large cities are intimate hotels with excellent kitchens, antiquarian bookshops, museums of every type and, of course, those spectacular Dutch skies – Delft blue with huge puffy clouds.

Picnicking and enjoying the view by the IJsselmeer.

RECLAIMED FROM THE SEA

If nature had been left to take its course, this small
nation wouldn't even be half its present size.

The pagan settlers who first colonised the
western shores of the Netherlands must
have eked out a wretched existence – even
by Dark Age standards. If they escaped starvation or drowning – both caused by frequent
floods – marauding Vikings would pack their
slave holds with them.

A thousand years earlier, inhabitants of the
inland dunes and bogs had survived through
marginal arable farming and raising livestock.
Tribal warfare following the collapse of the
Roman Empire forced many to move seaward
for a more peaceful existence.

Pushed to what are now Groningen and
Friesland provinces in the north, these people had to find a way to live with the tides.
As they could not stop the sea, their only
choice was to raise the land. They constructed
mounds anchored by long stakes driven
into the mudflats, surrounded by seaweed
and tidal debris, and covered with layers of
muddy clay. Finally, they built huts on top of
the hillocks, called *terpen*, many of which are
still visible today.

Kinderdijk windmills.

New lands

Until the early 11th century, the amount of
farming land in the Netherlands was little
more than half its current area. Over the centuries, dykes, canals, polders, windmills and,
ultimately, monstrous tidal barriers have been
used to reclaim thousands of square kilometres.
Without them, waves would be lapping at Utrecht, and half the country – 18,000 sq. km (7,000
sq. miles) and the habitat of more than 60 percent of the population – would either be under
water or subject to frequent flooding.

People began building small dykes (embank-
ments) to protect their homes and farms as early

as AD 700. As competition for farmland inten-
sified, they surrounded marshes and swampy
lakes with dykes and canals to drain the ground.
In those times, drainage was often a simple matter of opening a canal sluice gate at low tide,
letting water flow out into the river or sea.

The first major sea dyke was constructed in
1320, when residents of Schardam, northwest
of Amsterdam, built an embankment across
the Beemster basin to prevent the Zuiderzee
(today's IJsselmeer) from flooding their land.
Again in 1380, in the same region, farmers
built a dyke to separate the Purmer lake from
the Zuiderzee at Monnickendam. Without the
dykes, the soft, marshy land sank below sea
level when it was drained. Sea water swallowed

the freshwater lake and large bog northeast of Amsterdam, turning the entire area into a shallow, southern bay of the North Sea.

Protecting low-lying areas created polders – a word stemming from the old Germanic *pol*, referring to the stakes used to hold together dykes, dams and mounds. Now the term is used for reclaimed land.

Land reclamation methods have changed little in 600 years. Even using 21st-century drainage and pumping technology, and after the construction of dykes and drainage canals, the land that emerges a year or so later is still a

Amsterdam, began to expand. De[...] engineering expertise, the Dutch st[...] uphill battle against the forces of n[...] was exacerbated by the effects of peat in inland areas. With such a watery [...] few trees were available for fuel, and peat was the common alternative. But as this was dug from the earth, it left a wake of sterile, sandy deserts.

Despite great efforts, flooding was never completely controlled. Dykes and canals merely provided a breathing space between seasonal high tides, and were frequently breached by the surge of an angry sea. They gave some protec-

A big bulldozer works on a dredging project.

swampy morass. The next stage is the digging of many shallow run-off ditches. The land is then seeded with grass to help it dry, as well as to prevent the growth of persistent weeds and to draw the salt gradually out of the soil.

Drying takes about five years, and today, when this process is complete, roads, water, electricity and other infrastructure have to be provided. During this period the government controls the agricultural conversion process before turning the land over to selected farmers a few years later.

Slow progress

Land reclamation gathered pace during the 14th and 15th centuries, when many towns, such as

tion, though, and a measure of how important they were to the community can be seen from the cruel and unusual penalty for damaging a dyke: the guilty person had their right hand amputated before being banished.

Centuries of disasters

Records from as far back as 1287 indicate that great floods occurred practically every century. An estimated 50,000 people drowned in 1404, and on All-Hallows Eve, 1570, granite blocks protecting dykes were tossed aside like driftwood, and entire houses swept out to sea. The worst 20th-century flood occurred in 1953, when more than 1,800 people lost their lives and nearly 100,000 were left homeless.

The All-Hallows Eve flood of 1570 was the worst in the Netherlands' history; some estimates place the level of the floodwaters at more than 5 metres (16ft 6in).

Such disastrous inundations created a rich folklore of stories involving heroic deeds accomplished against all the odds. Sadly, there is no truth to the tale about Hans Brinker, the boy who saved all of Holland by sticking his finger in a leaky dyke, even though there is a symbolic statue of him at Spaarndam. There was, however, face the direction of the wind. Water could then be scooped out constantly and more efficiently. Around the year 1620, using some 20 windmills, the Beemster, Purmer and Wormer polders, created over three centuries earlier, were finally drained enough to allow arable farming.

Mills, then and now, work by scooping water from the drainage ditch, raising it, and emptying the water into a larger canal several feet higher up. To be effective on large polders, windmills are used in series, each one raising the water to a higher level. Every polder has a network of drainage ditches that flow into progressively wider and

'The Bursting Of The Dyke At Bommellerwaard', 1861.

a ship's captain who saw a dyke near Rotterdam about to be breached during the severe storm of 1953. At great risk to himself, and the ruin of his boat, he steered the vessel into the waters rushing over the dam, turning his vessel sideways so that the waters swept him broadside to plug the fast-growing gap. The dyke was saved and, in all probability, so were hundreds of people.

Permanent, substantial land reclamation did not emerge in the Netherlands until the late 16th century, when windmills were converted into windpumps. This allowed them to drive scoop-wheels, fitted with buckets for raising water from the drainage ditches.

A great leap forward came with the invention of a windmill with a top that could be rotated to deeper canals, and ultimately into the ring canal that surrounds the polder. From the ring canal, water drains either into the sea or into a freshwater reservoir. There are many such reservoirs around Amsterdam, which are used for recreation and for irrigation during rare periods of drought.

Menace from the sea

Around 1700, another disaster threatened, potentially as devastating as any flood. Wooden dykes became infested with shipworm, an aquatic termite. Foreign newspapers solemnly forecast Amsterdam's doom. Begged, borrowed and imported stone was the initial solution, and new materials, including metal, concrete and plastic, were gradually developed.

Land reclamation ceased during the early 18th century, when the Netherlands was continuously at war with England and France, and did not begin again in earnest until the mid-1850s, when steam – and later diesel – engines were used to power the pumps.

The first major area to be reclaimed using steam-powered pumps, beginning in 1852, was the Haarlemmermeer. The rehabilitation of this huge swamp west of Amsterdam created new road and rail connections and more farmland. Today, Schiphol airport and its surrounding high-tech distribution and printing businesses are located

Wind turbines on the IJsselmeer's coastline.

on the former marsh, some 4.5 metres (13ft) below sea level.

Zuiderzee dam

Plans for protecting Amsterdam by enclosing and draining parts of the Zuiderzee had been around since engineer Hendrik Stevin first proposed a scheme in 1667. Others flirted with the notion in subsequent centuries, but it wasn't until 1916 that work actually began.

This monumental project began by draining the 20,000-hectare (50,000-acre) Wieringermeer polder and constructing the Afsluitdijk, a 32km (20-mile) -long, 90-metre (300ft) -wide dyke across the Zuiderzee, which cuts off the tidal basin from the sea. It was completed in 1932, and the old sea, now a freshwater lake, has been known as the IJsselmeer ever since.

An artificial island and harbour, built from concrete caissons and dredgings, was created at the halfway point so that construction, involving 500 boats and more than 80 tugboats, could proceed from both directions. Huge willow 'mattresses' were first laid down so that subsequent layers of stone and pilings would not sink into the seabed.

At first, building in the shallow water went smoothly. But, as the gap between the two arms was reduced, the seemingly calm tidal pond began to cut a deep channel in the seabed as water rushed through the narrowing gap. By the time the opening was just 14 metres (45ft) across, the engineers began to have serious doubts about the project's feasibility.

In the end, they completed the final section in a matter of hours, racing against time, an incoming tide and an approaching storm. A

FUTURE DEVELOPMENTS

A potential super project for the 21st century remains on the drawing board: to provide further protection for the IJsselmeer and its many polder farms and communities, not to mention Amsterdam. The government hopes to link up the Frisian Islands in the northeastern tip of the country by means of a series of dykes. The project would cut off the Waddenzee (the waters that separate the islands from the mainland) from the North Sea, creating recreational freshwater areas while preventing further saltwater infiltration into groundwater and polders. Another major reclamation project – building a new Schiphol airport off the coast – is being considered. The cost would be formidable,

but Amsterdam's existing airport will reach its growth limit around 2020 and, as it is a vital component of the Dutch economy, new room for expansion will have to be found.

Some lobbyists question whether new land is needed at all. Why trouble to create new polders when simple flood protection might be enough? The answer cuts to the heart of the economy. While some oil reserves have been discovered offshore, the Netherlands has little in the way of natural resources. This small country – Europe's most densely populated – has no choice but to make increased use of all the land available for agriculture.

barrier of sorts was quickly built in front of the opening to slow the rushing water. This enabled willow mattresses and stones to be positioned properly to complete the dyke. Now, at the barrier's central point, large sluice gates and locks allow the passage of ships and marine life, in particular young migratory eels.

More than 1,800 sq km (700 sq miles) of polders were subsequently developed, with some reaching completion only in the 1980s. Two of the largest are the Noordoostpolder and Flevoland province, east of Amsterdam. The new town of Lelystad, Flevoland's provincial capi-

> *Despite their previous ubiquity, only about 1,000 windmills remain today – mostly as private homes or museums. No more than a handful are still in working order.*

rivers diverted or dammed. The project dwarfed all previous flood-control efforts. A short stretch of dam at Haringvliet needed 65 massive pilings, some driven as much as 53 metres (175ft) deep. The steel sluice gates are 12 metres (40ft) high and wide, and weigh 543 tonnes (535 tons); huge engines are needed to open and close them.

Sailing into the Hellevoetsluis sluice at Haringvliet.

tal, is named after the engineer I.C. Lely, who designed the Zuiderzee reclamation project at the beginning of the 20th century.

After the devastating 1953 storm, which flooded 185,000 hectares (460,000 acres) in the southwest, the government embarked on another massive scheme: the Delta Project. It took some 32 years and 12 billion guilders (£4 billion/US$6.5 billion) to complete this massive tidal barrier sealing off 700km (430 miles) of tidal flats and flood-prone estuaries where the Rhine, Maas, Waal and Scheldt rivers empty into the North Sea. Reinforcing the water defences is an ongoing process.

When the project began, few could have imagined the scale of the problems that would be encountered. Artificial islands had to be built;

Ecology and environment

Concerns about the environment soon became a serious and unforeseen stumbling block, particularly in the estuary between Noord-Beveland and Schouwen-Duiveland where a solid dam had been planned. Fishermen, backed up by Holland's formidable environmental lobby, warned against the loss of commercial oyster and mussel beds and the consequences of swamping miles of ecologically rich salt marshes. After an eight-year delay, the government eventually agreed on a smaller, movable barrier with gates that would permit a degree of tidal flow. As a result, although the marshes shrunk in extent from 16,200 hectares (40,000 acres) to 600 hectares (1,500 acres), the mudflats diminished by just one-third.

DECISIVE DATES

Early days (150 BC–AD1200)

circa 3000 BC
Stone Age people build megalithic burial chambers in Drenthe.

Mid-1st century BC
Roman period begins. Low Countries inhabited by Celtic and Germanic tribes: Frisii in the north, Batavii in the centre and Belgae in the south.

1st century AD
Romans establish a fortress at Nijmegen, a town at Heerlen and garrisons at Utrecht and Maastricht .

4th century
Saxons invade and settle the east; Franks invade and settle the south. Conversion from paganism to Christianity begins.

12th century
Herring fishermen settle beside the River Amstel, on the site of what is now Amsterdam.

The growth of nationhood (1200–1568)

1275
Floris V grants "Amestelledamme" freedom from tolls on transport of goods; first documentary record of Amsterdam.

1421
St Elizabeth's Day flood costs more than 10,000 lives and drowns polders and villages along the Maas and Waal.

15th century
Dukes of Burgundy gain control of Low Countries. After the last duke's death, power devolves on the Austrian Habsburgs.

1517–56
Charles V shifts the Habsburg Empire's centre of gravity from the Low Countries and Austria to Spain.

War and peace (1568–80)

1568
Low Countries revolt against Spanish rule, launching Eighty Years War.

1572
Dutch Revolt against Spanish rule, led by William of Orange, begins in earnest.

1579
Protestant refugees from Antwerp seek asylum in Amsterdam, helping to lay the foundations for the city's Golden Age.

The Golden Age (1580–1660)

1602
United East India Company founded.

1621
West India Company founded to trade with the Americas.

1652
First of numerous wars with the English for maritime supremacy.

A new consciousness (1660–1810)

1688
William III of Holland is crowned King of England and Scotland.

1702
William III dies without heir.

1744
France invades the southern provinces.

The Dutch West India Company was a chartered company of Dutch merchants.

1747
William IV is elected hereditary head of state of the seven northern provinces (the United Provinces).

1795
France invades the north and, in alliance with the Patriots, sets up a National Assembly.

1806
Napoleon establishes his brother, Louis Napoleon, as King of the Netherlands.

A period of transition (1810–50)

1813
After Napoleon's defeat, William VI is welcomed back from exile.

1814
William VI crowned King William I of the Netherlands.

1839
The Netherlands' first railway line, between Amsterdam and Haarlem, opens.

1848
A new Dutch constitution comes into force.

Europe in turmoil (1850–1945)

1870–6
Opening of North Sea Canal revives Amsterdam's position as an important port.

1890
Completion of Nieuwe Waterweg (New Waterway) to the North Sea begins Rotterdam's growth into the world's biggest port.

1914–20
The Netherlands remain neutral during World War I.

Statue of Anne Frank in Amsterdam.

1928
Amsterdam hosts the Olympic Games.

1940
Nazi Germany invades on 10 May. Holland capitulates on 15 May.

1942
Anne Frank and family go into hiding.

1944
Anne Frank and family betrayed and arrested. In September, liberation begins with Operation Market Garden.

1945
Anne Frank dies at Bergen-Belsen concentration camp. Canadian troops enter Amsterdam on 7 May.

The modern world (Post-1945)

1949
Indonesia wins independence.

1952
Holland joins five other countries to create the European Coal and Steel Community, forerunner of the European Union.

1992
Maastricht Treaty creates the European Union.

1999
European Monetary Union; the Netherlands is one of 11 countries to establish the euro.

2001
The Netherlands is the first country to legalise same-sex marriage.

2002
Outspoken right-wing politician Pim Fortuyn is assassinated.

2004
Ethnic tensions heighten after the murder of controversial film-maker Theo Van Gogh.

2007
After immigration issues force a governmental collapse, a new centrist coalition takes power.

2010
The Netherlands Antilles were dissolved and the Caribbean Netherlands created.

2012
A coalition cabinet was formed in the general election between the social-democratic Labour Party (PvdA) and conservative-liberal People's Party for Freedom and Democracy (PVV).

2013
Queen Beatrix abdicates and her son, Willem-Alexander, becomes King.

2016
500th anniversary of the death of artist Hieronymus Bosch.

Old stone grave in Drenthe, known as a hunebedden.

EARLY HISTORY

The story of the country's early development is
a tale of hardship, war and religious strife,
enlivened by dynastic empire-builders.

races of human habitation dating back
more than 30,000 years have been
found in the Netherlands, though it is
not until around 4500 BC and the palaeo-
lithic farming communities of Limburg that
a picture emerges of the prevailing culture
and lifestyle.

> Industrial relations were often fraught in
> 15th-century Amsterdam. Sometimes, entire
> groups of labourers would protest by simply
> leaving town en masse.

Between around 3000 and 2000 BC, construction of megalithic funerary monuments
called *hunebedden* flourished in Drenthe – 53
can still be seen along the Hondsrug (Dog's
Back) north of Emmen. Each *hunebed* must
have required considerable effort to build,
using giant stones deposited by a glacier
that had reached its endpoint in this area
and then receded. The megaliths and distinctive bell-beaker pottery found in the graves
connect their neolithic makers with the predominant cultural trend in Western Europe
at that time.

A new dawn

From about 2000 BC onwards, the mega-
lith-builders' civilisation disappeared. From
the onset of the Bronze Age, human settlers began to spread westwards towards the
North Sea and the low-lying deltas of the
rivers Scheldt, Waal, Maas, Rhine, IJssel and
Ems, burying their dead in funeral mounds,
individual graves and urns containing ashes.
Around 500 BC, settlers in coastal Friesland

Portrait of Philip I of Castile, known as The Fair.

and Groningen began to give themselves
some protection from the tides by constructing *terpen*, low earthen mounds on which
they built their huts and animal enclosures.
More than 1,000 *terpen* have been identified,
and some of them form the origins of contemporary towns and villages.

At about the same time as the Celts were
taking over further south, Germanic tribes,
including the Batavians and Frisians, occupied the area of the present-day Netherlands
and were firmly established by 50 BC, when
the Romans appeared on the scene. Julius
Caesar credited the Batavians with making a
spirited and fierce defence of their swampy
homeland.

In AD 12, the Roman general Drusus Germanicus brought the Batavians into the imperial fold in the role of an auxiliary cavalry to support the legions. But, in AD 69 the Batavian leader Claudius Civilis led an uprising. He was ultimately defeated, although he did manage to secure concessions for his people.

Frisian resistance

The Romans could make no headway against the Frisians, however, and were content to hold the line of the River Rhine. They estab-

Duke Philip of Burgundy, known as The Bold.

lished a legionary base at Ulpia Noviomagus (Nijmegen), a crossing of the Maas (Meuse) at Mosae Trajectum (Maastricht), and built baths at Coriovallum (Heerlen).

In 382, St Servaas (Servatius) became the Netherlands' first bishop when he moved the seat of his bishopric from Tongeren to Maastricht. The Germanic peoples erupted across the Rhine during the 5th century to tear the Western Roman Empire apart. The Franks, led by Clovis (466–511), defeated and absorbed the Batavians, but the Frisians were again too hot to handle. Not until 689 did the Franks, under Pepin II, defeat the still pagan Frisians.

Insurrection continued amongst the feisty Frisians, as attempts were made to convert them to Christianity. It took the heavy broadsword of Charlemagne during the late 8th century to finally subdue these proud and independent people, and thus integrate the Low Countries (the present-day Netherlands, Belgium and Luxembourg) into his wider European empire.

After Charlemagne's death in 814, the Frankish Empire was divided among his sons, and most of the Low Countries passed to the Middle Kingdom (Lotharingia/Lorraine), which later became a duchy of the Germanic Holy Roman Empire. As Frankish rule weakened during the 10th century, Vikings took the opportunity to invade and ravage the land.

Although nominally owing allegiance to the empire, from the 10th century to the 14th century, the Low Countries comprised a number of feudal states. The rulers of these states enjoyed many privileges and, in practice, were semi-autonomous. Among the feudal rulers were the bishops of Utrecht, the dukes of Brabant, the counts of Zeeland and the increasingly powerful counts of Holland.

The birth of Amsterdam

Born amid water, Amsterdam is surrounded by it still. The fishermen who built the first huts at the mouth of the River Amstel around 1200 must have earned a good living for that period from the rich Zuiderzee fishing grounds. Yet they and their families were at the mercy of wind and sea in that swampy delta, and many must have lost their lives when storm surges washed their dwellings away. Yet the community flourished, particularly when, around 1220, a dam was built to hold the Zuiderzee at bay. As a by-product, it also created a good anchorage at the point where Centraal Station now stands.

Named Amestelledamme, the settlement expanded as a commodities market, helped by an influx of Flemish weavers and Jewish merchants. In 1275, the year that is considered the city's foundation date, Count Floris V of Holland granted the people of Amestelledamme toll-free passage on the waterways – a sign of its growing importance and a move that spurred further growth in trade. Ships unloaded cargoes of timber, salt and spices on what is now the Dam, and sailed away laden with cloth and grain.

In 1300 the Bishop of Utrecht gave Amestelledamme its town charter, and in 1317 Count Willem III of Holland took over the town from the bishops. Another link in the commercial chain was forged in 1323, when Count Floris VI named Amsterdam as a tollpoint for the import of beer, which was an essential alternative to tainted water supplies. In 1369, Amsterdam began a period of maritime trade with – and at the same time competed vigorously against – the powerful Baltic-based Hanseatic League. Amsterdam and other Dutch towns eventually supplanted the league as Northern Europe's trading powerhouse. By 1414 Amsterdam was Holland's biggest town, with a population of around 12,000.

While its trading status became firmly established, Amsterdam itself remained on less secure ground, and the town's buildings proved susceptible to the ravages of fire. Indeed, in 1452 most of them were burned down. Following this catastrophe, the City Fathers ordained that all new buildings would be made from stone. Only two wooden houses remain today.

The good, the mad and the bold

In 1384 Count Lodewijk of Flanders died and was succeeded by his daughter Margaret, the wife of Duke Philip the Bold of Burgundy, beginning the Low Countries' dazzling Burgundian period. Over the next century or so the dukes of Burgundy gained possession of most of the Low Countries, partly through dynastic marriages and partly by conquest.

Duke Philip the Good was the family's top hand at acquisitions, taking over Limburg in 1430 and Holland and Zeeland in 1433. By 1473 his successor, Charles the Bold, controlled most of present-day Netherlands, plus Belgium, Luxembourg and territories in France. On his death in battle in 1477, he was succeeded by his daughter Mary, wife of the Habsburg Empire's Crown Prince Maximilian of Austria. Mary died aged 25 in a horse-riding accident in 1482, pitching the Burgundian Empire – and the Netherlands along with it – into Habsburg hands.

One of Maximilian's enduring acts was, in 1489, to grant Amsterdam the right to use the imperial crown on its coat of arms, a symbol you can see most prominently today gracing the summit of the city's Westerkerk tower.

Maximilian's son, Philip the Handsome, succeeded to the rule of the Low Countries when his father stepped up to become Holy Roman Emperor. He later married Joanna the Mad of Spain, thereby retaining the family penchant for bizarre monikers and bringing Spain into the Habsburg fold – a development that in due course would have grim repercussions for the Low Countries.

The high tide of Netherlandic influence would seem to have come when Charles V, born in Ghent, inherited the Low Countries in 1515, Spain in 1516 and the Holy Roman

Philip the Handsome, c. 1495.

Empire in 1519. But Charles was forced to engage in relentless warfare to preserve his unwieldy and scattered realm, and used the Low Countries as a reservoir of money and soldiers, while at the same time shifting the empire's centre of gravity southwards to Spain.

While blue-bloods and their dynasties came and went, a more fundamental change was brewing. Martin Luther's 1517 condemnation of the Catholic Church provoked the rise of Protestantism, a development that was reaching crisis proportions in the Low Countries by 1555, when Philip II, a fanatical Catholic, began to inherit the empire from the failing hands of Charles V.

THE GOLDEN AGE

The Netherlands' Golden Age of the 17th century was the zenith of its power – a glittering period of remarkable art.

O ne of the best ways to gauge the impact of the Dutch Empire is to walk into an antique map store almost anywhere in the world. Ask to see 17th-century Dutch world maps and watch the proprietor's eyes light up at the prospect of dealing with a connoisseur.

For much of the 17th century, when Dutch ships and banks ruled the commercial world, maps made in Amsterdam were regarded as the best, both for accuracy – Dutch ships sailed to more places and brought back more reliable geographical information than those of any other country – and beauty. Dutch 17th-century cartographers, artists, engravers and printers were to mapmaking what Dutch Masters were to 17th-century painting – perhaps the greatest collection of talent ever working at one time in a single country. Even today, many map collectors and dealers believe that Dutch Golden Age maps have never been surpassed for quality. So, if you visit an antique map shop, and don't plan to spend a fortune on an authentic Blaeu or Janszoon, dampen the proprietor's enthusiasm by adding, 'I'm just looking.'

Art flourishes

The growth of empire and the prosperity it brought spawned an extraordinary period of artistic and cultural production. The Golden Age, noteworthy by any nation's standards, was especially remarkable in that it occurred in a small, waterlogged land of stubborn people.

Many believe the Golden Age is unparalleled in world history. 'There is perhaps no other example of a complete and highly original civilisation springing up in so short a time in so small a territory', wrote the historian Simon Schama.

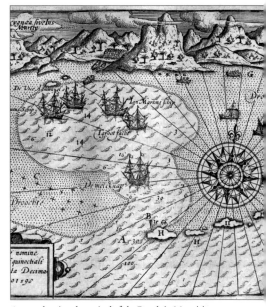

A map showing the arrival of the Dutch in Mauritius.

This was not due solely to the ambition and acumen of the merchant middle class that provided the empire's driving force. Those important qualities were there in abundance in the late 16th century, for the Dutch had already developed a thriving Baltic-based commodities trade in salt, herring, wine, bricks, cereal, wood, iron and copper.

Equal in importance to the merchant-trader's desire to get rich was an external event that triggered their determination to succeed – the 80 years of struggle against Spain that began in 1568. The conflict began with the anti-heresy campaign of the Spanish king, Philip II, who saw it as his duty to wipe out the Calvinist movement that had taken root in the northern

Netherlands. When Philip outlawed Calvinism, the northern provinces rebelled under the leadership of William the Silent, whom the Dutch regard as the father of their country.

Decades of strife with Spain were the result of religious differences, but there were also economic factors. Spain not only wanted to control religion, but also to restrain the Dutch economy. The Dutch reacted in typical hard-headed fashion, outlawing Catholicism and doing all they could to expand their economy, including setting up in trade competition with Spain across the globe.

other wars. England's destruction of the Spanish Armada in 1588 is an example. The Dutch were emboldened by knowing that many of the cannons that might have challenged them on the other side of the world were now safely in galleons at the bottom of the English Channel. As

> Unlike any other great artistic period in Europe, the big-name Dutch Masters were surrounded by many 'Little Masters', whose paintings are still in demand.

William the Silent.

The 1579 Treaty of Utrecht created the United Provinces and provided the foundation of the modern Netherlands through the alliance of seven northern provinces – the southern provinces remained subject to Spain and eventually became Belgium and Luxembourg. More significantly for the development of a Dutch empire, the treaty gave the United Provinces shipping control of the lower Rhine, and allowed Amsterdam to eclipse rival Antwerp as the region's principal commercial centre.

Trading advantage

Dutch sailors and merchants of the late 16th century were skilled, but they were also lucky that their enemies and competitors were distracted by

Spain's entanglements with England and France continued, more Dutch ships undertook ambitious voyages with little fear of reprisal, and set about opening new routes, establishing colonies and plundering other countries' trade.

At home, the Dutch were fast becoming the bankers of Europe. The Bank of Amsterdam was formed in 1609, and the Amsterdam Stock Exchange began trading in 1611. Favourable interest rates, reliable foreign currency exchanges and the willingness of Dutch bankers to loan money attracted investors and financiers from across Europe – and greatly spurred on the ventures of Dutch entrepreneurs.

Born out of religious repression, the United Provinces of the north provided freedom of conscience to all citizens. Protestants, Jews and other religious refugees poured in from France, Spain, Portugal and elsewhere. Anyone could immigrate to the United Provinces for 8 guilders – a year's pay for a Dutch sailor. The entry fee was often waived for refugees with a valuable skill or craft. In addition, the United Provinces boasted a free press – a rarity in those days – that attracted writers, thinkers and academics. The result was an infusion of the best and brightest talent from across Europe.

There were some constraints. Speaking Yiddish was illegal, and Catholicism was formally

enjoyed a longer period of sustained popularity than that of any other painter. But as well as painting, numerous other artistic disciplines – such as architecture, sculpture, furniture-making, silver-working and porcelain production – all flourished during the Golden Age of the 17th century. The country's success in trade was the great enabler, providing both the wealth with which Dutch citizens patronised the arts, and the artistic stimulus for new designs. In the early 1600s, a Dutch merchant ship returned from a voyage to China with a hold packed with late Ming Dynasty porcelain, which proved so

The Amsterdam Stock Exchange in the early 17th century.

banned, although the authorities allowed Catholics to worship as long as they didn't hold public services. The result was dozens of small private 'churches', often hidden in secret rooms in homes and warehouses. A fine surviving example can be seen at Amsterdam's Amstelkring Museum, a refurbished 17th-century merchant's home known as 'Our Lord in the Attic' because of its Catholic chapel under the roof. Later, the existence of so many hidden rooms would enable Jewish refugees to hide from the Nazis in Dutch homes.

Today, the Golden Age is best remembered for paintings by the three greatest Dutch Masters – Johannes Vermeer, Frans Hals and, of course, Rembrandt, whose work has probably

A CLASSLESS SOCIETY

The Golden Age was a time of great prosperity enjoyed by all – not merely the ruling classes. Openness and market competition existed in all spheres of life, not just in art, and attracted an exceptional number of skilled, ambitious citizens able to use their talent and determination to improve their lot in life.

Unlike in many other European countries at that time, it was possible for people to move from class to class. Members of the middle and even lower classes could become clergymen, artists, craftsmen, traders and merchants. They could get rich, and have an influence in provincial affairs.

Sailors' talk

Spoken by about 22 million native speakers in the European Union including Belgium, this West Germanic language has had a big influence on modern English.

Although the Dutch language is similar to German, it can sound strange and alien. Not for nothing was the term 'double Dutch' coined in the 18th century

Replica of the Amsterdam ship; the Dutch language got around.

to describe someone whose speech was incoherent or impenetrable. Even words you think you know turn out very different. Gouda, the town and the world-famous cheese, is pronounced something like 'chowda' – the *ch* sound being hard and guttural, as in the Scottish pronunciation of loch.

Vincent Van Gogh, known to the English as 'Van Goff', and to Americans as 'Van Go', is an almost unpronounceable Van Choch in his native tongue. Again, the *ch* sounds as if the speaker were clearing his throat – perhaps it is the phlegmatic effects of living with cold, damp air rising from a watery polder landscape that has resulted in such a guttural consonant.

On the other hand, written Dutch can be deceptively easy. Sue Limb weaves real Dutch words into

her entertaining autobiography, *Love Forty*, as in this conversation: '*Uur klogs aar bei de bakdor,*' called his wife as he went. '*Ij moovd dem uit ov de utilijtij-roem bekos ov de stink.*' '*Ja, dat wwas de pijg-schijt vrom de manuur-heep. Sorrij.*'

An influential tongue

Many Dutch words – most of them earthy and verging on the unprintable – have been assimilated into English. Robert McCrum, author of *The Story of English*, catalogues *fokkinge*, *kunte* and *krappe* as words that we euphemistically call Anglo-Saxon but which are, in fact, Low Dutch.

Poppycock, which has become an acceptable expletive, derives from the Dutch *pappekak* (literally, soft dung). Sailors from the Low Countries probably introduced these words to England and the Americas, along with purely nautical terms like smuggler (from *smuckeln*) and keelhaul (from *kielhalen*).

Dutch territorial influence in North America ceased when British settlers seized Nieuw Amsterdam and renamed it New York. But the Dutch linguistic contribution to American English lingers on in place names like Harlem and Brooklyn (originally called Haarlem and Breukelen).

Contemporary American English contains many words derived from Dutch. To quote McCrum: 'If you have a *waffle* for brunch, or *coleslaw* with your dinner, or a *cookie* with your coffee, you are using Dutch American. If you ride through the *landscape* in a *caboose* or on a *sleigh*, if you find your *boss* or neighbour *snooping* and accuse him of being a *spook*, you are also using words that came to America from the Netherlands'.

Future survival

Pessimists are concerned for the language's very survival. English (or its American variant) is widely understood and spoken and has become the language of popular music, the internet, satellite TV and advertising. The Netherlands is one of the world's biggest markets for English-language publications. In the past, Dutch absorbed many foreign words yet remained a distinctive tongue, despite Oliver Goldsmith's dismissive comment in 1759 that the Dutch were 'destitute of what may be properly called a language of their own'.

Today, some alarmists fear that without a determined effort to keep the language alive, Dutch could die, leaving a handful of (English) four-letter words as its only legacy. However, most Dutch people – young and old – are proud of their language; giving it up would be tantamount to losing part of themselves.

popular that it inspired the beginning of the national pottery industry, based in Delft.

The finer things

Material prosperity meant that ordinary citizens could afford the finer things in life, such as silver salt shakers and original paintings that they themselves had commissioned. Such paintings represented something new – non-classical art. The Dutch School launched realism in painting. Instead of merely forming the background, landscapes and seascapes became the central subject matter of paintings. And indi-

life and their environment, their country and their city sights so thoroughly that their paintings provide a nearly complete pictorial record of their culture. However, it was more than mere reportage. A sensitive feeling for the painterly

> There had been a practical side to the Dutch devotion to the arts: with the economy expanding as rapidly as the empire, work by well-known artists was a sound hedge against inflation.

'Cello Lesson', by Caspar Netscher (1639–1684).

viduals and families posed, and were painted, as themselves instead of in the guise of biblical or mythological figures.

The love of art was universal; visitors to the Netherlands during the Golden Age routinely remarked on how everyone, from blacksmith to baker to burgher, seemed to have original art, often personally commissioned, hanging prominently at home and in their business premises. Merchants commissioned paintings of their trade ships, and farmers of their prize cows – the scene often completed by an artistically rendered cowpat on the ground. Realism extended to street scenes and facial expressions that captured a moment or an emotion of everyday life. A modern critic sums it up: 'The Dutch described their

view of everyday life and nature not infrequently raised their production to the level of great art.'

Golden city

Amsterdam, which dominated Holland province, the richest and most important of the seven, is one of the most striking legacies of the Golden Age. In 1607, when the Singel canal was no more than a ditch around the 15th-century city walls, the council approved a plan for three new canals: Herengracht, Keizersgracht and Prinsengracht. Fine houses, built to strict requirements, were erected along the main canals, with shops along interlinking side canals. The Jordaan was added in 1612 as a self-contained community of artists and craftsmen.

The plan of central Amsterdam, which was completed in the late 17th century, remains one of the most successful examples of forward-looking town planning in history. One modern critic notes: 'It is not often that a town has been enlarged so sensitively as to increase its characteristic beauty. Its great claim is in the noble dimensions of the canals, in the wonderfully successful relation between the breadth of the water and of the quays on either side, and the height of the buildings.'

For a glimpse of how Golden Age merchants lived, visit the Willet-Holthuysen Museum, a refurbished canal house at Herengracht 605. Originally built as a wealthy family's gift to a pampered eight-year-old son, the museum displays furniture, glass, silver and Golden Age ceramics.

Many houses on Herengracht show how merchants, though constrained by strict building requirements and zoning laws, quietly tried to outdo each other with fancy gables and flourished façades. Other examples of the way that comfortable Dutch lived in 17th-century Amsterdam can be seen at Rembrandt's former house, Jodenbreestraat 4, which has a collection of the artist's drawings and rooms furnished in period

'The Old Town Hall of Amsterdam', by Pieter Jansz Saenredam (1597–1665).

THE WHIFF OF ELEGANCE

The city council used money raised by selling canal-front housing plots to finance the new canal system. It was believed that only the wealthy would be able to buy and build on the three main residential canals, but Amsterdam's prosperity was such that many middle-class merchants were able to afford to move in. Despite its undeniable grandeur, there was a serious problem with the new Amsterdam. No provision had been made for flushing out the canals, so they stank horribly in warm weather. In summer, wealthy people fled to their country houses, which were perhaps only a few miles away, but mercifully far from the stench.

style. Perhaps the grandest of all the architecture of the period can be seen in the Town Hall, now the Koninklijk Paleis (Royal Palace) in Amsterdam, and the Mauritshuis in The Hague, both designed by Haarlem-born painter and architect Jacob van Campen.

An empire in decline

At the empire's height, Dutch holdings encompassed parts of Brazil, Dutch Guyana (now Surinam) on the northeast coast of South America, a fistful of tiny but productive Caribbean islands, Manhattan Island, African outposts that provided slaves for Caribbean sugar plantations, parts of Sri Lanka, South Africa, Tasmania, and – the jewel of the realm – most of present-day Indonesia.

Little remains. Much of the empire was lost – even during the Golden Age. As traders, the Dutch were among the best; as colonists, they were among the worst. More interested in trade than migration, they exploited the people and resources of their colonies and returned home with wealth instead of putting down roots.

The end of the Thirty Years War, in 1648, allowed England, Spain and France to turn their attention to the marauding Dutch. Colonies stolen from the Spanish and Portuguese were taken back again. Neglect by the States General, the United Provinces' ruling body, as much as English

A curious historical footnote to the decline of the Dutch Empire and the fading of the Golden Age is that during the late 17th century and well into the 18th – a period known as the *Pruikentijd*, or 'age of wigs' – everything French became all the rage, and French was spoken instead of Dutch in the finer salons.

Francophilia failed to diminish – even after France had conquered the Netherlands in the late 18th century. French rule was maintained until the point of Napoleon's abdication in 1815, after which the Netherlands gradually evolved into a constitutional monarchy.

Golden Age artefacts at the Willet-Holthuysen Museum.

aggression, was to blame for the loss in 1664 of Nieuw Amsterdam – renamed New York.

Other factors at home added to the empire's decline. The Zuiderzee was silting up, making it difficult for ships to reach Amsterdam docks. This did not matter to many descendants of the original merchants, traders and bankers who had been responsible for building the empire. New generations seemed more interested in spending than making money, leading one Dutch historian to suggest that the 17th century should be called the Age of Wood and Steel because of its commodity-trading and shipbuilding, and the 18th century the Golden Age because of all the gold the Dutch locked away in strongboxes instead of investing in new ventures.

The end of empire

In shops and museums displaying Dutch maps, the decline of the Golden Age is very easy to see. By the turn of the 18th century, many Dutch maps were little more than plagiarised copies of French and English maps that were by then leading the way, reflecting the change in global influence.

Despite contrary evidence, many Dutch cartographers copying earlier maps continued to show California as a separate island up to the 18th century. It wasn't until 1704, when the French government formally declared California part of the American mainland, that Dutch mapmakers at last fell into line. The Golden Age was indeed over.

An old mill adorns a 1737 street sign in Amsterdam.

FROM COLONISTS TO CONQUERED

The Golden Age was all but over, and the Netherlands was to see a gradual but distinct turnaround in fortune.

You can still see and touch the Golden Age legacy all around you in Amsterdam and other Dutch towns. Even though the lustre has been dulled by the passage of four centuries, its glint is firmly embedded. But by the start of the 18th century, the reservoir of inspiration, confidence and wealth that was its wellspring had run dry. The Zuiderzee had begun silting up, making it difficult for ships to reach Amsterdam. But, perhaps more significantly, many wealthy citizens of the town, living in their fancy new canalside houses, no longer wanted ships sailing up to their front doors and disgorging cargoes into the attic.

The second and third generations of the merchant families did not share their ancestors' zest for chasing the guilder to the ends of the earth; they were more interested in spending money than in garnering it. The merchant fleet was depleted, the national debt grew, and peasants who had been wearing leather shoes went back to making wooden ones. The United Provinces went into a period of decline, losing commercial pre-eminence to England and France.

Wilhelm III.

William and Mary

In 1688, in what Protestants called the 'Glorious Revolution', England's Catholic monarch, James II, was deposed. In his place, William of Oranje-Nassau, *stadhouder* of Holland and Zeeland, and his wife, the English princess Mary Stuart – daughter of James II – were jointly crowned as William III and Mary II of England. William's wars against France in opposition to Louis XIV's expansionist policies strained the economy of the United Provinces, and the republic went into steep decline as a trading nation.

William III died without an heir in 1702, and the office of *stadhouder* was left vacant until

UNDERCOVER EMPEROR

In 1697, Russia's Tsar Peter the Great worked incognito for a few days at a shipyard in Zaandam, near Amsterdam, studying Dutch shipbuilding methods. He stayed at the humble wooden home of a local blacksmith, Gerrit Kist, whom he had once employed in Russia. The 'Czaar Peterhuisje' (Tsar Peter House) at Krimp 23 in Zaandam, enclosed in a brick shelter in 1895 by Tsar Nicholas II, is popular with Russian visitors and contains an exhibition and souvenirs of Peter's stays (he visited again in 1698 and twice in 1717), including the small box-bed into which the more than 2-metre (nearly 7ft) -tall Tsar of All the Russias squeezed himself.

1747, when William IV inherited it, for the first time unifying the republic under one leader. But between 1751 and 1788, the United Provinces were torn by civil strife between conservative supporters of the House of Orange and liberal reformers, called Patriots, demanding greater democracy and combining republicanism with the new ideas of the Enlightenment.

A side effect of this struggle was that in 1782 the Dutch were the first to recognise the United States and grant loans to the new democracy. The Patriots aimed to replace the United Provinces' patrician plutocracy and its Orangist

as his capital. Rather unexpectedly, Louis proved too sympathetic to his new subjects, and in 1810 Napoleon forced him to abdicate and incorporated the country into the French Empire. Throughout this period economic activity

> *You get a good idea of the style in which wealthy Amsterdammers of the fading Golden Age lived at the city's Museum Willet-Holthuysen and Museum Van Loon, both well-preserved patrician houses.*

King William I of the Netherlands in 1814.

traditionalism with a much wider democracy. What they did, however, was unite these former ruling-class foes, in particular after the Patriots seized power in 1785, and provoked a pro-monarchy Prussian invasion two years later that sent the Patriots packing, mostly to France.

They returned in 1795 when a French revolutionary army invaded and replaced the antiquated political institutions of the United Provinces with the French-sponsored Batavian Republic, a unitary state with its own National Assembly, named after the Batavii tribe that rebelled against Roman rule in AD 69. William V fled to England.

In 1806, Napoleon Bonaparte took over the republic and proclaimed his brother Louis-Napoleon King of the Netherlands, with Amsterdam

declined on a disastrous scale. The French requisitioned men and resources, and the Dutch lost most of their overseas trade because of the British blockade. Napoleon's failed 1812 invasion of Russia and his crushing defeat at Leipzig in 1813 spelled the end of the Napoleonic adventure. Prince William VI of Orange, son of William V, returned from exile and was crowned King William I of the Netherlands in 1814.

A new nation, a new voice

Dutch troops played a prominent part in the Duke of Wellington's decisive Allied victory over Napoleon at Waterloo in June 1815, earning the country a voice at the Congress of Vienna that same year. Austria renounced its claim to the southern provinces of the Low Countries – Belgium and Luxembourg – and the congress attached both regions to the Kingdom of the Netherlands. North and south were united again under one monarch for the first time in more than two centuries.

The Dutch managed to hold on to a good part of their empire when the Netherlands emerged from French rule at the end of the Napoleonic era. Trade in colonial products remained an integral part of the economy until World War II. William ruled as a constitutional monarch, though parliament's role was limited. His efforts to unify the two halves of the country, and the 1830 Belgian Revolution that followed years of unrest gave the southern provinces independence as the Kingdom of Belgium. William recognised Belgian independence in 1839, and abdicated the following year. Pro-democracy riots that took place in 1845 led to a constitutional convention under J.R. Thorbecke, and in 1848 William II accepted reforms that provided for a directly elected parliament; thus the Netherlands became a constitutional monarchy.

Prosperous ports

A period of rapid development, beginning in 1870, saw improvements in education and public health provision. The economy received a boost when in 1872 the Nieuwe Waterweg opened, strengthening Rotterdam's position as a port; in 1876 the Noordzee Kanal (North Sea Canal) opened, reviving Amsterdam's port and bringing fresh prosperity. Bicycles appeared in 1880 – the start of a passionate romance that continues unabated to this day. The first car put in an appearance in Amsterdam on 21 July 1897; a century later cars were guests who had overstayed their welcome in the city of Golden Age canals and narrow streets, and tough measures were put in force to control, and ultimately, to banish them.

Economically, the Netherlands concentrated on trade and agriculture well into the 20th century, then developed a large-scale industrial base. Politically, parliamentary authority was supreme, and the electorate was expanded when universal male suffrage was introduced in 1917 and women's suffrage after World War II.

The country remained neutral during World War I, but the combined effect of the blockade of Germany imposed by the Allied nations and the operation of German U-boats in the area choked off trade and caused food shortages that led to strikes, riots and support for the Communist

Party. Most of Belgium had been occupied by the Germans, and Belgians fled in large numbers to the safety of the Netherlands. As many as a million refugees sheltered with their northern neighbours, among them choirmaster Lieven Defosel of Brussels, whose efforts at Haarlem's Concertgebouw concert hall helped raise funds to care for the dispossessed.

Conditions slowly improved during the 1920s, and in 1928 Amsterdam proudly hosted the Olympic Games. This all too brief post-war high was then followed by the Great Depression of the 1930s, during which many thousands of unem-

Hinde Rijwielen Fabriek Amsterdam poster, 1896.

ployed people worked on job-creation schemes, such as the construction of the Amsterdamse Bos recreation park, to the south of the capital. Amid chronic shortages and massive riots, the government used the army to maintain public order. In 1932 the Afsluitdijk (Enclosing Dyke) was completed, closing off the Zuiderzee and creating the freshwater IJsselmeer.

The Netherlands had hoped to remain neutral once more at the outset of World War II, which began with Germany's invasion of Poland in September 1939. Hitler had little time for the Netherlands' neutrality, however, and on 10 May 1940 German air and ground units crossed the Dutch border, plunging the nation into the darkest chapter in its history.

Amsterdam:
An historical portrait

Since its marshy origins, the Dutch capital has been a bustling, prosperous, multi-cultural melting pot where all members of society could meet to rub shoulders in its narrow streets.

Battle between Dutch and Spanish ships.

'The pungent salt smell, the northern, maritime keynotes of seagull and herring, the pointed brick buildings, tall and narrow, with their mosaic of parti-coloured shutters, eaves, sills, that give the landscapes their stiff, heraldic look.' Nicolas Freeling, the Dutch crime writer, presents this romantic view of the city in his novel *A Long Silence*. By contrast, the historian Simon Schama smells the underbelly of the beast: 'In high summer, Amsterdam smells of frying oil, shag tobacco and unwashed beer glasses. In narrow streets, these vapours stand in the air like an aromatic heat mist.'

The reality

Amsterdam's elegance lies in its ingenious use of space. As Schama says: 'In Amsterdam, alleys attract, avenues repel. The Kalverstraat's din and cheerful vulgarity are the authentic Dutch response to the alienating breadth of a boulevard.'

Indeed, every inch of space seems to be accounted for. Statistics show that in terms of people per square metre, Amsterdam is as crowded as Hong Kong.

The sense of homogeneity suggested by the concentric canals is countered by the individuality of each neighbourhood, from the raffish waterfront district to the bohemian yet understated Jordaan, the melancholy (though in transition) Jodenbuurt (Jewish quarter) to the gentrified Museum District, the schizophrenic Oude Zijde (Old Side) to the sleazy red-light Wallen (quays).

The most appealing districts are, almost by definition, those with peculiar geography and the most chequered history.

The birth of a city

By the 13th century a flourishing community had built a dam across the River Amstel and settled on the land around the marshy mouth. Named Amestelledamme, the medieval town soon prospered as a commodities market, helped by an influx of Flemish weavers and Jewish merchants. Ships unloaded precious wood, wool, salt and spices on Dam Square and sailed away with fine cloth, furnishings and grain.

As the town expanded, the 14th-century city walls, built along Oudezijds and Nieuwezijds Voorburgwal, outlived their usefulness and placed constraints on Amsterdam's growth. In 1452, after a series of disastrous fires, the City Council decreed that all houses should henceforth be built of slate and stone rather than of wood.

Amsterdam prospered quietly under Burgundian and Habsburg domination but was politically marginalised until the end of the 16th century. The turning point in Amsterdam's fortunes came in 1578, when the city changed sides and supported the Dutch Calvinist, William of Orange, against Philip II and the Spanish Catholics.

This event, known as the 'Alteration', made Amsterdam a natural home for French Huguenot refugees and Flemish Protestants. After the declaration of the United Provinces in 1581, religious tolerance fostered the establishment of clandestine Catholic churches such as Ons' Lieve Heer op Solder on Oudezijds Voorburgwal.

Although Catholic worship was officially illegal, the authorities tolerated discreet observance.

Hitting new heights and eventual decline

Dutch maritime superiority and mercantile success helped usher in the Republic's Golden Age, and Amsterdam enjoyed unrivalled prosperity as a banking centre and the hub of a burgeoning Dutch Empire. During the 17th century, Amsterdam perfected its *burgerlijk* culture, an aspiration to the highest civic and moral values rather than a mere embodiment of bourgeois taste. The Republic saw itself as 'an island of plenty in a sea of want'.

In 1613, Amsterdam's wealthy ruling class embarked on an ambitious foray into town-planning with the building of the city's three greatest canals, the crescent-shaped Herengracht, Keizersgracht and Prinsengracht. These canals, the *grachtengordel* (canal belt), were soon adorned with magnificent warehouses and patrician town houses.

The 18th century saw Amsterdam's gradual economic decline, coinciding with a conservative reaction against the perceived excesses of the previous century. The decline was only reversed when the creation of the Noordzee Kanal in 1876 engendered a shadow 'Golden Age', with an architectural revival and population growth. The wealthy built neoclassical mansions, while the poor made do with good low-cost housing schemes in the De Pijp and Old South districts.

As a result of enlightened Dutch social policies, Amsterdam embarked on new low-cost housing schemes between the wars. The Jordaan was already well established as a working-class district, but the city's housing shortage was alleviated by the creation of garden suburbs in Amsterdam's Old South. Designed by architects of the Amsterdam School, these quirky yet utilitarian estates are characterised by multicoloured bricks, bulging façades and bizarre windows.

Young and old

More recently, the city has bucked the Dutch trend towards *cityvorming*, the clinical planning ethos that has blighted Rotterdam, The Hague and Utrecht. By contrast, conservation and anti-development measures are generally favoured by Amsterdam's left-wing City Council and supported by the city's predominantly young population.

Even so, cherished landmarks have been demolished. In the 1970s, Nieuwmarkt and a section of the Jodenbuurt were sacrificed to make way for a metro system. As for the completion of the Muziektheater and Stadhuis (City Hall) complex on Waterlooplein in 1987, the controversy lingers on.

Resistance to *cityvorming* is particularly strong in Amsterdam's most closely-knit neighbourhoods. The Nieuwmarkt, Jordaan, Western Islands and De Pijp districts are not about to be re-designed in a bland new international style. Nieuwmarkt's cultural identity is not cast in

A street in the Jordaan district with the Westerkerk in the background.

stone: the buildings have been altered frequently since the 16th century, but the neighbourhood's resilience and its mercantile spirit remain intact. The district has traditionally welcomed refugees, from the Jews of the 17th century to today's Chinese, Indonesian and Surinamese immigrants.

Elsewhere, Amsterdam's best-loved district, the Jordaan, is generally immune to outside pressure, despite gentrification. Its rebellious identity was forged in early industrial disputes, and this closely packed quarter has been home over the years to a rich mix of Huguenots, craftsmen, almshouse-dwellers, hippies, students and yuppies.

Dutch Resistance fighters armed with captured German weapons, 1944.

THE WAR YEARS

The Dutch thought they had little to fear from Hitler's Germany, but nothing could prepare them for the terrible consequences of Nazi ambition.

World War II began for the Dutch in the early hours of a beautiful Friday morning – 10 May 1940. As dawn broke over the flat, peaceful landscape, Junkers-Ju 52 transport planes flew in from the east carrying parachute troops, while ground forces, including an SS motorised regiment, swarmed over the German/Dutch frontier, dispelling any lingering hopes that the Netherlands could remain neutral. Later that same morning, Germany's ambassador to The Hague, Count Von Zech Von Burckersroda, wept as he handed over the official declaration of war to the Dutch Foreign Minister.

Hitler had pencilled in a one-day schedule for the complete occupation of the Netherlands, one of the important first stages of his master plan to overrun Europe. There was a slight hitch: the Dutch Davids, confronted with the Nazi Goliath, dared to fight back. The Dutch armed forces were hastily trained and poorly equipped. Many soldiers were still getting used to their army boots, and almost all of them were pacifists at heart and had no enthusiasm for war. Despite such circumstances, they kept their country out of German hands for five days – four more than Hitler had calculated.

The master plan

The Führer planned to launch his main offensive against Britain and France from Dutch and Belgian bases, after he had subdued the population. Later he would take care of what he euphemistically dubbed 'the Jewish problem'. While, tragically, he succeeded only too well with certain parts of his plan, he never quite managed to subdue the Dutch.

The combined Dutch forces of 350,000 men bought enough time to enable Princess Juliana,

German soldiers marching through a town in Holland during World War II.

accompanied by Prince Bernhard and their two children, to escape to Canada, and for Queen Wilhelmina, together with her Cabinet, to reach the safety of British shores.

Dutch losses during those first days of confrontation hardly mean much when set against the backdrop of the millions of Allied troops who lost their lives defending democracy during the struggle against the Nazis. But the five-day battle took its toll, leaving 2,200 soldiers and 2,159 civilians dead, and 2,700 wounded.

It is difficult to calculate the exact number of Germans who died; many lost their lives when the defenders blew up vital bridges, and others were shot down in the Ju 52s. Official

Despite fleeing Holland, fervent Nazi-hater Prince Bernhard did not sit out the war; after leaving his family safely in Canada he led the free Dutch forces from Britain.

records show that 1,600 Germans were taken prisoner. For 1,200 of them, shipped to Britain just before the capitulation, the combat years of World War II were very short.

The Dutch had been well aware of the developments in Germany in the 1930s that brought

Queen Juliana when she was heir to the throne, 1935.

Hitler to power and, ultimately, devastation to Europe. But the people of the Netherlands hoped that if they kept their heads down he would go away, or at least leave them alone.

Wall Street and the guilder

They had their own problems to contend with. The same economic shock waves that reached Germany from America in 1929 also reached the Netherlands. The Wall Street Crash had just as devastating an effect on the Dutch guilder as it had on British pounds sterling and the German mark. But the Dutch thought that stoicism in the face of adversity would be the solution that would win the day. The prime minister implemented belt-tightening measures and

curbed spending in order to maintain the strength of the guilder.

Neighbouring Britain devalued sterling, but the guilder held while unemployment soared. People concentrated on having a good time to avoid the economic issues and blocked their ears to the echoes of Hitler's ranting and to the sound of marching jackboots drawing uncomfortably close across the frontier.

Royal wedding

First came the World Jamboree Celebrations, then the marriage of shy young Princess Juliana to the German Prince Bernhard. The 24-year-old Princess had met the young German Prince in 1935. He was invited to lunch with the royal family at their Austrian ski resort, and, while Queen Wilhelmina did most of the talking, the two were busy falling in love.

Her innocence and euphoria could not have lasted long. Soon the young couple were confronted with Dutch reservations about the Prince's nationality, together with a Nazi witch-hunt against Prince Bernhard, who let it be known he would have no truck with the Nazis. In fact, three years after his wedding he would be found crouching on the roof of Soestdijk Palace, defiantly machine-gunning low-flying German planes.

The Dutch, who had previously avoided disturbing the enemy at the gate, finally showed their feelings on the day that the royal engagement was announced. Some Germans living in the Netherlands flew the swastika. In The Hague, seat of government and home to the country's well-behaved army of civil servants, people tore down the hated and feared insignia.

The German press blamed Prince Bernhard for the insult and started a campaign against him, and the German government withdrew the passports of nationals who had been invited to attend the wedding. The Dutch government opened talks and a compromise was reached, by which German nationals living in the Netherlands were advised not to display the swastika, while the Dutch agreed that Germany's national anthem and the 'Horst Wessel' song could be sung at the gala wedding evening. During the singing, some German guests gave the Hitler salute. Dutch and other guests responded by singing 'Rule Britannia'. It was a tense situation.

Dutch fascism

The early years of the 1930s had seen the emergence of Dutch fascism. The leader of the Dutch NSB (National Socialist Movement), whose members liked to strut around in black shirts and call themselves Nazis, was a short, vain man called Anton Mussert. A great admirer of Mussolini, he set himself up as the voice of order and solidarity which would unite the Dutch Aryan race and get rid of the enemy (Jews and any other undesirable foreigners), bringing the country back to prosperity.

Dutch troops, Colonel Pieter Scharroo. They came to deliver an ultimatum.

After smashing Waalhaven airport, where eight Fokker G-I fighters managed to shoot down two enemy bombers, the Germans met with fiercer opposition in Rotterdam itself. The city had a defence force of only 1,400 soldiers armed with just 24 light and nine heavy machine-guns between them.

Fuelled by desperation, anger and courage, these men fought the German infantry force, which had landed on the River Maas in seaplanes and was now heading for the

The devastated centre of Rotterdam lies in ruins after the German air raids of 14 May 1940.

Mussert hoped for power once the Germans occupied the Netherlands. He liked to quote Mussolini: 'The people are like a woman, they will go with the strongest.' He never tired of telling people that the Italian dictator was, 'like Hitler and me, not very tall.' Mussert faced a Dutch firing squad on 7 May 1946. He had not grown much in the interim and never achieved the position of power for which he yearned.

Rotterdam burns

At 10.30 on the morning of 14 May 1940, four days after the invasion, three German soldiers waving a white flag picked their way through the smoke-filled streets of Rotterdam, heading towards the headquarters of the leader of the

city. Rotterdam port was one of the Germans' main objectives and it was taking too long to conquer.

General Schmidt, commanding German troops at Rotterdam, Moerdijk and Dordrecht, sent Colonel Scharroo an uncompromising message. The city was to be surrendered or face a heavy infantry attack starting at 1pm on the same day, followed 20 minutes later by heavy bombardment from the air. Colonel Scharroo was given two hours to think it over.

Stay of execution

Neither Scharroo nor the city's mayor needed two hours. Their minds were made up: there would be no surrender. A quick call was made to a senior Dutch officer, General Winkelman. He contacted the queen's commissioner and Colonel Scharroo was ordered to send a message to General Schmidt stating that any ultimatum must be officially signed, giving the signatory's identity and rank. Meanwhile, General Schmidt sent a message back to Germany saying that the bombardment should be delayed while negotiations took place.

It was noon, and Rotterdammers, taking advantage of the lull in fighting, were shopping for food amid general relief that the shooting had stopped. Trams were running, children were on the streets.

A cyclist riding through the ruins of Rotterdam.

Meanwhile in Germany, the first squadrons of heavily loaded bombers were already moving down the runway at bases in Bremen and Westphalen on their way to their target – Rotterdam.

Hundreds of Rotterdammers had 90 minutes left to live – the time it would take to fly from Bremen and Westphalen on a clear day – and 14 May was another clear spring day. General Schmidt wrote and signed his latest ultimatum. The answer was to be in his hands by 4.20pm. The Dutch messenger, Captain Backer, accompanied by two German soldiers, set off again with a white flag. They may have exchanged remarks; certainly they looked up when they heard a deep sonorous sound in the air coming from the south and east. The German planes

had arrived. The raid commander had been told that if red flares were set off Rotterdam was to

> Though few in number, Dutch Nazis played a prominent role in occupied Holland by betraying Resistance members and rounding up Jews for the death camps.

be spared. Red flares went up – it appeared that the Rotterdammers had been given a reprieve.

Death from the air

The first group of planes changed course and flew off, their bombs still in their holds. However, a second wave remained on course, and dropped their bombs on thousands of screaming, panicked people who had never really believed the Germans would actually do this. It was 1.30pm, and many children were back at their school desks.

The Germans sent a message to Dutch headquarters in The Hague. Utrecht, a historic and beautiful city of many thousand inhabitants, would be next. All other Dutch cities would be bombed in turn. General Winkelman reluctantly decided to give in.

A message of surrender was sent to German headquarters at the Hotel des Indes in The Hague; it was a lovely old building, where Pavlova had died and Mata Hari used to meet her consorts. Word was sent to Dutch troops to destroy their weapons. Unwilling to believe the battle was lost and their country was now in German hands, they did not start to do so until the next day, Wednesday 15 May.

At the time, Queen Wilhelmina was staying in London, as a guest of George VI at Buckingham Palace. She was about to sit down to supper with the king when the terrible details

> A force of 10,000 Allied airborne troops was due to hold the bridge at Arnhem for just two days; in the event, against overwhelming odds, a mere 600 men held it for four.

reached her. That night, 125 Amsterdam Jews took their own lives.

Ten weeks later, the shattered ruins of Rotterdam were still smouldering. The death toll was recorded at 800, while some 80,000 people had been made homeless. Around 24,000 houses had been destroyed, along with 2,500 shops, 1,200 factories, 500 cafés, 70 schools, 21 churches, 20 banks, 12 cinemas and two theatres. The Nazis had truly arrived.

Dark days

Four years of misery descended upon the Netherlands. Each day brought new deprivations, degradations and sources of fear: shortage of food, lack of freedom, curfews, media censorship, death. Long cold winters had to be endured with no fuel for heating. In sudden *razzias* (round-ups), thousands of men were herded off to work in forced labour camps. For the country's Jewish population, it was a period of absolute and unadulterated terror.

But the Dutch, like so many others elsewhere in occupied Europe, never gave up hope. As time went on, acts of resistance grew in number, and by the end of the war, the Dutch Resistance was one of the most effective of any occupied country.

The Biesbosch marshes, a hard-to-penetrate area near Dordrecht, became a relatively safe haven for Resistance fighters and, by 1944, a transit route

Princess Juliana visiting the British King and Queen at Buckingham Palace on 13 May 1940.

THE DOCK WORKERS' STRIKE

A statue of a burly docker stands in Amsterdam's Jonas Daniël Meijerplein, commemorating the general strike of 25 and 26 February 1941, mobilised in protest at the Nazi deportation of the Jewish population.

Led by the city's dockers, it was Amsterdam's first open gesture of rebellion, as revulsion for the occupiers began to conquer collective fear. The strike has gone down in Dutch history as the 'day beyond praise'.

The Germans, who at first were taken aback by this brazen show of defiance, then moved quickly to stamp out what they saw as a dangerous undermining of their authority. Police patrolled the streets, shooting at passers-by, and notices were posted ordering the people to return to work immediately. Their message was unequivocal: 'There will be no meetings or gatherings of any kind, nor any political party activity. Anyone disobeying will be proceeded against under German military law. Hereafter, anyone who strikes, or who agitates for strikes will receive up to 15 years and, if the defence industry is involved, death.'

People slowly went back to work, but morale had been temporarily boosted by the fact that Amsterdammers had dared to resist the tyranny under which they laboured. There were no more posters urging the Dutch to trust their German friends. The kid glove was shown to cover a steel fist.

for Allied agents, downed airmen, refugees and arms between the occupied and liberated parts of Holland. The Germans tried to root the Resistance fighters from their hiding-holes among the reeds and marshes, but failed. Captured German soldiers were held as prisoners-of-war in the Biesbosch, under the occupiers' noses.

False dawn

September 1944 was a cruel month, marked by two particularly black dates. The first was *Dolle Dinsdag*, 'Mad Tuesday', which took place on 5 September. The German army had been routed in France and was fleeing in confusion through the Netherlands towards the German frontier. The Dutch thought freedom was at hand, their jubilation countered by the panic which broke out among collaborators, who joined the retreating Germans. Desperate people who had worked with the occupiers thronged railway stations. Hundreds left their luggage on the platforms in their rush to get on trains heading east.

Dutch citizens thronged the streets in Arnhem and surrounding villages, jeering the departing German troops and the flotilla of dispossessed traitors scurrying along behind.

Dutch resistance graffiti.

ANATOMY OF A BATTLE FAILURE

There are many theories as to exactly why Operation Market Garden failed. Was it a breakdown in communications? Overconfidence? Or the weather? A combination of all these reasons is probably the answer. Recriminations were thrown about, with each party blaming the other.

Cornelius Ryan, former war correspondent and author of *A Bridge Too Far*, which records every detail of the battle, once interviewed General Eisenhower, commander of Allied forces in Europe. Eisenhower, who insisted the interview should not be published until after his death, described Montgomery as 'a psychopath', 'egocentric' and 'a man trying to prove that he was somebody'.

Ryan also interviewed Montgomery. The Irishman was himself 'difficult' and admitted he did not suffer fools at all. But he did not think Montgomery a fool.

In an interview given at the launch of *A Bridge Too Far,* Ryan had this to say of General Montgomery: 'He was a vain, arrogant man. Ambitious as hell, popular with his men, a great publicist and highly intelligent, but Montgomery can never be forgiven for one act. This man knew that the 2nd SS Panzer Corps was in the Arnhem area yet still he sent his airborne troops in on top of them and, for that matter, so did Eisenhower. They both overruled the Dutch intelligence reports.'

People started to wave anything they could find that was coloured orange – the Dutch royal family's colour – and rumours were rife: Rotterdam had already been liberated, the queen was returning, the British were on their way.

Then, almost as suddenly as the flow of troops had started, it stopped. The next day the streets of Arnhem were still. A horrible realisation began to sink in. The British were not coming and the Germans were not going. They were recovering, regrouping and preparing to fight another battle, one of the most important of World War II, during which more Allied troops would die than in the Normandy landings. The tragic events that were to follow would go down in history as the Battle of Arnhem, or Operation Market Garden.

The Allied offensive, which began on 17 September 1944, was meant to open a corridor in central Holland from Eindhoven to Arnhem through which troops and tanks would sprint, and crossing the Rhine, head into the heart of Germany. Had it succeeded, the daring plan devised by Britain's Field Marshal Montgomery might possibly have brought the war to an end within weeks.

The plan was breathtaking in its simplicity. The Allied airborne operation involved flying in men, artillery and equipment of the 1st Allied Airborne Army. There were to be 5,000 fighters, bombers and transports, and more than 2,500 gliders. On the ground, the British 2nd Army's massed tank columns were poised along the Dutch/Belgian border.

Five major river and canal bridges and other minor crossings were to be seized by the airborne troops, opening up a long narrow corridor, with Arnhem the last gateway to the final goal, the Rhine, and Germany's heartland. The Third Reich would be toppled, bringing an end to the war in 1944.

A bridge too far

During the last conference at Montgomery's headquarters, Lt-General Frederick 'Boy' Browning, the British Deputy Commander of the 1st Allied Airborne Army, made the memorable remark: 'I think we may be going a bridge too far.' He was proved tragically right. When the Allied paratroopers arrived, the Germans, who were not supposed to be in the area in such strength, were waiting to meet them. The elite 2nd SS Panzer Corps had been quartered near Arnhem in the quiet, green area around Oosterbeek to rest and recuperate from recent combat.

While the US 101st and 82nd Airborne divisions succeeded in capturing Eindhoven and Nijmegen, when the battle for Arnhem began, the British 1st Airborne Division found itself cut off from help along the corridor: they fought bravely and desperately, but many were killed or captured. Dutch families around the area opened their doors and hearts to the wounded and dying. Many acts of individual heroism that day are recorded for history. But the saddest reminder of the battle must be the rows of simple white crosses in Oosterbeek War Graves Cemetery. Operation Market Garden left

In Arnhem Oosterbeek War Cemetery.

17,000 Allied soldiers, British, American and Polish, killed, wounded or missing.

The failure of Operation Market Garden had a further terrible legacy; thousands of people in industrial areas around Amsterdam, The Hague and Rotterdam died of hunger (because of a Nazi blockade), while in the death camps of Central Europe, hundreds of thousands of Jews died, as the Nazis, aware of the Allies' imminent arrival, tried to destroy evidence of the policy that would come to be called the Holocaust.

Freedom at last

Finally, on 5 May 1945, Germany capitulated and the Netherlands was liberated. The official document was signed in Wageningen. A jubilant Prince Bernhard was present, together with General Blaskowitz, Commander of the German troops in the Netherlands, and the Canadian General Faulkes.

There were scenes of ecstatic joy in Amsterdam, The Hague, Delft and Rotterdam (most of the south of the country had already been liberated before the winter). But there was a marked difference in the appearance of the cheering crowds to those, say, of Paris. The faces of many were grey and hollow; some people could hardly stand on their pathetically thin legs. Children were weak and

'fraternised' with German soldiers were rounded up and had their heads shaved. Dutch Nazis, and other collaborators who had not already fled, were arrested as the euphoria led to an explosion of bitter anger amongst the recently liberated. But the Dutch are a reticent people. There were no public

> The Battle of Arnhem left over 10,000 Dutch dead, most of them civilians, victims of the campaign itself or of the terrible 'hunger winter' that followed.

Liberation Day marks the end of the occupation by Nazi Germany during World War II.

had to be held. Many were suffering from tuberculosis.

After the Allied attack on Arnhem, the Germans had deliberately slowed down vital transport carrying food to the industrial areas of the Netherlands. Food and fuel supplies ran out during the winter. Many people were so desperate that they resorted to eating tulip bulbs. While the relief drops of Operation Manna did much to alleviate suffering, thousands died before spring finally arrived, bringing with it the long-awaited liberation.

Revenge and recrimination

On the evening of Liberation Day ugly scenes took place as terrified women and girls who had

lynchings. Of 154 death sentences passed only 42 were carried out. Practical as ever, the Dutch set most of the collaborators to work rebuilding damaged roads and buildings.

As the country slowly started to heal, a tally was made of the ravages caused by the war; hundreds of thousands were dead or missing, and the bill for damaged property reached billions of guilders. The list of destruction included 70,000 houses, 8,360 farms, 10,000 factories and 200 churches. There was a special figure for the Jewish population. In 1940, 140,000 Jews lived in the Netherlands, mostly in Amsterdam. At the end of the war less than a third of that number remained alive. Of those who had survived, most had lost everything. Then the struggle began to understand it all.

Operations Manna and Chowhound

Cut off from food supplies by the Germans, thousands of Dutch residents were saved from starvation by the Allies at the end of the war.

The bitterest months of the occupation began for the Dutch after the failure of Arnhem; life under the desperate and revengeful enemy was to prove horrific. Several thousand Dutch men, women and children died as a result of German reprisals, many killed in retaliation for kidnappings carried out by the Resistance. But the worst figure was the 15,000 who died from hunger in the last year of the war.

By October 1944, the war's front line ran right through the Netherlands; the northern part of the country was still in German hands and cut off from food supplies. Food was failing to get through because of rail strikes, and the Germans had blocked the waterways in retaliation for the strikes.

Desperate for food

The whole country suffered, but cities were the worst hit: The Hague, Rotterdam and Amsterdam. Pathetic streams of people made their way out of the cities to the countryside, pushing wheelbarrows laden with personal possessions to barter for food. They often returned empty-handed. Most tragic of all were the children, many of whom dropped dead from exhaustion on the streets. To compound the misery, it was a bitterly cold winter, and fuel had run out. People cut down trees in the cities' parks for firewood; the wooden blocks between the train rails disappeared overnight. By midwinter the death toll was high.

In December 1944, Minister Gerbrandy, head of the Dutch government in London, wrote to General Eisenhower: 'The Dutch government cannot accept that eventual liberators will be liberating dead bodies.' The letter pressed for an offensive to begin to free the north of the Netherlands. But on the day Mr Gerbrandy wrote his letter the Germans started their own desperate offensive in the Ardennes. Every available German soldier was needed for battle, so, to release them from occupation duties in Holland, Dutchmen were despatched in their thousands to camps in Germany.

In January 1945, the death rate in Amsterdam was 500 a week; as there was no wood for coffins, most bodies were buried in paper or rolled in a sheet.

Air-drops

That spring, the first weak sun shone on some very pathetic faces: some were green-tinged from eating too many tulip bulbs; infectious diseases, including typhoid and diphtheria, were rampant. Then, on 25 April, posters appeared promising relief from the months of relentless misery. The Allies were to start air-drops of food.

This risky exercise was called Operation Manna. On 29 April the skies above the north of Holland were suddenly filled with the deep sound of low-flying British Lancaster bombers; this time when their bomb-bay doors opened it was to release crates of

RAF pilots preparing to drop supplies of tea.

food rather than bombs. Pilots and crews risked their lives as they flew as low as 60 metres (200ft) above the dropping areas. People filled the streets waving to the planes; many were crying and waving sheets, shirts, anything that would flap in the wind.

Some crews emptied their pockets, throwing out chocolate and cigarettes. When the second wave of planes came, people had messages ready. Sheets were spread out reading 'God Bless You' or, in some cases, 'Cigarettes here please'.

From 1–8 May, American B-17 Flying Fortress bombers joined the exercise, known as Chowhound. To many Dutch, these operations were the sign that the misery was over. 'It was a wonderful sight, the great billowing parachutes, crates of food attached', said one Dutch woman who was there.

MODERN HISTORY

In the aftermath of World War II, the
Netherlands emerged as the very model of a
modern European nation.

As was the case elsewhere in newly liberated Europe – indeed, in many countries throughout the world – the immediate post-war period was difficult for the Netherlands. The priorities were reconstruction, in particular of war-shattered cities such as Rotterdam, Arnhem, Eindhoven and Nijmegen, and repairing the damage done by flooding when dykes had been damaged. As the economy slowly recovered, the foundations were laid for the country's cradle-to-grave welfare system, which, financed by high taxation, would become one of the most generous and comprehensive in the world.

Benelux, a customs union with Belgium and Luxembourg, came into force in 1947, followed by Dutch membership of the European Coal and Steel Community in 1952, and the European Economic Community (now the European Union) in 1958. Queen Wilhelmina abdicated in 1948 in favour of her daughter, Juliana. The following year, with the Soviet Union presenting the latest security threat to Western Europe, the Netherlands joined NATO.

In 1953, disaster struck. A devastating North Sea storm broke through the dykes in the southwest, causing catastrophic flooding, with substantial loss of life and property, in parts of Zeeland, Noord-Brabant and Zuid-Holland provinces. The Dutch government's response was the Delta Works), a 30-year engineering effort begun in 1958 to strengthen sea defences by sealing off river estuaries and coastal inlets, and raising dykes throughout the southwest. It reached its climax in 1987, with the opening of the colossal Oosterschelde Stormvloedkering (Eastern Scheldt Storm Surge Barrier). Land has continued to

Princess Christina during Golden Jubilee celebrations for her grandmother, Queen Wilhelmina, 1948.

be reclaimed from the sea, especially around the freshwater IJsselmeer.

End of the colonial era

After World War II, the East Indies emerged from Japanese occupation with a new determination to seek independence. The Dutch fought desperately to restore colonial rule, but yielded in the face of an insurrection led by General Sukarno, whose aims were supported by the US and most of Europe. Independence was granted in 1949, and the Dutch East Indies became Indonesia. Visitors to the Netherlands today cannot fail to see an influence, from the many citizens of ethnic Indonesian origin to the Indonesian restaurants that serve some of the best food in the country.

A few small Caribbean islands remain part of the Dutch realm, but the western colonies have had far less cultural impact on the Netherlands. Dutch Guyana gained independence

> As a fading echo of the cracker radicalism of the 1970s and 1980s, environmentally minded Amsterdammers voted in 1992 to drastically cut car use in the city.

Protests in Amsterdam reached a violent peak in 1975, as police confronted demonstrators over plans to demolish housing in the old Jewish quarter around Nieuwmarkt to build a new metro system. Similar battles broke out in the following decade in the adjacent Waterlooplein neighbourhood in an attempt to prevent construction of a new opera/dance venue and Town Hall complex. Despite the strong opposition, the metro opened in 1980, followed by the Muziektheater (now known as the Nationale Opera & Ballet) in 1986 – the Opera House is now one of the city's top cultural attractions.

A protester throwing a brick towards a line of charging riot police during an 1980 protest in Amsterdam.

as Surinam in 1975, after which 150,000 of a population of 400,000 exercised their right of immigration to the Netherlands. Surinamese immigrants have generally not assimilated as well as the Indonesians.

Fighting in the streets

During the 1960s Amsterdam was a hotbed of radical political activity, led by the anti-establishment 'Provos' (a term derived from provocateurs), dedicated to shaking Dutch complacency. The Provos won seats on the city council in 1965, and the following year led demonstrations that disrupted the wedding of Princess Beatrix to German Claus von Amsberg. The Provos disbanded in 1967.

Throughout the 1970s and 1980s, and even into the 1990s, a severe shortage of decent affordable housing fuelled the activities of squatters, called *crackers* in Dutch. The government's prioritisation of hotel construction – along with the aforementioned new Town Hall and Muziektheater – rubbed salt in the *crackers'* perceived wounds and provoked many homeless people into taking over unoccupied houses.

In 1980, violent disturbances rocked the city as 500 police, using armoured vehicles and CS gas, evicted *crackers* from properties in the heart of the museum quarter. That same year, the celebrations for Queen Beatrix's coronation were disrupted in a major way, with protesters and police once again slugging it out in Amsterdam's streets amid clouds of tear gas.

Such epic events are now little more than memories. In recent years the city's political and business leaders have tried to promote an image – and a reality – more in tune with the needs of commerce. Amsterdam has consolidated its position as an international business centre, the European headquarters of multinational corporations, and a transport and distribution hub. The country has the 18th-largest economy in the world, an incredible statistic given the nation's size.

An economic pioneer

During the 1990s, the Netherlands was the setting for two far-reaching European Union treaties: the 1992 Maastricht Treaty which created the Single European Market, and the 1997 Treaty of Amsterdam, which confirmed the course of European Monetary Union (EMU) and the creation of the euro. When the first EMU deadline arrived in 1999, the Netherlands was one of 11 countries to establish the euro.

The country was also one of the founding members of the G10 (Group of Ten) in 1962, which participate in the General Arrangements to Borrow (GAB) and introduced the 'floating exchange rate' in 1971.

An international tragedy

Wim Kok's government resigned shortly before the 2002 general election, following a critical official report on an affair that had been eating away at the country's self-esteem for years. In 1995, Bosnian Serb forces had stormed the besieged United Nations 'safe haven' of Srebrenica in eastern Bosnia, which was protected by a small battalion of lightly armed Dutch UN troops. The troops had little choice but to give way, and the Serbs proceeded to massacre 7,000 Bosnian Muslim prisoners, in the single greatest atrocity in Europe since the World War II. Wim Kok and his ministers accepted responsibility for the Dutch failure.

In the election that followed, a new political party zoomed to sudden prominence. The LPF, led by Pim Fortuyn, a flamboyant, right-wing, gay political newcomer, ran on a platform of opposition to immigration, a tougher response to crime and a radical shake-up of cosy, compromise-driven Dutch politics. The establishment took little notice until Fortuyn

was gunned down in the street in 2002, an event that shocked the nation. Further shock followed in 2004, when Theo van Gogh (great-grandson of Vincent's brother), a film-maker who had made a controversial documentary on the status of women in Islam, was murdered in the street by a violent extremist.

These two killings altered the political landscape of the country, heightening racial tensions and provoking much soul-searching. The genie of immigration – released from its bottle by Pim Fortuyn – and issues of multiculturalism have become hot topics, causing the

Wim Kok addresses the news media.

RACIAL TENSIONS

This continues to be an issue. In 2013 a white linesman was kicked to death by teenage Moroccans following a dispute after a youth football match in an Amsterdam suburb, bringing into sharp focus the problems with immigrant integration. In 2014, the country was the eighth most popular destination for asylum seekers in Europe. As a result of stresses on the welfare system and a public backlash over Muslim immigration, in 2015 the centre-right government toughened its laws by stopping food and shelter provision for people who fail to qualify as refugees; a rule that almost toppled the government following a clash with centre-left Labour.

centre-right government to implode in 2006. The centrist coalition that replaced it in early 2007 included the country's first Muslim senior ministers.

State of the nation

A small, densely populated country (the population tripled last century), with 16.9 million inhabitants in its 42,000 sq km (16,000 sq miles), the Netherlands probably needs every centimetre of sea floor it can lay its hands on. But statistics can be deceptive. Two-thirds of the population live in one-fifth of the country,

Schiphol airport, one of the world's biggest.

the western 'Randstad' area that includes Rotterdam, The Hague, Amsterdam and Utrecht.

In the remainder, population pressures are far less apparent. Farmland and national parks take up much of the available space, and cities like Maastricht, Eindhoven and Groningen are fewer and further between. Landscapes vary from flat polders to heaths and lakes, even including hills, while cultural differences ensure that the languages of Friesland and Zeeland co-exist with Dutch and a gaggle of local dialects. In place of the stress and aggression which might normally result, the Dutch have developed a tolerant, live-and-let-live attitude that has coloured their politics and culture.

In some countries, certain social groups or classes are described as the 'pillars of society', be it the middle class, the judiciary or religious institutions. The Netherlands took this idea a stage further by making all groups the *zuilen* (pillars) of society, any one of which could survive perfectly happily without reference to the others, yet which generally chose mutual co-operation over confrontation as a way of achieving goals.

Divisions in society

Today it remains true that the media, education, trade unions, hospitals and cultural organisations are divided according to religious and political groupings. That the system has worked owes much to the celebrated contradictions of Dutch society, where unity and diversity, conservatism and liberalism, stuffiness and adventure, are easy bedfellows. The Dutch are renowned the world over for their tolerance.

A lack of political angst has enabled the Dutch to concentrate on creating and sharing prosperity. In the decades since the war, the economy, motivated by a lack of raw materials and the loss of Indonesia, has been transformed from one based on agriculture to one where high-tech industries and trade predominate. Many multinational companies have established significant operations here.

The great middleman

'Gateway to Europe' and 'Holland Distribution Land' are slogans often used to underline the country's geographical advantages. Positioned as the transport hub of Western Europe, and possessed of such important assets as Schiphol airport and the port of Rotterdam, the Netherlands is considered the middleman par excellence.

But a simpler, more human concept underlines everyday life. When all the grand ideas of tolerance, Golden Ages and commercial acumen have been weighed in the scales of a nation's worth, you may still be struck more forcefully by the constant Dutch search for *gezelligheid*. This is an enigmatic word for that special something that makes a country friendly, cosy, comfortable, familiar, welcoming and memorable. Dutch, in fact. *Gezelligheid* may turn out to be the country's most important commodity.

A new era

After the fall of the government in February 2010, when the PvdA refused to allow the Dutch Army to continue its involvement in Afghanistan, snap elections were held in which the VVD took over as the largest party (from the CDA) followed by the PvdA. However, the biggest winner in these elections was the right-wing PVV, led by the charismatic Geert Wilders, which doubled its number of seats. A coalition between the VVD and CDA formed a minority government, with Mark Rutte becoming prime minister.

International importance

With its future assured, albeit with a reasonably turbulent government, the Netherlands remains one of the world's most desirable places to live. As well as having the best healthcare in Europe, it came fourth in the UN's 2013 World Happiness Report and the country has the 13th highest per capita income in the world after a 2013 report by the International Monetary Fund (IMF).

In March 2014, The Hague hosted an emergency meeting of G7 members to discuss Russia's annexation of the Crimean Peninsula in

King Willem-Alexander and Queen Maxima attend a 200th anniversary celebration of the Netherlands.

In October of 2010, the Netherlands Antilles was dissolved following a referendum after years of discontent. However, the islands of Bonaire, Sint Eustatius and Saba voted to retain links with the Netherlands and are now known as the Caribbean Netherlands.

Dutch elections went on to be held again in 2012, following the collapse of the minority government after Wilders and the PVV rejected proposed austerity measures. A new government was formed between the PvdA and VVD with Rutte remaining prime minister.

Like her predecessors, Queen Beatrix abdicated in 2013 and her son, Willem-Alexander, became king on 30 April in that year, continuing the legacy of the House of Oranje-Nassau.

Ukraine. The city is seen as 'the world's legal capital' as it is home to four international courts: the Permanent Court of Arbitration, the International Court of Justice, the International Criminal Tribunal for the Former Yugoslavia and the International Criminal Court. It is also the HQ of Europol, the EU's criminal intelligence agency.

Having produced some of the world's greatest artists and possessing some of the world's best museums, the country's cultural riches will be under the spotlight in 2016 for the 500th anniversary of the death of fantasy artist Hieronymus Bosch and again in 2018 when Leeuwarden in Friesland becomes a European Capital of Culture.

A Dutch family in Amsterdam.

THE EVOLUTION OF A NATION

Religious freedom, coupled with a hatred of being told what to do, has in many ways moulded the Dutch into a cosmopolitan and relatively classless society.

Many elements of Dutch society, like the Dutch themselves, are a study in contradictions. The Netherlands is a nation devoted to tidiness and a strong sense of order, yet its capital is known for pavements slippery with dog droppings, graffiti-scarred walls and dishevelled drug addicts. The Dutch hate taking orders and gleefully jeer the self-important, yet they revere their monarchy. It is a nation founded on religious tolerance, yet features a powerful religious lobby. The people fiercely guard their privacy, yet leave their living-room curtains open all evening, maintaining that they have nothing to hide.

The Dutch rarely try to explain; to them, the contradictions are simply part of being Dutch. Like their sense of humour: the Dutch revel in hearing or telling a good joke, yet they also admit they are a stolid, dull people ('but not as dull as the Belgians', they quickly point out). They are not prone to apologies (though they do offer a simple 'sorry' if they bump into you on the street). This remains a source of frustration to foreign visitors used to having their own 'space'.

But in such a crowded country, visitors are expected to go with the flow. And in anarchic cities like Amsterdam, that means dealing with cyclists racing through red lights and taxis permitted to drive along the tram tracks.

The break with Spain

The emergence of the Netherlands as a nation can be traced back to the late 16th century. The whole of the Low Countries was then under Spanish rule, but already divided by religion. The southern provinces (modern Belgium and Luxembourg) were staunchly Catholic and accepted Spanish sovereignty, unlike the Dutch

Clad in orange to mark King's Day.

in the northern provinces, who rebelled against Philip II's efforts to impose Catholicism on them and stamp out the Calvinist movement.

The northern, Protestant-dominated region came to be known as the United Provinces after the seven member provinces that signed the Treaty of Utrecht in 1579. From that time onwards, the United Provinces acted as a separate nation, though, until 1648, not one recognised by the Spanish. The alliance, which left each of the provinces with considerable independence, served as a model for the federalism that evolved in later nations, including the US.

Then, as now, the Dutch hated being told what to do, whether by a foreign king or by one of their own dukes. As a result, the seven provinces were run in much the same manner as the medieval city-states of Europe: each province made its own laws, and other states had little or no say in a province's internal affairs. The only real influence of the States General, the assembly to which each province sent representatives to discuss issues of common importance, came in military affairs and in drawing up economic policy when it was considered an integral part of military strategy. The United Provinces rarely recognised a national leader, except in dire necessity such as times of war.

Begijnhof buildings, Amsterdam.

CREATION OF THE WELFARE STATE

Some believe that the Netherlands transformed itself into a welfare state in the 1960s, but the roots go far deeper. Virtually every town has surviving examples of *hofjes*, the small houses often set around garden squares that were built by religious organisations and family trusts for the poor and elderly. In Amsterdam an example is the Begijnhof, a square just off Kalverstraat. Just as the unemployed, disabled and aged of the 21st century find succour in the welfare state, the poor of the 16th and 17th centuries were looked after by charities. About 25 percent of today's gross national product is redistributed by the government.

Wealth creation

There was another critical element in the way the United Provinces were run. Instead of allegiance to a king or prince or a set of ruling families, power rested with the commercial classes – the merchants, traders and bankers who created the wealth. And they did create wealth. The 17th century, despite continuing conflict with Spain, has become known as the Golden Age of the Netherlands; in that century the Dutch carved out a trading empire around the world and used their prosperity at home to create an era of achievement in fields as disparate as art, architecture and town planning.

Many believe that the Golden Age would have had no lustre if the United Provinces had not been founded on the principle of freedom of conscience. In one of the earliest examples of Dutch contrariness, Calvinism was the official religion and Catholicism was formally outlawed, but the United Provinces allowed anyone to practise any religion they wished in private, Catholics included.

This religious freedom, along with the then rare freedom of the press, drew refugees to the United Provinces from all over Europe – many of them the richest, most ambitious and best skilled in their own countries. Later, as the empire grew, many from the Dutch colonies, particularly from what is now Indonesia, came to settle in the Netherlands, often through intermarriage with the Dutch or working for Dutch companies. Consequently, the Netherlands has always had a cosmopolitan flair, mixing races and religions and a more or less equal chance of exploiting individual talents. One legacy of the Golden Age is that anyone could become a member of the clergy, an artist or an entrepreneur. Although not members of a completely classless society, most Dutch belong to one large, dominant middle class.

Social structure

For centuries Dutch society was built on *zuilen*, or 'columns', representing different components of the population. The members of each group kept to themselves but nonetheless held up the ideals of the nation. The two main columns consisted of Protestants and Catholics. They not only had their own churches, but their own schools, civic organisations and political parties. Parts of some towns would be Catholic, other parts Protestant, while some towns were completely one or the other.

Since World War II, the distinctions have faded. Some historians give Hitler the credit: the Nazi occupation forced Dutch who had never mingled – Calvinists and Catholics, city-dwellers and villagers, northerners and southerners – to work together. Today, the *zuilen* are still there but they are ineffective, and many Dutch are members of more than one column.

Perhaps the biggest change has taken place in religious attitudes. Church attendance has fallen dramatically, and polls indicate that more than half Dutch are now agnostics or atheists. Many only set foot in a church for one of the

criticise those who took part in the demonstration. 'We do not believe in holy men', he told one interviewer. 'The Pope came here as a man higher than others. That is not the Dutch way.'

His successor, Wim Kok of the Worker's Party (PvdA), received his political grounding in the hierarchy of trade unions, hence his Socialist view, and took a completely different approach.

Yet the Calvinists remain influential, using their powerful lobby to restrict aspects of everyday life, such as drinking laws and opening hours. Dutch television features some of the most biting satire in the world, which pokes

The Zuiderzee Museum, located on the Wierdijk in Enkhuizen, looks to preserve the area's cultural heritage.

non-religious talks, concerts or regular exhibitions that take place.

Religion and politics

In politics, the Protestant and Catholic parties merged in the 1960s, creating the Christian Democratic Appeal (CDA), which became the dominant centrist party. Significantly, in this mostly Protestant country, the charismatic Ruud Lubbers, a Catholic, became the leading Dutch politician of the late 20th century, with a series of Christian Democrat election victories that gave him repeated terms as prime minister. When protesters marched on Pope John Paul II chanting 'Kill the Pope!' during a 1985 visit to the Netherlands, Lubbers was reluctant to

> Despite a surface control by Calvinist ideals, the Dutch largely retain a live-and-let-live attitude to foibles in their society.

fun at all aspects of the Establishment – except God and religion, which are still largely taboo.

When laws are elastic

The role of religion and the Calvinist lobby may be partly responsible for the continuing contradictions – some might say hypocrisy, others just typical Dutch pragmatism – that continue to exist between Netherlands law and day-to-day practice. To visitors, prostitution and drug use are obvious examples. In theory, drugs are illegal, though you wouldn't know it from the way police calmly stroll past marijuana cafés ('coffee shops'). Brothels were only legalised in the 1990s, although they have been flourishing in many Dutch cities for centuries. A less well-known example is euthanasia. Now legal under certain controlled conditions, it was for a considerable time technically illegal, yet practised by doctors with the tacit approval of the authorities.

Prostitution and soft drugs remain illegal because any attempts to change the legal status quo would be strongly opposed by the Calvinist lobby. But such practices go on openly because the Dutch people, with their legendary tolerance, don't really care whether they're illegal or not. The café owners and prostitutes are even invited to become members of the local Chamber of Commerce.

This remarkable ability to look the other way can sometimes embarrass the Dutch. In recent years, for example, the Netherlands has been forced by pressure from other countries to act against its child pornography industry, which was supplying much of the rest of the world with explicit magazines and videos of young-

Out in Amsterdam's red light district.

LIBERAL PARENTING

One Dutch mother interviewed says she did not try to discourage her two daughters from teenage sex; she advised them on birth control. When the daughters dabbled in marijuana, the mother didn't harangue them; she had smoked pot herself. The junkies on the streets sent a stronger anti-drug message to the girls. When one daughter went through a punk phase, the mother agreed that it was ridiculous for people to be afraid of green hair. When the other daughter had her fourth bicycle stolen in one year, the mother didn't question her when she arrived home with another days later. 'I suppose she stole it, but who can blame her?'

sters in acts of sex and violence involving adults, other children and animals. 'People, normal people, did not realise how nasty or extensive this stuff is,' one Member of Parliament admitted. However, after the infamous Dutroux child-abuse scandal that rocked neighbouring Belgium in the late 1990s, closer attention is being paid to this subject.

At the same time, the Calvinist traditions of the Netherlands can be viewed as a contributing factor in some of the country's most progressive programmes, including a long-term National Environmental Policy Plan, which calls for water, air and soil pollution to be reduced by up to 90 percent before 2030 – a goal that would consume up to 3.5 percent of the gross national

> *Some believe one reason the Dutch keep their curtains open is that they want their neighbours to know that their homes are clean and that they have no reason to hide anything going on inside.*

product. It is a programme and a cost that few other countries would dare undertake, but as one financial analyst concluded: 'Gripped by Calvinistic guilt over lapsed stewardship of the earth, the Dutch are convinced that their country is the sink of Europe. They point out that it is a small, densely populated land, a third of which is covered with water, and close to what they regard as pollution-spewing Britain and western Germany.'

No doubt the Calvinist traditions have also played a role in the leadership the Dutch have assumed in the world peace movement since it began in the Netherlands at the end of the 19th century.

Order and respectability

The liberal attitudes of the Dutch – perhaps 'libertarian' would be a better word, though some critics might prefer 'libertine' – are one of the country's biggest contradictions. Despite a long history of religious intolerance, the Dutch willingness to let anyone do anything provided it doesn't hurt other people seems at odds with other basic elements of the Dutch character. They are a people in many ways obsessed with respectability and with a strong sense of order.

Women and family

Dutch feminism presents a number of other contradictions. At first glance, women in the Netherlands seem to be among the most broad-minded and outspoken anywhere in the world. Yet, until quite recently, relatively few Dutch women went out to work compared with other industrialised Western countries.

Formerly, Dutch women worked only until they got married, and then became house-wives and mothers. Today, increasing numbers of married women go out to work, although most wait until their children are at school. It is interesting to note that the majority of children in the Netherlands are born at home, rather than in hospital. Several weeks before any scheduled birth, a midwife is sent to inspect the mother-to-be's home to make sure the parents (or parent) are prepared. Mid-wives generally supervise the birth. On the day after the birth, the government sends a young woman to the home. For the next eight days, from 7am to 6pm she acts as a mother's helper: cleaning up, washing, taking care of the other children, shopping, making meals, receiving visitors, and so on.

Attitudes to royalty

The Dutch may occasionally joke about their monarchy, but in fact the royal family is

Queen Beatrix and Claus van Amsberg.

extremely popular. In typical Dutch fashion they live in much less ostentation than, say, the British royals, and treat the accident of birth as a lifelong job that fate has assigned to them. In Britain, the only reasonably recent monarch abdication (in 1936) was a major event; in the Netherlands abdication is routine.

The last three queens have retired in great dignity to let their younger heirs carry on. One of the reasons the Dutch royals are so popular is that they behave just like a modern family, and the Dutch people can therefore relate closely to their problems. Prince Claus, the late husband of Queen Beatrix, who abdicated in favour of her son, King Willem-Alexander, in 2013, has been widely praised for his courage in discussing publicly his battles, over a number of years, with depression.

Family life

The Dutch are very orientated towards family life, and visitors from other countries often remark on the healthy, friendly relationship that exists between Dutch parents and their children. The common emphasis, if there is one, seems to be on avoiding the sort of conflicts that can create a permanent rift, and issues are often approached from the child's perspective.

or 'cosiness, conviviality', as represented by the *schemerlampen*, the soft-shaded 'twilight lamps still found in many Dutch homes. There's even a word in Dutch for sitting up late and watching the fire die down.

The Dutch also have a reputation for hard-headed shrewdness in business (in the 17th and 18th centuries they sold weapons to, and even underwrote the ship insurance of, their enemies). Yet quality of life is not equated with prosperity, and the gap between the highest and lowest incomes is much less than in most other developed nations.

A family bike trip, Kinderdijk, Olanda.

Golden Age values

Dutch home life encompasses several values that seem to date back to the Golden Age. The television age has inevitably changed traditional trends as it has elsewhere in the world, but it is still not unusual for a Dutch family to turn off the television and spend an evening together making conversation or playing music.

Still important is the concept of *deftig*, which doesn't translate directly but can be described as 'dignity, respectability, stateliness' (see page 82). Visitors express surprise that most Dutch homes have no curtains in the front room, but the Dutch do not feel the need to hide the way they live. At the same time they attach importance to the concept of *gezelligheid*,

The Dutch may at first may seem a little standoffish or even gruff to outsiders, but this is a misleading impression. In fact, they love to go out to eat in large, noisy groups, following the Dutch adage, 'Pleasure shared is pleasure doubled'. The Dutch generally like to make friends and look for any excuse to chat: over coffee in the morning, tea in the afternoon and beer or *jenever* (gin) in the evening. A Dutch person who is dining alone in a restaurant is unlikely to be offended at an invitation to join someone else who is also seated alone. As a result, there is often ample opportunity for the solitary visitor with the appetite – or the thirst – to learn first-hand about Dutch society and its many contradictions.

The House of Orange

After a controversial past, the Dutch monarchy appears to be in safe hands thanks to a new young king and his vibrant Latin American wife.

It is easy these days to see the monarchy's appeal to Dutch citizens. Willem-Alexander, who became the first Dutch male monarch since 1890 in 2013 following the abdication of his mother Queen Beatrix, is a keen environmentalist and sportsman. His Argentinian wife, Queen Maxima, is equally popular, regarded as 'authentic'.

The appeal of the House of Orange remains linked to its role as a unifying force during the struggle for independence. The Oranje-Nassau dynasty dates back to medieval times, when the German Count of Nassau was granted estates in the Low Countries, but the dynasty only came of age in the late 16th century when William of Orange inherited these estates along with the southern French principality of Orange. The colour orange is displayed on all ceremonial occasions.

A German consort

However, the appeal of the royal family hasn't always been so obvious. In 1966, amidst social unrest, Princess Beatrix married German diplomat Claus von Amsberg, previously a member of the Hitler Youth and the German army. The wedding, in Amsterdam, was the occasion for smoke bombs, tear gas and violent demonstrations. A decade later, Queen Juliana's consort, Prince Bernhard, was found guilty of being 'open to favours' and accepting a million dollars from Lockheed in connection with defence contracts. Even so, tolerance and esteem for the royal family ensured that a constitutional crisis was avoided.

In 1980 rioting disrupted Queen Beatrix's investiture in Amsterdam. The city was in the throes of a housing crisis, while 84 million guilders were being spent on the royal residence in The Hague. The protesters' slogan was '*Geen woning, geen kroning*' ('No home, no coronation').

The royal role, enshrined in the Constitution, is 'above politics', and the monarch is the only fixed factor in a fast-changing, pluralist political scene. But the monarchy can be abolished at any time by Act of Parliament. The Dutch are no blind loyalists, and should the Orange dynasty die out, would not hesitate to proclaim a republic.

Despite loyalty to the House of Orange, much credit is due to the influence of recent monarchs. During Queen Wilhelmina's 50-year reign (from 1898 to 1948), moral leadership was the keynote. She was a member of the Reformed Movement and, as a pious Calvinist, encouraged the Church to resist secularisation.

A low-key queen

In true Dutch fashion, Queen Juliana rebelled against her mother's imperiousness. During her reign, from 1948 to 1980, she proved a natural communicator with a common touch. Her successor, Beatrix, often

King Willem-Alexander And Queen Maxima.

said that if she hadn't been queen, she too would have been a social worker. Although marriage to a German was not popular, Beatrix endeared herself to the public with her egalitarianism, low profile and conscientiousness. The second-richest woman in Europe, she showed social restraint bordering on parsimony. The royal family resists ostentatious limousines and will drink cheap Luxembourg sparkling wine rather than fine French champagne.

Likewise, Beatrix was careful not to inflate her role in the public's eye. In return for toeing the line, the royal family expects a level of privacy envied by members of other European royal families. Today's House of Orange offers the nation a peaceful continuity, symbolic unity, moral leadership and, in a country of faceless governments, an identifiable brand name.

PROVINCIAL LIFE

The Netherlands may seem like a nation
divided between town and country but
the population's values are closely linked.

In his famous poem *In Nederland*, J. Slauerhoff presents the typical metropolitan view of provincial life. Such disparaging sentiments are probably endorsed by many would-be sophisticates in Amsterdam or Rotterdam, but the poet's criticism is clearly the view of a privileged outsider from Randstad Holland.
The Netherlands is not where I want to live,
you always have to keep your urges in check
for the sake of good neighbours,
who peer eagerly through every crack.
You always have to be striving for something,
thinking of the well-being of your fellow man.
Only on the sly may you give offence.

The Randstad

Literally the 'Rim City', but better translated as the Western Conurbation, the Randstad is the crescent-shaped area embracing Amsterdam, Utrecht, Dordrecht, Rotterdam, The Hague, Leiden and Haarlem. Although it is not a geographical region and has no official status, the term encompasses the Netherlands' most powerful urban centres in North and South Holland and Utrecht. This is the hub of the country; elsewhere tends to be dismissed as 'the provinces'.

This Randstad bias emerged with the mighty Dutch Republic in the 17th century. Before then, the distinction was between town and country: an inhabitant's sense of identity was bound up in the municipality; and, unlike today, the southern cities were more powerful than those in the west. Towns relegated to provincial obscurity today were then in the ascendancy. In the south, Middelburg, Maastricht and the old Flemish towns were important dukedoms, trading or religious centres. Nijmegen, in the heart of the country, was a

Rounds of traditional Dutch cheese.

member of the medieval Hanseatic League, while Groningen and Leeuwarden, in the north, were prosperous merchant cities trading in spices, tobacco and cloth.

With the creation of the Dutch Empire, metropolitan Amsterdam and South Holland province acquired a disproportionate weight that they still retain today. Despite modern government's attempts at decentralisation, the Randstad reigns supreme economically. However, unlike the provinces, the Randstad is vulnerable to encroaching internationalism. The small-town flavour of the region is endangered by silicon flatlands, dormitory suburbs, chain hotels, cosmopolitan culture and fast-food outlets. Of course, this pessimistic view ignores the concentration of cultural riches in the Randstad, from Rembrandts to Delftware, gables to Van Goghs, international ballet to experimental jazz – the provinces can rarely compete on this scale. Even so, in looking at the glittering shop window of the Randstad, it

> In summer on the Wadden Islands there may be sightings of locals practising the odd sport of wadlopen, 'mudwalking' across the tidal mudflats of the Waddenzee.

Carvings of Dutch emblems in Marken.

is all too easy to miss the more old-fashioned goods in the stockroom. Despite the surface gloss of metropolitan culture, the provinces offer a truer picture of traditional Dutch culture and values.

There is, then, a strong case for seeing the Netherlands as two separate nations: the Randstad and the rest. In broad brushstrokes, the distinction is between modernity and authenticity.

Compared with the hectic metropolis, the southern and eastern provinces and the islands are more traditional, insular and agricultural. Stepping outside the Randstad enables one to peer through the curtains into the world of small-town Holland, where the pace of life is much slower.

The provinces

Starting in the north of the country, on the remote Wadden Islands, you might encounter Texel boat repairers, conservationists or fishermen. In rural Friesland, dairy farmers can be spotted chatting outside huge pyramid-shaped farmhouses. Their local language, Frisian, bears relation to both English and German. In the capital of neighbouring Groningen (city and province share the same name), university students can be seen gossiping in trendy chrome-clad cafés.

To the southwest, in Flevoland province, Urk is a poignant reminder of the price traditional fishing villages have had to pay for the damming of the old Zuiderzee (now called the IJsselmeer). Since the building of the Afsluitdijk and the ban on trawling in the IJsselmeer, local fishermen have had to sail further for their catch. EU quotas have made life even more difficult, yet old values, including the wearing of traditional costumes, are still prevalent. The inhabitants of Flevoland can also be viewed as victims of the Randstad. The province's new polder landscape was intended to provide housing for the adjoining metropolis, but commuters have proved reluctant inhabitants in places such as Emmeloord, which is little more than an overgrown housing estate.

Just east, in Overijssel province, the lake district based on the water-locked village of Giethoorn has been developed as a boating centre. Giethoorn's relative openness to outsiders contrasts with the insularity of the farming communities located to the south of the lakes. Staphorst, for instance, has a strict church-going community whose members discourage the use of cars on Sunday and reject many aspects of modern life.

Negative impacts

The eastern part of the province, known as Twente, is another casualty of Randstad economics. The old textile towns have declined pitifully, deprived of reinvestment and commercially marooned.

Just west of Flevoland, Noord-Holland province embraces the Randstad with happier results. Despite bordering the metropolis, the cluster of former fishing villages has a clear sense of identity. Volendam, for instance, has exploited its picturesque past as a modern-day tourist trap, while Marken remains a traditional fishing village to all appearances – the only element it lacks is the fish.

South of the former Zuiderzee, most of Utrecht province falls into the urban Randstad, but lesser-known Gelderland is a snapshot of suburban Holland. Apeldoorn advertises itself as 'the biggest garden city in the Netherlands' but is in reality a collection of gentrified garden suburbs, the slightly snobbish inhabitants forming the last vestiges of empire.

South of Gelderland lie Noord-Brabant and Limburg, the Catholic southern provinces. These regions differ from the north in religion,

Zeeland, just south of the Randstad, has elements of both the north and south provinces. Its proximity to old Flanders has given the region more exuberance than its northern neighbours, while the watery isolation has helped preserve intact its Protestant idiosyncrasies. Contradictory Zeeland is home to costumed farmers' wives in Middelburg, struggling fishermen on the coast and prosperous yacht-owners at Veere.

Provincial architecture

Building up the provinces has not always been successful. Lelystad was built in the 1960s as a

A sightseeing boating trip along a canal in Giethoorn, know as the 'Venice of the North'.

temperament and economic success. Breda and Bergen op Zoom are hearty commercial towns with lively carnivals and a Burgundian flavour. As for the Noord-Brabant countryside, Van Gogh's village of Nuenen and its surrounding heathland and peat bogs are still recognisable from many of the painter's early landscapes.

Although both Limburg and Noord-Brabant are dotted with unspoilt villages, the region has also proved that international business can succeed outside the metropolis: Eindhoven, for instance, is home to the giant Philips electrical company, while Limburg has benefited from the relocation of several government departments – a move that has transformed the former coal-mining town of Heerlen.

dormitory town for Amsterdam and Utrecht and as a recreation centre for city-dwellers. Lelystad followed what was then known as 'the mathematics of space', the obsessively geometrical lines of De Stijl architecture (see page 95). Although it was heavily criticised in its early years for lacking character, this experiment is getting renewed attention from innovative young architects intent on making it more liveable. In nearby Almere, built on the edge of the Randstad in the 1970s, architects attempted to counter the anonymity of high-rise blocks with a construction resembling an open chest of drawers, intended to create the feeling of an old Dutch *buurt* (neighbourhood). Although Almere was dismissed as a 'modern ghost town'

> *Gambling is popular in the provinces. A visit to one of Heerlen's casinos shows that the old Dutch dictum remains true: 'I invest, you speculate, they gamble.'*

and an impersonal, characterless suburb, it too is receiving renewed attention, largely due to its proximity to Amsterdam.

Dutch planners have since realised that provincials prefer vernacular architecture to monofunctional creations. In this vein, there has been an interesting development on the Oostelijk

traditional gabled town houses. Because of the high cost of land, houses tend to be small and rather minimalist in style, almost regardless of the relative wealth of their inhabitants. Certainly there are differences in social status between a modest fisherman's cottage in the Biesbos marshes and a grand villa on the wooded outskirts of The Hague, but extremes of affluence are less visible in the Netherlands than elsewhere in Europe.

This was even the case with Amsterdam's 17th-century architecture: the gabled working-class houses in the Jordaan are almost as

Cycling through tulip fields.

Islands just east of the Amsterdam Maritime Museum, called the 'New East'. The Java, Borneo and KNSM islands have architecture that offers residents a waterfront view just a few minutes by bike or ferryboat from the city centre. A relatively new area called IJburg, further southeast, is also contributing to solving housing problems. In particular, the Dutch dislike tower blocks: over 70 percent of the population live in family houses and reject the credo of the De Stijl movement: 'No more masterpieces for the individual... but mass production and standardisation with a view to providing decent housing for the masses'.

Elsewhere in the provinces, new bourgeois garden suburbs are popular, as are well-restored

impressive as the prosperous merchants' houses that line Herengracht.

Domestic life

The provinces have long been a shrine to family values, and it can be argued that, since the 17th century at least, the Dutch have worshipped domestic culture. As historian Simon Schama says: 'The predominant perception among Dutch people is that for all their international orientation and progressiveness, there is still something of the mentality of the village or the small town: one's image is important, an eye must always be kept on what the neighbours are doing, what they think, and anything that breaks out of the comfortable small-scale pattern is to be treated with suspicion.'

The Dutch adore their children but, in return for the attention lavished upon them, children are expected to be both polite and respectful. Critics claim that far too much emphasis is placed upon being '*normaal*' – conforming to parental expectations. A common expression is 'Act normally and you're conspicuous enough,' an indication of the level of decorum expected.

Psychologists characterise the Dutch as an introverted family culture, one in which the well-being of the family is paramount and the home is a fortress against the world. Provincial family life is essentially low-key, comforting, conservative and conformist. The domestic cocoon is easily mocked but seldom pierced by outsiders. In fact, a predilection for cosy domesticity is often cited as the fundamental flaw in Dutch literature.

Provincial culture

Visitors who restrict their travels to Amsterdam could be excused for thinking that the Dutch spend their leisure time at the National Ballet, fringe theatres and nightclubs. But this

A Kortenhoef farmhouse.

RURAL ARCHITECTURE

In the countryside residents favour neat, barn-like farmhouses adorned with mottoes or decorative gables. Any comparison between the Randstad and the provinces must take account of the importance of land to the provinces – farming is the one occupation that the provinces have in common. The fact that the Netherlands is the world's third-largest agricultural producer is, with the exception of bulb-growing, thanks to provincial efforts.

Although specialisation is increasing, most farms are still family-run and passed down the generations. The type of farming varies regionally: horticulture on the polderland, cattle and dairy farming in Friesland, fruit farming in Gelderland and mixed farming in Noord-Brabant and Limburg. The farm buildings also differ: T-shaped farms in Gelderland and Overijssel, while Noord-Brabant favours farms with long, low façades. Limburg boasts white half-timbered farmhouses and fortified farms built around a courtyard. Friesland has long, pyramid-shaped or granary-style barns, raised on *terpen* (artificial mounds).

All Dutch farmhouses exude an air of security and dependability, the epitome of Dutch rural values. Old farms in Flevoland often have mottoes adorning the façade. One typical motto, *Werklust* (joy in work), makes the point that this is serious hard-working countryside.

is not true of provincial culture, and in a small village in Friesland, entertainment is more likely to involve singing in a local choir, skating or fishing.

A mirror of provincial culture is presented by Heerlen, an unexceptional commercial town in Limburg. On a typical day, an amateur group will be performing a play in local dialect, various brass bands will be rehearsing for the Carnival and an experimental ballet will be on at the Stadsschouwburg. For those in need of a simple night out, there are bowling clubs, multiplex cinemas, pancake houses and rustic-style

Regional costume at home in Hoorn.

THE ROLE OF WOMEN

Most provincial housewives believe that cherishing the home is a virtue that outweighs a second wage. As a result, fewer women work full time here than in any other European Union country.

Feminists point out that the Dutch government was the last to sign an EU directive granting equal pay and rights to women and that legislation discriminates against women. Moreover, Dutch social services assign benefits on a family basis. Although these criticisms are well founded, it is still a fact that the home remains the cornerstone of Dutch life for many provincial women.

bars. There, the regulars drink, socialise or just read the evening newspaper.

Provincial culture is essentially populist and in this respect is heir to the hearty alehouse scenes painted by Jan Steen. Burghers in the 17th century used to claim that 'the first little glass is for health, the second for a toast, the third for a nightcap and the next can only be for pleasure'. Smoking, then as now, remains a popular pastime. Although the smoking of tobacco indoors is nationally banned, some small pubs are exempt from this rule and smoking, like coffee-drinking, seems to be the national pastime. And the traditional way of rolling one's own cigarette continues.

Outside the Randstad, the survival of regional dialects, costumes, folkloric festivals and traditional sports indicates the diversity and depth of provincial culture. Even though there are few remote areas in the Netherlands, regional accents are proudly retained. Dialects are spoken in the Veluwe, Groningen, Drenthe and Gelderland. Frankish is spoken on the German border, while dialects of Vlaams (Flemish) survive in Noord-Brabant and Limburg. The province of Friesland has its own language, Frisian, quite distinct from Dutch, and it would be a foolhardy visitor to Zeeland who argued that the province's tongue, Zeeuws, is not a language in its own right, too.

Costumes

Regional costumes are another sign of local identity preservation. Costumes are most common on the shores of the IJsselmeer, in Overijssel and on the islands of Zeeland. However, even within the Randstad costumes have not disappeared completely. In Scheveningen, formerly a small fishing village near The Hague but now a holiday resort, matronly fishwives still wear their black costumes with pride; by contrast, young locals refer to their elders with embarrassment as 'the black stockings'. In touristy Volendam, you will see men in baggy trousers and women in black striped or pleated skirts posing for pictures. In neighbouring Marken, the costumes are entirely different and worn more naturally, though only on special occasions. Women's dress includes bonnets, long-sleeved blouses, cotton waistcoats and embroidered bodices, while men wear a red sash and a blue smock over their baggy black trousers.

Sport and festivals

Traditional sports and regional festivals continue to draw enthusiasts. Many activities such as skating, walking, fishing and sailing arose naturally from the landscape. In Friesland, duck-trapping, once the 'poor person's hunting', is widely enjoyed, and in Middelburg (Zeeland), a curious form of bowling called *krulbollen* is still played. Friesland boasts the greatest variety of quaint sports, including *fierljeppen* (pole-vaulting over a canal) and *skûtjesilen* (races in flat-bottomed sailing boats). Even within the Randstad, traditional

Leisure

Given the importance of domestic values, leisure is often family-orientated or home-based. Gardening is so popular that even families without gardens attentively cultivate allotments. Even the smallest community has a music group or choir with its own banner, motto and public performances.

On a daily basis, the streets of many provincial Dutch towns (and even those of Amsterdam) are filled with a variety of music, ranging from muzak to Flemish carillons and street organs.

Making skating a feature of everyday life.

pursuits remain. Every year, in the North Sea near Scheveningen, a five-day pole-sitting marathon takes place: the winner is the last person left sitting on the pole.

Ordinary sports are popular throughout the provinces, and the emphasis is always upon group involvement. Football (*voetbal*), the country's biggest spectator sport, is worshipped nationally, as is the case across most of Europe. Cycling is another common pursuit, particularly on the polderland and in Gelderland's national parks.

Walking events, such as the four-day Nijmegen marathon, are professionally organised, but it is generally felt that community spirit is more important than competition.

THE ELFSTEDENTOCHT

The Elfstedentocht (11-cities race) is a skating marathon through Friesland. The race begins in Leeuwarden and covers 200 km (125 miles) and 10 other cities before ending in national exhaustion, watched on television by the whole population. There are about 300 serious competitors, but over 18,000 skaters try to complete the gruelling eight-hour course. The ritual begins and ends in darkness, and skaters endure harsh winter conditions. The competition is only held in severe winters, but its infrequency alone cannot explain its cathartic effect on the nation. Perhaps it is a reminder to the Dutch of national struggles against ice and water.

Folklore fairs, cheese markets, herring festivals and carnivals have survived all over the provinces. In the time of the Republic, the *Middenstand* ('bourgeoisie') had a taste for public festivities, and little has changed today.

Morality and class

The Dutch are a relentlessly moral people, in their aspirations at least. The 17th-century battle to put 'honour before gold' continues, as does the struggle between puritanism and sensuousness. New moral dilemmas seek out the balance between individuality and conformity, tolerance and righteousness, merit and grace.

There are, however, significant differences between the moral values of the Randstad and the provinces. In practice, the Randstad weights the balance in favour of tolerance and individuality rather than conformity. Metropolitan intellectuals have even coined the term 'Hollanditis' to describe the 'Dutch disease' of excessive liberality. In The Hague and Amsterdam new protest groups emerge daily to challenge the authorities on the housing crisis, environmental issues or unem-

The church of Den Hoorn on the island of Texel at sunrise.

LOVE OF THE LANDSCAPE

A deep appreciation of Dutch landscape unites painters as various as Brueghel, Hieronymus Bosch, Ruysdael and more recently, Mesdag and the Dutch Post-Impressionists. It is best expressed in Ruysdael's moody paintings: he places the horizon so low that cities and human life appear submerged in the cloudy skies. This attachment is both proud and sentimental, but hard to fathom, since nature dealt the Dutch an indifferent hand. The puritanical reply is that through God-given grace they have redesigned the watery landscape: having valiantly fought against countless floods, they feel proprietorial about their achievement.

ployment. The provinces are far less confrontational and view situations with classic Dutch earnestness.

The provinces think of themselves as holding the moral high ground, usually supported by their religious faith and old-fashioned domestic virtues. The cornerstone is the belief in *deftigheid* (decorum), which masks the provincial yearning for respectability. The younger generation, however, even in the provinces, often equates the term with excessive civility, stiffness and even hypocrisy.

For the older generation, *deftigheid* can take the form of an obsession with propriety. Some 'rules' of etiquette include not laughing too heartily and making as few gestures as possible. Greeting with a big hug is not done. Certainly, provincials attach great importance to manners: there are set times when coffee should be served to guests; when coming into a room, the newcomer must greet the others who are present by turn; and at a birthday party or other social function, they must be sure to shake hands with everyone and introduce themselves formally.

In business letters, men and women often use only their initials in order to protect their privacy. Such propriety and reserve can expose the provincial to the charge of a rather mindless conformity, but luckily individuals have their ways of escaping this straitjacket – often by way of a broken outburst of bluntness. *Nivellering*, the trend towards equality, has helped blur class barriers, particularly in the larger cities. However, in the north of the country and out on the islands, social hierarchy is noticeably more rigid. In Friesland, Overijssel and Zeeland, for instance, social cachet still belongs to the bigger farmers, landowners and wealthy shopkeepers. The term *Boerenslim* (farmer's intuition) is used as a compliment.

As if to counteract differences in wealth and status, there is little display of affluence or conspicuous achievement. Because of their Calvinist roots, wealthier citizens still tend to play their status down, although this does not always hold true when they are abroad. Then the Rolex watches are worn with pride and the expensive sports cars are driven to impress. It is a strange paradox. The Dutch are a nation often accused of having the good life – but of not knowing how to enjoy it.

Certainly, the old battle between puritanism and sensuousness still rages in the provinces, while the struggle between godliness and greed remains as fraught in the countryside as it is in the midst of the city.

Religion

Although Randstad residents are not as church-going as in the past, provincial Dutch remain tied to their religious landscape as a matter of course: religion is a key pillar in the traditional Dutch scheme of compartmentalising society.

Known as *verzuiling*, the practice of dividing society into denominational groups still pervades the provinces, influencing the choice of school, newspaper, leisure pursuits, political party, hospital and pension scheme. It is still common for, say, a young Catholic teacher living in Noord-Brabant to be educated at a denominational college, join a Catholic brass band or chess club, listen to a Catholic radio station, read a Catholic newspaper and go on a holiday organised

Flea market finds in Leeuwarden.

by a Catholic club. By the same token, it is quite common for a Protestant member of the Reformed Church (Hervormde Kerk) or Orthodox Reformed Church (Gereformeerde Kerk) to follow a completely separate yet parallel path. A farmer from Zwolle in Overijssel might typically subscribe to a Protestant weekly, shop at a Protestant grocer, be innoculated at a Protestant hospital, meet his future wife at a church dance and end his days in a Protestant old people's home.

Given the importance of these religious distinctions, people are skilled at reading the visible clues of affiliation. Catholics, for instance, distinguish themselves from Protestants by wearing their wedding ring on the third finger of the left hand instead of on their right hand, as is more common in the Netherlands.

Church services vary considerably in both style and content. Compared with the sober tone of Protestant services, the services of the Catholic Church have much more ritual, and Catholics also favour melodic hymns over more sombre psalms.

Protestant distinctions

Approximately 8 percent of the Protestant population are Dutch Reformed, 4 percent are Calvinists and 6 percent belong to the Protestant Church in the Netherlands (PKN).

Dutch Catholic opinion often conflicts with Rome's, and it is little wonder that Ruud Lubbers's Christian Democratic Party enjoyed so much power during the 1980s and 90s. A public protest during one of the Pope's last visits proclaimed: 'The Church, once built on a rock, is slowly sinking into the marshy soil of the provincial Netherlands.'

Even though 56 percent of the population has no religious affiliation, 70 percent of Dutch schools are religiously segregated, though this paradox has more to do with academic achievement than anything else. In Amsterdam and

Toy ships for sale in Veere.

Out in the countryside the Orthodox Reformed Church has great power and its power base comes more from the working class. By contrast, the Reformed Church is perceived as being more liberal on social issues, but is also seen as being more vulnerable to the modern trend, leaning towards secularisation.

Catholicism

While Protestants dominate the northern provinces, Catholics are in the majority in the south and form a majority nationally (26 percent). In Catholic terms, the Dutch are most liberal, favouring contraception and women priests, as well as attending to Third World issues.

other major cities, churches are being turned into exhibition centres, but a Dutch Sunday is still sacrosanct. Very few newspapers publish a Sunday edition, and most shops and petrol stations are closed. A Sunday visit to any rural community presents a scene little changed for decades.

But attachment to place, God, domestic virtues and a moral code are not uniquely provincial. Most Dutch subscribe to these values in part, and difference is more in emphasis than essence: the Randstad presents an international face but retains a provincial heart. In a Dutch home, you may notice the family Bible, piano, home-made *appeltaart* and handmade toys – all clues to the fact that few nations are more domesticated than the Dutch.

A scenic cycle

Cycling might be a quick and fun way to explore a city but head out into the countryside if you're looking for a quieter life.

Whatever it is that makes the Netherlands tick, the bicycle must be a vital part of the mechanism, for there are 13 million bikes in this country of 16 million people. Most are humble stadfietsen (city bikes), and many of them will have been stolen any number of times and then put back into circulation again. Despite the absence of any mountains, Dutch cyclists generally have a second bike in their locker, a smart racer, touring bike or even a mountain bike for heading out into the wide green yonder at the weekend or on holidays.

The bicycle might have been invented with the Netherlands in mind. Not only is there a vast network of bicycle paths and signposted cycling routes, but myriad tiny roads lead into the heart of polders, farming country, forests and heathland.

Cycling in the Netherlands is a sociable business, not least because so many people do it. Not a few are of an age at which they might ordinarily be thinking of slippers, warm fires and quiet evenings in. Don't underestimate these older riders, who are willing and able to keep going in all weather, often long after the young hotshots have hung up their Lycra racing suits for the day.

Explore the countryside

If you've resisted the temptation to join the legions of cyclists in towns and cities for fear of swirling traffic, head out into the countryside. Hire a bike in town, then take a train to almost anywhere you fancy; or hire a bike from the railway station at your destination – most main stations and many small ones have hire facilities. Flopping aboard a train at the end of the day is also a good way to get you, your bike and your weary legs back to base.

Once aboard your trusty steed, watch for blustery winds threatening to separate you from the saddle. Wind is a fact of life on the spirit-level-flat polders near the coast, and anyone not up to the challenge is advised to seek a more sheltered experience on inland forest trails. Take heart, though: even if you set off into the teeth of a strong wind, you may find that on the way back it is now behind you, allowing you to fly with the wind in your sails.

In places where inhabitants and tourists are thin on the ground, and the pace of life slackens off a gear or two, you may be the only thing moving in the landscape – apart from whirling windmill blades. There is an exhilarating sense of freedom and mobility on a bike. From your saddle, the countryside drifts past at a pace you can absorb. You feel like part of the process, instead of a four-wheel interloper.

Cycling from Amsterdam

For an easy, four-hour round trip avoiding most of the city traffic, cycle southwards along the banks of the River Amstel. After a half-hour or so, you emerge sud-

A Dutch symbol.

denly into the countryside on the way to the pretty village of Ouderkerk aan de Amstel.

A far tougher proposition is cycling round the IJsselmeer. Until the 1930s, this big lake on Amsterdam's doorstep was not a lake but a sea, the Zuiderzee, which the Dutch penchant for reshaping their country has transformed. Who can resist cycling round a sea? For a cyclist, it is the perfect Dutch experience, immersed in wind, sun or rain, following a narrow track between the polders and the lake.

Experienced racing cyclists can do the 320-km (200-mile) round trip in a day. If you're not getting as many miles to the gallon as you used to, set yourself a more modest target of four to six days. The IJsselmeer is one of the most beautiful areas in the country, and a leisurely cycle can be most rewarding.

A FEAST OF FESTIVALS

The Netherlands has a year-round calendar of events, from lively pre-Lenten carnivals in February to raucous New Year's Eve celebrations.

The Dutch enjoy a celebration and love to sing, dance, make music and dress up in costume. Thanks to its rich history and multicultural population, there are hundreds of festivals held throughout the year in the Netherlands. These celebrate everything from film and music to sports, poetry, tall ships, flowers and plenty more besides.

In February or March, the festive pre-Lenten carnival in the provinces of Noord-Brabant and Limburg celebrates the arrival of spring. Three days of organised anarchy reigns, with spectacular parades and plenty of dancing, eating and drinking. From mid-March to mid-May, the world's largest flowering-bulb show (tulips!) is on at Keukenhof Gardens near Leiden. In May, more than 600 windmills around the country welcome the public on National Windmill Day. The Summer Carnival Street Parade snakes its way through Rotterdam at the end of July and the city also hosts the world's largest jazz festival, North Sea Jazz Festival, in the same month. The Amsterdam Gay Pride Festival is held on the first weekend of August while the Grachtenfestival (Canal Festival), featuring classical-music concerts on barges, takes place in the capital in the second half of the month. The annual Bloemencorso in September is a colourful parade of flowers and music that makes its way from Aalsmeer to Amsterdam. Contact the local tourist offices for further details.

Live music at the North Sea Jazz Festival.

Boat-loads of people congregate on the canals for Koningsdag or King's Day, in central Amsterdam, the best place to witnes the festivities for this day of celebration.

See blooms afloat at Westland Floating Flower Parade (Varer Corso), held in August.

A young vendor at the Koningsdag free market with her wares.

A RIGHT ROYAL CELEBRATION

Koningsdag (King's Day), the king's official birthday, should certainly be experienced at least once. For those who arrive in Amsterdam on 27 April unaware of the festival, it could be quite a shock to discover thousands of people swarming into the city and heading towards the centre.

Although every city and village has a King's Day celebration, the capital is the place to be. There is music in the air, with bands at nearly every major intersection, and food vendors offering a medley of international snacks. In honour of the House of Orange, people drape themselves In orange scarves, hats, ribbons and other adornments, and often paint their faces orange, too. Even the red, white and blue Dutch flags are decorated with orange pennants.

The canals play host to an unofficial boat parade, which is a show within a show. And there is a so-called free market, a tradition that allows people to set up vending stands. The event ends in the evening with a fireworks display.

ostumed float at Carnival in Maastricht.

ebrating Gay Pride in Amsterdam.

Carnival costumes for all the family.

THE ART OF THE GOLDEN AGE

**The most glittering period in The Netherlands'
history is also one of the most culturally rich
the world has ever seen.**

The 17th-century Golden Age was a time of excellence in politics and economics as well as in the arts. The Dutch Republic ruled the seas and was one of the most powerful countries in Europe. The Treaty of Westphalia (also known as the Treaty of Münster), concluded with Spain in 1648, merely sealed the formal independence that the seven northern provinces of the Netherlands had seized almost a century earlier.

Painting exhibited a distinctive national character, and many artists took their subjects from their own experiences and the environment that surrounded them, athough generally they confined themselves to a single type of subject matter, such as portraiture, still lifes, landscapes or domestic scenes of everyday life.

Many 17th-century Dutch and Flemish artists improved on the techniques of their predecessors, painting on skilfully cut thin oak panels which rarely warped or cracked. Besides wood, other materials such as copper were used, though canvas predominated as it was better for large paintings, allowing a freer and bolder style – even if the weave occasionally showed through. The different surfaces and their preparation had an important influence on the techniques and styles of the artists of the Golden Age. Wooden panels with a white chalk ground gave a smoothness that was conducive to minute detail and the meticulous finish that led Gerard Dou (1613–75) to found the important school of genre painting at Leiden known as the Fijnschilders.

Dou painted *Young Mother* (now in the Mauritshuis, The Hague) 'so finely as hardly to be distinguish'd from enamail'. The Rijksmuseum in Amsterdam has fine examples of most of the painters of that splendid era, and all the works mentioned here are in that museum, unless otherwise noted.

'Still Life with a Turkey Pie', Pieter Claesz.

The greatest of the era

Though Rembrandt is today regarded as the most outstanding 17th-century painter, Frans van Mieris and Adriaen van der Werff were considered the greatest painters of the day by their contemporaries. Others, such as Cesar van Everdingen, the brothers Gerrit and Willem van Honthorst, and Hendrik Terbrugghen, were equally talented and highly regarded. But unlike the prolific painters whose work is on public view, such artists have been more or less forgotten, their paintings either lost or destroyed, or held in private collections.

The still-life painting of the Golden Age was initially very sober, as the works of Pieter Claes (1597/8–1661) and Willem Heda (1594–1680) demonstrate. Their work is characterised by the rendering of a combination of objects carefully chosen for their symbolism. Gold and silver cups and fragile glasses and jugs often feature, serving as a warning against excess and acting as a reminder of the transitory nature of life – a favourite theme of the still-life genre.

As the century progressed, the Eighty Years War came to an end, prosperity increased and Calvinism turned away from depictions of religious themes. More elaborate fruit bowls and flower vases, ever more splendid gold and silver cups and rich tapestries appear in portraits and sumptuous

'The Night Watch' by Rembrandt.

COLOURS OF THE AGE

The Dutch artist of the 17th century employed a fairly limited palette. Certain colours, like blue and green, were difficult and expensive to get hold of, and were therefore used sparingly and to dramatic effect. Natural ultramarine (lapis lazuli) was the most expensive, and azurite, a blue copper carbonate mineral, very scarce. Poor-quality artificial azurite, indigo for underpainting and smalt (ground-up blue cobalt glass) were often used instead. Green was obtained from a mixture of blue and a lead-tin oxide or vegetable-dye yellow. The yellow has often faded, leaving some Dutch paintings of this era with blue foliage and grass in woods and fields.

still lifes, such as those by Willem Kalf (1619–93) and Abraham van Beyeren (1620/1–90).

Institutional patronage

It was also customary to paint group portraits of the regents of institutions, *hofjes* (almshouses for the elderly), orphanages and hospitals. Frans Hals (1581/5–1666) was a masterly portrait painter who captured the essence of his models, as shown in his famous *Merry Drinker*. The Frans Hals Museum, in a 17th-century (men's) almshouse in Haarlem, the town in which he lived, exhibits most of his group portraits, which are also known as Corporation Pieces.

Rembrandt van Rijn (1606–69) is undoubtedly one of the world's greatest artists. He can certainly be called the painter of humanity, since he always emphasised the human element, not only in his portraits, but also in his biblical and historical paintings. Until 1631, he worked in Leiden, his birthplace. The first paintings of his early period, such as *The Musical Company* and *Tobias Accusing Anna of Stealing the Kid*, are very colourful. Later on, Rembrandt's preference for strong contrasts between light and shade becomes apparent, as in his *Old Woman Reading* and *Jeremiah Lamenting the Destruction of Jerusalem*.

Rembrandt left Leiden in 1631 to move to Amsterdam, where he worked until his death in 1669. There he abandoned the meticulous style of his Leiden period for a broader manner, in which light and shadow merge into each other, and his greys and browns display a deep, warm glow.

A world-famous work of his Amsterdam period, which Rembrandt completed in 1642, was originally called *The Company of Captain Frans Banning Cocq and Lieutenant Willem van Ruytenburch*, and depicts the moment when the captain gives his lieutenant the order for the guards to march out. The painting was given the title *The Night Watch* in the 19th century. This large work, originally installed in the Arquebusiers' Guildhall, now hangs in the Rijksmuseum.

Dutch landscapes

It is understandable that at a time when the country was fighting for its independence, painters would choose that land, their own immediate environment, as a subject for their pictures. A good example of this genre is the large *Winter Landscape with Ice-Skaters* by Hendrick Avercamp (1585–1634). Other good examples are Jan van

Goyen's (1596–1656) majestic *Landscape with Two Oaks* and Esaias van de Velde's (*c.*1591–1630) sombre *Cattle Ferry*.

> Restored Dutch paintings look clean and crisp – even when dark colours were used – because they were covered with a turpentine-based varnish which can be easily removed by restorers.

Landscape painting reached its zenith in the 17th century in the work of Jacob van Ruisdael (1628/9–82). In *The Windmill at Wijk bij Duurstede* and his grand *View of Haarlem*, van Ruisdael presented the impressive expanse of the flat Dutch countryside under enormous cloudy skies. Other landscape painters worth looking out for are Adriaen van de Velde (1636–72), Aert van der Neer (1603/4–77) and Paulus Potter (1625–54) who painted animals in extensive landscapes.

The painters' decision to concentrate on their own surroundings was particularly well suited to the rendering of church interiors. The impressive *Interior of St Mary's Church at Utrecht* by Pieter Saenredam (1597–1665) is one of many fine examples.

Merry company

Another favourite theme was Dutch scenes from daily life, divided by subject matter into groups – what we know as 'merry company' scenes (*gheselschapjes*), outdoor scenes (*buitenpartij*) and brothel scenes (*bordeeltjen*), most containing a hidden moral. These subjects are characteristic of Dutch genre painting, yet there is no Dutch word – past or present – that directly corresponds to the present-day English sense of the word 'genre'.

Dutch genre painting originated in the 16th century with Patenir and his Flemish followers, the greatest of whom was Pieter Brueghel the Elder (1525–69), who developed landscape into a subject of its own rather than using it merely as a background to religious, mythological or historical scenes. Brueghel left Antwerp during the Spanish occupation and moved to Amsterdam, where his work gave impetus to the development of new forms of Dutch painting.

Although Brueghel's paintings retained a moralistic tone, he depicted scenes from peasant life, *kermisses* (fairs and carnivals) and weddings. By contrast, other early 'merry company' paintings

showed elegantly dressed and cosmopolitan young men and women eating, drinking, playing music and embracing in taverns or in landscape settings; Dirck Hals (1591/2–1624), the lesser-known younger brother of Frans, was a great exponent of these 'merry company' scenes until the 1630s. His contemporary, Jan Miense Molenaer (1609/10–68), painted children, often in theatrical settings, symbolising freedom from care.

The witty and perceptive Jan Steen (1626–79) also depicts the behaviour of children in, for example, the typically Dutch Feast of St Nicholas, and that of adults at a fair or an inn. Adriaen

'Ice-skating in a Village' (detail), Hendrick Avercamp.

van Ostade (1610–85), from Haarlem, specialised mainly in scenes taken from peasant life.

The public were well aware of how to read these paintings: a map frequently indicated the absence of the head of the household, gone travelling overseas on trade; a dog in inns and brothels pointed to gluttony and licentiousness; a cat and a mouse reinforced the sense of the transience and uncertainty of human existence, while the ploy of a painting within a painting often pointed out a moral or a warning.

Canvas nasties

Amsterdam was a vigorous centre of genre painting in the first three decades of the 17th century. Particularly popular were barrack-room scenes and tavern interiors with soldiers drinking, fighting and womanising. It is curious that Amsterdam merchants should have chosen to hang scenes of brawling soldiery on their walls. Perhaps they wanted a contrast to their relatively peaceful lives (after all, very little fighting ever took place in Amsterdam) – or perhaps they enjoyed these pictures for much the same reasons that people today like to watch action movies or the portrayal of violence on television – the vicarious thrill.

The talented Willem Duyster (1599–1635) specialised in these active yet delicately painted scenes, and Gerard ter Borch (1617–81), con-

'Girl with a Pearl Earring', Vermeer.

sidered by some to be as great as Rembrandt, began his career as a painter of barrack-room scenes. His later, more refined art, of which his *Gallant Conversation* and *Seated Girl* are remarkable examples, represents a distinct departure and stands in a class of its own.

It goes without saying that painters in Holland – a country dependent on the sea – found water a natural subject for their pictures. Willem van de Velde the Younger (1633–1707), of *The Cannon Shot* fame, is the best-known Dutch marine painter, but another master of the genre, Jan van de Capelle (1626–79), was by no means his inferior.

Light plays a crucial part in the work of the Delft master Johannes Vermeer (1632–75), and,

because he is sparing in his use of shadow, he achieves a great translucency of colour. Despite their small size, his paintings belong among the most monumental works in Dutch art. You'll find four in the Rijksmuseum – *The Kitchen Maid*, *Woman Reading a Letter*, *The Love Letter* and *The Little Street*.

Painters often chose a townscape or a single street as a subject, as in the work of Gerrit Berckheyde (1636–98) and Jan van der Heyden (1637–1712). The domestic interiors of Pieter de Hooch (1628–1684 were similar to those of Vermeer, though less serious and less strong in form. *Woman with a Child in a Pantry* and *Courtyard behind a House* are among his best works.

The explosion of artistic talent in the 17th century is truly remarkable, yet the popularity of painting in the Golden Age did not obscure other forms of achievement – architecture, sculpture, silver, porcelain and furniture – which demonstrated a high standard of individual craftsmanship. Beautiful objects then being created were integrated into the houses of the wealthy. Chairs, tables and cabinets, even birdcages and doll's houses, were as much on display as the works of art.

Imitation and flattery

Delft is now known for the blue-and-white painted pottery which Italian potters introduced to the region, although early production centred on Antwerp. In the 17th century the descendants of these potters, now Protestant refugees, moved from Antwerp into the northern provinces, where they made Rotterdam and Haarlem their main centres. Not long after, the city of Delft began producing its characteristic tin-glazed tiles, plates and panels, painted with blue decoration copied from Chinese wares imported by the East India Company. By the mid-17th century, Delft jars, vases and bowls, and even door portals and lintels, were everywhere, ornamented with landscapes, portraits and biblical or genre scenes.

During the 17th century large quantities of silver were also made – not only in cities such as Amsterdam and Rotterdam but also in the smaller towns where traditional forms were kept. One such was the characteristic Friesland marriage casket or *knottekistje*, shaped like a knotted handkerchief.

From the first decade of the 17th century silver drinking horns used on ceremonial occasions, as well as vessels, basins, urns and saltcellars, began to be decorated with a new ear-shaped form. This 'auricular' design, created by Paulus van Vianen (1570–1613) of Utrecht, was soon joined by flowing patterns of sea creatures and molluscs developed by van Vianen's brother Adam and his nephew Christian. Later in the century, a profusion of flowers found their way into the decorative armoury, including the newly imported and highly prized tulip. Adam and Paulus both excelled in the production of representational scenes. The German painter Sandrart said of Paulus that 'with the hammer alone he could make whole pictures... with animals and landscapes, all perfect in their decoration, design and elegance.'

The Dutch Renaissance

Innovation in architecture and sculpture was largely due to the influence of one stonemason employed by the city of Amsterdam – Hendrick de Keyser (1565–1621). He developed his own characteristic style, freeing Dutch sculpture from its former rigidity and symbolic quality, which resulted in a softer, anatomic style, full of movement, and became known as 'Dutch Renaissance.'

Moving on to be an architect, he related the interior spaces of buildings to the exteriors, integrating the ornament to the structure rather than applying it superficially. His masterpiece is the Mausoleum of William the Silent, Prince of Orange, built on the site of the former high altar of the New Church in Delft (1614–21). The bronze figure of William the Silent is surrounded by tall obelisks, linking it to the High Gothic interior of the New Church. Two of his most impressive and characteristic buildings that survive in Amsterdam are the Zuiderkerk (1603) and the Westerkerk (1620), where Rembrandt is buried. With an imposing build-up of Dorian, Ionic and Corinthian columns, and the imperial crown of the Holy Roman Emperor Maximilian I adorning the 85-metre (280-ft) high steeple, the Westerkerk is the most monumental example of Dutch Renaissance architecture.

The architect Jacob van Campen (1595–1657) designed the Mauritshuis and the Huis ten Bosch in The Hague, and the New Church at Haarlem in the spirit of 'Dutch Classicism,' but his major project of the century was the construction of a new Town Hall for Amsterdam. This imposing building, now the Koninklijk Paleis (Royal Palace), was built on a massive scale and is one of the few classical buildings in the Netherlands. Solid and rational, it seems the ultimate expression of the values of the Golden Age. Built when

Despite being one of the most celebrated of all Dutch painters, Vermeer was far from prolific; only 30 works by him are known.

the Netherlands was at the height of its powers, the new city hall reflected the wealth of the city. The first foundation stone was laid in 1648. The artist Artus Quellien of Antwerp was appointed as sculptor and, together with other skilled craftsmen, executed the designs of van Campen. Artists such as Ferdinand Bol and Govert Flinck, both

Delft Town Hall, as rebuilt by Hendrick de Keyser.

pupils of Rembrandt, painted large chimney pieces for the major rooms.

In 1808, Louis Napoleon, King of Holland and brother of the French Emperor Napoleon Bonaparte, took over the building and converted it into a royal palace, furnishing it with a valuable and extensive collection of Empire (or Napoleonic-style) furniture. Eventually King William I returned the building to the city government, and it still remains in use as a royal palace, which the king uses for special ceremonial occasions. With its painted wall reliefs, sculptures, Empire-style furniture, chimneypieces and marble inlaid map of the world, it is no wonder that the 17th-century poet Constantijn Huygens described the building as 'the eighth wonder of the world.'

MODERN ART

It's not easy to follow in the footsteps of Rembrandt and Van Gogh, but today's artists have carved their own path.

When one thinks of Dutch art, the great masters of the 17th century come to mind: Rembrandt, Ruisdael, De Hooch, Steen, Cuyp, Hals and Vermeer, among others. The quiet strength of serene, detailed works; the powerful chiaroscuro portraits; the cluttered naturalism of rustic still lifes; intense raging seas and pastoral Dutch landscapes. The 18th century reflected earlier achievements in art, with no new directions taken. It was a time of contentment and the good life *à la française*. Rather than the grand imagery of the past, a lighter attitude prevailed in the 18th century, with anecdotal portraits by painters like Troost and De Lelie. In the 19th century, Van Gogh's expressionism contrasted with Breitner's visual realism and, in retrospect, can be seen as one of the many starting points of modern art.

However, if the importance of Van Gogh seems assured now, it certainly wasn't during his lifetime. He famously sold just one painting and led an impoverished life that is still seen as the epitome of what it means to be an entirely and hopelessly impassioned artist. It is staggering to think that his entire output – around 800 paintings – was completed in just 10 years, from first taking up the brush at 27 to ending his life with a bullet at 37. It is no exaggeration to say that the instability of Van Gogh's mind is reflected in his visceral canvases, which swirl with thick brushstrokes. Such works can never be adequately reproduced, so the Van Gogh Museum in Amsterdam and the Kröller-Müller Museum in the Hoge Veluwe National Park near Arnhem are the perfect places to get closer to his work.

Mondrian and De Stijl

Although the preceding centuries were a tough act to follow, there was no turning back for

'Sunflowers', Van Gogh.

20th-century art. In 1917 the artists of the De Stijl movement emerged, intent on seeking a new and contemporary tradition, staking new territory, making new visual statements. Piet Mondrian was its most prominent member. But it was Theo van Doesburg, founder of a polemical magazine called *De Stijl (The Style)*, who would start rumblings towards the subsequent development of modern art in the Netherlands. Its purpose was 'to state the logical principles of a style now ripening, based on a pure equivalence between the age and its means of expression.'

The basic problem being addressed by individual painters throughout Europe was what to paint and how to paint. This was the problem that De Stijl intended to address, based on a coherent theory that if the individual was the measure of all things, then anything could be art if the artist presented it as such.

Mondrian's œuvre would mark him as one of the greatest of the 20th-century Modernist painters. Although his early work portrayed a romantic symbolism, his canvases made a radical shift over the next few years until he reached the easily identifiable 'contra-compositions' in red, yellow and blue. In those classic paintings produced during the 1920s and 1930s, space is evoked and structured with the use of black lines and small blocks of primary colour.

Mondrian's well-known *Victory Boogie Woogie* painting, which dates from 1943, can be seen in the Gemeentemuseum Den Haag in The Hague, along with five other canvases.

In his book *Dutch Painting* (1978), Rudi Fuchs states that with the exception of Van Gogh, Expressionism never really caught on in The Netherlands. 'Whether that is because the Dutch character is not given to the display of strong emotion (Van Gogh after all found his own style in France) is difficult to decide. In fact, Dutch art between the two wars, with the exception of De Stijl, found itself curi-

'Victory Boogie Woogie' by Mondrian, at the Gemeentemuseum.

'Vrouw met hond', Constant, 1949.

MAGIC REALISM

A group of original artists who painted in a cold, precise, realist style labelled 'Magic Realist' were Carel Willink, Pyke Kock and Raoul Hynckes. Similar in style were painters Charley Toorop and Dick Ket.

Carel Willink's description of their work is perhaps the most insightful of this brief fling with expressionism: 'Our vision is the confrontation with the never reassuring, never completely comprehensible world of phenomena in which the smallest and most familiar object can suddenly turn into something frightening; a world stranger and more dreadful in its haughty impenetrability than the most terrifying nightmare.'

ously apart from international developments. The Dutch either did not know about them or rejected them.'

The COBRA movement

After World War II, greater social involvement seemed to be an essential requirement for the newly evolving art. Socialism brought together a group of free-wheeling personalities intent on creating a fresh, vivid style of painting. Exhibitions of 20th-century masters such as Picasso, Braque, Léger and Chagall served as inspiration to these young, creatively restless artists. Constant, Corneille and Karel Appel joined forces with their Belgian and Danish counterparts Christian Dotremont, Joseph Noiret and Asger

Jorn in 1948 to form an international group which took its name, COBRA, from the first letters of their three European capitals (Copenhagen, Brussels, Amsterdam).

The movement's artists experimented – playfully at times – drawing on the influence of folk art, primitivism, Naïve painting and the drawings of children and the mentally ill. As Constant summarised COBRA: 'A painting is no longer a construction of colours and lines, but an animal, a night, a cry, a man, or all of these together. Suggestion is boundless, and that is why we can say that, after a period in which art represented nothing, art has now entered a period in which it represents everything.'

In 1995, the COBRA Museum voor Moderne Kunst opened its doors in Amstelveen, a suburb of Amsterdam. The main focus of the collection is modern art from 1945 onwards, and it features leading works from the short-lived COBRA movement. There is also a collection of abstract and semi-abstract Netherlandish art from the 1940s and 1950s.

Challenging art-making

In the early 1960s other artists emerged, like Jan Schoonhoven, influenced by Duchamp and the emerging Tachism movement in Paris – a variation on post-war abstract expressionism.

The Pop Art movement was another influence for Schoonhoven and others such as Armando, Daan van Golden and J.C.J. van der Heyden, who, according to Rudi Fuchs, would 'come to terms with the fact that they were producing simple visual objects, the artistic importance of which did not reside in a 'content' but an ideological position. In an extremely and even disturbingly offhand manner, their works questioned the nature of art, and the nature of art-making.'

Other artists such as Peter Struycken, Ad Dekkers and Bonies 'sought a way out of the deadlock by going back to Mondrian's claim that art should not be based on private intuition, but that art-making required continuous and strict analysis of one's procedures.' They maintained the position that 'everything could be art, that art was in the mind of the beholder... Continuing Mondrian's search, in a sense, they proposed that a painting should be analysed and broken down into its basic elements – such as colour, form, scale, surface and so on.'

Co Westerik is more of a realist painter, with quite a large following, and Reinier Lucassen's

highly imaginative work has many recognisable visual elements. Jan Dibbets and Ger van Elk have included photography and photomontage in their paintings. Stanley Brouwn and Rene Daniels are other important contemporary artists with an international following.

On a more 'commercial' note, Jan Cremer, a 1970s writer of the Henry Miller ilk who added painting to his colourful achievements, has had his share of successful one-man shows in recent years, as has the Dutch rock musician Herman Brood. On the distaff side, Marlene Dumas's provocative paintings and drawings are often

Marlene Dumas painting at the Gemeentemuseum.

included in major international exhibitions in Venice and Kassel, and she has managed to be accepted into the 'boy's club' in terms of her work being purchased by museums. Although she was born in Cape Town, South Africa, she adopted Holland as her home in 1976. Marijke van Warmerdam has also been invited to exhibit her work at the Venice Biennale.

Today a new (and slightly younger) generation of artists is emerging whose work is being taken seriously by collectors: among them, Winneke Dijkstra, Arnold Mik, Liza May Post, Joep van Lieshout, Sylvie Fleurie, Job Koelerij, Gerald van der Kaap and Ronald Ophuis. These days, when it comes to art in the Netherlands, there is much to discover.

ARCHITECTURE

The architectural heritage of the Netherlands is not restricted to antiquity; the country was at the vanguard of the modern movement.

When one thinks of architecture in the Netherlands, it is the timeless buildings of the 17th century which spring most readily to mind: Amsterdam's patrician canal houses and stately churches with their crown-bearing towers, which are also found in many of the country's larger cities. But there are other important architectural periods in the Netherlands – and examples are not only to be found in its capital.

Over the ages, there have actually been three periods of serious growth in architecture: the Middle Ages; the Golden Age between 1550 and 1700; and the first half of the 20th century. The last of these enjoyed two peak periods: in the first three decades, and during the major building activity after World War II, with its massive housing projects designed on a human scale by socially committed architects like Aldo van Eyck and Herman Hertzberger.

Contemporary architecture

In looking at Amsterdam's architectural tradition, it's hard to imagine that not all that much has changed since P.J.H. Cuypers (1827–1921) built his monumental neo-Gothic churches and other grand landmarks. The city's Centraal Station and the Rijksmuseum are two buildings of huge national significance.

Fin de siècle architecture in the Netherlands was not based on the same motifs as seen in the more organic Art Nouveau creations in Belgium and France. The Dutch 'New Art' was influenced more by geometric, abstract motifs with a Far Eastern bias. Many artists and architects became attracted to the socialist and anarchist movements as well as to the esoteric approach of theosophy, and the distinction between art and life was getting blurred.

De Resident, an area in the city centre of The Hague.

It was a time to return to craftsmanship and innovation. Architects were at the helm of new design, not only in their buildings, but in the creation of furniture, ceramics, glassware and the graphic arts which were often integrated into their projects. The Beurs van Berlage (Amsterdam Stock Exchange) is a good example of architectural design, with its striking red-brick exterior, imposing clock tower and skylit interior with built-in and carved wood elements.

Modern master

Hendrik Petrus Berlage (1856–1934) is regarded as the father of modern Dutch architecture. A visionary who managed to break from the past and approach architecture more rationally,

> The most important thing about the influential
> De Stijl group was exactly that: their influence.
> Few of their designs were actually built.

Berlage's craft finds its purest manifestation in his Gemeentemuseum Den Haag (Municipal Museum) and First Church of Christ, Scientist, both in The Hague. His Stock Exchange building has additional elements of Cuypers's Dutch Renaissance influence, while a trip to America also acquainted him further with the work of Frank Lloyd Wright. Even more important are his

Modern houses in Amsterdam.

contributions to Dutch urban design, in Amsterdam, the Hague, Rotterdam and Utrecht.

The Housing Act of 1901 was a pivotal point in Dutch architecture, which opened up the possibility of subsidised housing to meet the needs of the working class. This found its conduit in Berlage's ambitious development plan in Amsterdam South, notable for its decorative use of brickwork with detailing in wood, sculpture, iron and distinctive window shapes, doors and even mailboxes. This form of craftsmanship, or façade architecture became officially known as the 'Amsterdam School' in 1916, and would alter the appearance of the city quite dramatically. Defined by its elegance and creativity of design, local variants on this theme soon appeared elsewhere in

the Netherlands. Each project gave the architect – Berlage, De Klerk, Kramer, Staal and many others – the opportunity to explore ideas that added novelty and a playful sense to constructed forms.

The Dada-inspired De Stijl movement (Dutch for 'The Style'), founded in the early 1920s, had more of a utopian approach towards a unity of the arts: to create a balanced environment that would dominate all aspects of life. The group's leader, architect Theo van Doesburg, spoke of creating a new consciousness of beauty aimed at the universal. Painters Piet Mondrian and B. van der Leck were other proponents of the movement, along with mathematicians, poets and sculptors. Influenced mainly by Berlage and Wright, the De Stijl architects were joined by Gerrit Rietveld (1888–1964), a cabinet-maker known for his red-blue wooden chair, whose design was years ahead of its time. Resembling a toy construction, it is actually comfortable. After World War II, De Stijl continued to be an inspiration for architects who aspired to the avant-garde direction of modernism.

The Nieuwe Bouwen (New Building) movement, or Dutch functionalism, developed during the 1920s, and was based on rational and economic considerations rather than the craftsmanship approach of the 'Amsterdam School'. Architects Mart Stam, J. Duiker and J.B. van Loghem (among others) were inspired by Berlage's ideas on normalisation in housing, and were vehement proponents of an industrialised system of building affordable housing in large quantities. Their ground and first-floor housing projects in Haarlem and The Hague proved that their functionalist principles could be put into practice.

The contemporary landscape

The 21st century is already witness to another boom in architecture. The Hague is being reinvented with its revitalised city centre, while Rotterdam is a city literally on the rise with development in both its 'downtown' and harbour areas. Many of the buildings have been designed by leading Dutch talents such as Rem Koolhaas and Jo Coenen, as well as architects of international repute like Sir Norman Foster and Frank Gehry.

However, no matter how much land has been – and continues to be – reclaimed, housing remains a problem in the Netherlands. The VINEX project was launched in 1992 by the Minister for Housing to create a million new homes over the following 25 years. Another architectural golden age may well be around the corner.

Inside story

From Golden Age mansions to modern apartments, the Dutch are masters at accommodating the smallest of spaces creatively and stylishly.

In the Golden Age, Dutch canalside mansions were very different from Venetian *palazzi*: the grandest Dutch rooms were always on the ground floor, while the depth of the building was always greater than its breadth.

Inside a gabled mansion in Amsterdam, Delft or Leiden lay a cornucopia of treasures. Marble fireplaces would be surrounded by Delftware tiles, while heavily embossed sideboards indicated the burghers' taste for exuberant Flemish design. Oriental porcelain, Venetian glassware and mirrors shone brightly – despite the clergy's denunciation of such 'devilish vanity'.

A love of order

Superficially, the modern Dutch home would appear to be a complete break with the past. However, despite the love of order, there are occasional sentimental lapses into houses that are cloyingly sweet and twee. An immaculate front garden is often complemented by well-trained hanging baskets, matching window boxes and topped, perhaps, by a mailbox masquerading as a bird house or dolls' house. There is often a plaster replica of a *kabouter*, or gnome, or an eerily authentic-looking heron.

The house itself is also left open to inspection, as passers-by will note from the only partly drawn frilly lace curtains. This goes along with the ideology that the Dutch have nothing to hide. The provincial Dutch home often treads a fine line between sweetness and kitsch – before accidentally crossing it. Closer examination, however, reveals shades of 17th-century values and tastes in the solid furniture, soft lighting and cut flowers, not to mention the orderliness, cleanliness and propriety. Sir William Temple, the British ambassador to the Netherlands during the Republic, was puzzled to find that spitting at banquets was frowned upon. Thomas Nugent, a 17th-century traveller, agreed, reporting that the Dutch were 'perfect slaves to cleanliness... for the streets are paved with brick and as clean as any chamber floor'. There is still a low shame threshold as far as cleanliness is concerned: until about 10 years ago, it was common to see doorsteps scrubbed daily.

Interior design

As for interior design, furniture is generally solid, imposing and, although shunning flamboyance, contains intricate details. Flowers are essential to the Dutch concept of homeliness. In provincial homes you will find a far greater variety and profusion of pot plants and cut flowers than in the more contemporary environs of the Randstad. Most guests still visit with flowers rather than wine. Contrary to expectation, the most popular flowers are not tulips, but a mixed bouquet.

Comfort is the main factor in a Dutch home, although Dutch interiors began a transition after

Dutch home design in Amsterdam.

World War II from a pseudo-Bauhaus period with ultra-modern elements to the '*Goede Wonen*' concept of the 1960s and early 1970s. This was spearheaded by a group of designers and furniture companies who promoted pure, airy and light interiors with no frills.

As Dutch design continued to develop with more emphasis on style, function and aesthetics, interiors became more distinctive. Beauty and simple elegance are more important to a Dutch household than glitzy objects. And it is no surprise that the Dutch have a great affinity for colour, which they often use in subtle and original combinations. Flea-market finds sit quite comfortably next to a designer chair. Because of the variety of old and unusual buildings, often with minimal space, the Dutch are masters at improvising and at accommodating the smallest of spaces creatively.

Tulips in the Keukenhof.

FLOWERS – A WAY OF LIFE

The tulip is perhaps the most definitive image of the Netherlands, and Dutch horticulturalists work hard to retain this reputation.

In a country where land is precious, the majority of city-dwellers take great pride in their interior gardens. Rare is a Dutch house or apartment that doesn't have flowers on the table, an array of pot plants or window boxes in constant bloom. In rural areas, a house isn't a home without a garden. Only the Japanese buy more flowers per annum than the Dutch. In the Netherlands, people spend an average of 60 euros per year (about £40/US$70) on cut flowers alone, whereas in the United Kingdom and the United States the average is around half that.

Bouquets are bought and presented for almost any occasion, often complete with their own mythology and hidden meaning, depending on flower type, colour and presentation. A bouquet of fewer than 10 flowers is always a social blunder – in spring, when tulips are plentiful, they are sold in bunches of 50. Yellow tulips, for example, are the specified flower for birthdays that occur on 21 May. Legend has it that on this day yellow flowers also signify unrequited love. If presented upside down, however, this unhappy situation may well be remedied.

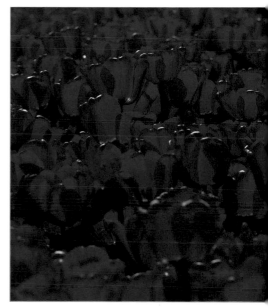

A bulb field.

The flower industry

Today the specially cultivated flowers, bulbs, fruits and vegetables that comprise Dutch horticulture bring in more than 16.2 billion euros a year (£12 billion/US$18 billion) as an export. Horticulture accounts for more than 39 percent of Dutch agricultural production. With this boost, the Netherlands is the second-largest agricultural exporter in the world after the United States, with most of its production going to European Union nations.

The Netherlands and, in particular, the Westland area between Amsterdam and Rotterdam, export more cut flowers than the rest of the world combined (52 percent global market share). In potted plants, the market domination is the same.

Cultivating the landscape

More than 10,000 hectares (25,000 acres) are under glass in modern greenhouse production. About half of this area is devoted to flowers and plants, the rest to hydroponic fruits and vegetables. The Dutch were quick to take advantage of this modern method of growing tropical or seasonal produce year-round. It works without soil by anchoring the plants in porous gravel and flooding them frequently with highly enriched, inorganic nutrients. Dutch hydroponically grown produce ends up in supermarkets the world over. (In recent years, however, consumers have complained that these high-tech fruits and vegetables are lacking in flavour.)

More than 54 percent of available land in the Netherlands – 2 million hectares (5 million acres) – is used for agriculture. The specific activity is dictated by soil type. The abundance of sandy soil means that over 60 percent of this agricultural land is used as pasture for feeding livestock to support the enormous Dutch dairy industry. Another 35 percent is rich enough for arable farming.

Outdoor production of flowers and house plants occupies the rest: about 2,000 hectares (5,000 acres) in total. With so much space for livestock, it is not surprising that the Netherlands has almost as many pigs as people. The nation's 50,000 livestock and poultry farmers between them keep more than 12 million pigs, 4 million cattle and some 103 million chickens.

However, what is also not surprising for this small, densely populated country, with a very high water table, is its monumental manure problem. These animals produce more than 90 million tonnes of waste annually, about twice

Arcen Castle gardens.

CAROLUS CLUSIUS

From the 1570s a Flemish botanist called Carolus Clusius (or L'Ecluse in French) was advising gardeners all over Europe on the care, cultivation and scientific aspects of gardening and flower care, with special attention to the newly imported tulip. In 1587, the Dutch enthusiasm for flowers combined with their appreciation of scientific study led to the foundation in Leiden of one of the first European institutes for botanical study. Clusius was its second director and went on to lead the institute into the successful propagation of many new plant varieties, including tulips, crocuses and irises, thereby laying the foundation for today's horticulture industry.

as much as is needed for fertiliser. Unfortunately, all of it has been going back onto the ground. The result is diminishing soil fertility, nitrate poisoning of the ground water and even acid rain as a result of the gases given off by the manure.

For the moment the government has restricted the wholesale spreading of manure, set herd limits and established 'manure banks' for farmers to deposit their excess while scientists search for alternative uses for the unavoidable by-product.

Landscape gardening

As far back as the late 1500s, Dutch gardeners and botanists were setting European standards for horticulture and the design of stately gardens. As Dutch merchant vessels began to sail the world's oceans in search of tradeable goods, they regularly brought back new species and varieties of plants never seen before in Northern Europe. The Dutch reputation for horticulture spread internationally and, in particular, to England.

During this period, and for centuries to come, Dutch and French garden styles set the standard for the rest of Europe. This was especially true for the English where, during and after the Civil War, Royalists and Catholic decoratively trimmed trees as well as ornamental hedges have always been considered typical Dutch features.

Tulip development

The roots of Dutch horticulture and garden influence can equally be traced back to the import and development of the tulip, the Netherlands' most famous flower.

The tulip originated in the Caucasus and spread as far as present-day China. In the wild, the flower grows along a corridor on either side of the 40th Parallel. Explorers

North Holland bulb field.

sympathisers favoured the French garden style, while Parliamentarians and Protestants leaned toward the Dutch.

In Britain, the reign of the Dutch Protestant King William III of Orange and his wife Mary (1688–1702) also had a large influence on English and European garden styles. Their royal gardener, a Dutchman named Bentinck, designed one of the best surviving examples of a Dutch-style enclosed garden at the magnificent Hampton Court near London. Dutch gardens (ironically called English gardens in the Netherlands) were typically enclosed by a wall and divided internally by hedges. Brilliant and colourful floral patterns, topiary designs, tightly ordered and

were sending back new varieties from this area until the beginning of World War II.

The first recorded instance of the tulip being successfully cultivated for garden use was in Turkey. By the 18th century, Turkish growers had registered more than 1,500 different tulip varieties and were the undisputed masters of tulip-growing in the world. Strict standards for shape, colour and production were maintained, and Constantinople was the only place where Turks could legally sell their tulip bulbs. For several Turkish sultans, this precious flower held a position of courtly honour, and festivals involving at least 500,000 tulips were spectacular annual events.

Tulips came to Europe in the middle of the 16th century through trade and diplomatic channels, which is how Clusius obtained his first bulbs. With the growth of the East India Company, trade and prosperity increased in the Amsterdam area. The bulbs travelled easily, and the rare and colourful flowers became a natural way for the increasingly wealthy merchants and nouveaux riches to flaunt their wealth. A garden full of expensive tulips was a sure sign of prestige and social standing.

Mysterious petals

During this period and long after, the most valued tulip had petals that were known as

At the Flower Market, Amsterdam.

'feathered' for their broken or striated colour patterns. For centuries no one could determine what made the unusual and beautiful petals. Botanists were especially confounded because the patterns of one generation of bulbs would produce seedlings whose flowers often did not resemble their parental generation at all. Only much later did scientists discover that the breakage in colouring was due to insect-borne viruses attacking the bulbs. Experts also say that the tulips of this period did not resemble the familiar shape we know today. Paintings of the time depict them with larger, often ragged heads with more petals, less graceful leaves and overall a less streamlined look.

Growers in the Netherlands now produce more than 4 billion bulbs annually, two-thirds of them grown for export. Export bulbs are split into two markets: dry sales and the forcing market. Dry sales are simply propagated bulbs harvested from the fields. For the forcing market, bulbs are sold to greenhouses for year-round cultivation to produce cut flowers.

Flower auctions

Hundreds of different species of flowers are sold daily at the Aalsmeer Flower Auction (the world's largest flower auction housed in the world's largest building in terms of footprint) near Schipol Airport.

Visitors are welcome at this open auction from Monday to Wednesday and Friday from 7 to 11am and on Thursday from 7 to 9am (for more information, see www.floraholland. com – guided tours are available). Here, the vast majority of produce – 90 percent of all bulbs

TULIPOMANIA

Because of the unpredictability from one crop to the next and rising demand, rabid speculation on bulb prices took hold in the 1630s. The craze became known as 'tulipomania' or 'the wind trade' by Dutch florists, satirists and historians alike – nothing in the market reflected any true value of the bulbs; hence, trading the wind.

As wealth trickled down to the middle classes, the speculative frenzy in the bulb trade increased. Family fortunes were made and eventually wiped out in the bidding fever that gripped Amsterdam and the western Netherlands. At one point, one white-flamed Semper Augustus bulb reportedly sold for 6,000 florins (the average annual salary at the time was around 150 florins).

Churches echoed with sermons on the evils of bulb gambling, and politicians tried to prohibit it, no doubt fuelling prices even more.

Eventually, prices returned to more reasonable levels, and other bulb and corm flowers, such as daffodils, lilies, crocuses, irises and hyacinths, dahlias and gladioli, became popular, though none rivalled the tulip. Greenhouses, which began to multiply rapidly at the turn of the 20th century, changed the nature of the industry. In due course the rose displaced the tulip as the best-selling flower, a trend that continues, with the tulip relegated to fourth on the sales charts, behind roses, chrysanthemums and carnations.

and flowers and 85 percent of other fruits and vegetables – are sold through the unique Dutch 'clock' auction system.

There are three auction halls with a total of 14 clocks. The buyers are exporters, wholesalers, shopkeepers and street traders who are seated on benches and can purchase via all the clocks in their halls by pressing a switch. Under this system, the pointer turns round a large dial indicating the price of a lot.

The clock starts at 'noon', which represents the highest prices, and sweeps downward. The auctioneer calls out which flowers are on offer, specifying their grower and the minimum quantity which the buyer must purchase. Prices start high and decrease as the pointer turns. Bidders can stop the clock at the price which they are willing to pay.

Across the country 39 separate auctions use this system for selling flowers, fruit and vegetables, including Aalsmeer. Each year on the first weekend of September, the Bloemencorso (parade) takes place from the centre of Aalsmeer via Amstelveen to Amsterdam and Zaandam with festive, colourful floats that delight the thousands of spectators who throng the route. In Aalsmeer, the celebration continues with a range of activities and flower exhibitions.

In the old days, buyers used to gather in the growers' fields to inspect the crop in the ground before the bidding would start. Today these so-called 'green' auctions have become exceedingly rare. With the technical precision and predictability of greenhouse-growing, produce and bulbs are now 'sold forward', meaning that the bulbs are still in the ground or the produce still on the vine at the time of purchase. At the auctions today, brokers acting for buyers and sellers from around the world do all the bidding, while thousands of packers and shipping agents wrestle with the millions of flowers in other parts of the auction hall.

New techniques

Most plants are still cultivated vegetatively, by sowing or striking off young buds from the more mature and strongest plants. But tissue culture and meri-stem culture are used increasingly as methods of ensuring quick, identical and disease-free flowers.

Under a microscope, laboratory technicians cut tiny stems from selected young plants. The cuttings are then grown in test tubes for a set number of weeks depending on the plant. The process then starts all over again, with the best samples used for breeding, and the rest sold. These plants have not seen a rainy day for dozens of generations, and black dirt, to them, is ancient history.

Growers prefer test-tube methods because they increase productivity and speed up the search for new colours, qualities and varieties of plant. Methods are now so well developed that 1 million seedlings per year can be produced from a single plant. This method also guarantees that the plants are bred disease-free, which

Aalsmeer Flower Auction, the world's largest.

opens up new export markets, such as Australia and New Zealand, for example, both of which have strict import regulations.

With the rising cost of natural gas needed to heat the greenhouses and of electricity to run every other automated and computer-controlled climatological aspect, growers are now hunting for plant strains that can be grown without the consumption of so much heat and light. Many Dutch laboratories are also working hard to produce infertile plants so that competitors cannot profit from their research and produce new generations of flowers virtually identical to the seedlings they have purchased. One can only imagine what these vegetative eunuchs might be called.

FOOD AND DRINK

As well as hearty traditional dishes, you can enjoy more recent imports, like the delicious cuisine of the Netherlands' former colonies.

In years gone by, Dutch cuisine was synonymous with potatoes, cabbage, bread, cheese, potatoes, herring, endive and more potatoes – with some sausage thrown in for good measure. To bear this out, you only have to look at Dutch still-life paintings, with their bountiful buffets, any number of Old Master paintings with the family gathered round a sumptuous meal and, of course, Van Gogh's celebrated portrait of the *Potato Eaters*.

Because the Dutch prefer to eat their national dishes in their own homes, restaurants offering Dutch specialities are often hard to track down. However, there's been something of a resurgence, and many Amsterdam restaurants now take pride in serving traditional food – dishes like *hutspot met klapstuk* (hotchpotch of meat, carrots and potatoes), *stamppot van zuurkool en worst* (sauerkraut mashed with potatoes and sausage) and *bruine bonen* (brown bean) soup. And several newer places offer a diverse menu based on the 'new Dutch cuisine', which features fresh local produce prepared seasonally from traditional recipes, but cooked with a light touch in terms of fat content.

Eating out

Happily, when dining out in the Netherlands these days, there is plenty of variety. In Amsterdam and a few of the larger cities, it is possible to dine in almost any language thanks to the proliferation of ethnic restaurants – from Vietnamese to Ethiopian. And just as the Dutch explorers once brought back spices from around the world, innovative chefs are combining East with West to create unique and delicious 'fusion' dishes. In other cities, the choice is more limited to the local pancake house, the ubiquitous pizzeria or Chinese and Indonesian restaurants. Food from Surinam,

Traditional herring preparation.

the former Dutch colony in South America, offers a spicy mixture of Creole and Indian, a kind of soul food, with hearty curries and roti bread, peanut soup and *pom*, a type of sweet potato. But there is also a lot to enjoy about hearty Dutch cuisine, especially in winter months.

Severe winter weather and travel by foot, on skates or by boat necessitated large meals rich in fats and carbohydrates to provide energy and retain body heat. But vast meals are a thing of the past, and thick soups and mashed vegetable dishes omit the extra fat in deference to the health-conscious. The most traditional winter dish, still popular among the older generation, is *boerenkool stamppot met worst* (cabbage mashed with potatoes and served with smoked sausage or *rookworst*). There is a Dutch saying that *boerenkool* ('farmer's cabbage', or kale) is best when taken from the ground after the first frost. But young people tend to prefer international fast food chains, which have become a very visible part of the national foodscape in recent years.

Other specialities of the Dutch kitchen include white asparagus served with ham and chopped egg (in May and June), smoked eel, special puddings with whipped cream, pancakes and the famous herring, known as 'the poor man's oyster'. Herring are eaten as a snack, raw or salted, with plenty of chopped onion. Herring stalls are a feature of Dutch life, especially in May, when everyone wants to try the mild *nieuwe* (or *groene*) *haring* – the first green herring of the season. These stalls or wagons attract a variety of clients, many of whom eat them the traditional way, holding them expertly aloft by the tail between thumb and forefinger of the right hand, head lifted, mouth open and then swallow! Others may prefer a *broodje haring*, slices of herring in a soft roll, or just slices of herring. If you prefer another sort of fish, the stalls also sell smoked

Bacon and fresh veg pasta at Luden in Amsterdam.

The Netherlands is known for its frites.

FOOD ON THE GO

If you fancy a quick snack, there are a number of options, from the simple shop selling *broodje* (filled bread rolls), or the Vietnamese *loempia* (spring roll) vendor, to the Middle Eastern takeaway stand that sells *shoarma* (roast lamb) or falafel in a pitta. However, the most popular Dutch snack is Belgian-style *patat* chips (or *frites*). Instead of eating them smothered in the usual tomato ketchup, the Dutch dip them in mayonnaise or exotic sauces – a habit satirised by John Travolta's character in the film *Pulp Fiction*. They have little to do with their fast-food counterparts, so make sure you try them. And don't skimp on the mayo.

salmon, smoked eel and two varieties of succulent Dutch shrimp, the *Noordse* or *Hollands garnalen*, the North Sea's finest.

Drinking habits

Many people drink beer, especially pils, a light beer, though the favoured drink is *jenever* or Dutch gin, made from distilled malt wine with juniper berries. At about 5pm people drop into their local café for a *borrel*: a small glass of either the colourless *jonge* (young) *jenever*, less creamy than the *oude* (old), which has a pale yellow colour and a noticeably heavier, muskier flavour. The Dutch are known for their liqueurs and fruit brandies, although these are now losing popularity to imported drinks. Beer, mineral water and wine are drunk with meals. A favourite New Year drink called *Bisschopswijn* ('Bishop's Wine') may have been named after St Nicholas. This mulled wine is used for a Dutch toast – *Gezondheid* (Your health!) or *Proost*.

If you get hungry while in a café before the dinner hour, try a plate of *borrelhapjes* (snacks) like *kroketten* (meat or shrimp croquettes) or *bitterballen*, meatballs coated with bread-crumbs, deep-fried and served with mustard. Make sure to let them cool before taking a bite; the inside is notoriously hot, and the Dutch

Bitterballen are a tasty snack.

always enjoy a perverse chuckle watching foreign guests innocently tuck into them. Later in the evening, a *tosti*, or grilled cheese sandwich, often combined with a slice of ham, usually hits the spot and helps temper the effects of a potential hangover.

Coffee is the Dutch national drink, and 'koffiedrinken' is the national pastime. A cup of strong coffee, a *bakkie*, is usually served black. Espresso is a popular alternative, and *koffie verkeerd*, or 'wrong coffee', is a popular choice, a kind of *café au lait*, with a lot of steamed milk and a little coffee. Hot chocolate is mostly a winter drink, and when people go skating, stands are set up on the ice with large urns on stoves.

Breads and pastries

The bread basket on a breakfast table holds a varied selection of bread, from pre-cut white to heavy, black rye, and perhaps wholewheat, raisin and seed bread. A spiced cake, known as *ontbijt-koek* or *peperkoek*, and often eaten just with butter, varies according to each province. Some towns

> *The tradition of eating at home is entrenched, and only in recent years have the Dutch started leaving work to have business lunches.*

A rich variety of loaves.

have their own special recipes for *peperkoek*, which are closely guarded by local bakers.

In larger towns croissants are overtaking the *broodje* as a snack food, and are sold filled with combinations of cheese, ham, liver, shrimp, smoked eel, steak tartare, salad or herring. The *koffietafel* (coffee table) lunch, which is served in homes and in office canteens, includes a variety of breads, cheeses and meats. The drink of choice is usually milk or *karnemelk* (buttermilk).

Pastries are light and inventive and not too heavy on the sugar, although the *boterkoek*, Dutch pound cake, is quite rich in butter. On St Nicholas's Eve (5 December) chocolate-covered alphabet letters are made and given to friends

Drinking

Lager, gin and liqueurs are on the drinks menu in the Netherlands' cafés and bars; just make sure you know what the volume is first.

Drinking in Holland should always be a pleasurable experience, but before embarking on a big night out, it's advisable to be acquainted with the beverages available. Beer is invariably served in a 25cl. glass

Jenever drinking in Hoppe Brown Bar, Amsterdam.

called an Amsterdammer or *vaas* (vase). A smaller glass of 20cl. is known as a *fluitje* (pronounced 'floutcha', meaning whistle). Finally, anything resembling a pint is known as a *pul* (50cl.), but locals humorously refer to it as an *emmer* (bucket).

Lager

Most cafés serve Heineken or Amstel, although Grolsch, Brand and Oranjeboom are popular too. The beer-drinking public favours these lagers, all of which are around 5 percent volume. Traditionally lager is served with froth, so don't be offended; locals would not consider the beer fresh any other way. There are many other beers available; *witbier* (white beer), a cloudy concoction usually served with a slice of lemon, is made from wheat and has a bitter-sweet

taste. Other alternatives include darker, sweeter beers, often on draught and served in semi-spherical glasses. De Koninck and Palm (both from Belgium) are the most popular. At this juncture it's worth bearing in mind the importance of measuring beer strength in percentage alcohol by volume, an extremely reliable indicator of price and potency. The more adventurous drinker will be easily seduced by the superbly rich and diverse amount of Belgian beers, often brewed in monasteries, the effects and flavours of which may be as celestial as the price after too many temptations.

Dutch gin

Jenever (pronounced 'yurnayver'), and commonly known as Dutch gin to English speakers, is a beautifully subtle spirit often called a *borrel*. There are three sorts: *jonge* (pronounced 'yonger') young *jenever*, *oude* (pronounced 'owd') old *jenever*, and *korenwijn* (pronounced 'corenvain'). Ironically, the difference between old and young *jenever* is not age. *Jenever* is distilled from grain (usually barley and rye) and malt, the resultant distillate being malt wine (50 percent alcohol by volume). The law stipulates that young *jenever* contains no more than 15 percent malt wine, old *jenever* no less than 15 percent and *korenwijn* no less than 40 percent.

Traditionally the young *jenever's* strength is raised by the addition of molasses alcohol and, unlike the others, is delicately flavoured with juniper berries. Only some old *jenevers* are aged in vats (*korenwijn* always is) and take on the hue of a distinguished malt whisky. Beer drunk in combination with a *jenever* is aptly named a *kopstoot*, meaning 'headbang'.

Liqueurs

About 300 years ago, when distilling was developed in The Netherlands, pure alcohol wasn't considered palatable. With the newly arrived choice of spices and other goodies, courtesy of the Dutch East India Company, were all sorts of splendid 'remedies' with names that still reflect their dubious qualities.

Bruidstranen or 'Bride's Tears', for example, served directly after marital vows, is a pure orange liqueur containing 22-carat gold leaf and silver leaf tears. Probably the most famous of all is *Oranje Bitter*, made of steeped Malaga orange peel, an esprit of Valencia peel plus a touch of aniseed esprit, and served on King's Day (27 April), a big national holiday. On this day one could consume all of the above and recover with a *Bittere Lijdenstroost* or 'Bitter Consolation', a liqueur made of vanilla, cinnamon, Malaga orange and a hint of Amsterdams bitters. *Proost!*

and family. The *boterletter*, made from old-fashioned puff pastry and almond paste filling served hot, is still a traditional part of the festivities. For a Christmas wreath (*kerstkrans*) the Dutch shape the *boterletter* into a ring instead of a letter. It is then spread with icing and decorated with candied cherries, orange and lemon peel and a red bow.

Sweets and biscuits

The Dutch are also fond of sweets and biscuits. *Stroopwafel* consists of two thin wafers sandwiched together with syrup, best eaten when

New Year's Eve, but are now a popular street food all year round.

Although vegetarianism has been on the increase in recent decades, meat is still a basic staple in the daily diet, supplemented in winter by potatoes, red and white cabbage, kale and *zuurkool* (sauerkraut). In spring, there is an abundance of asparagus, fennel and various green beans, peas, courgettes, aubergines, artichokes, carrots, onions, spinach and various salad foods, many of which are produced in quantity by the hothouse horticulturalists of the Netherlands. In the 17th century the

Stroopwafel – and how best to eat them.

warm and traditionally served with afternoon tea. Spiced cookies, *speculaas*, often windmill-shaped, are sold in packets or by weight and usually eaten with coffee. In the past they were made on *koekplanken* ('cookie planks'), moulds hollowed out into the shapes of windmills, mermaids, elephants or whatever; today, genuine *koekplanken* are sold in antiques shops and modern copies, made as souvenirs, are widely available.

The classic *appelgebak* (apple pie), made with special rum-soaked raisins and apples, is generally served in the afternoon rather than after an evening meal. *Oliebollen*, spicy doughnuts sprinkled with powdered sugar, were traditionally made to eat around Christmas time and on

RIJSTTAFEL

The Indonesian *rijsttafel*, or rice table, has anything from 16 to 30 side dishes based around rice. Dishes, which might include such favourites as *ayam goreng* (Indonesian fried chicken), *sambal oedang* (shrimps in a red sauce), and *pisang goreng* (fried bananas), are accompanied by crunchy prawn crackers known as *kroepoek*.

If you prefer to eat less or are watching the budget, order *nasi rames*, a miniature *rijsttafel* with generous spoonfuls of various side dishes. If you prefer noodles instead of rice, order the *bami rames* instead. And be careful with the *sambal*, which is Indonesian chilli sauce – a little goes a long way.

Dutch, inspired by their East Indies Company, began to cultivate as many exotic fruits as they could induce to grow. In 1636 the great still-life artist Jan Davidsz de Heem even chose to live in Antwerp (now part of Belgium) because, Sandrart recorded, 'There one could have rare fruits of all kinds, large plums, peaches, cherries, oranges, lemons, grapes, and others, in finer condition and state of ripeness to draw from life.' These days, fresh fruits abound, but are generally imported.

The main hunting areas lie in the province of Limburg, particularly the woods between

A passion for pancakes

Dessert menus in restaurants might well feature the traditional Dutch *flensjes* (thin pancakes), but given a fancy French name – such as *crêpes Suzette* or *crêpes Brésiliennes*, the latter filled with vanilla ice cream coated with a warm sauce made from half chocolate and half coffee. Ordinary plate-sized pancakes of the savoury variety are made with a meat, tomato, cheese or mushroom ragout, or some other such topping, and served at dinner. A sweet version may be topped with Grand Marnier, strawberries or chocolate sauce and whipped

Partridge dish at fine-dining de Kromme Watergang restaurant in Sluis.

Maastricht and Venlo. However, restaurant customers are used to a distinct game season in the cold months. Quail, partridge, pheasant, hare and rabbit are all popular winter dishes, mostly cooked in beer, wine or cognac. Another traditional game recipe is *Jachtschotel* ('Hunter's Dish'), made from stewed venison covered with mashed potatoes and topped with sliced apples and breadcrumbs. It is served with red cabbage.

In all country areas, free-range poultry is plentiful – many families rear their own chickens, guinea fowl, turkeys, ducks and geese. In restaurants fowl is often accompanied by apple sauce or *stoofpeertjes* (little 'stewing pears' cooked in red wine and cinnamon), or redcurrant sauce.

cream, or else served up the no-frills way with maple syrup or *stroop*, a type of treacle. *Poffertjes*, or mini pancakes, are another variation on the same theme.

At home, dessert might consist of a delicious and filling bread pudding made from slices of stale bread, eggs and dried fruit. *Vla* is also a popular country dessert, similar to custard. You'll seldom find it in restaurants, but supermarkets sell many different kinds flavoured with vanilla, chocolate or fruits.

Another favourite when dining out is the traditional *Dame Blanche* – vanilla ice cream with chocolate sauce. Cheese platters are an option as a final course, with some cheeses made from sheep and goat's milk.

Local flavours

Each region has its own food specialities. The southern provinces, for instance, are well known for Burgundian pleasures of the table. In Maastricht, in the province of Limburg, the local dish is a stew resembling Hungarian goulash. Raw vegetable salads served with sausages are also popular. Their local pastry (*vlaai*) is either filled with seasonal fruits (ranging from apricots and cherries to apples or plums) topped with a lattice pattern or filled with rice and cream.

The people of Leiden eat *hutspot* on 3 October to commemorate the town's liberation from

restaurants, where you can sit and enjoy the outlook over the beach as you tuck into the delicious seafood on your plate.

In both the polder lands in the north of the country, and in the new province of Flevoland, country-dwellers keep their own cattle, pigs and hens. Traditionally, these hard-working people eat more meat than city-dwellers; a family might, on average, eat more than 2 kg (4 lb) of meat every day. Then again, some farmers might dine exclusively on potatoes, with each family member eating around 1 kg (2 lbs) worth, dipped into an

Black mussels.

Oysters in Alphen aan den Rijn.

the Spanish in 1574. Leiden had been under siege for several months and the townspeople were starving. Then Prince William of Orange ordered the sluices to be opened to flood the surrounding land, and, faced with the prospect of drowning, the invaders retreated. When a Leiden boy climbed up to explore the deserted ramparts he found an iron pot left by the Spanish containing a stew of beef and vegetables. Now, they make their own commemorative *hutspot* with *klapstuk* (boneless beef short ribs), carrots, potatoes and onions.

In Zeeland, seafood predominates, especially mussels, oysters, sole and turbot. Many local restaurants are built on stilts at the water's edge. There are also a good many glass-fronted

individual bowl of gravy from the meat dish of the previous day.

Colonial legacy

Because of the country's colonial legacy, Indonesian food is extremely popular, so much so that the cuisine has become entirely integrated into the Dutch way of life. Most restaurants specialise primarily in dishes from the islands of Java and Sumatra, and you'll find the best in the larger cities such as The Hague, Amsterdam and Rotterdam.

Because it is home to the highest population of Indonesians (and Dutch resettled from Indonesia), The Hague justifiably lays claim to the most authentic restaurants, and certainly offers the spiciest food.

A classic Dutch landscape.

Amsterdam canal at sunset.

INTRODUCTION

A detailed guide to the entire country, with principal
sites clearly cross-referenced by number to the maps.

Gabled houses.

T he Netherlands is a small country, approximately
255 km (160 miles) north to south, and 180 km
(112 miles) east to west. English-speakers habitu-
ally refer to the country as 'Holland'. The Dutch know
the country as Nederland (the Netherlands). Strictly
speaking, Holland refers only to the two provinces of
Noord- (North) and Zuid- (South) Holland. Most of
the best-known cities of the Netherlands are located in
these two areas, including the capital, Amsterdam; the seat of government, The Hague ('s-Gravenhage, or Den Haag, in Dutch); plus
Rotterdam, Delft, Leiden, Gouda and Haarlem.

This densely populated region appears to be
almost one unbroken conurbation. The Dutch call
it the Randstad: ring-town, but a better, if less literal
translation, is 'the big village'.

The remainder of the Netherlands comprises 10
provinces: Zeeland, Utrecht, Noord-Brabant, Limburg, Gelderland, Flevoland (created in the 20th
century from reclaimed land and declared a province only in 1986), Overijssel, Drenthe, Groningen
and Friesland.

The landscape and character of these more rural
provinces is surprisingly varied and conforms little to the cliché-ridden image of flat, monotonous

River Dinkel in Twente.

polder. Zeeland is a region of islands, peninsulas, sandy coastline
and bird-filled marshes. The southern provinces of Noord-Brabant
and Limburg have a distinctly Catholic culture, a more flamboyant,
Gothic-inspired architecture and wooded hills.

Further north, the great rivers (Rhine, Maas and Waal) cut through
the heath and woodland landscape of the central provinces, while
Gelderland and Overijssel form a region of meadowlands, orchards
and streams, known as the Achterhoek (back corner).

In Drenthe a wilder landscape is dotted with megaliths, marking
the giant communal graves of prehistoric settlers; where the province
merges into Groningen, man-made hillocks rise from the peat levels as further evidence of early settlement. Finally, Friesland, with its
thatched barns and farmhouses, gives way to the shallow Waddenzee
and a chain of often remote but completely unspoiled islands.

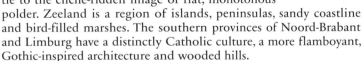

Netherlands

0 20 km
0 20 miles

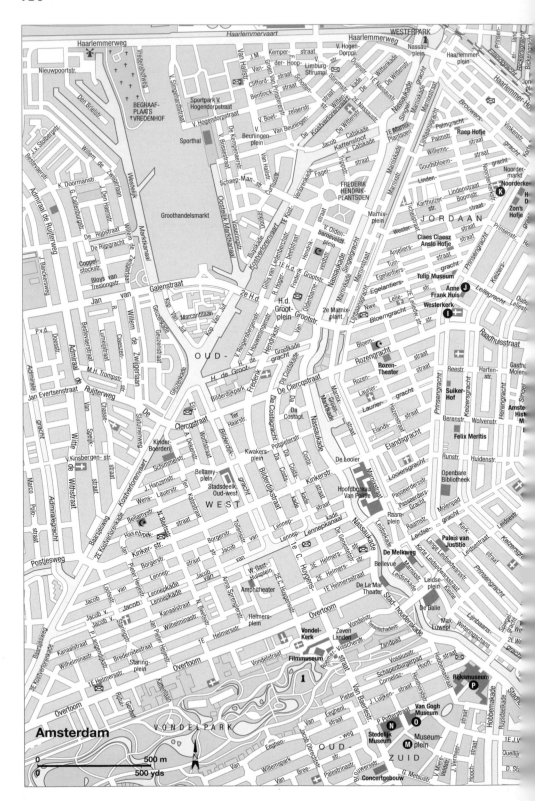

Amsterdam

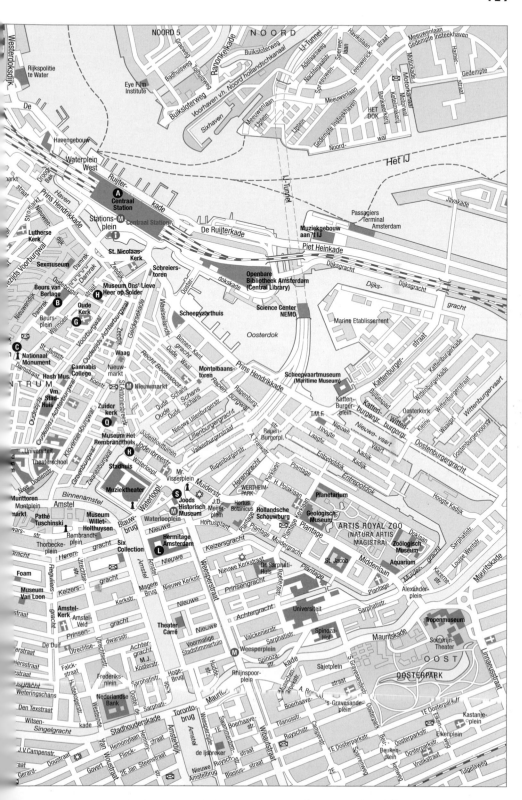

Expect to see bicycles everywhere you go in Amsterdam.

AMSTERDAM

Modern Amsterdam offers something for everyone: from world-class art and stunning architecture to colourful streets that buzz with life.

For most visitors, an encounter with Amsterdam begins among the organ-grinders, street musicians, jugglers, harried commuters, weary travellers (and pickpockets) on Stationsplein, in front of **Centraal Station Ⓐ**. This is a disconcerting yet appropriate beginning, in keeping with the district's voracious appetite for novelty, trade and travel.

Since 1855, however, the city has been severed from the sea by Centraal Station and now looks inward for its identity. Built on an artificial island in Het IJ, the city's old inner harbour, the station gives little sense of its watery origins until you cross Prins Hendrikkade towards Damrak. Only then are you aware of the redundant stretch of water (on the left) that was once the cutting edge of the Dutch Empire, its quaysides and warehouses disgorging goods on their way from the East Indies to Germany and the Baltic.

Today, commuters shuttle back and forth across the IJ between Amsterdam North and Centraal Station. Both the number of ferries and the routes they serve have grown, and this seems likely to continue as the old harbour waterfront is opened up for new housing developments.

A good reason to cross the IJ is to visit the **Eye Film Institute** (IJpromenade 1; tel: 020-589 1400; www.eyefilm.nl; exhibition open Sat–Thu

A cheeky young Amsterdammer.

10am–7pm, Fri until 9pm), a futuristic film institute which opened in 2012. As well as temporary exhibitions and screenings in its four state-of-the-art cinemas, there is a bar-restaurant with stunning views over the harbour. This part of town has become particularly hip in recent years with youth brands such as MTV and Red Bull moving into the area, resulting in old warehouses being transformed into stylish offices and studios and a slew of waterside bars, restaurants and clubs springing up.

Main Attractions
The Jordaan district
Anne Frankhuis
Stedelijk Museum
Van Gogh Museum
Rijksmuseum

The Royal Palace on Dam Square.

From the Beurs

Just as the city has turned its back on the sea, so too do the visitors who rush down busy **Damrak**. This tawdry thoroughfare, bordered by smoky cafés, tacky souvenir shops and a fleet of canal boats, pumps tram and taxi traffic south to the heart of Amsterdam. Ignore the 'change' shops and cheap fast-food storefronts on the right – although you might want to pop into the **Sexmuseum** (www.sexmuseum amsterdam.nl; daily 9.30am–11.30pm; over 16s only) at No. 8 – and focus instead on the stately **Beurs van Berlage** Ⓑ (www.beursvanberlage.com, the former Stock Exchange, on the left. The Dutch have always been a nation of gamblers, and when, in the 17th century, they would lay a wager on anything from the gender of a baby to the profits of a tulip harvest, much of this speculation centred on the Beurs.

The origins of the Beurs lie in informal dealings in neighbouring Warmoesstraat, but in 1608 a Stock Exchange was created on Rokin and, at the end of the 19th century, a new Beurs replaced it on Damrak.

The greatest Dutch poet, Joost van den Vondel, railed against the first Exchange as a 'bringer of misery; sunlight never penetrates thy building'. Inside the spacious main hall of the Beurs, one can admire plain ironwork, narrow arcades and Romanesque and neo-Renaissance motifs. Designed by architect H.P. Berlage, the remarkable Dutch Modernist building is now a unique conference centre and event venue with an attractive café.

Royal connections

It is better to continue along Damrak into the Dam rather than to turn into **Nieuwendijk**, a snaking street of vulgar shops running parallel to Damrak. The **Dam**, the city's only unencumbered square, was long a public and political forum, thanks to the presence of the Royal Palace, once the Town Hall (Stadhuis), and a space large enough for medieval executions, Republican processions and 1980s demonstrations against cruise missiles. Today, demonstrations, carnivals and various cultural and political events

are held on the site. The most notable event takes place on 4 May at 8pm, just across the square at the **Nationaal Monument ⊙**, when two minutes' silence is observed in honour of those who died in World War II. This event, which is televised across the country, is attended by the king and many notables, and watched by thousands who arrive hours ahead to secure a good view of this moving ceremony.

The obelisk-shaped monument is a war memorial containing urns of earth from each of the Netherlands' 11 provinces (it predates the creation of Flevoland, the 12th province) and from Indonesia. The sculptures of naked war victims surrounding the obelisk bear the message 'Never again.' Vivid memories and marks of World War II are ever present in Amsterdam, from the excellent Resistance and Jewish Historical museums to the Anne Frank House (see page 142).

Although now sliced by shuttling trams, the Dam has kept some of its public character, although today its political role is marginal. The **Koninklijk Paleis** (Royal Palace; tel: 020-620

4060; www.paleisamsterdam.nl; opening times vary), built in the Classical style between 1648 and 1655 by Jacob van Campen, maintains a stately presence on the Dam, opposite the equally impressive **Nieuwe Kerk**. The king still welcomes heads of state and other VIP guests to the palace during the year (look for the guards surrounding it and the curious crowds of onlookers). The sombre exterior is embellished with pilasters and pedimented windows, with sea gods and unicorns representing the oceans. In contrast, the interior is light and elegantly ornamented, awash with white marble. It features an array of sumptuous state rooms.

Proud symbol

At its inception the former Stadhuis (Town Hall) was a celebration of Dutch independence and renewed peace. Poet Constantijn Huygens praised it as 'the world's Eighth Wonder. With so much stone raised high and so much timber under,' a reference to its creation on 13,659 wooden piles. The Stadhuis's symbolic importance

SHOP

One of the nicest areas for shopping in Amsterdam is De 9 Straatjes (The 9 Streets; www.de9straatjes.com), on the canal belt behind the palace. As well as hip men's and women's fashion boutiques, there are vintage shops, home decoration and lifestyle stores, plus bars, restaurants and cafés.

National Monument.

THE EASTERN DOCKLANDS

The area to the east, just a few kilometres further on from Centraal Station, known as the Oostelijk Eilanden (or Eastern Islands), comprising man-made KNSM, Java and Borneo islands, has undergone extensive development in recent years to provide innovative housing for people wishing to live just outside the city. Also here are two museums: **Het Scheepvaartmuseum** (National Maritime Museum; Kattenburgerplein 1; tel: 020-523 2222; www. hetscheepvaartmuseum.nl; daily 9am–5pm), which is situated in an 18th-century naval warehouse and has a replica of a Dutch East India Company ship outside, and the green sinking ship-shaped **NEMO Science Center** (Oosterdok 2; tel: 020-531 3233; www.e-nemo.nl; daily 10am–5.30pm) whose sloping roof has an outdoor café and a pop-up beach in the summer. At Oosterdokskade 143 is the new 10-storey **Openbare Bibliotheek Amsterdam** (Amsterdam Central Library; daily 10am–10pm). The east is a 'must visit' for fans of contemporary classical music and jazz too, who flock to the Muziekgebouw aan 't IJ (Piet Heinkade 1; tel: 020-788 20 00; www.muziekgebouw.nl). Further out, a group of six man-made islands along the IJsselmeer called the IJburg is being developed to provide new housing for at least 45,000 inhabitants.

to 17th-century Amsterdam is emphasised by the innumerable paintings of the building that hang on the walls of the city's Historical Museum.

A distinguished neighbour of the Koninklijk Paleis, the **Nieuwe Kerk** Ⓓ (tel: 020-638 69 09; www.nieuwe kerk.nl; daily 11am–5pm) is new in name only. Built in 1400 after a series of fires, the New Church received grand 17th-century additions to its late-Gothic structure. Then, however, it was forbidden from having a tower because the regents feared competition with the Town Hall. Today, the church's fine interior and importance as a cultural centre have helped it emerge from the Town Hall's shadow. Temporary art exhibitions often make it difficult to see the 17th-century organ, choir rail and pulpit or to admire the marble mausoleum of Admiral de Ruyter, so it is worth trying to attend one of the many concerts which are offered throughout the year. Since 1815, Dutch kings and queens have been invested here, most recently King Willem-Alexander in 2013.

In Dam Square, with Nieuwe Kerk (New Church) in the background.

Brief interlude

Tacked on to the church are several minuscule shops and a quaint café. However, for the more genuine article, try *De Drie Fleschjes* on Gravenstraat (No.18), a 17th-century tasting house tucked behind the church. Known as *proeflokalen*, such atmospheric bars originally allowed customers to sample *jenever* (Dutch gin), but now serve an extraordinary range of spirits and cocktails.

Wynand Fockink (www.wynand-fockink.nl) on Pijlsteeg (No.31) was the most famous, but it closed in 1990 after failing to compete with the rash of brown cafés and designer bars. In 1992 it reopened its doors under new ownership and continues to be a stopping point for connoisseurs of Dutch gins and liqueurs.

Thus rejuvenated, cross the Dam and walk down commercial **Kalverstraat** past countless clothing and snack shops. Avoid the endless stream of pedestrians by turning into a lopsided gateway adorned with the triple-cross arms of Amsterdam. Notice the figures of chubby children dressed in red and-black uniforms, a reminder that the gate once led to the City Orphanage. Founded in 1578 on the site of St Lucy's, a former convent the orphanage was a tribute to the enlightened rule of the city fathers. On reaching adulthood, successful orphans were supposed to show their gratitude by becoming benefactors of the orphanage, but the majority of would-be entrepreneur had already been recruited as lowly errand boys by local fishwives. The orphanage was moved out in 1960 and the site was transformed into the **Amsterdams Historisch Museum** Ⓔ (Amsterdam Historical Museum Kalverstraat 92 or Sint Luciënsteeg 27, tel: 020-523 1822; www.amsterda museum.nl; daily 10am–5pm).

Before entering the museum itself prolong the sense of solitude by entering the adjoining **Begijnhof** Ⓕ

Amsterdam's finest almshouse court and one of the city's most spiritual enclaves. In the 15th century this religious quarter was literally an island and, although the once-polluted Beguinensloot moats were filled in 1865, the Begijnhof remains a place apart. First recorded in 1389, the almshouses were home to the Sisters of St Lucy, a Franciscan order that replaced the once popular lay Beguine way of life for women. Beguines chose to lead a partial form of convent life, including the vow of chastity. The last Beguine died in 1971 but the almshouse continues as a residential sanctuary for 'unmarried women of good repute'.

Timber house

The Begijnhof, reached through a number of inner courtyards, comprises a series of brick-and-stone gabled houses built between the 14th and 17th centuries. Het Houten Huys, No. 34, was built in 1460, making it the oldest surviving dwelling in Amsterdam. It is one of only two remaining wooden houses, erected before fire regulations forbade such flammable building materials.

Amsterdammers are fondest of the Begijnhof in spring, when the lawn becomes a carpet of daffodils and crocuses. No. 26, one of the grandest houses, was the home of Sister Antoine, the last Beguine, and has been preserved as she left it. The small church on the square, given to the city's English and Scottish Presbyterians over 300 years ago, hosts intimate concerts.

Opposite the church is one of the city's many clandestine Catholic chapels, a dark, Italianate church, which still smells of candles and serious prayers. From here, walk back through the courtyards of the former orphanage and through the unique Schuttersgalerij (Civic Guards Gallery) which leads to the Historical Museum. Stop at the Mokum café and consider the original residents: the cows that were kept here by the nuns at St Lucy's convent.

Historical Museum

Inside the Historical Museum itself, the trail through Amsterdam's history

The Begijnhof.

FACT

Amsterdam has more than 1,200 bridges and the prettiest is said to be Magere Brug or 'Skinny Bridge'. Linking Nieuwe Kerkstraat with Kerkstraat, this white-wood crossing was built in 1934. Access is only for pedestrians and cyclists and it opens several times a day to let river traffic through. At night, the bridge is illuminated by 1,200 light bulbs.

is imaginatively presented both chronologically and thematically, and not restricted to a particular order. The strength of the collection lies not only in its accurate portrayal of social history through paintings, furniture and cleverly juxtaposed artefacts, but in its creative, changing exhibitions which reflect the city's evolving character.

Highlights of the collection include *het groeikaart* ('the growth map') tracing Amsterdam's growth over the centuries. Amsterdam DNA, a multi-media exhibition, takes visitors on a tour of 1,000 years of history, while kids can find out what life was like in a 17th-century orphanage. 'New York meets the Dam' is a new exhibition focusing on graffiti art in the two cities.

There are also early works by Jan Luyken, Rembrandt and Van Gogh, and other fascinating tableaux of time past, but the museum is famed for its 16th-, 17th- and 18th-century group portraits of the civic guards (employed from the 14th century onwards to protect Amsterdam's citizens), which are hung on the street

inside a glassed-in gallery leading to the Begijnhof. The presentation of Dutch 'anti-democratic movements' deals frankly with the existence of Dutch fascist sympathisers and with the later Jewish deportations.

Contrasting moods

For something completely different, find the doorway between the houses numbered 37 and 38 in the Begijnhof and follow the passageway to **Spui** (pronounced 'spow'), the lively university quarter and home to numerous brown cafés. Café Hoppe (Spui 18) is perhaps the city's most celebrated brown café, frequented by artists and writers, with an intimate, slightly louche atmosphere, in tone with the nicotine-stained walls. Opposite, bankers and businesspeople in suits stand with their beers in warm weather. For elegance and great people-watching, try Café Luxembourg (Spui 22–24), or cafés along the nearby Singel canal. On Fridays, an antiquarian book market offers a good selection of English-language books at reasonable prices. Just opposite is the Athenaeum Book

Athenaeaum Book Store.

Store and News Centrum, which offers a range of books, newspapers and magazines in English.

If you have the energy for extended café-crawling or nightclubbing, follow Kalverstraat south to Rembrandtplein, the most frenetic part of town. En route, call in at the **Pathé Tuschinski Cinema** on Reguliersbreestraat (No. 26), which shows some films in their original language, and admire its splendid Art Deco interior. Further up, around Reguliersdwarsstraat (behind the Flower Market), a predominantly gay quarter, with dining, cruising and clubbing, offers yet another new dimension to city life.

If dinner in a less lively but more stylish district appeals, avoid the tourist-crammed Rembrandtplein and Leidseplein quarters with their piano bars, fast-food restaurants and overpriced tourist traps and walk down any of the four main canals (Singel, Herengracht, Keizersgracht, Prinsengracht), where you will discover many fine, reasonably priced restaurants along the small streets that crisscross the canals, such as Runstraat, Reestraat, Hartenstraat and Wolvenstraat. There are inexpensive ethnic restaurants, elegant dining establishments with well-known chefs, as well as charming brown cafés.

Oude Zijde (Old Side)

Affectionately known as 'Mokum' (the Yiddish word for 'place'), the historic heart of Amsterdam contains the Old Church and the Amstelkring, a 'clandestine' church on Oudezijds Voorburgwal. The red-light district crowds around the north end of the latter canal. The area also harbours more subtle attractions, including the Waag, or Weigh House, and East Indies House.

After the space of the Dam and Damrak, turning into cramped, dingy Warmoesstraat is a shock. In the 17th century, this narrow street (running parallel with, and to the east of, Damrak) was the centre of the fabric and furnishing trades. The shops stocked Nuremberg porcelain, Lyons silk and Spanish taffeta as well as delftware and Haarlem linen. Fallen on harder times, the narrowest shopping street

Visiting the distinctive Pathé Tuschinski Cinema.

TIP

You can't come to Amsterdam and not take to two wheels. Yellow Bike (tel: 020-620 6940; www.yellowbike.nl) is the city's longest-established bike-tour company and offers a two-hour Small City Bike Tour, a three-hour Big City Bike Tour, a three-hour tour of the eastern docklands and a four-hour trip out into the countryside.

Oude Kerk.

in town now relies on cafés and restaurants (De Bakkerswinkel at No. 69 is good for a snack), but a smattering of traditional trades retain a presence here. Despite these pockets of respectability, **Warmoesstraat** glows, if not red-hot, at least a warmish pink hue. The Condomerie Het Gulden Vlies (The Golden Fleece) is a tasteful, reputable outlet for sex toys and condoms – from run-of-the-mill to novelty wear – with sales assistance from sensitive and helpful staff. From here, any alley east leads to the heart of the **red-light district** in Oudezijds Achterburgwal and Zeedijk. If you want to have an inside look at the *walletjes* (red-light area), visit the **Prostitutie Informatie Centrum** (Engekerksteeg 3; www.pic-amsterdam.com; Wed–Fri 10am–5pm, Sat 10am–7pm). They offer walking tours of the area in English on Saturdays at 5pm and Wednesdays at 6.30pm.

The Old Church

Although the Oude Zijde has been blighted by the sex industry, the district's dilapidated condition should not blind visitors to the wealth of architectural treasures hidden behind uninviting façades.

At the Damrak end of Warmoesstraat the WijdeKerksteeg alley leads to the **Oude Kerk** Ⓖ (Old Church; www.oudekerk.nl; Mon–Sat 10am–6pm, Sun 1–5pm), Amsterdam's oldest building, and the original church of the Amestelledamme fishing community. Despite a number of fires, the church's 13th-century tower remains, along with a chapel added in the 15th century. Before the 'Alteration' in 1578, many windows and paintings were destroyed by Protestant iconoclasts, but enough treasures remain to make this the best-preserved of Amsterdam's churches. In the 17th century, the Oude Kerk was the city's first experiment in transforming churches into community centres, a secular tendency that is most marked in today's Nieuwe Kerk. By contrast, the Oude Kerk continues to attract a congregation, even if many who attend services are partly drawn by the excellent organ recitals. You can hear the bells being rung on Tuesdays and Saturdays at 4pm.

Inside this often cold church, the dusty medieval misericords, heavy grey flagstones, half-erased family crests and faded murals give the interior a forsaken feel; look out for the gravestone of Rembrandt's wife, Saskia. There is much to admire, from the ornate organ to the wooden vaulted ceiling and cherubic statues. Some of the stained-glass windows, a kaleidoscope of reds, blues and purples, date from the 16th century. The best time to see the church is in winter, when the light is low and shining through the coloured glass. Temporary art exhibitions are held here, including the Pride Photo Award, an international photography competition about sexual diversity.

The church is also the starting point for the Drugs Tour (www.drugstour.nl; free; over 18s only), which explores sites associated with the city's cannabis culture and departs every Friday at 6pm.

Hidden church

Lucky visitors may hear the church's 15th-century bells before crossing the canal on Oudekerksbrug to the right bank of Oudezijds Voorburgwal. Turn left and follow the canal a little way north, then cross the Leidsesluis bridge back to the left bank. Beside the bridge is **Museum Ons' Lieve Heer Op Solder** ⊕ (Our Lord in the Attic; tel: 020-624 6604; www.opsolder. nl; Mon–Sat 10am–5pm, Sun 1–5pm), one of Amsterdam's most charming and least-explored museums.

This 17th-century merchant's house conceals the finest of the city's 'clandestine' churches, and offers many other surprises, from the cellar to the attic. The lower part of the house, however, gives an accurate glimpse of its more ordinary past. It was used by Catholics from 1650 until 1795, when the French rulers restored the Catholics' right to worship openly. Jan Hartman, a Catholic sympathiser, linked the top floor of three gabled houses to

form two galleries with space for 400 worshippers.

Upstairs, a tiny chaplain's room nestles on the landing, but right under the eaves lies the large church itself. The size of the lower gallery, not to mention the creaking floor, makes the secrecy of the services rather fanciful. Apart from the sweet Maria Chapel, decorated with fresh flowers and 18th-century paintings, the charm lies in odd details such as the revolving mahogany pulpit, ready to be hidden at a moment's notice. From the upper gallery, views over the rooftops embrace the sombre St Nicolaaskerk and the garish promise of a Live Sex Show – just another paradox in this neighbourhood of contrasts.

Seediness and gentility

From here there is a choice of routes. The faint-hearted can avoid the brashness of the red-light area by walking south down Oudezijds Voorburgwal towards **Rokin**. Known in the 16th century as the Velvet Canal, because of its prosperous air, Rokin retains refined traces in the unusual gable

On Rokin.

stones of the houses lining the canal. From the canal-boat dock on Rokin, the red-light area can be viewed in the evening from the comfort of a candle-lit boat cruise.

The fearless, as well as those who are soon offended by the tasteless patter of sex-show hawkers and the line of gawking tourists outside windows displaying scantily dressed women, can cross to the right bank of Oudezijds Voorburgwal and the even narrower Oudezijds Achterburgwal canal in order to see some more of the city's architectural gems, like Zeedijk. At No. 2 is a well-restored gabled house, the second of the city's remaining wooden houses. Vistors who are curious to find out about the city's drugs scene should pause here to check out the **Hash, Marijuana and Hemp Museum** (Oudezijds Achterburgwal 148; www.hashmuseum.com; daily 10am–10pm) and the **Cannabis College** (Oudezijds Achterburgwal 124; www.cannabis-college.com; daily 11am–7pm; free), which has a cannabis garden (charge). At its opposite end, Zeedijk ends in

The Hash Marijuana and Hemp Museum.

Nieuwmarkt, a broad, interesting square surrounded by **Chinatown** and some prize-winning social housing. Historically it bordered the Jodenbuurt (Jewish quarter), and during World War II, Jews were assembled here to await deportation to transit camps.

Have a look at the imposing **Waag** (Weigh House) on the square. In its time, this medieval gatehouse has been a civic weighing house, a guild house for both the militia and the surgeons, and the predecessor of today's Jewish Historical Museum. An *eetcafé* on the ground floor is worth a visit. Also along Zeedijk are several good budget-priced Chinese restaurants. In fact, the entire Nieuwmarkt area has a distinct vibrancy, a big change from its former days as a virtual drugs ghetto. If you follow Zeedijk towards Centraal Station, you'll also find many good Japanese, Portuguese and Malaysian restaurants.

Ruling elite

Nieuwmarkt can also be reached by a less tawdry route via **Koestraat**. In passing, notice the optimistic carvings of Faith, Hope and Charity on Nos. 7 to 11, and the wine-merchants' guild house at No. 10. Koestraat ends in Kloveniersburgwal and the 17th-century mansion (No. 29) known as the **Trippenhuis**. Military insignia on the façade indicate that this was once the home of the Trip family of armament manufacturers. The Trips were powerful members of the Magnificat, the ruling clique of families who governed the city during the Golden Age. Opposite, at No. 26, is the so-called smallest house in Amsterdam, once owned by the Trip family's coachman. From here, you can turn left into Nieuwmarkt or follow the canal to the right until you reach **Oostindisch Huis** (East Indie House), the imposing red-brick building by the next bridge. This was the headquarters of the East India Company and, as such, frequently received deliveries of precious commodities, such as spices, coffee, ebony and mahogany.

Further down Kloveniersburgwal, a small alley lined with bookstalls, Oudemanhuispoort, passes through former almshouses to the photogenic **Huis op de Drie Grachten** (House on the Three Canals). On the right is the Agnietenkapel, the cradle of Amsterdam University.

The best way to discover a city is to people-watch, and if you need a break from sightseeing, head for one of the modern grand cafés. **De Jaren** (Nieuwe Doelenstraat 20) has two of the most popular outdoor terraces in town, overlooking the River Amstel. There is a salad bar at lunchtime, and at dinner a reading table, with English periodicals. For more elegance and intimacy, opt for the **Sofitel Legend The Grand** (Oudezijds Voorburgwal 197). A century ago it was the City Hall, and a century before that a hostelry for distinguished travellers. Now transformed into a five-star hotel, it's a good spot for (an expensive) lunch or afternoon tea.

The Jordaan

The area to the west of the Dam known as the **Jordaan** is a tight grid of narrow streets bounded by Brouwersgracht, Prinsengracht, Rozengracht and Lijnbaansgracht. With its bouquet of streets named after flowers and plants, the Jordaan probably takes its name from the French word *jardin* (garden). This French connection has been present since Huguenot refugees settled here in 1685, but the Jordaan's history dates back to the preceding century. Then, the city was bounded by the Singel canal, and the Jordaan – outside the city walls – was a district inhabited by immigrants and the lower classes. Many of the early residents were employed to dig Amsterdam's great concentric canal system in 1607. As a mere suburb, the Jordaan was outside the city's jurisdiction and prey

to property speculators, resulting in diverse architectural styles and standards.

By the 19th century, the Jordaan housed the city's industrial working class and was a hotbed of political activism. With 83,000 people living in this cramped district, protests and strikes were frequent, provoking the Netherlands' first asphalt road programme – the original cobbles had been thrown at Queen Wilhelmina during an official visit in the 1930s.

Despite the Jordaan's humble roots, the now popular streets surrounding the canals have been gentrified in recent years, sending property prices sky high. This process began in the 1980s, when the district was given a major face-lift and began to attract professionals as well as arty and alternative Amsterdammers. With property prices on the increase and rent control on the decrease, a good portion of the local population was forced to relocate to newly developed areas outside the city, such as Almere. However, the Jordaan still retains much of its atmosphere.

Market by the Waag.

EAT

If you're too busy sightseeing to relax in a restaurant for lunch, try some of the local snacks. Buy *kroketten*, ham and cheese croquettes, from Van Dobben (Korte Reguliersdwarsstraat 5); fries from Vleminckx (Voetboogstraat 31) or a herring sandwich from Rob Wigboldus Vishandel (Zoutsteeg 6). Then comes the challenge to find a quiet spot.

Jordaan North, the area above Westerstraat, is a maze of small alleys, quiet restaurants and thriving workshops, and retains many of its working-class roots. The North has many 'true' Jordaaners, independent-minded students, artisans and tradespeople born and bred in the quarter. **Jordaan South**, situated below Westerstraat, is more gentrified, with highly individualistic shops on delightful side streets adjacent to the larger canals and a variety of renowned brown cafés.

Specific routes through the Jordaan are unnecessary, since its appealing canals and geometric alleys entice strollers to abandon fixed plans and instead fall into the nearest brown café, book store, art gallery or trendy shop. Apart from mandatory visits to the Westerkerk and the Anne Frankhuis, which are technically beyond the edge of the Jordaan, aimless wandering is the order of the day.

Outdoor life

Enjoying alfresco drinks.

Starting from hectic Leidseplein, head into central Amsterdam along Leidsestraat and turn left at Prinsengracht. Soon you cross Leidsegracht and (five streets beyond) reach **Looiersgracht**. At the first sign of sunshine hitting the city's streets, locals bring their chairs out into the roadways, and those lucky enough sit sunning themselves on balconies. The low-key cafés on Looiersgracht typify the city's laid-back atmosphere.

Just north of Looiersgracht, **Elandsgracht** is best known for its idiosyncratic indoor market (the Looier), a mass of stalls selling anything from 1950s memorabilia to handmade pottery, old dolls and toys; but there are no great bargains to be had here. If you subscribe to the adage 'you get what you pay for', however, take a stroll down Oude Spiegelstraat, Amsterdam's antiques row, where discerning antiquaries do business (see page 146). **Lauriergracht**, the next real canal north, has gabled houses towards the eastern end, and check out somewhat seedy **Lijnbaansgracht**, at the opposite end, where music blares out at night from a clutch of vibrant bars.

Around the Westerkirk

Continue along Prinsengracht and across hectic Rozengracht, with its variety of shops, ethnic bakeries and *traiteurs* (from Turkish to Spanish) and several modern furniture galleries. Look skyward and you will see the familiar spire that is the landmark of the Westerkerk (West Church). The small canals and streets radiating from the Westerkerk are distinctly chic and occasionally over-restored. Even so, the neighbourhood remains eclectic, and attractions around here range from the elegant French restaurant Christophe at 46 Leliegracht to cosy lunch rooms, minimalist architects' studios and second-hand bookshops.

The **Westerkerk** ❶ (West Church; Mon–Sat 10am–3pm; free), which dates back to 1630 and was renovated in 1990, is the city's finest church, a masterpiece in Dutch Renaissance style by the talented father and son Hendrick and Pieter de Keyser. Its soaring spire, the highest in the city at 85 metres (275 feet), is crowned by a glinting yellow-and-blue crown, a reminder of former Habsburg rule. If you are feeling energetic, the view from the tower is remarkable, stretching to the Rijksmuseum in the south and the harbour in the north. The house where Anne Frank and her family hid from the Nazis is just a few doors away, at 263 Prinsengracht, and she described Westerkerk's carillon chimes in her diary. Today you can still hear them toll on the hour, and there are occasional outbursts of a popular or classic refrain, depending on the occasion.

Compared with the Oude Kerk, the Westerkerk's interior is slightly disappointing, but its popularity with tourists is secured by the fact that Rembrandt was buried here, although the site of his tomb is unknown (indeed his bones were probably removed to a charnel house some 20 years after his interment in the church). Classical music concerts are held on certain days (Monument Day, for instance). Look for the statue of Anne Frank on Westerplein near the entrance to the church and, if you want a snack, there are several stands nearby selling herring and Dutch fries, known as *patat*.

In remembrance

Beside the Westerkerk is the **Homomonument**, a sculpture group of pink marble triangles – a reference to the symbol homosexuals were forced to wear by the Nazis. The memorial commemorates homosexuals who died in the Nazi camps, or suffered persecution in the past.

For an insight into life in Amsterdam during the Occupation, visit the **Anne Frankhuis** ❶ (263 Prinsengracht, tel: 020-556 7100; www.annefrank.org; Nov–Mar Mon–Sat 9am–7pm, Sun 9am–9pm; Apr–Oct Mon–Sat 9am–9pm, Sun 9am–10pm, July–Aug daily 10am–10pm). From 1942 to 1944, the Frank family hid in a secret annexe here and were sustained by helpers who provided them with food bought on the black market. In 1944, German police raided

The canalside Westerkerk.

Anne Frank

Translated into 70 languages, the teenage diary of the world's most famous Holocaust victim is more relevant than ever in today's social and political climate.

On Monday 6 July 1942, Anne Frank accompanied her family into the Achterhuis (the back annexe) of 263 Prinsengracht. In February 1941, the Nazis had begun their first round-up of Amsterdam's Jewish community. Otto Frank was already planning an escape. Forced by the Germans to leave his prosperous business, he was still able to prepare several rooms on the top floors and back of 263 Prinsengracht, a combined warehouse and office, as a secret hiding place.

The safety of his family and four Jewish acquaintances was to hinge on a swinging cupboard concealing the stairs to the back portion of the building. Otto Frank had planned to disappear on 16 July, but on 5 July a deportation order for his daughter Margot arrived. At 7.30am the next day the Frank family made their way to 263, where the others later joined them.

The statue of Anne Frank at the house.

The diary

Anne's record of life in their secret refuge is remarkable, not just as a diary of a Jewish family in hiding, but as a record of the intellectual growth of a young girl already blessed with obvious literary talents, as she passes through her formative adolescent years under fearful circumstances. As you turn the pages, it is her steadily maturing mind that proves to be the real source of interest.

The second entry of her diary could have been written by any 13-year-old. She writes: 'I had my birthday on Sunday afternoon. We showed a film *The Lighthouse Keeper* with *Rin-Tin-Tin*, which my school friends thoroughly enjoyed. We had a lovely time.' In July 1944 the same diarist, now 15, wrote: 'It is a great wonder that I have not given up all my expectations because they seem absurd and unfeasible. But I still cling to them, despite everything, because I still believe in the inner goodness of humanity. It's absolutely impossible for me to base everything on death, suffering and confusion.'

Just 20 days later the refugees in the annexe were discovered by the Gestapo and sent to concentration camps. Only Anne's father Otto returned. Anne died of typhus at Bergen-Belsen in March 1945 aged 15, only three weeks before British troops arrived to liberate it. Her diary had been left behind among old books, magazines and newspapers lying on the floor and recovered by Miep Gies, one of the family's helpers.

The complete version

A complete version of the diary, *The Diary of a Young Girl: Definitive Edition*, was published in 2007. Of the many mature and perceptive passages written during the last weeks she spent in hiding, the most famous quotations come from the final paragraphs of her entry for 15 July. Ironically, three months previously, on 4 April, she had written: 'I want to live on after my death'. With over 70 translations of her book reaching millions of people, she has achieved the immortality she desired.

Anne's spirit provides the key to the real significance of 263 Prinsengracht. The Anne Frankhuis is more than a place where a world-famous diary was penned. It is both a living monument to all those who were victims of racism, fascism and anti-Semitism in World War II, and a warning to the modern world that intolerance and racial violence are still with us.

the house and discovered their hide-out. They deported the entire Frank family, first to the transit camp at Westerbork, and then to Auschwitz and Bergen-Belsen. An adjacent building has space for temporary exhibitions, as well as an educational department, multi-media resource centre, bookstore and café. With the crowds that queue for admission all day, it's a good idea to buy tickets online in advance.

Now cross over Prinsengracht into the Jordaan proper. Beyond Egelantiersgracht turn left and look for the 17th-century almshouse court in Eerste Egelantiersdwarsstraat. Known as the **Claes Claesz Anslo Hofje**, these beautifully restored houses offer fine examples of step, spout and neck gables. Nearby, at the **Tulip Museum** (Prinsengracht 116; tel: 020-421 0095; www.amsterdamtulipmuseum.com; daily 10am–6pm), you can find out about one of the country's most famous exports and buy some to take home.

On neighbouring Egelantiersgracht is Café 't Smalle, a cosy brown café that is one of Amsterdam's oldest. During summer months boats pull up to its outdoor landing and join the terrace crowd. Smoking and drinking have been part of the Jordaan's charm since the 17th century.

Quiet courtyards

If hidden almshouses appeal, the Jordaan district is the right place to be. However, due to too many visitors disturbing the peaceful ambience, doors tend to remain locked. If they happen to be open, do tread quietly and respect the inhabitants. From Claes Claesz Anslo, a short walk northwards along Prinsengracht takes you to Zon's Hofje at Nos. 157–171 and the Van Brienen Hofje at Nos. 9–133. Stemming from the early Dutch Republic's belief in the virtue of personal charity, such almshouses nowadays represent the institutionalised form, but nevertheless manage to retain a tangible spirituality.

A short walk across Prinsengracht leads to **Noordermarkt**, and Hendrick de Keyser's last great church, the Noorderkerk, built in 1620 and restored in 1998. En route, you may find distraction in the cafés and stylish shops along Prinsenstraat.

Around the Noorderkerk the atmosphere is more laid-back Jordaan than upmarket chic. In summer, several festivals are held here, and on Mondays and Saturday mornings this friendly square is home to a market. The Monday flea market sells everything from fabric and sewing items to books, toys, tools and ethnic snacks, while Saturdays feature a popular farmer's market which specialises in organic produce, natural breads, grains and other health-oriented products. Adjacent is a small flea market offering second-hand clothes, vinyl records, books and ethnic jewellery. It attracts a lively crowd of shoppers, street musicians and curious tourists.

On market days the long queue on the corner will doubtless be outside the Winkel lunch café, famed for its

Flowers at the Tulip Museum.

apple tart, baked on the premises and served warm with whipped cream.

The North Church

The dignified **Noorderkerk** (North Church; Mon 10.30am–12.30pm, Sat 11am–1pm; free) stands aloof from the surrounding fuss. Like the Westerkerk, this church is owned by the state and was renovated following a public fund-raising initiative. Organ concerts are held every Saturday at 2pm from mid-September to mid-June (charge). The building itself is notable for its subdued atmosphere and a stark statue outside. In keeping with such a radical area, this statue of chained figures is a monument to the *Jordaanoproer* of 1934, the Jordaan unemployment riots during the Depression years. 'The strongest chains are those of unity', reads the moving inscription.

Jordaaners still commemorate the uprising every year with poems, posters and floral tributes. On the church itself is a memorial to another significant event in local history. A sign commemorates the 400 local Jews who were deported as a reprisal for the killing of a single Dutch Nazi-sympathiser during a street battle.

Waterside walks

From Prinsengracht, you can walk east to the grand canals of **Keizersgracht** and **Herengracht**. Alternatively, continuing north along Prinsengracht leads to an entirely different cityscape. The **maritime quarter**, beginning at Haarlemmerstraat, and bordered by parallel Brouwersgracht (Brewer's Canal), with its picturesque old converted *pakhuizen* (warehouses), is one of Amsterdam's most picturesque areas. Long Haarlemmerstraat is filled with small shops and restaurants, and an independent cinema, appropriately called The Movies, which shows films in their original language.

But for those who love the bohemian Jordaan, the decision is easy: lunch at a popular *eetcafé* like Café de Tuin (13 Tweede Tuindwaarsstraat) or Café de Prins (124 Prinsengracht), or dinner in Jordaan North (perhaps near Westerstraat) at a simple ethnic restaurant. Choose from a variety of cuisines, including Spanish tapas, Greek, Italian, Indian and seafood.

It is inexcusable to leave the Jordaan before discovering a final brown café. On Lindengracht, De Kat in de Wijngaert (No. 160) offers classical and blues music from its extensive CD collection. For a more eclectic clientele, the owners of De Doffer on Runstraat (Nos. 12–14) promise that 'In the Jordaan, we serve tramps as well as lawyers.'

The grachtengordel

Each of Amsterdam's three main canals is approximately 3km (2 miles) long, so it may not be an attractive proposition to walk the entire length of each one, although many enjoy the scenic stretch. As with the Jordaan, you can select small sections or, better still, simply follow your instinct. Since the waterways are not far apart, an

Nightfall over Herengracht.

are linked by side streets, it's easy to meander and switch between canals.

The **grachtengordel** (canal belt) network was created in the early 17th century to cater to a wealthier and expanding population. As grand houses materialised along the canals, the merchant class gradually moved from the insalubrious Oude Zijde to the relative opulence of these new canals. The City Council imposed strict regulations to preserve the tone of the neighbourhoods: barrel-making was forbidden because of the noise, brewing was forbidden because of the bad smell, and sugar refining was out of the question as it posed a severe fire hazard. But trade was not excluded altogether: these steep-roofed houses were also intended to double as warehouses, with storage space in the attics and basements. Taxes were levied according to the size of the frontage, a system which often encouraged ostentation and vulgarity. The maximum permissible width was 10 metres (30ft), but the depth could extend to 60 metres (190ft).

Gable architecture

If these canal houses remain special today it is partly due to their decorative gables. The old-fashioned pointed or spout gable was gradually replaced by the simpler step gable, while in the 1630s the gracious neck gable became fashionable and remained so until the mid-17th century. From about 1660 onwards, the flowing bell gable was popular, but in grander houses was superseded by the Italian-style straight or triangular cornice. By the end of the Golden Age, the most ostentatious patrician houses had broad pedimented façades decorated in neoclassical style with garlands or extravagant sculptures.

The grandest of these 17th-century mansions were built with a warehouse in the basement, lavish reception rooms on the ground floor and, above, a dining room and banqueting room. Inventories from the time describe Persian silk furnishings, Turkish rugs, Japanese lacquerware, Venetian or ebony-framed mirrors as well as oil paintings or alabaster statues in most rooms. All in all, the greatest houses

Beautiful houses on the Prinsengracht.

PRINCE'S CANAL

From the Noorderkerk, it's just a few steps to the measured, bourgeois calm of **Prinsengracht**; the elegant clusters of typical façades range from grey to ice-cream pink. Guessing the meaning of the gable stones provides an interesting game: Jesus and the loaves and fishes give way to the Three Wise Men, two turtle doves, and finally to St Paul blowing a trumpet. Note the large hooks placed just below the gable on each and every home. Purely functional, these serve to lift furniture and other household goods by rope to and from the house when the inhabitants are relocating. Most front doors are painted a dark Amsterdam green – a colour chosen long ago (though not mandatory) for its compatibility with the colour of the canal water.

outshone even the *palazzi* of Venice – in a republic which claimed to put virtue before gold! Although they might not have the best interiors, the **Museum Willet-Holthuysen** (Herengracht 605; www.willet-holthuysen.nl; Mon–Fri 10am–5pm, Sat–Sun 11am–5pm) and **Museum Van Loon** (Keizersgracht 672; www.museumvanloon.nl; daily 10am–5pm) are fine examples of stylish 17th- and 18th-century burghers' households. On the opposite side of the canal at No. 609 is **FOAM** (tel: 020-551 6500; www.foam.org; daily 10am–6pm, Thu and Fri until 9pm), a photography museum featuring exhibitions by some of the world's leading snappers. Walks along the three concentric canals, which were added to the Unesco World Heritage List in 2010, reveal significant differences in style. **Prinsengracht** (Princes' Canal) is perhaps the humblest of the three, with a greater number of warehouses. **Keizersgracht** (Emperors' Canal) is the most approachable and varied waterway, especially the stretch of renovated gables near No. 324. It is **Herengracht** (the Gentlemen's

Canal), however, that contains the most elegant and expensive mansions. The stretch between **Brouwersgracht** and **Raadhuisstraat** has a number of fine converted warehouses, as well as the Bartolotti mansion (Nos. 170–172), a Renaissance cascade of decoration. The east bank, from Huidenstraat to Leidsestraat, provides the greatest variety of gables spanning Renaissance and classical styles.

But it's the elegant **Golden Bend** section, between Leidsestraat and Vijzelstraat, to which wealthy 17th-century merchants most aspired. There is much to enjoy here in the quirky sculptural details and gables decorated with dolphins or mermaids. Outsiders might find this stretch a vain exercise in grandeur. Great double-fronted mansions compete with each other in size, while a sumptuous copy of a classical Loire Valley chateau (380 Herengracht), its gables and windows embellished with reclining figures, cherubs and various mythical characters, dwarfs the adjoining Renaissance gables. Most of these mansions now house opulent hotels, offices and banks, and one of them is the residence of Amsterdam's *burgemeester*, or mayor.

While you're in this area, cross the Blauwbrug bridge over the River Amstel (giving you one of the city's best views) and head to the **Hermitage Amsterdam** ⓛ (Amstel 51; tel: 020-530 8755; www.hermitage.nl; daily 10am–5pm). This branch of the Hermitage Museum in St Petersburg in Russia, which opened in 2009, hosts two temporary exhibitions a year from the main museum's collection and also has two permanent collections, one relating to Netherlands-Russia relations and another one about the 17th-century Amstelhof building, originally a retirement home for elderly women.

The Museum District

For art lovers, the real centre of Amsterdam is **Museumplein** ⓜ

Garden at Museum Van Loon.

situated to the southwest of the canal circle's Golden Bend, in an area known as Oud Zuid (Old South). This is a broad, open public space which links the city's three major museums and the century-old Concertgebouw concert hall. Grassy areas extend uninterrupted, offering a pleasant refuge for relaxation. A large pond behind the Rijksmuseum is good for winter skating, and various events continue to take place on site, including the Uitmarkt cultural festival every August. Although hundreds of trees were chopped down to accommodate a new underground car park for some 600 cars, the controversy over this project might just turn into contentment over the next few years.

For a different type of relaxation, there is the popular **Vondelpark**, a year-round haven for joggers, cyclists, dog-walkers and skaters, where lively concerts and dance events are held in summer. Avid shoppers may prefer a stroll along P. C. Hooftstraat, the home of designer labels, though it's nothing special compared with major shopping streets in other European capitals. Your money is better spent on **Spiegelgracht**, at the heart of the city's antiques shopping quarter, Spiegelkwartier, where each shop resembles a mini-museum. Asian antiquities, old Dutch tiles, Art Deco objects, Russian icons and pewter are just some of the specialities here.

Modern art

The **Stedelijk Museum** Ⓝ (Museumplein 10; tel: 020-573 2911; www.stedelijk.nl; daily 10am–6pm, Thu until 10pm) specialises in modern art, from the mid-19th century to the present day. The museum reopened in 2012, with a new wing for temporary exhibitions, after being closed for nine years for renovation. Foreign highlights include works by Chagall, Braque and the German Expressionists, as well as many new names from the US and UK. For a Dutch flavour, however, Mondrian and Karel Appel

are outstanding, as are contemporary artists like Jan Dibbets, Rene Daniels and Stanley Brouwn. Exhibits from the permanent collection are constantly changing, so if you come looking for your favourite Picasso, don't be surprised to find a Matisse in its place. There are free tours in English on Sundays at 3.45pm.

Note that the Mondrian collection in The Hague is even more comprehensive, and the focus on Appel, Constant and Corneille, members of the celebrated COBRA movement, has been shifted to the **COBRA Museum voor Moderne Kunst** (COBRA Museum of Modern Art; Sandbergplein 1; tel: 020-547 5050; www.cobramuseum.nl; Tue–Sun 11am–5pm) in Amstelveen. Take tram 5 to the end of the line and visit this modern building filled with the work of these experimental painters who, by breaking away from constructions of traditional art, proved to be ahead of their time.

The **Van Gogh Museum** Ⓞ (Museumplein 6; tel: 020-570 5200; www.vangoghmuseum.nl; daily 9am–5pm, Fri until 10pm), next door to the

Relaxing in the Vondelpark.

Stedelijk, is an essential stop. The main building, designed by the Dutch architect Gerrit Rietveld, remains devoted to the world's largest collection of works by Van Gogh and also houses paintings by his contemporaries, including Gauguin. The new wing, designed by Japanese architect Kisho Kurokawa, is being used exclusively for changing exhibitions. With its austere style, inspired by geometric elements such as cones, ovals and squares, and its titanium roof and side wall, the building gives a very firm nod to the 21st century. The use of natural stone on the curved gable is also an original gesture. A tranquil pond makes a strong Zen statement and serves as a resting place between the two buildings, linking old with new.

The permanent collection, at once chronological and thematic, is, like Van Gogh's art, eminently approachable. The main focus is on Van Gogh's development, from his dark landscapes painted in the Dutch provinces of Noord-Brabant and Drenthe, to his light-strewn Parisian Impressionist phase, and finally to the climax of his life's work in th visionary Mediterranean atmospher at Arles. To avoid the queues, boo tickets in advance online.

Packed with treasures

The **Rijksmuseum** ⓟ (Museumstraa 1, tel: 020-674 7000; www.rijksmuseum nl; daily 9am–5pm) just to the north a vast, unwieldy collection that draw much of its inspiration from the cit itself. This national, cultural treasure house reopened in 2013 after under going 10 years of renovation. This wa followed by the new Phillips Wing, i 2014, which includes temporary exh bition space, a photography galler and a restaurant. In all, 8,000 objec in 80 galleries tell the story of 80 years of Dutch art and history fror the Middle Ages to Mondrian.

It's best to concentrate on the Dutc Masters. Time permitting, there is als the renovated Dutch History colle tion, a vast sweep from the Middl Ages to 1945, and Painting: 18th–19t Century, a glance at Dutch Impre sionism and the schools of Amste dam and The Hague. The main cours however, has to be the 17th-centur Golden Age, which is accommodate in more than 30 galleries. The star the show is *The Night Watch* by Ren brandt, housed in its own room o the second floor. Next door in the Er galerij (Gallery of Honour) highligh include *Kitchen Maid* by Rembranc van Rijn, *The Merry Drinker* by Frar Hals and *The Merry Family* by gen painter, Jan Steen, whose work humo ously captures the lower orders at pla (even the baby looks drunk). With th exception of Rembrandt, Dutch pain ers tend to rehearse the same litany facial expressions, from circumspect t careworn, complacent to vain, virt ous to lascivious. Morality is never f away in 17th-century Dutch paintin

The collection of Delftware potter also on the second floor, is particular good. In the garden is the Asian Pav ion, surrounded by water, to house th collection of Asian art. Again, it's be

Amsterdam's pride and joy, the Rijksmuseum.

to book tickets online in advance to avoid the queues.

A short stroll east of the Rijksmuseum along Singelgracht is the **Heineken Experience** (Stadhouderskade 78; tel: 020-523 9222; www.heineken.com; Mon–Thu 10.30am–7.30pm, Fri–Sun 10.30am–9pm). The world-famous lager was brewed in this building until 1988. Now visitors can enjoy a 1.5-hour self-guided tour before sampling some of the liquid gold.

Jodenbuurt (old Jewish quarter)

Admirers of Rembrandt's work might like to visit the remains of Amsterdam's Jewish quarter, where the artist lived for much of his life. The **Jodenbuurt** (sometimes called Jodenhoek) stretches east of the Dam and waterfront area. Even though the quarter has been sadly neglected and, in recent years, partly demolished, a sense of Jewish spirit seeps through the ruins.

From Centraal Station, an intriguing walk leads southeast to Rembrandt's House and the Jewish Historical Museum on Jonas Daniël Meijerplein. The quickest route on foot is via increasingly colourful Zeedijk, but far quicker would be to take Tram 9 or the metro to Waterlooplein.

By the 17th century, up to 10 percent of Amsterdammers were Sephardic Jews from Spain and Portugal who, although relatively prosperous and well integrated, were not allowed to join trade guilds. They worked in the cloth, tobacco, sugar or book industries. From 1620 waves of poorer Ashkenazi Jews from Poland and Germany settled in the east of town and, unable to speak Dutch, turned to menial ghetto jobs around Sint Antoniesbreestraat. Still, in polyglot Amsterdam, it was possible to be at once an insider and an outsider. Poet Andrew Marvell recorded this religious melting pot in the 17th century: 'Hence Amsterdam, Turk-Christian-Pagan-Jew/Staple of sects and mint of schism, grew.'

By 1900, 95 percent of the residents in this area were Jewish and played a visible role in Dutch society until World War II. However, between 1940

At the Van Gogh Museum.

Van Gogh Museum
Amsterdam

and 1945, the area became a sealed ghetto (the Joodse Wijk), and over 70,000 Jews, 90 percent of the Jewish population, met their deaths in Auschwitz, Sobibor or Bergen-Belsen. Amsterdam, once known as the 'Jerusalem of the West', today has a Jewish population of about 15,000.

Sint Antoniesbreestraat is now a shadow of its former colourful self. Even so, among the shoddy modern buildings you can still see several original gables, and there is even a Jewish bakery. Although it is still a working-class area, many new residents include an international alternative crowd, often congregating in the trendy Tisfris café' or at the nearby Muziektheater.

At No. 69 is the **De Pinto House**, once owned by a Portuguese merchant but now a public library. After admiring the decorative scrollwork around the windows, glance inside at the elaborate painted ceiling.

Urban renewal

Museum Het Rembrandthuis.

Just over the road is one of Hendrick de Keyser's famous gateways, surmounted by a skull and crossbone It leads to another de Keyser maste piece, the **Zuiderkerk** **Q** (Sout Church), whose elegant spire rise above the surrounding *nieuwbou* (new housing). This was the city's fir purpose-built Calvinist church, begu in 1603 and completed in 1614, as th date above the tower clock poin out. Three of Rembrandt's childre are buried here and the building w painted by Claude Monet in 1874. Th church currently serves as a centre f urban renewal with an exhibition o housing and environment. In 1945 was used as a temporary morgue f Jews killed in Nazi raids.

Sint Antoniesbreestraat cross Oude Schans by means of a wind swept bridge. On the near side a quaint lock-keeper's house and cluster of gabled houses; on the f side, to the right of the bridge, th edges of Waterlooplein market spi over the quayside, and it is worth ta ing a stroll through the surroundir neighbourhood and exploring quai Staalstraat, with its welcoming caf and bookshops.

HET TWISKE RECREATIONAL PARK

To the north of Amsterdam, between Zaanstad and Purmerend, lie the recreational parklands known as Het Twiske, which takes its name from the River Twisck, a tributary of the River Wormer.

This vast park has something for everyone, be they fisherman, sailor, diver, swimmer, cyclist or ornithologist. If fishing or birdwatching proves too strenuous, you can always set up a barbecue or picnic in one of many designated areas. The landscape came into being as a result of centuries of turf-cutting, and more recently sand-quarrying, which left a lake with many islands. Eventually it was converted into a multiple-use recreational area. It is not uncommon to see Scottish Highland cattle and Shetland ponies grazing in the meadows amongst the splendid and sometimes rare flora and fauna. With so much water, it is a logical location for a sailing school, where sailing craft, canoes and rowing boats can be hired.

In keeping with its natural charms, motorised craft are banned. By far the most pleasant way to get there from Amsterdam is by bicycle from the back of Centraal Station, with a free ferry crossing to Amsterdam North, around 12km (7.5 miles) round trip. The route is well marked. For further information, see www.hettwiske.nl. The parklands never seem crowded, so you are almost guaranteed a peaceful day.

Jodenbreestraat takes over from Sint Antoniesbreestraat, but the only vestige of its 17th-century self is the **Museum Het Rembrandthuis ®** (Rembrandt House Museum; Jodenbreestraat 4; tel: 020-520 0400; www.rembrandthuis.nl; daily 10am–6pm). The painter lived here from 1639 to 1660, until bankruptcy forced him to move. The mansion, restored to look as it would have done when Rembrandt lived here, contains over 250 of his drawings and etchings, including a portrait of Jan Six, one of Rembrandt's patrons. In painting his patron as a refined art lover, instead of the ostentatious merchant that he was, Rembrandt won a permanent place in the magnificent Six Collection (Amstel 218; tel: 020-642 7777; www.collectiesix.nl; visits Mon–Fri mornings by request). Along with Van Gogh and Vermeer, Rembrandt continues to be one of the Netherlands' most beloved, as well as most famous, painters. Among the best works in the Rembrandt House are the sensitive portraits of his wife Saskia and his homely portrayals of beggars, barrel-organ players and a rat-catcher. The trades have long gone, but Rembrandt's physiognomies are recognisable in the faces of present-day Amsterdammers.

Diamonds and dockers

From here, make a brief sortie into **Uilenburg**, formerly a maze of back alleys and sweat shops. The building on the right was the Boas diamond-polishing works, a major source of employment for Jewish residents in the 19th century. Today, it is the site of the **Gassan Diamond Factory** (Nieuwe Uilenbergerstraat 173; tel: 020-622 5333; www.gassan.com; daily 9am–5pm), where there are free tours for visitors; being able to try on some rings at the end of a visit is particularly fun.

Jodenbreestraat peters out in busy Mr Visserplein, but it is worth negotiating the traffic hazards to see Mari Andriessen's statue of a docker. *De Dokwerker* commemorates the round-up of 425 Jews in February 1941. The event provoked a general strike, led by the dock workers, in which outraged Amsterdammers expressed solidarity with their fellow citizens using the slogan: 'Keep your dirty

Gassan Diamond Factory.

hands off our rotten Jews.' The short-lived strike was a unique protest against Nazi inhumanity in occupied Europe. On the far side of the traffic island is the **Portuguese Synagogue** (Visserplein 3; tel: 020-531 0380; www.portugesesynagoge.nl; open Sun–Fri from 10am, closing times vary) which, in the 1670s, had the distinction of being the largest synagogue in the world. Originally a 'clandestine' synagogue, it had the same status as the 'secret' Catholic churches (see page 137).

On Nieuwe Amstelstraat, just opposite the synagogue, is the **Joods Historisch Museum ⑤** (Jewish Historical Museum; tel: 020-531 0380; www.jhm.nl; daily 11am–5pm), housed in a complex of four former Ashkenazi synagogues. Beginning in the domed New Synagogue, the exhibition traces the spread of Judaism through the Netherlands, from its humble beginnings to the years of prestige in the 18th century, the decimation of the community during the Holocaust, and continuing right up to the present day. The displays are fascinating and extremely touching. Highlights include an 18th-century Ark, the ritual

The Joods Historisch Museum.

baths and wartime memorabilia. The gift shop offers an interesting selection of books and Judaica. And you can call in at the museum's kosher café for a sandwich or slice of cheesecake before leaving. Tickets are valid for one month and also give access to the Portuguese Synagogue as well as the Children's Museum (in the JHM) and **Hollandsche Schouwburg** (National Holocaust Memorial; Plantage Middenlaan 24; tel: 020-531 0380; www.hollandscheshouwburg.nl; daily 11am–5pm).

By Sint Antoniesbreestraat is a statue of a turtle, representing Time and its loss for the Jewish community. Towards the Artis Royal Zoo (Plantage Kerklaan 38–40; www.artis.nl; daily Mar–Oct 9am–6pm, Nov–Feb 9am–5pm), the Hortus Botanicus (Plantage Middenlaan 2a; www.dehortus.nl; daily 10am–5pm) botanical gardens and Plantage Middenlaan is a prosperous 19th-century Jewish neighbourhood, where doorways are occasionally adorned with pelicans. According to Judaeo-Christian legend, the pelican will, in adversity, feed its starving young with its own blood.

Streetwise in the city

Renowned for its sex and drugs, Amsterdam is slowly cleaning up its act; making another good reason to visit one of the world's safest cities.

The Netherlands is one of the world's safest countries, with crime rates falling year on year. However, as with all major cities, Amsterdam has problems with thieves and pickpockets, especially around stations, major attractions and on public transport. The red-light district is probably best avoided after dark.

Drugs

Drugs continue to be a controversial issue. In the early 1990s the number of registered 'coffee shops' was reduced from 750 to 250 (there are now fewer than 200) to stem the tide of hard drug dealing, and to maintain the line between soft and hard drugs, thus making it easier for the authorities to observe and control. A registered coffee shop now displays a green and white licence plate in its window instead of the tell-tale cannabis-leaf logo. It cannot hold more than 500 grams of soft drugs in stock, or sell more than 5 grams per deal, and the lower age limit is 18.

In 2012 a new law stated that only residents of the Netherlands could buy cannabis in coffee shops from then on. However, realising the effect that this would have on tourism (around 35 percent of tourists visit a coffee shop), this law is not enforced in Amsterdam.

Coffee shop names – and aromas – are a giveaway: Smokey, Mellow Yellow and The Otherside continue to puff away peacefully. To avoid any misunderstanding, genuine coffee shops often display 'No smoking' notices in English. Yet there is no need to be alarmist about drug-related issues. The majority of Dutch soft-drugs users are tolerated provided that they don't infringe on others' rights.

Prostitution

The same tolerance has always applied to sex in the city. Known as the *walletjes*, the red-light district offers every variant on pornography and prostitution. Rembrandtplein and Thorbeckeplein, just south of the red-light district, provide a hint of things to come. Peep shows and pick-up clubs, boisterous gay bars and saucy striptease shows give way to no-frills sex in brash Oudezijds Achterburgwal around the corner.

There are an estimated 7,000 prostitutes in Amsterdam, but most first-time visitors are drawn inexorably to the titillating prospect of the girls in the goldfish bowls (although, the windows are slowly being shut down in a bid to clean up the area). Energetic Thai women dance to music only they can hear behind their glass cages, others sit on padded red window seats and, between clients, paint their fingernails, smoke, or desultorily flip through a paperback. In 2000 the government legalised brothels, restricting prostitution to non-residential areas, but in the past few years there has been a policy shift, with the focus very much on brothel owners, who are regularly checked. Key issues of concern are age, nationality, health and safety of the girls or boys. The brothel proprietors are compelled to ensure that their employees are over 21, have regular health checks, are not press-ganged into prostitution and are not illegal immigrants. The last item is very important, since the opening of eastern and other borders did for a while stimulate sex-slavery and the exacerbation of HIV and AIDS-related problems. Any breach of these conditions results in the proprietor losing their licence.

Gay districts

Amsterdam is second only to San Francisco in its social acceptance of homosexuality. Today, the city has a number of gay districts; the friendliest is centred on Kerkstraat and Reguliersdwarsstraat.

The glow of windows in the red light district.

AMSTERDAM CAFÉ CULTURE

The Netherlands is big on cafés, and half the fun for visitors lies in wandering in and discovering them for themselves.

The Netherlands has a long café tradition. Some claim that the first bar, euphemistically called a café, opened its doors in Amsterdam in the 13th century, when two men and a dog in a boat drifted ashore on the marshy banks of the River Amstel. By the 17th century, there were countless taverns in Amsterdam and other cities. Dutch cafés have as much cultural value as museums and a visit to one is essential.

Traditional brown cafés (so-called because walls and ceilings have turned brown from age and smoke) are identified by dark, cosy, wooden interiors. Coffee is generally brewed, not machine-made, and if you fancy a snack to go with your beer or spirit, there is usually a plate of olives or cheese. These cafés epitomise the Dutch word *gezelligheid*, which means a state of cosiness or conviviality. This is where locals come for a few beers after work, to play cards, engage in political debates and tell tall tales.

The more elegant and stylish grand cafés serve lunch and desserts and tend to have high ceilings, more light, reading tables and a variety of music. There are men's cafés, women's cafés and even night cafés, which close around 5am. There are also cafés where you can play chess, throw darts, or play pool or billiards. Take your pick.

Classic brown café style at De Ooievaar in the Jordaan.

Making the most of some sunshine to enjoy some outdoor refreshments.

A trendy barrista.

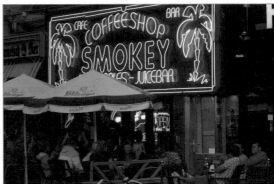

Get some healthy juice with your legal high.

WHAT'S THE ALTERNATIVE?

Hash cafés attract their own mellow public, and most tourists who fancy a walk on the wild side place a visit to a hash coffee shop at the top of their itinerary. The best-known ones are Dampkring (www.dampkring-coffeeshop-amsterdam.nl) at Handboogstraat 29, award-winning Green House Centrum (www.greenhouse.org) at Oudezijds Voorburgwal 191, which is a favourite with visiting celebs, and Abraxas (www.abraxas. tv) at Jonge Roelensteeg 12. Although the police have clamped down in recent years, due to a rise in hard drug selling, you won't have to look too far to find one. There are currently around 180 but plans are afoot to reduce this number to 155 by 2016. Once inside, punters are presented with a menu, which outlines the taste and effect. You have to be over 18 to partake and, similar to pubs, an establishment is subject to sanctions if anyone underage is found to be there. Alternative cafés attract their own clientele by hanging green-and-white placards in the window to distinguish themselves from regular ones. No alcohol is sold on the premises, following a law passed in 2007.

...ore ...dard – ...still ...l – café ...ulgence.

...ed up outside a coffeeshop, but you should avoid driving ...hing after indulging at one of these spots.

A marijuana cultivation and head shop in Amsterdam.

AMSTERDAM ENVIRONS

You don't have to travel far from Amsterdam to discover a wealth of worthwhile sights, like historic Haarlem and cheese-producing Edam.

This section covers the rest of the province of Noord-Holland, bounded to the east by the IJsselmeer, to the south by the provinces of Utrecht and Zuid-Holland, and to the west by the North Sea. **Haarlem** is the provincial capital. It is an attractive old Dutch town on the edge of the Kennemerduinen (Kennemer Dunes) National Park, with a famous collection of paintings by Frans Hals. Further north is **Alkmaar**, a pleasant (cheese) market town. The towns along the River Zaan, known collectively as the Zaanstad, lie only a few miles northwest of Amsterdam. The flat landscape of Noord-Holland is familiar from paintings by Dutch Masters such as Ruisdael. Large areas in this province consist of reclaimed polder lying below sea level.

Schiphol airport, 13 km (8 miles) southwest of Amsterdam, lies 4.5 metres (15ft) below sea level on a former lake, the Haarlemmermeer, where a great sea battle took place against the Spanish during the Dutch Revolt. Three huge pumping houses were built in the 19th century to drain the lake. These distinctive neo-Gothic industrial buildings still stand; a museum which charts the Dutch struggle against the sea is housed in the former pumping house, **De Cruquius**, in Heemstede, a suburb of Haarlem.

Tulip fields by a typical Dutch church.

Bulbs to bookshops

The most rewarding areas for walking or cycling in the Amsterdam environs are the dunes along the west coast and the woods of Het Gooi. Bulb fields extend along much of the eastern fringe of the dunes. The area's main flower and plant auction takes place in a vast complex at **Aalsmeer** ❶ 19 km (12 miles) southwest of Amsterdam. Another curious auction, the Broeker Veiling, is held in **Langedijk** ❷ village, near Alkmaar, where boats laden with

DRINK

The local beer is called Jopen, which dates back to 1407 and is named after the 112-litre barrels in which it was originally transported. Revived in the 1990s, the beer is now brewed in a former church, Jopenkerk (Gedempte Voldersgracht 2; www.jopenkerk.nl), where there is also a café and restaurant.

vegetables are navigated through the auction sheds.

Haarlem ❸ is an interesting historic town on the River Spaarne, and it has clung to its ancient character more than any other town in the Randstad – the great conurbation, also known as the Big Village, that spreads south to Rotterdam and embraces Leiden and Utrecht, Delft, Gouda and Amsterdam as well as Haarlem itself.

Although only a 15-minute train journey from Amsterdam, Haarlem still seems very much under the sway of sober 17th-century virtues. It has an abundance of antiques dealers in the brick-paved lanes to the south of Grote Markt, and many curious old shop interiors, such as the violin-seller, found at 16 Schagchelstraat, the comic-book store at 8 Jacobijnestraat, and the cheese shop at 39 Nieuwe Groenmarkt.

H. de Vries's bookshop at 3 Jacobijnestraat has a Dutch Renaissance interior, reminiscent of paintings by Pieter de Hooch. Also on this street, at No. 22, is Galerie Année, which exhibits contemporary art. But the most curious shop in Haarlem is the chemist A. J. van der Pigge at 3 Gierstraat, where you can buy herbal teas or *drop* (liquorice), in a dark interior crowded with ancient apothecary jars.

Haarlem was the birthplace of many Dutch artists, including Geertgen tot Sint Jans (who lived in a monastery on Sint Jansstraat) and the landscape painters Salomon van Ruysdael and Jacob van Ruisdael. Jacob painted the dramatic *View of Haarlem* seen from the dunes at Overveen, now in the Mauritshuis in The Hague.

Renowned artist

The most famous artist of Haarlem was Frans Hals. Probably born in Antwerp, Hals spent most of his life in Haarlem, where he specialised in group portraits of military guilds and governors and governesses of charitable institutions. Eight of these extraordinary works, which inspired the French Impressionists and Van Gogh, are now hanging in the town's Frans Hals Museum.

The best place to begin a tour of Haarlem is the **railway station Ⓐ**, a

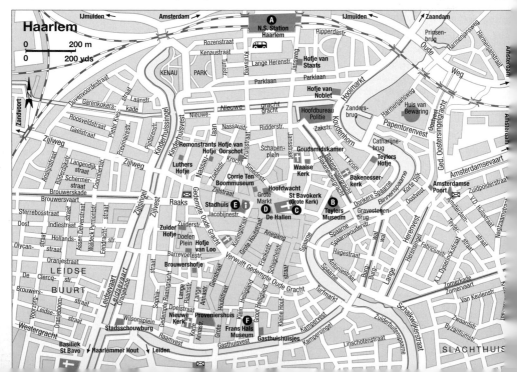

handsome Art Nouveau building of polished wood and tile pictures dating from 1908. Now head down Jansweg and turn left to reach the **Bakenessergracht**, named after a Gothic church whose delicate 16th-century spire overlooks the canal. Groenebuurt (a lane to the right) brings you to the former Begijnhof quarter, of which all that survives is the church, a curious edifice with several houses built within the nave.

The Netherlands' oldest museum

Continuing along Bakenessergracht brings you to the broad River Spaarne. Standing on the waterfront nearby is the **Teylers Museum ❸** (Spaarne 16, tel: 023-516 0960; www.teylersmuseum. nl; Tue–Sat 10am–5pm, Sun noon–5pm), the oldest museum in the Netherlands. This magnificent relic of the Dutch Enlightenment has been preserved in its original state.

The museum was founded in 1778 by Pieter Teyler van der Hulst, a prosperous silk merchant who amassed a large collection of fossils and scientific instruments. The round entrance hall of the museum, with its marble statues and bas-reliefs depicting the sciences, has all the grandeur typical of a country house. More splendid still is the Oval Hall, a two-storey neoclassical hall built in 1779, with glass cabinets filled with antique scientific instruments and bizarre pyramid-shaped display cabinets for minerals. The museum also houses an important collection of Dutch and Flemish prints, and 19th-century romantic paintings.

Damstraat leads from the Spaarne to the **Sint Bavokerk ❸**, also known the **Grote Kerk** (Great Church; Mon–Sat 10am–5pm). This enormous Gothic church was a favourite subject of 17th-century artists such as Pieter Saenredam and Gerrit Berckheyde. It dates from the 15th century, though the ornate bell tower above the crossing is a 16th-century embellishment.

The church is a marvellous jumble of roofs and gables, with several low buildings attached, and several tiny 17th-century houses (rented out by the church authorities to raise revenue) along the south wall.

The entrance to the church is through one of these little shuttered houses, which adds to the dramatic impact of the vast nave. Though the church seems rather empty, it contains many fascinating features, including some curious medieval misericords, and several decorated graves of shoemakers in the ambulatory. Sint Bavokerk is renowned for its 18th-century Müller organ, which brought Mozart (aged 10), Händel and Liszt to this town.

The Grote Markt

Haarlem's imposing and atmospheric main square is worth more than a few minutes of your time. The **Grote Markt** (Main Square) still looks very much as it did in the 17th-century townscapes of Gerrit Berckheyde in the Frans Hals Museum. The Vleeshal (Meat Hall) on the south side was

Haarlem.

designed in 1602 by Lieven de Key in a crowded Dutch Mannerist style, with a giant ox head to indicate the building's function. Along with Verweyhal, the former fish market, it is now an exhibition space for contemporary art called **De Hallen** (www.dehallen. nl; Tue–Sat 11am–5pm, Sun noon–5pm). Opposite, exhibiting the more restrained classicism typical of the mid-17th century, is the **Hoofdwacht**, a guard house.

The **Stadhuis** (City Hall) on the west side, standing on the site of a banqueting hall of the Counts of Holland, is an attractive mixture of buildings dating back to the medieval and Renaissance periods. The old town is dotted with some 18 *hofjes* (almshouse courts) founded by wealthy burghers, mostly situated in quiet streets to the west of Grote Markt, though there are three stately 18th-century almshouses on the east side (including one on the Spaarne founded by Pieter Teyler in 1787). The other main reason to visit Haarlem is the **Frans Hals Museum** (Groot Heiligland 62, tel: 023-511

5775; www.franshalsmuseum.nl; Tue–Sat 11am–5pm, Sun noon–5pm), which is easily reached from the church down Warmoesstraat (notice the curious patterned pavements of brick), Schagchelstraat and Groot Heiligland.

The museum occupies a Dutch Renaissance building which was designed by Lieven de Key in 1608 as a hospice for old men, but two years later was converted to an orphanage. It contains several attractive period rooms and a detailed dolls' house, but its principal treasure is the collection of eight group portraits by Frans Hals.

Three paintings show members of the Guild of St George, and two depict the members of the Guild of St Adrian – whose guild house (the Kloveniersdoelen) is still standing in Gasthuisstraat. These military guilds seem to have been more interested in banqueting than in exercising, and Hals's portraits marvellously capture the slightly tipsy guild members, with their distinctive pointed beards and flowing orange and pale-blue silk sashes. The other

Exhibition sale on the Grote Markt in Haarlem.

LIE OF THE LAND

To the south of the old town, the large wood **Haarlemmerhout** is all that remains of an ancient forest that once extended from Haarlem to The Hague, where the Counts of Holland were fond of hunting; it is the oldest public park in the Netherlands. An extensive area of bulb fields extends along the eastern edge of the dunes from Haarlem to Leiden. These intensely cultivated fields are mainly situated on the polder that was created when the Haarlemmermeer was drained. This new land is extremely fertile, and provides enormous yields of tulips, daffodils and chrysanthemums. A visit to the busy Aalsmeer Flower Auction, near Schiphol Airport, provides a marvellous glimpse into the workings of this efficient Dutch industry.

group portraits are extremely sombre by comparison. One shows the
governors of St Elizabeth's Hospital,
and the other two are rather embit-
tered portraits of the governors and
governesses of the old men's home,
painted when Hals, aged over 80,
was an inmate.

Beside the seaside

Just west of Haarlem is the brassy
North Sea resort of **Zandvoort** ❹,
where you can see what Amsterdammers get up to at the beach. It is just
30 minutes by train from Amsterdam's
Centraal Station – there is a train at
least hourly, and you normally need to
change at Haarlem.

On a hot, sunny day, you might want
to pack swimming gear and suntan

lotion. When you arrive, go straight
ahead out of Zandvoort Station, for
the 5-minute walk to the beach. Top-
less bathing in summer is pretty well
de rigueur, and the southern end of
the long stretch of sand is where gay
beachgoers and naturists congregate.
Beach bums hang out either here or
at the areas frequented by windsurfers
and catamaran enthusiasts.

Even in bad weather, many Amsterdammers like to take an invigorating
stroll along the beach before retiring
to one of the resort's cafés or restaurants for something restorative. In
summer, the beach is lined with dozens of *paviljoenen*, temporary beach
cafés, where the food is mostly, but
not exclusively, of the burger-and-fries
variety. In compensation, the mobile

EAT

Alkmaar is a good place for treats. Ijssalon W Laan (Koorstraat 45) only serves vanilla-flavour soft ice cream but you can have it in a variety of sundaes. Friethuis De Vlaminck (Voordam 2) is the place to go for delicious Belgian-style fries, which can be topped with a choice of sauces.

seafood stalls that trundle down to the water's edge are generally good. Away from the beach you can tour the Nationaal Park De Kennemerduinen (Kennemer Dunes National Park), where rolling dunes form a vital part of Amsterdam's sea defences.

Cheese capital

The town of **Edam** ❺, 22 km (14 miles) northeast of Amsterdam, is a cheerful, interesting little place with attractive canals crossed by narrow wooden bridges. Like many towns of the region known as Waterland, Edam was once an important whaling town, as the quay named Groenland (Greenland) recalls. In the 17th century it was an important port, with large shipyards situated on the waterway to the east of the town. Edam is now world-famous for its round cheeses, which are produced by farms on the fertile Beemster and Purmer polders. Edam cheeses, wrapped in a protective skin of red wax for export, can still be bought in the 16th-century Kaaswaag (Weigh House; Jan Nieuwenheizenplein 5;

Edams Museum.

www.edamcheeseshop.com; Apr–Sept daily 9am–6pm, Sat 8.30am–5pm, Sun 9.30am–5pm).

The main attraction

The main attraction in the town is the curious **Edams Museum** (Damplein 8; tel: 0299-372 644; Tue–Sat 10am–4.30pm, Sun 1–4.30pm). This occupies a late-Gothic house with a curious floating cellar that rocks to and fro as you walk across it. Opinions differ as to the purpose of the cellar; the romantic theory is that it was built by a retired captain to remind him of the sea, while a more prosaic explanation is that it was built this way to keep it dry in times of flooding.

The museum proudly displays the portraits of three eccentric local characters: Jan Claeszoon Clees, who was extremely fat; Trijntje Cornelisdochter Kever, who was very tall; and Pieter Dirkszoon Langebaard, who (as his name suggests) had an extremely long beard. 'Long Beard' toured the country displaying his beard to raise money for the local **Weeshuis** (Orphanage) which is still standing on Kerkstraat.

The museum faces an unusual square; **Damplein** is built in the form of a long arched bridge to allow ships to pass beneath. South of here stands the solitary tower of a 15th-century church, with a beautiful 16th-century carillon of bells from Mechelen. Further south, you come to Edam's most attractive canal, the Schepenmakersdijk (Shipbuilders' Dyke), with curious tea houses on the water's edge on one side.

Exploring Alkmaar

Alkmaar ❻ is a modest inland town 40 km (25 miles) north of Amsterdam, whose one moment of glory came in 1573 when it successfully withstood a Spanish siege, prompting the quip 'from Alkmaar to victory'. It is now a busy market town where a traditional cheese market is staged on Friday mornings during the tourist season. The yellow-skinned cheeses are piled

onto wooden sledges by porters in traditional garb, before being taken to the Waaggebouw, a 14th-century chapel which was converted to a weigh house in the 16th century by the addition of a Renaissance gable and a jaunty bell tower. It now contains a small museum of cheese-making techniques. To explore Alkmaar on foot, take Stationstraat from the station, then follow the moat to the right, which brings you to a bridge leading to the **Grote Kerk**.

This imposing 15th-century church, was built of mellow Brabant limestone by the Keldermans family of Mechelen. The 17th-century organ was designed by Jacob van Campen, the architect of the Amsterdam Town Hall. Heading into town along Langestraat, you come to the **Stadhuis** (Town Hall). The east wing and tower were built in late-Gothic style around 1510; the west wing was added in 1694 in Baroque style.

North of here is the **Stedelijk (Municipal) Museum Alkmaar** (Canadaplein 1; www.stedelijkmuseumalkmaar. nl; Tue–Sun 10am–5pm), which has a local collection of guild group portraits, antique toys, tiles and paintings. Situated in a recently renovated modern building, it is worth a visit solely to see the panoramic view of the *Siege of Alkmaar*, painted by an unknown Master in the 16th century, and including nice touches of typical Dutch humour such as a drunken soldier and a couple making love as the battle rages on.

Heading east from here, you will eventually come to the **Waagplein**, scene of the Friday cheese market. A short walk north is the **Nationaal Biermuseum de Boom** (National Beer Museum; Houttil 1; www.bier museum.nl; June–Aug Mon–Sat 10.30am–4.30pm, Sept–May 1–4pm), with a bar in the cellar. Further east, the canal Verdronkenoord leads to the Noord-Hollands Kanaal, which has an animated maritime atmosphere. The curious **Accijnstoren** was built in 1622 to collect tolls on local shipping. In a delicate operation in 1924 the tower was moved by some 4 metres (13ft), using a system of rollers, thereby (but only temporarily) improving traffic flow.

Carriers in the famous Dutch cheese market, Alkmaar. The event takes place in the Waagplein square.

Zaandam

The industrial towns of Zaandam, Koog aan de Zaan and Zaandijk are strung out along both banks of the River Zaan, forming the conurbation of **Zaanstad** ❼. In 1592 a windmill-powered sawmill was invented in the Zaan region, leading to the development of a large timber industry which supplied nearby shipyards. Other windmills were built along the river-banks to supply power for oil-mills, paint-mills, flour-mills and mustard-mills (which produced the celebrated Zaanse mustard). By the 18th century there were more than 1,000 windmills slowly turning in the breeze.

In 1697 Tsar Peter the Great travelled incognito to Zaandam to visit the famous shipyards on the river Zaan. A tiny wooden house is preserved in Zaandam, the **Czaar-Pieterhuisje** (Krimp 23; Tue–Sun 10am–5pm), where he stayed with Gerrit Kist, a local smith he knew from St Petersburg. The building developed an alarming tilt and is now propped up by a 19th-century frame. Occasionally large groups of Russian

Fishing by the harbour in Ijmuiden.

sailors descend upon Zaandam to see the small wooden bed into which the Tsar used to squeeze his 2-metre (7ft) frame.

Zaandijk, a few miles north, has the sole surviving example of a complete street built in the old Zaan district style, with a small museum, the Zaanlandse Oudheidkamer, in an 18th-century merchant's home. The adjacent river was once the region's main thoroughfare. The abundance of timber in the Zaan region led to a distinctive local style of green wooden houses decorated with pointed or bell-shaped gables. In the 1950s many of the surviving houses and windmills in Zaan style were relocated to an open-air museum, the **Zaanse Schans**, situated on the river bank opposite Zaandijk. A working windmill here produces local mustard, and a clog-maker demonstrates his craft. The **Zaans Museum** (Schansend 7, tel: 075-681 0000; www zaansmuseum.nl;daily 10am–5pm) use: locally themed collections.

To the east of Amsterdam is the restored **Muiderslot** (Herengrach 1, tel: 029-425 6262; www.muiderslot

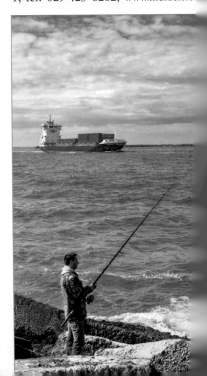

nl; (guided tours) Apr–Oct Mon–Fri 10am–5pm, Sat–Sun noon–5pm, Nov–Mar Sat–Sun noon–5pm), situated where the River Vecht enters the IJsselmeer. This attractive brick castle was built in 1285 by Count Floris V of Holland, the founder of many Dutch towns. Floris V was murdered here 11 years later by a group of nobles enraged by his policy of encouraging urban development. In the 17th century the poet and historian P.C. Hooft occupied the castle in his capacity as bailiff of Gooiland, and it became the meeting place for the illustrious Muiderkring (Muiden Circle) group of poets and writers; members included jurist Hugo Grotius and poets Constantijn Huygens, Joost van den Vondel and Maria Tesselschade.

From Amsterdam, you can take bus 110 or tram 26 from Amstel train station. Alternatively, enquire at the Amsterdam VVV about boat excursions (Apr–Oct Tue–Sun) to Muiden as well as to the Fort Pampus Island fortification. In Muiden, the Rederij Toman ferryboat landing is next to the castle.

Also worth a visit is **Oudekerk aan de Amstel**, a picturesque village just 4km (2.5 miles) southeast of Amsterdam that is too beautiful to miss. At the spot where the Bullewijk tributary joins the River Amstel, this pastoral landscape of windmills and farmhouses dates back to the 12th century, making it the oldest village in the Amstelland region. Its name is derived from the Catholic church which was founded in the area in AD 1000, and which now houses a row of charming houses built around 1733.

Remembering a massacre

Further east along the IJsselmeer coast the historic town of **Naarden** ⑧. In 1572 the Spanish army under Don Frederick of Toledo murdered almost all the inhabitants. The massacre is commemorated by a 17th-century stone tablet on a building at 7 Turfportstraat. The town fortifications

were demolished by the Spanish, and Naarden became a virtual ghost town.

More advanced defences were erected in the 17th century. These fortifications still completely encircle the town and are fascinating to explore. Their history is explained in the **Vestingmuseum** (Westwalstraat 6, tel: 035-694 5459; www.vestingmuseum. nl; Tue–Fri 10.30am–5pm, Sat–Sun noon–5pm) which is within a bastion connected to underground passages and casemates, themselves now home to a complex of upmarket restaurants and interior design shops known as the Arsenaal.

The woods of Het Gooi, south of Naarden, attracted wealthy Amsterdam merchants in the 17th century. Dutch Impressionist Anton Mauve lived in Laren and painted the surrounding Gooiland countryside. **Hilversum** ⑨, the main town of the area, is the home of Dutch national radio and TV. Its Town Hall was designed by W. M. Dudok in 1931. The town also has two fine gardens: the Pinetum Blijdenstein and the Costerustuin Botanical Garden.

Authentic Dutch wooden houses in the open-air museum, Zaanse Schans.

THE HAGUE AND ENVIRONS

The home of the Dutch government, The Hague, and its neighbours Delft and Leiden, have much to offer discerning visitors.

T he Hague and the neighbouring cities of Leiden and Delft lie in the prosperous northern part of Zuid-Holland province. Each of these venerable Dutch cities has played a crucial role in the Netherlands' history and the development of Dutch painting, and, not surprisingly, they have some of the best museums and art galleries in the country. Unlike most Dutch cities, The Hague does not owe its existence to trade or the sea; its principal activities are government and administration.

The seat of government

As the third-largest city in The Netherlands, with some 482,000 inhabitants, The Hague ❶ (Den Haag, or in full, s-Gravenhage, in Dutch) is referred to as the political capital of the Netherlands. Its government buildings cluster round the Binnenhof, and it is also home to the majority of the Dutch ministries, the residence of the queen, various royal palaces, the International Court of Justice, the world famous Peace Palace, and some 80 embassies and consulates. It is also known as the 'widow of Indonesia', the former Dutch colony which gained independence in 1945. Between 1850 and 1900, the Archipel residential area was built to accommodate thousands of returning Dutch and also Indonesians who chose to adopt Dutch nationality

and settle in the Netherlands. This accounts for the number of fine Indonesian restaurants throughout the city, such as Garoeda and Djawa.

For a feel of Old World Indonesia, visit the Hotel des Indes for afternoon tea. The Russian ballerina Anna Pavlova spent her last night in this stylish hotel, in 1931. A combination of culture and history, monumental and modern architecture, museums, stately hotels, antiques shops, gastronomy and natural beauty lend The Hague an air of sophistication and elegance.

Main Attractions

Ridderzaal, The Hague
Mauritshuis, The Hague
Vredespaleis, The Hague
Museum De Lakenhal, Leiden
Vermeer Centrum Delft, Delft

The Binnenhof entrance.

The city centre is manageable on foot, and public transport – both trams and buses – makes travelling from town to the sea quick and comfortable.

The Hague is also easily accessible from Leiden and Delft – under 15 minutes by train and not much longer from Rotterdam and Amsterdam, making day trips a pleasant possibility. It borders two seaside resorts, Scheveningen and Kijkduin, giving it a second reputation as a seaside city with miles of dunes and woods to explore.

The Hague was originally a hamlet close to the castle of the Counts of Holland, built in the 13th century. The hamlet grew up around a hunting lodge that belonged to the counts, and this gave rise to The Hague's curious Old Dutch name, 's-Gravenhage ('the Count's hedge'). The village first became important in 1586 when the Staaten-Generaal (States General, or parliament) of the new Dutch Republic met here, and The Hague gradually assumed the role of political capital, even though it was not officially a town, since it had no city walls or medieval privileges. Although The

Hague was never granted a charter (it still doesn't have one), it does have its own Town Arms; officially laid down in 1861, these depict a stork with an eel held tight in its beak. It is thought that this image pays tribute to the medieval storks which used to build their nests on the small island in the Hofvijver pond. Their presence was seen by The Hague residents as a sign of good fortune, as the storks would finish off all the remains from the fish market that would otherwise rot and possibly cause infectious diseases to spread amongst the town's inhabitants. Thus, in appreciation of the bird, the stork is now depicted on all municipal institutions.

Village life

The main attraction of this 'village', which is still referred to as 'the largest village in Europe', was that it offered a neutral meeting ground for representatives of the seven United Provinces who each jealously guarded their independence. Attractive streets and squares were laid out around the old castle in the 17th century, including

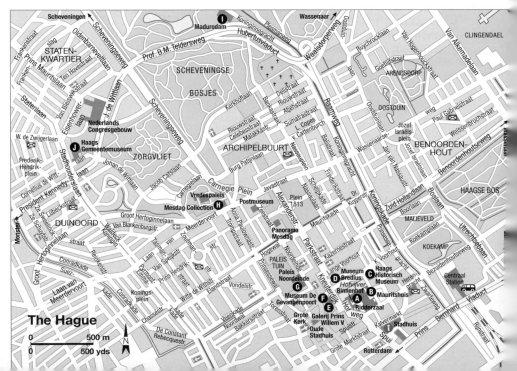

Plein and Korte Vijverberg, which were designed by the diplomat and poet Constantijn Huygens. Further improvements were made in the 18th century along Lange Vijverberg and Lange Voorhout.

The gracious style of the 18th century reached its highest expression in the former Royal Library at 34 Lange Voorhout, begun by Daniel Marot in 1734 with wings added in 1761 by Pieter de Swart. By the 19th century The Hague had become a fashionable literary and artistic centre, while the nearby village of Scheveningen was one of the most elegant resorts on the North Sea.

During the post-war years, The Hague lost much of its allure, due to the disappearance of many of its canals and the unchecked development of roads and office blocks. Fortunately, the extensive woods where the Counts of Holland hunted have been preserved, and the windswept dunes where the Impressionists of the Hague School painted remain as wild as ever.

Modernisation

The Hague celebrated its 750th anniversary in 1998. In the 1980s, it began an extensive plan to create a modern city centre with such projects as the Anton Philipszaal concert hall on Spuiplein, which is the home of The Hague Philharmonic Orchestra and host to many other cultural events. The Danstheater, designed by acclaimed architect Rem Koolhaas, is the home of the equally acclaimed Netherlands Dance Theatre.

The latest additions to The Hague offer considerable improvements, thanks to the contributions of such respected architects as Michael Graves, Cesar Pelli, Richard Koek and Rob Krier. This area between Utrechtsebaan and Rijnsegracht complements The Hague's historic centre, with new shops, modern housing developments and office buildings. Existing streets are being renovated, department stores given a facelift and overall accessibility greatly improved.

The impressive new Stadhuis (Town Hall), designed by the award-winning architect Richard Meier, also houses the public library and municipal records department, which employs a staff of more than 1,000 civil servants. With its two office wings forming a wall to the glass-covered atrium, the Town Hall has become a meeting place for locals and visitors alike.

The most attractive area of the city is situated around the old castle of the Counts of Holland. The gateway on Buitenhof leads into the Binnenhof, the former courtyard of the castle. The building that resembles a chapel in the middle of the courtyard is the **Ridderzaal** Ⓐ (Hall of the Knights; Mon–Sat 10am–5pm; audioguides are available from the ProDemos Visitor Centre at Hofweg 1), a 13th-century hall built by Count Floris V and heavily restored in the 19th century. This small building has come to be a symbol of the Dutch Parliament, although it is now used only for ceremonial occasions. A new building has been designed for the Tweede Kamer (Second Chamber), on Hofsingel. Its glass

Anton Philipszaal.

Inside the Mauritshuis.

façade is intended to give the public a glimpse of the government in action.

The Mauritshuis

There is another gateway behind the Ridderzaal that leads to the **Mauritshuis** Ⓑ (Plein 29; tel: 070-302 3456; www.mauritshuis.nl; Mon 1–6pm, Tue–Sun, 10am–6pm, Thu until 8pm), which rises out of the water like a Venetian palace. This was the former home of Count Johan Maurits, an enlightened governor who ruled over Brazil on behalf of the Dutch West India Company. Built between 1633 and 1644 by Pieter Post, using plans drawn up by Jacob van Campen, the classical building perfectly embodies the Dutch principles of reason and balance. In a letter to Johan Maurits, Constantijn Huygens praised 'the beautiful, very beautiful, and most beautiful building'.

The Mauritshuis was once famed for its 'cabinets of curiosities' – rooms filled with exotica brought back by Dutch trading ships. In the 19th century the Koninklijk Kabinet van Schilderijen (Royal Picture Cabinet) was moved here to create one of the most beautiful small picture galleries in the world. More like a private house than a museum, the Mauritshuis has a choice collection of Flemish, Dutch and German Old Masters. Works are hung in a series of handsome period rooms, ranging from grand gilded salons to intimate wood-panelled chambers.

The permanent collection on the ground floor is mainly devoted to Flemish paintings, including *Descent from the Cross* by Rogier van der Weyden and *Portrait of a Man* by Hans Memling. The rooms on the first floor contain some of the finest works of the Dutch Golden Age, including a number of Rembrandts. The most famous of these is *The Anatomy Lesson of Dr Tulp*, the artist's first major commission in Amsterdam, executed in 1632. The figure of Susanna painted in 1637 was probably modelled on his wife Saskia. There are also several self-portraits from different periods of Rembrandt's life. In the earliest, dated 1629, he looks almost arrogant, but by the time of the 1669 portrait (painted the year he died), the artist's face has weathered to an expression of infinite sorrow.

One of the more unusual paintings in the collection is *The Goldfinch*, by the brilliant Carel Fabritius, a pupil of Rembrandt, whose work inspired artists like Jan Vermeer, Pieter de Hooch and Emanuel de Witte. It is one of the few works by Fabritius to have survived, and was painted in 1654, the year the artist was killed in a gunpowder explosion in Delft at the age of 22 (see page 181). The explosion also destroyed many of his paintings.

Six years later, Vermeer painted *View of Delft*, which shows no evidence of the destruction. In 1994, this painting, as well as his famous *Girl with a Pearl Earring*, were restored. The Mauritshuis also has a striking *View of Haarlem* by Jacob van Ruisdael, and several white church interiors by Pieter Saenredam.

More museums

Wandering through the Mauritshuis, you are inevitably struck by the impressive views of the Hofvijver, all that remains of the castle moat. Several small museums overlook this lake, including the **Haags Historisch Museum** **C** (The Hague Historical Museum; tel: 070-364 6940; www.haagshistorischmuseun.nl; Tue–Fri 10am–5pm, Sat–Sun noon–5pm) on the east side. This museum of local history occupies the Sebastiaansdoelen, a Dutch classical building commissioned by the archers' guild in 1636. In Room 1, which looks out on the Hofvijver, you can see several old paintings of the lake, almost invariably featuring the distinctive 15th-century octagonal tower still standing alongside the Mauritshuis. You also see the archers' *doelen*, or firing range, that once stood on the east side of the lake. The museum's other main attraction is a dolls' house beautifully furnished in 19th-century style.

The **Museum Bredius** **D** (Lange Viverberg 14; tel: 070-362 0729; http://www.museumbredius.nl; Tues–Sun 11am–5pm) is in a handsome 18th-century house on the north side of the Hofvijver.

Its collection of paintings was formed by Dr Abraham Bredius, a director of the Mauritshuis at the turn of the 19th century, and contains works by both well-known names and unknown artists of the Dutch Golden Age.

A pleasant walk around the lake brings you to the **Galerij Prins Willem V** **E** (Plein 29; tel: 070-302 3456; www.mauritshuis.nl/discover/prince-william-v-gallery/;Tue–Sun noon–5pm), the oldest picture gallery in the Netherlands. Founded in 1774 by Prince William V, this small stately gallery has been restored to its original appearance, and paintings are crammed on the walls in several tiers (as they are in the painting in the Mauritshuis by Willem van Haecht of Alexander the Great Visiting the Studio of Apelles). The collection of Dutch Old Masters of the 17th and 18th centuries does not compare with the Mauritshuis, but this eccentric gallery is well worth a visit. In the same building is the **Museum de Gevangenpoort** **F** (Prison Gate Museum; Buitenhof 33; tel: 070-346 0861; www.gevangenpoort.nl; Tue–Fri 10am–5pm, Sat–Sun noon–5pm),

The Mauritshuis.

TIP

If you're going to the Gemeentemuseum Den Haag, don't miss the Photography Museum, Foto-Museum Den Haag (www.fotomuseumdenhaag. nl; Tue–Sun noon–6pm) also on site. Opened in 2002, it hosts around four exhibitions a year featuring new and established talent from the Netherlands and around the world.

which has a collection of instruments of punishment and torture.

Royal shopping street

Buitenhof divides the government quarter from the old town, now an area of pedestrianised shopping streets. The Passage, off Buitenhof, is an elegant shopping arcade dating from 1885. Groenmarkt, not far from here, is the centre of the old town. Here stands the **Grote Kerk**, a 15th-century Gothic church with an early 16th-century choir. The Oude Stadhuis (Old Town Hall) opposite was built in 1564–5 in spirited Renaissance style, and a large wing was added in the 18th century.

Noordeinde is the most elegant shopping street in The Hague, and has a number of well-preserved Art Nouveau shopfronts. There are many fine restaurants in the neighbourhood, including It Rains Fishes and Les Ombrelles. This is where you will find the 16th-century **Paleis Noordeinde** Ⓖ, also known as the **Binnenhof**. The history of the palace goes back to 1559 when Emperor Charles V assigned Prince William of Nassau to the post of stadhouder of the provinces of Holland, Zeeland and Utrecht. It is now the royal residence of King Willem-Alexander.

Trompe l'œil seascape

Continuing down Noordeinde and across a canal, you reach the **Panorama Mesdag** (Zeestraat 65; tel: 070-310 6665; Mon–Sat 10am–5pm, Sun 11am–5pm). Inside, you enter a darkened tunnel and ascend a spiral staircase to a mock pavilion, from where it's possible to view a lifelike panoramic scene of the coast and dunes at Scheveningen. The panorama was painted in 1881 by the Hague-based Impressionist painter Hendrik Willem Mesdag on a canvas 120 metres (400ft) long by 14 metres (46ft) high. In executing this work, Mesdag was assisted by his wife (who painted the village of Scheveningen), Theo de Bock (who was delegated to paint the sky), and the Amsterdam-based Impressionist George Hendrik Breitner (who added his favourite theme – a group of cavalry officers charging on the beach). The astonishingly realistic effect is obtained by the indirect daylight falling from above and the artificial foreground strewn with real objects.

Not far from here is the **Mesdag Collection** Ⓗ (Laan van Meerdervoort 7F; tel: 070-362 1434; http://de mesdagcollectie.nl/en/; Wed–Sun noon–5pm), occupying a house built in 1887 by the artist. This once neglected museum is now under the same management as the Van Gogh Museum in Amsterdam. It contains Impressionist paintings by Mesdag himself and other members of the Hague School, as well as a large collection of dark, melancholy works by members of the Barbizon School, including paintings by the likes of Corot and Millet, who greatly inspired Mesdag. The **Vredespaleis** (Peace Palace; Carnegieplein 2; tel: 070-302 4242; www. vredespaleis.nl; Tue–Sun 10am–5pm) is just north of the museum. Built

Paleis Noordeinde in the Hague city center.

house the Permanent Court of Arbitration set up after the 1899 Hague conference on the suppression of war, this stately pile was paid for by the Scottish millionaire and philanthropist Andrew Carnegie. Completed in 1913, its work failed to prevent the hostilities that led to World War I. The building is now used as the seat of the International Court of Justice – the 'World Court' – and contains a curious miscellany of objects donated by member states. It is only accessible on guided tours, which must be booked in advance.

Scheveningseweg runs north of here towards the sea, cutting a path through the vast wooded area of the Scheveningse Bosjes. On the edge of the woods to the east is **Madurodam** ❶ (George Maduroplein 1; tel: 070-416 2400; www.madurodam.nl; daily but times vary), a miniature reproduction of a Dutch town. With its precise – albeit tiny – reproductions of historic buildings in the Netherlands, it provides a handy shortcut to a sightseeing itinerary. It also has a 'working' port, an extensive railway network

and some interesting details reflecting contemporary Dutch life.

Art to science

The elegant quarter to the west of the woods contains a cluster of interesting museums. The **Gemeentemuseum Den Haag** ❶ (The Hague Municipal Museum; Stadhouderslaan 41; tel: 070-338 1111; www.gemeentemuseum.nl; Tue–Sun 11am–5pm) houses an excellent collection of modern painting and decorative art in an attractive low brick building overlooking an ornamental pond. This was the last work designed by the founder of Dutch modern architecture, H.P. Berlage (see page 99), who died a year before its completion in 1935.

Berlage's modern masterpiece provides an appropriate setting for an extensive collection of works by Piet Mondrian, ranging from early paintings in the style of the Hague School to abstract works composed of blocks of red, yellow, blue and white, with black lines delineating the pictorial space. Especially popular is Mondrian's *Victory Boogie Woogie* painting,

The statue of William I (Prince of Orange or Willem van Oranje).

A WALK AMONG THE SCULPTURES

Admirers of royal statues can take a leisurely 90-minute walk starting from Plein 1813 and ending at Lange Voorhout. Head out from Sophialaan at the Independence Monument of King William I. Proceed along Bazarstraat to Anna Paulownastraat and the site of the seated statue of Queen Anna Paulowna (1795–1865), the wife of King William II.

A short way along the road are the Royal Stables, home to some beautiful horses and the King's golden coach. The eclectic neo-Renaissance complex has a façade with horses' heads in the pediments, an imposing carriage gateway and an octagonal tower crowned with a spire above the mansard roof.

Along Noordeinde by Kneuterdijk Palace, a remarkable building which has served a number of functions since it was built in 1716 as the Palace of the Oranges, is an extraordinary statue of Queen Wilhelmina (1880–1962). Its robustness and lack of detail symbolise the queen's strong personality and steadfastness; she was, after all, the longest reigning Dutch monarch. Paleis Noordeinde has a history closely associated with the House of Orange and has been the royal residence since the 17th century. Today King Willem-Alexander uses it as his workplace and for receptions. Look for the large statue of Prince William I of Orange (1533–84), thought to be the oldest free-standing statue in The Hague.

which was purchased from a collection in America in 1998 for US$40 million.

The museum also has a renowned Delftware collection, an exquisite Dutch dolls' house, a large collection of musical instruments and a section devoted to fashion. In recent years, the collection has been revitalised and is well worth a visit for the building itself, let alone its eclectic contents. The nearby **Museon** (Stadhouderslaan 37; www.museon.nl; Tue–Sun 11am–5pm), which is built in a style that echoes Berlage's Gemeentemuseum, is a modern science museum with many working models. Also in this area is **Omniversum** (President Kennedylaan 5; www.omniversum.nl; daily from 10am, closing times vary), where films are projected onto the surface of a planetarium dome to achieve a striking visual effect.

Scheveningen

If you are keen to follow in the footsteps of the Hague Impressionists, the coastal resort of **Scheveningen** is just a short tram ride from the city centre.

The trams follow Scheveningseweg, a broad straight road created to link The Hague to the coast in the 17th century by Constantijn Huygens.

Like most resorts on the sea, Scheveningen is a mixture of faded elegance and brash modernity, in recent years increasingly dominated by ugly high-rise buildings. The most striking buildings are the Kurhaus, a grand 19th-century hotel, and the modern Pier, which has an observation tower, a children's playground and a several bars and restaurants. In the dunes is the **Museum Beelden aan Zee** (Harteveltstraat 1; www.beeldenaanzee. nl; Tue–Sun 10am–5pm), which is a private museum dedicated to contemporary sculpture. There is a Holland Casino opposite the Kurhaus hotel if you prefer more lively entertainment.

The **Scheveningen Sea Life Centre** (Strandweg 13; tel: 070-354 2100; www.visitsealife.com; daily 10am–6pm, July–Aug until 8pm) exhibits underwater life of the North Sea by presenting it in its natural habitat. Walking through an underwater tunnel, visitors can experience life in the blue depths of

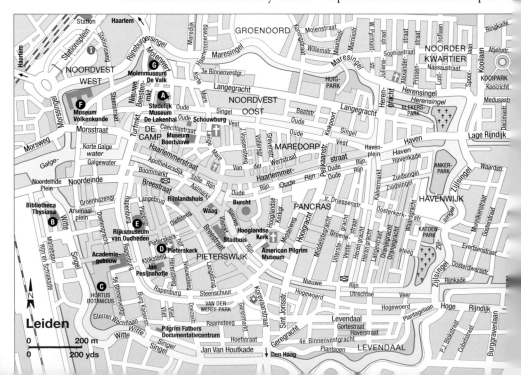

on the seabed itself without ever getting wet. If you want to avoid the bustling resort atmosphere that thrives along the frantic promenade, head in the opposite direction to **Kijkduin**, a smaller, more peaceful seaside resort, with expansive dunes and miles of sandy beach. Whichever beach you go to, be sure to try some *poffertjes*, delicious miniature pancakes.

University town

Leiden ❷, on a branch of the Rhine in the bulb-growing region between The Hague and Haarlem, is a likeable university town full of cafés and student bookshops. Leiden University is the oldest and most renowned in the Netherlands. It was founded in 1575 by William of Orange in recognition of the town's heroic resistance to the Spanish. Despite hunger and disease, the townspeople withstood a siege of 131 days. They were finally liberated by a drastic measure; the sea dykes were broken, allowing the sea to flood a large area to the south of Leiden, so that Admiral Boisot could sail a fleet of ships up to the city walls. A magnificent tapestry

in the Lakenhal Museum depicts this historical episode.

Cradle of talent

Many distinguished academics have taught at Leiden University, including Herman Boerhaave, professor of medicine, and Carl Linnaeus, the Swedish botanist. Several notable Dutch artists were also born in the city, including Rembrandt, Lucas van Leyden, Jan van Goyen, Gerrit Dou and Jan Steen. The **Museum De Lakenhal** ❹ (Oude Singel 28; tel: 071-516 5360; www.lakenhal.nl; Tue–Fri 10am–5pm; Sat–Sun noon–5pm) provides an interesting introduction to the history and art of this important Dutch town. The museum occupies a distinguished canalside building designed in Dutch classical style in 1640 by Arent van 's-Gravesande. The windmill flanked by cloth and wool above the entrance symbolises the building's original function as a cloth hall. Cloth making, which was introduced to Leiden by Flemish weavers fleeing the Black Death in the 14th century, was the town's main industry until

Enjoying a sunny spring day by the North Sea, with Scheveningen Pier in the background.

Rembrandt

After a successful start, the greatest artist of the Dutch Golden Age died a lonely pauper following family tragedy; but his influential legacy lives on.

Rembrandt Harmenszoon van Rijn was the greatest painter of the Dutch Golden Age. He was born in Leiden in 1606, the eighth child of a prosperous miller. Rembrandt was sent to the Latin School, a 1599 Renaissance building that still stands near the Pieterskerk. In 1620 he enrolled as a student at Leiden University, but soon abandoned his studies in favour of painting. His father sent him to study under Jacob van Swanenburgh, who owned a step-gabled house still to be seen at 89 Langebrug. After three years, Rembrandt moved to Amsterdam and spent six months in the studio of Pieter Lastman, a famous painter of classical and historical subjects.

Young and confident

In 1625, by now an ambitious young artist, Rembrandt was advised by the diplomat Constantijn

A portrait of the artist, by himself.

Huygens, an early admirer of his work, to study in Italy. He replied that he was too busy and said he could see all the Italian work he wanted in Holland. The self-portrait in the Mauritshuis painted in shows the young Rembrandt as supremely confident and slightly haughty.

In 1632, and now settled in Amsterdam, he received his first major commission, *The Anatomy Lesson of Dr Tulp*, painted for the Amsterdam guild of surgeons and now displayed in the Mauritshuis in The Hague. Two years later Rembrandt married Saskia van Uylenburg, the daughter of a prosperous burgomaster. He painted Saskia many times, including once as Flora in a marvellous painting now hanging in London's National Gallery.

Success and tragedy

In 1639 Rembrandt moved to a handsome Renaissance house in the Jewish quarter of Amsterdam (now the Rembrandthuis Museum). But Saskia fell ill and died in 1642, having borne four children. Only one, Titus, survived. A stone simply inscribed 'Saskia' in Amsterdam's Oude Kerk marks her grave.

Ironically, this was the period of Rembrandt's greatest triumph, *The Night Watch*, now his most famous and valuable work. The work was completed in 1642 for the Amsterdam guild of arquebusiers (marksmen), and now hangs in the gallery of honour in Amsterdam's Rijksmuseum. At about this time, Rembrandt appointed Geertghe Dircx as a nurse for Titus. Living together as a couple, they never married, as this would have deprived Rembrandt of income from Saskia's will. They parted in 1649 after a quarrel.

A sad ending

In 1656 Rembrandt was declared bankrupt, and was forced to move to a more modest dwelling in the Jordaan. Though beset by personal and financial problems, Rembrandt painted one of his greatest works in 1656 – the now damaged *Anatomy Lesson of Dr Deyman*, which hangs in the Amsterdam Rijksmuseum. His work continued to mature, and in 1661 he executed the famous *Syndics of the Drapers' Guild* – also to be found in the Rijksmuseum.

Titus died at the age of 27 in 1668, and 11 months later, in October 1669, Rembrandt also died. He was buried in an unmarked pauper's grave in the Westerkerk in Amsterdam, and his exact burial place is unknown. In all probability, his bones were removed after about 20 years to make way for new burials.

the 18th century. Five stone tablets on the façade illustrate the stages in cloth-making, beginning with spinning and ending with the inspection by the *Staalmeesters* (syndics, who applied a metal seal to certified Leiden cloth).

Lakenhal's art

A small art gallery in the Lakenhal contains works by 16th and 17th-century Leiden artists. Pride of place is given to Lucas van Leyden's *Triptych of the Last Judgement*, a faltering early Dutch Renaissance work painted in 1526 for the Pieterskerk. There is also an interesting scale model of the chapel of Marienpol Abbey, illustrating the locations of two altarpieces by Cornelis Engebrechtszoon now in the museum.

The Lakenhal has just one painting by Rembrandt, an unremarkable historical work dating from 1626, which is hung for comparison alongside a somewhat better work by Jan Lievens, with whom he probably shared a studio in Leiden. There is also a gloomy painting by Jacob van Swanenburg, Rembrandt's teacher in Leiden. But probably the most alluring work in the collection is the *View of Leiden* painted by Jan van Goyen in 1650 eschewing bright colours in favour of muddy brown tones.

The Lakenhal also has a number of period rooms rescued from old buildings in Leiden, including an 18th-century kitchen and a room in Biedermeier style. The most attractive rooms are in the wings on the first floor. The room in the east wing comes from the brewers' guild house, and is decorated with five murals depicting different steps in the brewing process. The Staalmeesterskamer in the west wing, which is hung with sumptuous gilt leather, was the chamber in which the syndics of the cloth guild used to meet.

The best view of Leiden is from the **Burcht**, a 12th-century castle surmounting an ancient artificial mound built at the convergence of two branches of the Rhine. From the battlements, you can see the two vast churches of Leiden which appear in Van Goyen's painting in the Lakenhal. The nearer of the two, the Hooglandse Kerk, has a very curious

The Burcht.

Pieterskerk in Leiden.

appearance. Its 16th-century nave was never completed in length or height, and is dwarfed by the 15th-century Flamboyant Gothic choir.

To reach the university area, head down Hartesteeg to the Nieuwe Rijn, then continue along Gangetje. The park you pass stands on the site of several houses destroyed in 1807 when a barge laden with gunpowder exploded. The park contains a statue of Burgomaster Pieter van der Werff, who refused to surrender the city to the Spanish army in the siege of 1574.

University quarter

On to Rapenburg, a handsome canal enlivened with many university buildings in Dutch classical style – the finest undoubtedly being the **Bibliotheca Thysiana** ⓑ at No. 25, which was built in 1655 by Arent van 's-Gravesande. The university began in the former chapel facing the Nonnenbrug. A lane alongside leads to the **Hortus Botanicus** ⓒ (www.hortus leiden.nl; Apr–Oct daily 10am–6pm, Nov–Mar Tue–Sun 10am–4pm), one of the oldest botanical gardens in the

world. Founded in 1587, it was originally stocked with numerous exotic species brought back from the Dutch East Indies and from the Americas.

Across the Nonnenbrug, an attractive lane leads to the **Pieterskerk** ⓓ (www.pieterskerk.com), a 15th-century Gothic church containing the tombs of Leiden academics, including Herman Boerhaave and the Remonstrant theologian Jacobus Arminius. There is a café with an attractive courtyard.

The university law faculty is opposite the church in the Gravensteen, a gloomy former prison of the Counts of Holland. The attractive cobbled lanes around the Pieterskerk contain antiquarian bookshops and pleasant cafés.

This lane emerges on **Breestraat**, the principal street of Leiden. The long façade of the **Stadhuis** on the right was designed in Dutch Renaissance style by Lieven de Key in 1595. The **Rijnlandshuis** to the left was designed by the same architect one year later for the powerful local water authority. De Key also built the beautiful **Stadstimmerwerf** on Galgewaard, which when floodlit at night is particularly striking

Egyptian treasures

Several outstanding national museums are situated in Leiden, including one of the Netherlands' oldest, the **Rijksmuseum van Oudheden** Ⓔ (National Museum of Antiquities; Rapenburg 28; tel: 071-516 3163; rmo.nl; Tue–Sun 10–5, also open Mon during school holidays; free for children under 5) founded in 1818. This attractive museum has an extensive collection of archaeological finds from the Netherlands, ancient Greece, Rome and Egypt. The mysterious floodlit Temple of Taffel in the entrance hall was presented by the Egyptian government in gratitude for Dutch aid in rescuing buildings threatened by the Aswan High Dam project. Renovations are in progress, scheduled to be completed by October 2016, so until then some parts of the museum will be temporarily unavailable.

The national ethnographic collection housed in the **Museum Volkenkunde** Ⓕ (Steenstraat 1, tel: 088-004 2800; Tue–Sun 10am–5pm) was founded in 1837. The museum has particularly interesting displays on the Dutch East India Company and

the countries with which it traded, such as China, Japan and the islands of Indonesia. Anyone for whom a trip to Holland is not complete without seeing a windmill should visit the **Molenmuseum De Valk** Ⓖ (2e Binnenvestgracht 1, tel: 071-516 5353; https://molenmuseumdevalk.nl; Mon–Sat 10am–5pm, Sun 1–5pm). Like the mill owned by Rembrandt's father, this 18th-century working windmill was erected on the site of a bastion, and contains several unusual rooms once occupied by the miller and his family.

Picturesque town

Delft ❸ is on the River Vliet, midway between The Hague and Rotterdam. This pleasant old town has changed very little since Vermeer painted the *View of Delft*, now in the Mauritshuis in The Hague. Standing on the Hooikade, where, one day in 1660, Vermeer painted his home town under a sky that threatened a summer storm, you can still recognise many features from the painting, such as the dusky red brick of the Armamentarium and the slender white spire of the Nieuwe Kerk.

Pretty Delft is popular with tourists.

THE PILGRIM FATHERS

The Pieterskerk quarter also has associations with the Pilgrim Fathers, who spent 12 years in Leiden before setting sail from Delfshaven on the *Speedwell*. John Robinson, the spiritual leader of the English religious community, lived on the south side of the Pieterskerk in the Jan Pesijnshofje. He had hoped eventually to join the Pilgrim Fathers in America, but died in 1625 in Leiden and was buried in the Pieterskerk. A plaque in the nearby Pieterskerk-Choorsteeg commemorates the Pilgrim Press run at No. 17 by William Brewster. You can find out about this fascinating piece of history across the river at the **American Pilgrim Museum** (Beschuitsteeg 9; tel: 071-512 2413; www.leidenamericanpilgrimmuseum.org; Wed–Sat 1–5pm).

Delftware

Brought to the Low Countries by Italians, Delftware reached its apogee in the 16th century but its beauty can still be seen around the country.

Delftware is the name given to a distinctive blue-and-white tin-glazed pottery produced in Delft and other Dutch cities. The earliest known tin-glazed pottery in the Netherlands was called majolica, after the Mediterranean island of Majorca where it was produced. The Italians were the main majolica producers in the 16th century, using techniques derived from Moorish and Spanish craftsmen. The term *faïence*, which is sometimes applied to Delftware, derives from the Italian town of Faenza, another important centre of majolica production.

The origins

In the early 16th century, the Italian potter Guido da Savino moved to Antwerp, where he established the first majolica workshop in the Low Countries. After the fall of Antwerp in 1585,

Classic Delftware.

skilled craftsmen fled from the Spanish terror to Holland or England. The Antwerp majolica workers mainly settled in Dutch towns such as Delft and Haarlem, where they began to produce wall tiles for kitchens and fireplaces. These provided protection against damp and dirt, the two great enemies of the Dutch housewife. Gradually new motifs were introduced to suit Dutch tastes.

In the early 17th century trading ships of the VOC (United East India Company) returned from the Far East laden with delicate Chinese blue-and-white porcelain, leading to a drop in demand for the coarser Dutch majolica. Many pottery workshops went bankrupt, while others responded by producing blue-and-white pottery modelled on Chinese porcelain, often decorated with biblical episodes or scenes from Dutch life. In 1645 civil war in China caused a sharp decline in imported supply and a temporary upswing in demand for local pottery.

Collections

In the mid-18th century the Dutch pottery industry suffered another major blow when cheap mass-produced English creamware began to flood the market. By the mid-19th century 'De Porceleyne Fles' (founded in 1653) was the only pottery left in Delft. In 1876 Joost 't Hooft revived the art of hand-painted blue decoration. Traditional designs were reintroduced, and later Art Nouveau motifs began to appear. Today many museums in the Netherlands possess large Delftware collections. The Gemeentemuseum Den Haag in The Hague has one of the finest in the world, mostly from the famous Van den Burgh legacy. The Rijksmuseum in Amsterdam also has a splendid collection, including curious tulip vases which were especially popular in Britain and the Netherlands during the reign of William and Mary. There is an interesting collection of Delftware tiles in Delft's own Rijksmuseum Huis Lambert van Meerten. In particular, the collection illustrates the wit of Dutch tile painters.

The Museum Het Prinsenhof in Leeuwarden contains the world's largest collection of tiles, with examples from Persia, Spain, France and Holland. The visitors' centre at Royal Delft, De Koninklijke Porceleyne Fles, exhibits numerous vases, plates and tiles and ceramic architectural details made in Delft. But the most remarkable decoration made at the pottery is the tiled interior of the bodega in the Hotel Die Port van Cleve, Amsterdam.

In the Middle Ages, Delft was a typical Netherlandish town of weavers and brewers, with numerous monasteries and convents within its walls. But its tranquil mood was shattered during the Dutch Revolt when William of Orange chose the town as his military headquarters, taking up residence in the Prinsenhof, a former monastery. He was assassinated here in 1584 by Balthasar Gerards, a fanatical Catholic, and is buried in the town's Nieuwe Kerk.

In the 17th century Delft had the dubious distinction of being the main arsenal of the Dutch Republic. In October 1654, the town was devastated by an explosion in the Secreet van Hollandt (a gunpowder store hidden in the garden of a former convent), which destroyed one-third of the houses in the city and killed 200 people. One of the victims was Rembrandt's gifted pupil Carel Fabritius, the painter responsible for the beautiful study, *The Goldfinch*, in the Mauritshuis in The Hague.

A canalside walk

A walk along **Oude Delft**, a narrow leafy canal, takes you past some of the most interesting buildings in the city. The letters VOC marked on a Renaissance house at Oude Delft 39 are a reminder that Delft was once one of the cities that bonded together to form the Verenigde Oostindische Compagnie – the United East India Company.

The massive brick building rising up from the water opposite is the **Armamentarium**, formerly the arsenal of the provinces of Holland and West Friesland. Its function is symbolised by the bearded figure of Mars, the god of war, perched awkwardly on a lion and a heap of weapons. The bridge at the end of Oude Delft marks the site of a medieval city gate, the Rotterdamse Poort, which appears in the foreground of Vermeer's *View of Delft*. You can learn about his work and see an imagined recreation of his studio at the **Vermeer Centrum Delft A** (Voldersgracht 21; tel: 015-213 8588; www.vermeerdelft.nl; daily 10am–5pm), housed in the former HQ of the painters' guild, of which the artist was Dean for many years.

Vermeer lived on **Markt B**, Delft's broad market square lined with cafés

TIP

To capture something of the atmosphere of medieval Delft, veer away from the centre and follow the canal east along Oosteinde to Oostpoort. Built around 1400, this is the only one of Delft's eight medieval gates still standing.

Delft's architecture has been beautifully preserved.

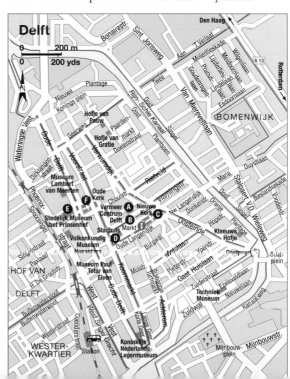

Delft

and restaurants. The **Nieuwe Kerk** **C** was begun on the east side of this square in the 14th century on the site of a medieval miracle. The slender spire of the church manages to appear harmonious, though it was built in separate stages from the late 14th to the early 16th centuries, and subsequently damaged several times by fire.

Founder of the Dutch Republic

The lofty late-Gothic choir, which dates from the 15th century, contains the marble and bronze **Mausoleum of William the Silent**, founder of the Dutch Republic. Begun by Hendrick de Keyser in 1614 (long after William's assassination) and completed eight years later by his son Pieter, it is richly decorated with uplifting motifs for the young Dutch Republic; the dog at William's feet symbolises fidelity, and the four female figures represent liberty (holding a hat), justice, religion and courage. The epitaph was composed by the statesman and poet Constantijn Huygens. The tombs of subsequent *stadhouders* and monarchs are in the crypt of the Nieuwe Kerk.

The jurist Hugo Grotius, who was born on Nieuwe Langedijk in Delft in 1583, is commemorated by an 18th-century memorial. In 1618 Grotius was imprisoned in Slot Loevestein for his support of the Remonstrants, but two years later his resourceful wife helped him to escape in a book trunk (possibly the one that is now displayed in the Prinsenhof Museum in Delft, though the Rijksmuseum in Amsterdam also has a chest which is claimed by some historians to have been the jurist's historic hiding place). Grotius spent the rest of his life in exile, and died in Rostock in 1645. His most famous work, *De Jure Belli et Pacis*, laid the foundations of modern international law. A plaque was attached to the monument by delegates to the International Peace Conference in The Hague in 1899. In recent years the writings of Grotius on justifiable warfare have been cited to shed light on the nuclear weapons debate.

The Renaissance **Stadhuis** **D** (Town Hall) opposite was built in 1618 by Hendrick de Keyser. It is decorated with ferocious lions' heads, a characteristic feature of buildings of the early Dutch Republic. This square building incorporates the stone tower of a medieval town hall gutted by fire in 1618. Botermarkt, a covered canal, leads to the most fashionable quarter of Delft. The weathered stone house at Oude Delft 167, built in the Flamboyant Gothic style of Brabant in 1510, was one of the few houses to survive the great fire of 1536.

Scene of the crime

A lane north of here leads to the **Museum Prinsenhof** **E** (Sint Agathaplein 1, tel: 015-260 2358; www.prinsenhof-delft.nl; Tue–Sun 11am–5pm) which contains an excellent collection of topographical paintings of Delft (frequently commissioned to illustrate one calamity or another), medieval sculpture, portraits of prominent

Historic Delft Markt with the Nieuwe Kerk and City Hall.

figures of the Dutch Revolt, Delftware and maps that give a clue to the history of the Netherlands and the development of its cities.

The museum occupies a beautiful 15th-century Burgundian Gothic convent with ancient tiled floors and leaded windows looking out on leafy gardens. This nunnery was the unlikely setting for the murder of William the Silent in 1584 by the Spanish sympathiser Balthasar Gerards. The bullet holes in the wall of the Moordzaal have been carefully preserved behind glass.

Opposite the convent stands one of Delft's finest buildings, the Gothic **Oude Kerk** ❻ (opening times vary). The tower, which dates from the 14th century, has a pronounced lean, and its bell sounds a suitably melancholy note. The church was built over the course of the 14th and 15th centuries, and a magnificent Flamboyant Gothic north transept was added in the 16th century by Anthonis Keldermans of Mechelen (though the effect is rather weakened by the absence of a south transept).

Illustrious residents

Within the whitewashed interior, the **tomb of Admiral Piet Hein** is given pride of place on the site of the main altar. Admiral Maarten Tromp, the hero of some 50 sea battles, is also buried in the Oude Kerk. His memorial is decorated with a marble relief depicting a sea battle. The most famous deceased resident is Vermeer; although the exact location of his tomb is unknown.

Another monument commemorates the Delft scientist Anthonie van Leeuwenhoek, who is credited with inventing the microscope, thus enabling him to observe such organisms as bacteria, red blood corpuscles and spermatozoa for the first time. A modern sculpture symbolising a yeast cell in the park at the end of Oude Delft commemorates Van Leeuwenhoek's discoveries. Perhaps fittingly, the air is now filled with a pungent yeasty smell from a neighbouring biochemical factory.

In a nearby clump of trees lies the derelict tomb of Karl Wilhelm Naundorff, who claimed he was the son of the executed King Louis XVI of France.

Museum Prinsenhof.

Rotterdam's Markthall.

ROTTERDAM AND ENVIRONS

From bombed-out ruin to dynamic, modern port, Rotterdam has exceeded its ambition to become one of The Netherlands' major urban centres.

The southern part of Zuid-Holland province is dominated by the port of Rotterdam, which extends for 37km (23 miles) along both banks of the River Nieuwe Maas, from Rotterdam to Hoek van Holland (Hook of Holland). The port activities, however, hardly impinge on the city of Rotterdam, which is unexpectedly quiet and attractive.

Dordrecht to the south retains much more the atmosphere of an old Dutch river port, with crumbling brick warehouses and canals lined with barges. The eastern part of this region is still largely rural, with several pleasant small towns, such as Gouda to the northeast of Rotterdam, and Schoonhoven and Nieuwpoort on opposite banks of the River Lek to the east.

In recent years, the face of **Rotterdam** ❹ has changed almost beyond recognition. With its dynamic modern skyline, it is now one of the largest and busiest ports in the world. Strolling along the Weena, the bustling downtown area, it is easy to see that this is a city on the move. One interesting landmark is the World Trade Center (completed in 1986), a flattened green ellipse built on top of the Koopman Stock Exchange building. Another is the 161.2-metre (529ft) -high Maastoren building (completed in 2009) by the south side of the Erasmus Bridge, which is the highest office block in the Netherlands.

Re-emergence

This is not the first time in its history that Rotterdam has undergone major redevelopment. It emerged as an important shipping centre towards the end of the 17th century when the Dutch were prospering from trade in the East Indies. After a period of decline, its status as a European trade centre was elevated again in the 19th century by the construction of the

Main Attractions
View from Euromast, Rotterdam
Museum Boijmans van Beuningen, Rotterdam
Boat trip to Rotterdam Port
Dordrechts Museum
Cheese Market, Gouda

A festive fair in Dordrecht.

Nieuwe Waterweg (New Waterway) canal to the sea (1866–72). In 1898, the 10-storey, 45-metre (148ft) -high Witte Huis (White House) was erected beside the old harbour.

After the port was bombed in 1940 (the Witte Huis was one of the few buildings that didn't crumble), it was rebuilt, with massive investment, to meet modern requirements. The spacious, pedestrianised streets of the Lijnbaan quarter, completed in 1953, inspired similar developments elsewhere.

No longer in the shadow of Amsterdam and The Hague, Rotterdam has resolved its identity crisis and is now the second-largest city in the Netherlands. It has a prestigious orchestra and hosts an internationally respected film festival. In summer, free dance, music and theatre festivals are staged in its parks and squares. The city centre reflects a fascinating cultural and culinary diversity.

Architectural highlights

The **Oude Haven**, Rotterdam's former harbour, has some exciting modern architecture. For many years after the bombardment of the city in 1940, the devastated area around the old harbour remained a wasteland. In the late 1980s it was rapidly transformed by the construction of a huge public library in glass and steel. The building offers fantastic views over the port and the modern city as well as its own hanging gardens. A collection of redundant Rhine barges owned by the Maritime Museum is also on permanent display here.

The only medieval building still standing is the **Grote Kerk** Ⓐ (Grotekerkplein; www.laurenskerkrotterdam.nl; Apr–Oct Tue–Sat 11am–5pm, Nov–Mar Tue, Fri and Sat 11am–5pm). Also known as Sint Laurenskerk, the church was gutted during the war, but subsequently restored with great skill. On a bleak square in front of the church stands a statue of Erasmus, the philosopher and scholar noted for his satire, who was born in Rotterdam in 1469. Although Erasmus left home at the tender age of six to study in Deventer and later Oxford, he spent most of his life in Rotterdam, and

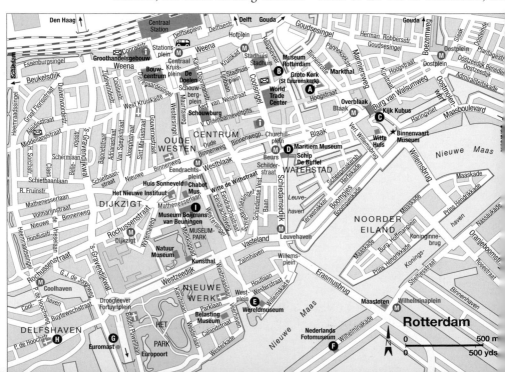

the city's university is named after him. The bronze statue by Hendrick de Keyser in front of the church dates from 1622. Behind the church is the **Markthall** (Binnenrotte 1), a spectacular food market in the centre of an arched block of apartments, which opened in 2014.

A five-minute walk northwest will bring you to **Museum Rotterdam** Ⓑ (Meent 119; www.museumrotterdam. nl; see website for details). The city's history museum moved to this purpose-built home in January 2016 and explores a variety of themes including the development of the port, local industry and World War II.

To the south east, the **Blaakse Bos** is a bizarre cluster of tilted cube houses supported by tall concrete columns, designed by Piet Blom. A raised pedestrian street lined with shops (Promenade Overblaak) runs beneath the houses to create a modern version of the Ponte Vecchio in Florence. You can visit the exhibition house **Kijk Kubus** Ⓒ (View Cube; www. kubuswoning.nl; daily 11am–5pm) for an impression of life in these strange futuristic dwellings, where all the furniture has to be adapted to the sloping walls. You can also stay here as a few of the houses have been turned into the Stayokay Hostel (tel: 010-436 5763; www.stayokay.com).

On the waterfront

The waterfront promenade along Boompjes brings you out on **Leuvehaven**. The **Maritiem Museum** Ⓓ (Leuvehaven 1; tel: 010-413 2680; www.maritiemmuseum.nl; Tue–Sat 10am–5pm, Sun 11am–5pm, July and Aug also Mon 10am–5pm), located behind a disused red lighthouse, is a modern museum devoted to Rotterdam's maritime history. The interior is reminiscent of a ship, with long steel gangplanks leading to the upper floors. The café terrace offers one of the best views in Rotterdam, looking down the Leuvehaven to the river. The museum also displays a number of exhibits on the quayside, including a reconstructed rope walk. In the middle of the windswept square beside this museum stands the sculpture *De Verwoeste Stad* (The Razed City).

TIP

Line 10 (www.lijn10.nl) takes visitors on a 'hop on-hop off' sightseeing trip aboard an historic tram during the summer months. Starting at Willemsplein by the Maastoren, it goes past all the main sights including the new train station, and ends at Euromast. Buy tickets on board (no credit cards).

Cube houses (Kubuswoningen) are a set of innovative dwellings designed by architect Piet Blom and built in Rotterdam.

WHERE

Every July the famous North Sea Jazz Festival weekend attracts visitors and top musicians to Rotterdam from all around the world.

Designed by Ossip Zadkine in 1953, it symbolises the destruction of Rotterdam in 1940. A figure contorted with fear holds up his arms to the sky; the large hole in the sculpture represents the destruction of the city's heart.

Occupying a pastel neoclassical building further along the waterfront, the **Wereldmuseum** Ⓔ (World Museum; Willemskade 25; tel: 010-270 7172; www.wereldmuseum.nl; Tues–Sun 10.30am–5.30pm) regularly organises stimulating temporary exhibitions on non-Western cultures and has its own highly-regarded restaurant, which serves Mediterranean cuisine. The building was originally the Royal Yacht Club of Prince Hendrik (1876–1934), the husband of Queen Wilhelmina, where he would meet with his friends to discuss their travels and show each other what they had brought back. Drop in at the Grand Café-Restaurant Loos on Westplein for lunch or dinner in a chic ambience. Or you can walk across the street to the small yacht harbour and take a speedboat ride across the River Maas to visit the Hotel New York. Although it keeps a very low

One of the few parts of Rotterdam not destroyed by German bombs in World War II.

profile, it is one of the liveliest places in town to have a drink or something to eat. Located in the former offices of the Holland America Line, most rooms have magnificent views of the river and all are uniquely furnished.

Near the hotel, as well as the Maastoren, is the **Nederlands Fotomuseum** Ⓕ (Photography Museum; Wilhelminakade 332; tel: 010-203 0405; www.nederlandsfotomuseum.nl; Tue–Fri 10am–5pm, Sat–Sun 11am–5pm), which is responsible for the archives of around 160 important historical and contemporary Dutch photographers.

Old and new

Overlooking the small **Veerhaven** beyond are several 19th-century shipping offices decorated with telling maritime details. Westerkade leads from here along the waterfront to the attractive English-style **Het Park**, with a curious wooden church for Norwegian seamen. On the west side of the park, the **Euromast** Ⓖ (Parkhaven 20; tel: 010-436 4811; www.euromast. nl; Apr–Sept daily 9.30am–11pm

Oct–Mar daily 10am–11pm) rises above the trees to a height of 185 metres (600ft). It was built in 1960 to celebrate the Floriade international flower and garden exhibition. The observation platform at 100 metres (330ft) offers a panoramic view of the city and port. The restaurant is an excellent spot to enjoy Sunday brunch with a view, although there is also a café-deli on the ground floor for those without a head for heights.

With the opening of the Erasmus Bridge in 1998, the city centre was extended further into the harbour area, where an ambitious, well-conceived dockside development of shops, cafés and housing has been created. Trams and the metro line provides easy access to the area. Further downstream, beyond the park, lies **Delfshaven ⓗ**, founded in the 14th century as the port of Delft, but now part of the municipality of Rotterdam. On the waterfront is **De Delft Museum** (Schiehaven 15; Tue–Fri 10am–4pm, Sat–Sun 11am–5pm), where a replica of an 18th-century warship is being built. Delfshaven survived the bombardment in 1940,

and most of its buildings are protected monuments. Admiral Piet Hein, who seized the Spanish silver fleet in a daring escapade in 1626, was born here. The port also has associations with the Pilgrim Fathers, who set sail for the New World (via Plymouth where they joined the *Mayflower*) in 1620 from the Middenkous quay.

Museum Park

The best-known of Rotterdam's museums is the **Museum Boijmans Van Beuningen ❶** (Museumpark 18; tel: 010-441 9400; www.boijmans.nl; Tue–Sun 11am–5pm). Founded in 1847, it houses one of the best art collections in the Netherlands (though many of the paintings donated by Frans Boijmans were destroyed by fire in 1864). The original museum was rebuilt in 1935 and extended in 1972. An ambitious renovation has created more space for its permanent and changing exhibitions. The museum owns a number of well-known early Flemish paintings, including *The Prodigal Son* by Hieronymus Bosch and one of the two versions of *The Tower of Babel* by Pieter

EAT

Both kids and adults will enjoy savoury and sweet pancakes at Pim's Poffertjes en Pannenkoeken (Nieuwstraat 19; www.pimspofenpan.nl; Wed and Fri noon–7.30pm, Thu and Sat until 8.30pm, Sun 1–8.30pm). Sit in a cosy booth or on the terrace and tuck into bacon, apple and raisin or chocolate and coconut.

View of the Museum Boijmans Van Beuningen.

Rotterdam Port

Europe's largest port, ranked in the top 10 in the world, has even bigger ambitions in the works for its future and visitors can find out all about them via a range of boat trips from the city.

The port stretches for 42km (26 miles) along the waterfront of the Nieuwe Maas. Each year it handles over 450 million metric tons of goods, and each year Rotterdam sees around 30,000 seagoing vessels and 100,000 inland vessels. About 85 percent of the citrus fruit consumed in Europe passes through the port, while more than half of Europe's tobacco imports and 40 percent of all the tea drunk in Britain arrives via Rotterdam.

Direct links

It was the completion in 1890 of the Nieuwe Waterweg between Rotterdam and Hoek van Holland that provided Rotterdam with a direct link to the North Sea; previously ships were

Large container vessel unloaded in Port of Rotterdam.

compelled to navigate a series of notoriously difficult channels. The port has several natural advantages, the most important being its situation on the main branch of the Rhine (called the Lek – 'Leak' – in the Netherlands), the world's busiest river. Rotterdam is also connected with France and southern Belgium by the River Maas, and with northern Belgium by the River Scheldt.

The Waalhaven, a predecessor to the modern port, was completed in 1930, and was then the world's largest harbour. Much of the Waalhaven is now devoted to container ships, a form of mass transport pioneered by Rotterdam. In 1972 the first container ship between Europe and Japan docked in the Waalhaven. Container ships can transport up to 18,000 containers since the arrival of 0.4km (0.25-mile) -long Triple E ships in 2013.

Rotterdam is also one of the world's most important oil, chemical and gas terminals, with several major companies maintaining storage tanks and refineries in the port. There are currently 78 wind turbines on site.

Boat trips

The harbour now constitutes about 50 percent of the area of Rotterdam. The best way to see the wharfs, quays, docks and silos is to take a 75-minute Spido (tel: 010-275 9988; www.spido.nl) harbour tour from Willemsplein 85 (next to the Erasmus Bridge). Each kilometre of the Rhine is numbered, beginning at kilometre 0 on Lake Constance and reaching 1001 at the Spido quay. At kilometre 1008 the boat turns across the busy shipping lanes and enters the Eemshaven, then heads back upstream to enter the Waalhaven.

Although covering only 7km (4 miles) out of the 37km (23 miles) of quays between the city and the North Sea, the trip provides a fascinating glimpse of port activities, as it darts between ships stacked with containers, or passes vessels in dry dock for repair.

A day trip takes visitors to see Maaslakte 2, an extension of the existing port which opened in 2013, and includes a tour of the Futureland Visitor Centre, where you can learn about the advanced technologies used at the Euromax Terminal, its innovative communication system and sustainable ambitions.

There are dinner cruises year round by The Pancake Boat (010-436 7295; www.pannenkoekenboot.nl), which is moored by the Euromast, for either 75 minutes or two and a half hours.

Brueghel the Elder. The collection of Old Masters includes Rembrandt's tender portrait of his son Titus, painted in 1655. The modern collection features canvases by Monet, Van Gogh and Kandinsky, and several Surrealist works by Magritte and Dalí. The collections of industrial art and arts and crafts span an extensive period from the 14th century to the present day.

The Boijmans stands on the edge of Museum Park, an innovative project linking a green oasis known as the 'people's park' with cultural institutions like the Kunsthal, Het Nieuwe Instituut, the Nature Museum and the Chabot Museum.

The **Kunsthal** exhibition gallery (West Zeedijk 341; tel: 010-440 0301; www.kunsthal.nl; Tue–Sat 10am–5pm, Sun 11am–5pm), focuses on contemporary art, occupying a building by renowned architect Rem Koolhaas. The logo on the tower is inspired by the 'This Way Up' sign stencilled on crates. The Kunsthal has no permanent collection of its own, but presents a wide choice of exhibitions ranging from art (Picasso), photography

(Helmut Newton and Alice Springs) and architecture to jewellery, cars and football clubs. Next door is the **Natuurhistorisch Museum** (Nature Museum; tel: 010-436 4222; Tue–Sun 11am–5pm), which has a collection of 25,000 objects, from dried plants to fossilised mammoth remains.

Het Nieuwe Instituut (Museum Park 25; tel: 010-440 1200; Tue–Sat 10am–5pm, Sun 11am–5pm) is worth visiting just to admire the glass building itself, designed by Jo Coenen. A striking installation by Peter Struycken illuminates the gallery under the long archive section and is particularly impressive at night. The Instituut focuses on design and innovation in the areas of architecture, design and e-culture. The stylish New Café, which was voted the best museum café in the country in 2015, serves (mainly) organic, seasonal food and has one of the most attractive terraces in the city.

Most of Rotterdam's private art galleries are concentrated either in the streets bordering the Boijmans Van Beuningen Museum or in Delfshaven. Witte de Withstraat is the

The Chabot Museum, dedicated to the Dutch painter and sculptor Hendrik Chabot.

NEW CONSTRUCTION

Near the Nieuwe Instituut are two architectural gems worth visiting. The **Chabot Museum** (Museumpark 11; tel: 010-436 3713; www.chabotmuseum.nl; Tue–Fri 11am–4.30pm, Sat 11am–5pm, Sun noon–5pm) is a listed villa built in 1938 in the 'Nieuwe Bouwen' (New Construction) style of architecture. It was the home of expressionist painter and sculptor Henk Chabot, whose works are exhibited within. **Huis Sonneveld** (Jongkindstraat 12; Tue–Sat 10am–5pm, Sun 11am–5pm) is one of the best-preserved houses in this 'Nieuwe Bouwen' style. It was designed by Brinkman & Van der Vlugt, also responsible for the Van Nelle Factory (www.ontwerpfabriek.nl), which produced tobacco until the 1990s and was made a Unesco World Heritage Site in 2014. A visitor centre is being developed there.

heart of Rotterdam's art scene and a good place to go for a hip night on the town: try Grand Café NRC (No. 63), De Witte Aap (No. 78) or Café de Schouw (No. 80), which is popular with writers. During the day, check out the contemporary art exhibitions at TENT (www.tentrotterdam.nl) and Witte de With (both at No. 50; www.wdw.nl; Tue–Sun 11am–6pm). Conveniently close to the Boijmans Van Beuningen Museum, the **Café De Unie** at 35 Mauritsweg is a faithful reconstruction of a building designed in 1924 by the Rotterdam architect J.J.P. Oud. Like the Rietveld-Schröder House in Utrecht, it obeys the tenets of the De Stijl movement, using vertical and horizontal lines and blocks of primary colour for decoration. The quayside of the Oude Haven is another good spot for attractive cafés.

Historic Dordrecht

The old river port of **Dordrecht** ⑤ lies at the confluence of three busy waterways, about 15km (10 miles) southeast of Rotterdam, and provides a pleasing contrast to the modernism

of Rotterdam. A castle was built here by Count Dirk III in the early 11th century to control vital shipping routes into and out of Holland. The town that grew up around the castle was granted a charter by Count Willem I in 1220.

Dordrecht played an important role in the emergence of the Dutch state; in 1572 this was one of the first towns to side with the Protestant rebels, and later the same year the United Provinces met in the Statenzaal (still standing in a courtyard known as the Hof, which once belonged to an Augustinian friary).

Dordrecht was also the scene of the Synod of Dordt, held in 1618–19, at which the hardline Dutch Calvinists rejected the more moderate tenets of the Remonstrants. This led, in 1619, to the imprisonment in Slot Loevestein of Hugo Grotius, a leading Remonstrant, and the execution in The Hague of the statesman Johan van Oldenbarnevelt.

These days the town is well known for its excellent award-winning weekend market, which is held every Frida

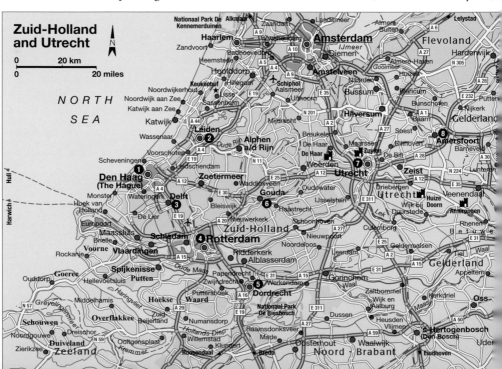

and Saturday around Statenplein, and its three-day Christmas market in December.

Dordrecht's waterfront

The waterfront at Dordrecht is the town's most interesting area, though many of the old warehouses are abandoned and decaying. A number of them are inscribed with the names of German towns or rivers, a reminder that Dordrecht was once a major port for the shipment of German wine.

The best approach to the harbour is down **Wijnstraat** (whose name recalls the wine trade). This is an old street lined with damp warehouses and curiosity shops, including an interesting antiquarian bookshop crammed with dusty novels in many languages, old records, faded prints, framed paintings and second-hand navigation maps. The overspill stock is stored in old St Emilion crates, suggesting that Dordrecht is still a wine port of some importance.

Turning left at the end of this street, you come upon the **Groothoofds Poort**, a magnificent city gate built in the 17th century on the site of its medieval precursor. Once the principal entrance to Dordrecht, it is designed in grand Renaissance style, with a large cartouche depicting the Maid of Holland, symbolised by a plumpish woman behind a wicker fence. The gate occupies a spectacular site at the confluence of three major waterways. To the right, the Beneden Merwede carries river traffic east to Gorinchem and the River Maas. Straight ahead, the Noord is used by barges travelling north to the Lek (Rhine) and Rotterdam, and to the left, the Dordtse Kil carries shipping bound for the Hollands Diep and Antwerp. An estimated 1,500 barges and ships pass by this spot every day, making it the busiest river junction in Europe.

The Van Gijn collection

Turning left along the waterfront, then across the little drawbridge, will bring you to **Nieuwe Haven**, a picturesque harbour filled with creaking boats and surrounded by the cluttered premises of ships' chandlers. This harbour is overlooked by the **Museum Simon van Gijn** (30 Nieuwe Haven; tel: 078-770

SS Rotterdam.

8709; www.huisvanguijn.nl; Tue–Sun 11am–5pm), a richly furnished merchant's house built in 1729. In 1864 it was acquired by the banker and art collector Simon van Gijn, who lived here until his death in 1922. Although it is now a museum, the house still has a lived-in feeling, and its handsome period rooms convey a sense of quiet prosperity. The kitchen, with its tiled walls and gleaming brass pots, dates from the 18th century, while a room on the first floor contains a Renaissance fireplace dating from about 1550. Decorated with curious figures of savages, it once heated the banqueting hall of the guild of arquebusiers (marksmen). Also of interest is the study on the first floor built by Van Gijn in neo-Renaissance style to evoke the 17th-century interiors of Vermeer.

The Van Gijn collection includes paintings, Flemish tapestries, glass and historical relics. On the first-floor landing is an attractive 17th-century shop sign, thought to have been painted by Albert Cuyp for a relative who sold wine. The most popular exhibition is the delightful collection of antique Dutch toys displayed in the attic and garden house, which includes dolls' houses, miniature shops, mechanical models (some still working) and magic lanterns. The museum also contains a model of Dordrecht as it was in 1544.

From the top of the tower of the nearby **Grote Kerk** (www.grotekerkdordrecht.nl; Apr–Oct Tue–Sat 10.30am–4.30pm, Sun 10am–4pm, Nov–Mar Sat 1–4pm), you can see how the town has changed since then. The Grote Kerk itself was built in the 15th century by Evert Spoorwater of Antwerp in a subdued Brabant Gothic style. The distinctive squat tower dates back even further; it was begun in 1339, but never completed. The size of the first tier indicates that it was intended to support a very lofty edifice, but instead it is surmounted, rather oddly, by four 17th-century clocks.

Voorstraatshaven is the narrow canal running alongside the church that leads into the centre of town. The view of the old **Stadhuis** (Town Hall) from the Visbrug is particularly impressive. This 19th-century building spanning the canal rests on the foundations of a 14th-century exchange

Gouda Markt.

established by Flemish merchants. Just across the bridge at 3–7 Visstraat is an attractive café, **Crimpert Salm**, which occupies a Renaissance building, dating from 1608, where the guild of fishmongers used to meet.

Dordrechts Museum

The **Dordrechts Museum** (Museumstraat 40; tel: 078-770 8708; www.dordrechtsmuseum.nl; Tue–Sun 11am–5pm), in a former lunatic asylum, has a fine collection of paintings by 17th-century Dordrecht artists, including Albert Cuyp, Samuel van Hoogstraten, Nicholas Maes and Ferdinand Bol. The self-portrait by Ferdinand Bol clearly shows the influence of Rembrandt, under whom he studied. Jan van Goyen, though not a local, painted an alluring *View of Dordrecht* in 1651, seen from the north bank of the Oude Maas. The low horizon and threatening sky are characteristic of 17th-century Dutch landscape painting.

A panoramic view of Dordrecht by Adam Willaerts hanging on the staircase shows the busy waterfront in 1629. A room of 19th-century works

by the Dordrecht-born artist Ary Scheffer is furnished attractively in Victorian style. An interesting painting by a fellow artist portrays Scheffer in his Paris studio working on one of the paintings now in the Dordrecht collection. The museum has several 17th-century 'vanity paintings', still lifes depicting symbols of mortality such as snuffed candles and pipes. This popular Dutch motif of human mortality is echoed on the portal of the nearby Arend Maartenshof, a 17th-century almshouse at 56 Museumstraat, where a Latin inscription above the entrance reminded its elderly residents *Vita Vapor* – roughly translated it means 'Life is but a wisp.'

A five-minute walk to the east, in a former Augustinian monastery, is **Het Hof van Nederland** (Hof 6; www.hethofvannederland.nl; Tue–Sun 11am–5pm), a new museum about one of the most important events in the country's history. In 1572, a meeting was held here by representatives of the Free Estates of Holland (adversaries of King Phillip II Spain), which eventually led to the establishment of the Republic of the

View on Dordrecht from the mouth of the Noord by Adam Willaerts.

In Gouda city centre.

United Netherlands. Visitors can learn about the influence of The Synod of Dordrecht on Dutch language and culture, as well as the story of the making of the Netherlands, via an entertaining film and multi-media exhibition.

Gouda

Gouda ❻ is a pretty little town on the River Gouwe, at the point where it enters the Hollandse IJssel, about 25km (16 miles) northeast of Rotterdam. Though its harbour activities have ceased, Gouda remains a lively market town, especially on Thursday morning (10am–1pm) from June to August, when a traditional cheese market is staged at the Markt. Local farmers bring their home-produced cheeses here to be weighed and graded. The town's main activity revolves around the **Markt**, which is unusually spacious by Dutch standards. In the middle stands the Stadhuis, built in 1450 in a Gothic style reminiscent of Flemish town halls, with numerous statues of Burgundian dukes and duchesses, and lofty step gables sprouting pinnacles. The **Waag** (Weigh House) on the north side of the square

is an imposing Dutch classical building, built in 1668 by Pieter Post, which has been converted into a **Cheese and Crafts Museum** (Apr–Oct Fri–Wed noon–5pm, Thu 10am–5pm). An interesting relief in the tympanum depicts the weighing of Gouda cheeses.

Kerkstraat leads from the Markt to a beguiling medieval area of quiet cobbled lanes surrounding **Sint Janskerk** (www.sintjan.com; Mar–Oct Mon–Sat 9am–5pm, Nov–Feb Mon–Sat 10am–4pm). This elongated Gothic church, rebuilt after a fire in 1552, is renowned for its exceptional stained-glass windows. Most of these were given to the church during its reconstruction by a wide range of donors, including municipalities, abbeys, guilds, princes and burgomasters. The 14 finest windows were designed by the brother Wouter and Dirck Crabeth in 1555–77 in a transitional style between Gothic and Renaissance art. The guilds usually commissioned representations of biblical episodes that were connected in some way with their trade. The window depicting *Jonah and the Whale* (window 30) was presented in 156

by the guild of fishermen, while the butchers' guild donated *Baalam and His Ass* (window 31). The *Last Supper* (window 7) was donated by Philip II in 1577, when Gouda was still a Catholic city, while in 1561 William of Orange presented the church with *Christ Driving the Moneylenders out of the Temple* (window 22).

A number of other interesting windows were executed after Gouda fell to the Protestants. Window 25, illustrating the relief of Leiden in 1574, was given by the city of Delft in 1603. In 1596, the city of Haarlem donated window 2, showing the capture of Damietta by Dutch Crusaders, while Dordrecht proudly presented window 3, illustrating its own attractions, the following year. In the 19th century, Jan Schouten of Delft added three very curious windows (numbers 1A, 1B and 1C) made from old fragments of glass.

Gouda museum

Opposite the church is the **Lazarus Gate**, a handsome sandstone portal, dated 1609, that leads into the leafy garden of the **Catharina Gasthuis**.

Founded in the 14th century as a hospice, it was later used as a hospital. Today the complex is used to display objects from the varied collection of the municipal **Museum Gouda** (www.museumgouda.nl; Tue–Sun 11–5pm). Several of its rooms are furnished in period style, including a Dutch kitchen. The collection of paintings is remarkably good for a town of this size, and includes several works by the Gouda-born artist Pieter Pourbus the Elder, a moving portrait of a dead child by Bartholomeus van der Helst, a series of civic guard group portraits, and some Impressionist paintings by members of the Barbizon and Hague schools.

Achter de Kerk street leads to a curious brick chapel modelled on the Church of the Holy Sepulchre in Jerusalem. Turning right here down Spieringstraat takes you past the ornate 17th-century portals of the orphanage (on the left) and an almshouse (opposite). Turning right along Minderbroederssteeg, a narrow street with some old warehouses, you reach Oost Haven, a former harbour now bereft of shipping.

A cheese-lover's dream at Museum Gouda.

UTRECHT

From tower-top views to cartoon characters and from castles to art, Utrecht and its neighbour Amersfoort have much to offer.

The small province of Utrecht owes its existence to the Christian Church. In the late 7th century, Pepin II, King of the Franks (a recent convert to Christianity) consolidated his power here by defeating the Frisian King Radboud at Wijk bij Duurstede. He then set out to convert his lands to Christianity and appointed a Bishop of Utrecht. Het Sticht, as the see was called, gradually extended its power, and by the 11th century its boundaries reached as far north as Groningen.

The most striking symbol of the power of the Church in Utrecht province today is the 14th-century tower of the Utrecht Domkerk (cathedral), which can be seen from as far away as Culemborg. The numerous other churches, monasteries and convents that have survived in Utrecht and Amersfoort are further evidence of the extent of Het Sticht's influence.

City of churches

Utrecht ❼ itself is one of the oldest cities in the Netherlands. It stands on a tributary of the Rhine, and was founded in AD 47 as a Roman garrison. A posting to Trajectum ad Rhenum (the Ford on the Rhine) must have seemed a bleak prospect to any soldier used to sunnier climes. This frontier was constantly being attacked from the east, and the Roman

settlement at Utrecht was destroyed five times before it was totally eradicated by Germanic tribes in the 3rd century. All that now remains to show for two centuries of Roman occupation are a few pottery fragments in the Centraal Museum.

King Pepin II took control in 689. He appointed Willibrord, a missionary from Northumberland, his first bishop (commemorated by a statue opposite the Janskerk). Willibrord built two churches on this strategic site and set about converting

Main Attractions

Domtoren
Centraal Museum
Kasteel de Haar

A bridge perch.

the people of his bishopric to Christianity.

In the 11th century Utrecht flourished under the protection of the German emperors. Bishop Bernold embarked on an ambitious project to make Utrecht a great spiritual centre of Northern Europe and drew up a plan to create a cross of four churches, with the Domkerk at the centre. Only two of these remain standing – Janskerk to the north and Pieterskerk to the east – but the position of the other two is easily identified. The cloister on Mariaplaats belonged to Mariakerk, the church at the west end of the cross, while a portal on Nieuwegracht leads to the ruined transept of the Paulusabdij, built at the southern point.

Numerous other churches and monasteries were built within the city walls, and the skyline of Utrecht was once a mass of spires. But many of these were toppled by a hurricane that struck the city in 1674.

The old canal

Oudegracht, the oldest canal in the city, is a good starting point for a tour of the old city. It was dug in the 11th century below street level to allow for sudden changes in the level of the Rhine. The canal is lined with brick quays and cavernous cellars that extend back to connect with the houses on the street above. Once used to store goods shipped from the Rhineland and Flanders, the vaulted cellars are now occupied by student restaurants and bars. In summer, café terraces are crammed into the short stretch of sunlit quayside between the Bakkerbrug (Baker's Bridge) and the Stadhuis (Town Hall). Out of season these quays remain silent and unused.

Several medieval town houses still stand on Oudegracht. **Oudaen** (No. 99) is a stern, fortified house built in 1320, when the Netherlands was gripped by an obscure dispute between two rival factions called the Hoeken (Hooks) and Kabeljauwen (Cods), rather like the 14th-century quarrel in Verona that ensnared Romeo and Juliet. Now restored, it has a magnificent café on the ground floor and a restaurant above. Opposite there is an even older building called

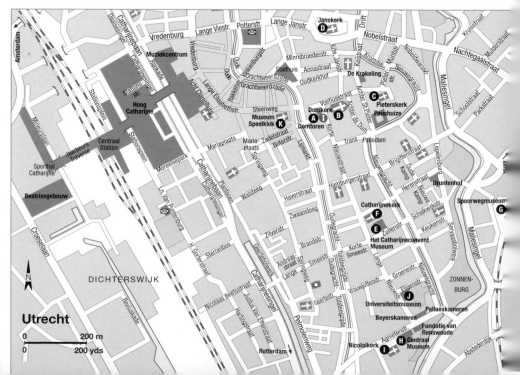

Utrecht

0   200 m
0   200 yds

Drakenborch (No. 114), dating from 1280 and restored in 1968.

The Domtoren

From the Bakkerbrug there's a good view of the **Domtoren Ⓐ** (cathedral tower; tel: 030-236 0010; www.domtoren.nl; Tue–Sat 10am–5pm, Sun and Mon noon–5pm), one of the architectural marvels of the Gothic age. Built between 1321 and 1383, it rises to an ethereal octagonal lantern 112 metres (376ft) high. It was for several centuries the tallest spire in the Low Countries, and even today it is impossible to remain unmoved by the elegance and sheer daring of the structure. Imitations of the Domtoren were built in Amersfoort, Delft, Groningen, Maastricht and Breda. Its unmistakable silhouette also appeared in several medieval paintings, such as the Van Eyck altarpiece in Ghent (a reproduction can be seen in the Janskerk). The 465-step climb up the tower is worthwhile if only for the panoramic view. Tickets, which include a guided tour, are available from the **Tourist Information Office** in the square, which also provides information about the museum quarter and a film of the history of Utrecht. Underneath the square is **Domunder** (Domplein 4; www.domunder.nl; Tue–Sun 11am–pm), where visitors can explore ,000 years of architectural remains by torchlight on an hour-long tour.

By following Oudegracht as it ends southwards, then turning left to Servetstraat, you come to the foot of the tower. A Renaissance gate on the right leads into the secret Bishop's Garden, where you get a superb view of the soaring tower. The archway beneath the Domtoren once led into the cathedral of Utrecht. A road now runs under the tower, and any traveller examining the Gothic vaulting runs the risk of being hit by a bus.

All that remains of the **Domkerk**, which was begun in 1254, are the choir and transepts on the far side of the road (www.domkerk.nl; May–Sept Mon–Sat 10am–5pm, Oct–Apr Mon–Fri 11am–4pm, Sat 11am–3.30pm, Sun 2–6pm). The nave, which had been built with inadequate buttressing, came crashing down during the freak hurricane in 1674.

Bishop Bernold's cross

The **Pieterskerk Ⓒ** (July–Sept Tue–Sat 11–5pm; free), the first church of Bishop Bernold's cross, was the bishop's favourite, and he elected to be buried here rather than in the Domkerk. Completed in 1048, it stands on the Pieterskerkhof, a tranquil square near the Domkerk. It is a rare example of the German Romanesque style. Utrecht was then part of the Holy Roman Empire, and the building materials were shipped here from the Eiffel: grey tuffa walls and red sandstone columns form a striking contrast to the ubiquitous Dutch brick.

Sadly, the storm of 1674 brought down both of the Pieterskerk's spires and caused considerable structural damage. The necessary repairs to the church were funded rather drastically

Quays and wharf cellars on Oudegracht canal.

by demolishing the westwork (an important architectural element of Romanesque church design) and selling the stone.

Turning right along Achter St Pieter brings you to an unusual house called De Krakeling (The Pretzel) at No. 8. It was built in 1663 by Everard Meyster, an eccentric local aristocrat who once laid a bet that he could persuade the people of Amersfoort to haul a nine-ton boulder, the *kei*, into the town. He won his bet and spent the money on a lavish feast of beer and pretzels for the 400 people who dragged the stone into Utrecht. The pretzel-shaped bell pull on the front door recalls this curious event.

Keistraat (renamed to commemorate Meyster's triumph) leads to the second of Bishop Bernold's churches, the **Janskerk** ❶ (Mon–Fri 1–5pm; free). Completed about 1050 in a similar German Romanesque style to the Pieterskerk, it originally had red sandstone columns, but these had to be encased in brick when the church showed signs of collapsing. One of the original columns has since been laid

bare in the nave. As with the Pieterskerk, this church lost its Romanesque westwork: one tower fell in the 14th century, the other followed on that bleak day in 1674.

After the Reformation, the choir – which had been rebuilt in the 16th century in Flamboyant Gothic style – was used to house the university library. In 1660 one of the chapels in the north aisle was converted into a guard house and adorned with a brightly painted coat of arms bearing the motto of the Dutch Republic: *Concordia res parvae crescunt* (Unity makes small things great).

New canal

Back on Drift, you can turn off down the elegant Kromme Nieuwegracht, the canal which bends along the former course of the Rhine, to reach Pausdam. This attractive bridge is overlooked by the **Paushuize** (Pope's house), a Flamboyant Gothic building dating from the early 16th century. It was built for Adriaen Floriszoon of Utrecht, who was appointed Pope by Charles V in 1522

The Domtoren.

Pope Adrian VI, the first and only Dutch Pope, immediately made himself highly unpopular in Rome by embarking on a vigorous programme of reform; none of his proposals was implemented before he died in the following year.

Nieuwegracht (new canal), a deep narrow canal, runs south of here. Not exactly new, it was built in 1393, in the same century as the old canal. Like Oudegracht, it has a lower quay lined with cellars, but these have all been abandoned. Nieuwegracht has some attractive examples of Dutch domestic architecture, such as the tiny classical house at No. 37.

Several religious orders built monasteries and convents on this canal. A former Carmelite convent now houses the **Museum Catharijneconvent** **E** (Lange Nieuwstraat 38; Tue–Fri 10am–5pm, Sat–Sun 11am–5pm). It has the finest collection of art from the Middle Ages in the Netherlands, with displays of illuminated manuscripts, statues, altarpieces and paintings by Jan van Scorel, Rembrandt, Frans Hals and Pieter Saenredam among others. Liturgical and other religious objects demonstrate the cultural and social differences between the Dutch Protestants and Catholics.

The adjacent **Catharijnekerk** **F** occupies a curious place in Dutch ecclesiastical history. Formerly the chapel of the Carmelites, it became the national cathedral of Dutch Catholics in the 19th century, when the ban on Catholic worship was officially lifted. The jubilant Catholics attempted to improve the chapel by adding a spire modelled on that of Kampen Stadhuis, and decorating the interior in rich neo-Gothic style. This offended the Dutch Protestants, who insisted that it be restored to its pristine whiteness.

Across the bridge from the Museum Catharijneconvent, Brittenstraat leads to a park bordering the city moat. Across the park, over an ornate iron bridge is the

Spoorwegmuseum **G** (Railway Museum; Tue–Sun 10am–5pm), housed in a disused 19th-century railway station. It has more than 50 historical locomotives, trains, wagons and coaches. You can take a short ride on an old steam train, or try your hand at driving a diesel locomotive, switching points, or driving an inter-city train on a simulator.

Almshouses

Outside the museum, turn right along the cobbled lane to reach the **Bruntenhof**, a row of whitewashed almshouses founded in 1521 by Frederik Brunt. A Renaissance portal leading to the Governors' Chamber (No. 5) bears a reminder of mortality in the form of an hourglass and skull. Three more almshouses at the southern end of the old town are worth a glance. Twelve homes known collectively as the **Pallaeskameren**, after their founder Maria van Pallaes, stand on Agnietenstraat. The date of foundation, 1651, and the Pallaes family coat of arms appear on every door lintel. In Lange Nieuwstraat, the

TIP

Explore Utrecht after dark on a Trajectum Lumen (www.trajectum lumen.nl) tour, organised by the VVV. Tours take place on Saturday evenings at either 8.30pm or 9pm from September to May for visitors to make the most of the city's artistic light installations; the Domtoren is particularly impressive.

The Railway Museum.

Beyerskameren consists of 16 terraced houses founded by Adriaen Beyer. The foundation date, 1597, is cut in the keyhole casing of the Governors' Chamber (No. 120).

When Maria Duist van Voorhout, Baroness of Renswoude, decided in 1757 that she was going to found an institution to educate poor boys, she spared no expense. The **Fundatie van Renswoude** on Agnietenstraat is a magnificent sandstone rococo building, decorated with the coats of arms of the founder and of the 13 members of the original board of trustees.

The former convent next door houses the **Centraal Museum** ⊕ (Agnietenstraat 1; www.centraalmuseum. nl; Tue–Sun 11am–5pm), which has an excellent collection of local history, furniture, costumes, sculpture and paintings. Highlights include paintings and artworks by Saenredam, Van Scorel (the most notable of Utrecht artists), Bloemaert, Moesman, Koch, Toorop and Droog Design, and the largest Gerrit Rietveld (1888–1964) collection in the world. Nearby, you can visit (by reservation) a house he designed in 1924 in 'De Stijl' style, which is on the Unesco World Heritage List (Prins Hendriklaan 50; tel: 030-2362 310 (for last-minute reservations on the day itself only); email: rshreserveringen@centraalmuseum.nl (for general reservations); Tue–Sun 11am–5pm). On the top floor of the museum is the studio of Utrecht-born children's author and artist Dick Bruna, who created the character 'Miffy'. There is also a multimedia information centre as well as a children's museum. A recreated medieval garden contains various moss-covered fragments rescued from demolished buildings. A path leads through the museum garden to the **Nicolaikerk** ⊕, built in 1150, which once boasted two spires, although one was replaced by an octagonal bell tower in 1586 and the other was felled by the storm in 1674.

Utrecht has the largest student population in the country and a five-minute walk north is the university's science museum, **Universiteitsmuseum** ⊕ (Langenieuwstraat 106; www.universiteitsmuseum.nl; daily

A summer canal boat trip.

ON THE WATER

The tourist office promotes a variety of tours on the canals. The most romantic way to explore Utrecht's waterways is on a traditional Venetian gondola, which departs from Oudergracht 177 (Mar–Nov 11am–6pm, summer until 8pm). Schuttevaer offers one-hour excursions in a covered boat (heated in winter) with commentary in English, leaving from Oudegracht 85 (daily 11am–5pm); while Utrecht Sloep Rondvaarten at Oudegracht 177 has daily tours with commentary in smaller, open-top boats. Alternatively, you can hire your own boat from several companies, the most fun being Canal Bike at Oudegracht 167, which has pedaloes, and Kanoverhuur at Oudegracht 4, which rents out canoes and electric boats.

10am–5pm), which also has a botanic garden with a lovely café terrace.

Along the ramparts

The most pleasant route back to the centre is along the landscaped ramparts. You will pass an abandoned Gothic Revival church, the **Sint Martinuskerk**, which overlooks a series of 19th-century workers' terraced houses known as **De 7 Steegjes** (the Seven Lanes), where patterned brick pavements create the impression of an outdoor carpet. The fact that the huge church is now neglected, while the humble dwellings alongside have been saved from demolition by a vigorous campaign, shows how the Dutch aspire not to grandeur but to *gezelligheid* (snugness).

Heading down Springweg, past a row of 11 almshouses founded in 1583 (Nos. 110–130), you come to the **Mariaplaats**, where a cloister is all that remains of the fourth of Bishop Bernold's churches. Turning right down Zadelstraat, then left into Buurkerkhof, brings you to the **Buurkerk**, the oldest parish church in Utrecht, where one Sister Bertken was walled up for 57 years at her own request, in order to escape the evils of the world.

Begun in the 13th century, it was converted into a hall church with five aisles in the 16th century. The church now houses the delightful **Museum Speelklok** ⓚ (Steenweg 6, www.museumspeelklok.nl; Tue–Sun 10am–pm), a collection of mechanical musical instruments, ranging from a glass case of twittering birds to several ear-splitting dance-hall organs.

Guided tours are given by enthusiastic music students from the university, whose job includes playing the piano and singing a lusty Berlin to the accompaniment of a street organ. English-speaking guides are available, and music is played on the our every hour with a repertoire ranging from classical and torch songs to waltzes and house music. Those who want to compose their

own little ditties can have lots of fun in the 'pling-plong' room. The presentation is unforgettable, though one wonders what Sister Bertken would make of it all.

Castles

The Bishops of Utrecht erected a number of castles to defend the region from the Dukes of Gelderland to the east and the Counts of Holland to the north. Many are still standing along the Rivers Kromme Rijn and Vecht. **Huis Doorn** (Doorn; off the A12 between Utrecht and Arnhem; www.huisdoorn.nl; Wed–Fri 1–5pm, Sat–Sun noon–5pm), built in the 14th century and rebuilt in the 18th century, was the residence of the deposed Kaiser Wilhelm II of Germany (1859–1941), who lived here from 1921 until his death. The Kaiser's former garage houses an exhibition on Dutch neutrality during World War I.

Before moving to Huis Doorn, the Kaiser lived (from 1918 to 1920) in **Kasteel Amerongen** (Amerongen; 8km/5 miles east of Doorn; www.kasteelamerongen.nl; Apr–Oct Tue–Sun

Castle Amerongen.

DRINK

Amersfoort used to be an important centre for brewing and its oldest pub, In den Grooten Slock (Zevenhuisen 1), is still open for business. You can try the town's current brews at Drie Ringen Bierbrouwerij (Kleine Spui 18; tel: 033-465 6575; Wed–Thu 2–7.30pm, Fri–Sun 1–7.30pm).

The medieval fortress city wall gate at Koppelpoort over the Eem River.

11am–5pm, Nov–Mar Thu–Sun 11am–5pm). This medieval castle, rebuilt in the 17th century, is one of the most interesting in Utrecht province, rich with furnishings and curiosities.

The aristocratic Van Zuylen family occupy a prominent place in Utrecht's history. Of their many castles in the province, the most interesting is **Kasteel De Haar**, 20km (12 miles) west of Utrecht (www.kasteeldehaar.nl; daily 11am–5pm). In the 19th century the ruined medieval castle was transformed into an ornate Gothic Revival edifice by Cuypers, architect of Amsterdam's Rijksmuseum. An entire village was demolished to create the extensive castle gardens. Just north of Utrecht on the River Vecht lies Slot Zuylen, another family pile. The castle is a curious mixture of medieval turrets and 18th-century Baroque.

Medieval Amersfoort

Amersfoort ❽ is a sober provincial town on the River Eem, 23km (14 miles) northeast of Utrecht, with small, neat houses and simple Gothic chapels. Its traditional industries were brewing, weaving and tobacco, and in the Middle Ages it was an important place of pilgrimage. The main reason to come here is to visit **Het Mondriaanhuis** (Kortegracht 11; Tue–Fri 11am–5pm, Sat–Sun noon–5pm), the home of leading De Stijl artist Piet Mondrian (1872–1944), which includes a reconstruction of his 1920s Paris studio.

An old town by Dutch standards, Amersfoort's first wall dates from about the 12th century. It was presumably a prosperous place, as a new wall was begun in the 14th century, enclosing a much larger area. The **Muurhuizen** (wall houses), which stand on the foundations of the inner city wall, are an unusual feature. They form an almost complete circle of lanes, which makes a very attractive walk through the old town (beginning from the Museum Flehite). The outline of the old wall can still be seen quite clearly in the façade of Groot Tinnenburg at 25 Muurhuizen.

At the northern end of Muuirhuizen is the **Museum Flehite** (Westsingel 50; Tue–Fri 11am–5pm, Sat–Sun noon–5pm). It contains a local history collection, including painful reminders of a camp for deportees built during World War II in the suburbs of Amersfoort. When the second town wall was demolished in the 19th century, some parks were laid out on the site, as in Utrecht. Several medieval gates are still standing from the second ring, including the unusual **Koppelpoort** near the Museum Flehite, a 15th-century watergate on the River Eem defended by two towers. Amersfoort's main church, the **Onze Lieve Vrouwekerk** (Church of Our Lady), was destroyed in the 18th century by an accidental explosion. All that is left is the 98-metre (320ft) -high **tower**, a replica of the Domtoren in Utrecht, which can be climbed with a guide (book via the VVV next door).

Rebels with a cause

Utrecht has a history of producing unconventional women, from hermit nuns and revolutionaries to aristocratic authors and a wannabe architect who influenced 1920s house design.

Utrecht may seem strait-laced compared with Amsterdam, yet it counts many radical women among its citizens. In 1529 a certain Zuster (Sister) Bertken made the bold resolution, at the age of only 30, to retreat from the world in a bricked-up cell in the choir of the Buurkerk. At that time, this part of the church was older and considerably lower than the nave, and the church authorities decided they should replace it. They had to wait until 1586, however, when Sister Bertken finally died at the age of 87.

Catharina van Leemputte was a spirited local woman who, in 1577, headed a band of women in an attack on Vredenburg citadel, which had become a symbol of Spanish tyranny during the Dutch Revolt. As a result of this women's revolt, little remains of Vredenburg except for some fragments of masonry near the tourist office.

Isabella Agneta van Tuyll van Serooskerken was born in Utrecht in 1740. She came from a powerful local aristocratic family, which owned numerous castles and houses in Utrecht province. Adopting the pen-name of Belle van Zuylen, she published *Le Noble*, a satirical novella involving a foolish aristocrat who inhabited a crumbling castle clearly modelled on one owned by her father, who promptly forbade Belle to write any more novels; she reverted to letter writing.

Architectural trailblazer

Truus Schröder was a 20th-century rebel. Her burning ambition was to be an architect, but there were no openings for women when she was young. When her husband died in 1923, she decided to build herself a new house, and enlisted the help of the Utrecht architect Gerrit Rietveld. Together they designed a small family house that permanently changed the direction of Dutch architecture. The Rietveld-Schröder house was tacked on to the end of a row of dull 19th-century houses in a calculated attempt to shock the bourgeoisie of Utrecht. The exterior is

reminiscent of an abstract painting by Mondrian, with flat surfaces rendered in red, blue, yellow and various shades of grey. To give the house a truly modern appearance, the external brick walls were concealed under a layer of plaster.

The interior design is equally radical, and its most striking feature is the ingenious method by which all the dividing walls can be folded away to create a single room. Rietveld was particularly adept at inventing space-saving solutions, such as a bathroom door that doubles as a slide projector screen and a cupboard in the hall that holds a child's wooden beach cart (designed by Rietveld and now in the Centraal Museum in Utrecht).

This unconventional partnership took a more personal turn when Gerrit Rietveld moved into the house, working in a studio on the ground floor originally intended as a garage. Up until 1963, the house enjoyed an enviable situation on the southern edge of the city. In 1963 this situation was shattered by the construction of an elevated section of the N222 ring road a few yards from the house. This proved too much for Rietveld, who died the following year – a victim of the modern age that he and Truus Schröder had done so much to create.

The Rietveld Schröder House.

Cadzand-Bad beach huts.

ZEELAND

This cluster of islands, linked to the mainland by dykes and dams, is Holland's sunniest spot, with beaches and nature reserves.

Zeeland ('Sealand') is well named. The southwestern province seems more part of the North Sea than of the Netherlands, to which it is so tenuously attached. Even in a country where a close, stormy relationship with the sea is the stuff of legend and everyday life, Zeeland seems a place apart, isolated from the mainstream of Dutch life, slashed by great jagged stretches of water.

In the past, this detachment was even more pronounced, as illustrated by old maps of Zeeland. The further back in time you go, the more the landscape breaks up into a pattern of little islands, all below sea level, uncertainly protected by dykes and dunes. As the centuries rolled past, the Dutch patiently stitched these islands together with typical ingenuity and hard work. That process is as complete as it is ever likely to be. The former islands now form long peninsulas connected to the mainland and Zeeland has emerged from isolation. Two factors more than any others have accounted for this: disaster and tourism. Disaster struck – not for the first time – during the night of 1 February 1953, when a deadly combination of tide and storm sent the North Sea crashing through the protective dykes and across the spirit-level-flat landscape beyond. More than 1,800 people lost their lives and there was immeasurable destruction.

Cycling in Zeeland.

Protection plan

The Delta Plan, a decades-long project subsequently launched to shut out the North Sea for ever, has, as a by-product, given Zeeland superb road links along which visitors pour from the rest of the Netherlands and neighbouring countries. They discover a land of vast horizons infiltrated on every side by lakes and sea channels, a water wonderland of beaches and harbour towns. There are few urban centres, though now sleepy villages once sent their adventurous spirits as

Main Attractions
Delta Park
Zierikzee Old Town
Yerseke mussels
Stadhuis, Middelburg

TIP

Take a boat tour.
Rondvaart Middelburg
(Achter de Houttuinen 39;
tel: 011-864 3272;
wwwrondvaartmiddelburg.nl)
takes passengers on a
tour of the Middelburg
canals, past the old Dutch
East India Company
warehouses, in a 54-
seater open-top boat
from April to October.
Frisia Rondvaarten (Het
Luitje 2; tel: 016-665
4321; http://frisiarondvaar
ten.nl) in Zierikzee regularly offers seal safaris
and other boat trips.

explorers and merchants to the farthest reaches of the globe. New Zealand is just one legacy of Zeeland's seafaring traditions. Tourism, fishing and farming are Zeeland's main sources of wealth. The first two depend on the ever-present sea, which, though it has threatened much, has given much in return. The third comes from superb farmland created by centuries of land reclamation. Fields that stretch endlessly under broad skies, market garden centres and orchards ensure that Zeeland will never go hungry.

Two-wheel benefits

There is no better way to explore Zeeland than on a bicycle. At the busiest times in summer, traffic is often bumper-to-bumper on the main roads. This gives a misleading impression of a congested province – Zeeland is too big to get congested and its back roads are a largely unused resource. On a bike you can escape from sweltering traffic jams in minutes, and pedal into another world of pretty villages and quiet cafés, little islands of civilisation in a sea of green fields. Zeeland has

no hills so it is perfect for cycling, but watch out for unobstructed winds that make the going harder.

You can hire bicycles in most towns and at main railway stations. There are signposted cycling routes all over Zeeland; you can get information on these from most local tourist (VVV) offices. If touring by car, the signposted **Delta Route** combines all aspects of the Zeeland experience – town, country, coast, history and the Delta works. The province-wide route breaks down into easily managed segments covering each of the islands and Zeeuws Vlaanderen. Information is available from VVV offices.

The Delta works

The Delta stretches across the mouths of the Rhine, Maas, Waal and Schelde rivers that all drain into the North Sea. What were once islands are now linked to each other and the mainland by the giant causeways of dams, barriers and raised dykes. Begun soon after the 1953 disaster, these huge dams and movable barriers that form the Delta works have become tourist attractions in their own

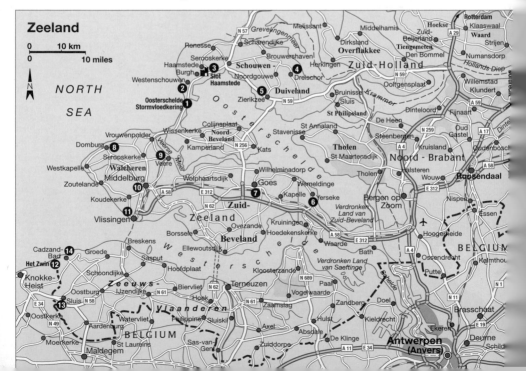

right. Over a period of 30 years and at immense cost, sea inlets that pierced Zeeland's coast were closed off, leaving it at the mercy of the North Sea, shortening the coastline by 700km (440 miles) and forming sheltered lakes that are a paradise for watersports and nature lovers. Coastal and river dykes were also raised and strengthened. The scale of these engineering works defies the imagination.

On the highways that sit on top of them, travellers flow effortlessly from one former island to another. Pride of place goes to the **Oosterschelde Stormvloedkering** ❶ (Eastern Schelde Storm Surge Barrier), which opened in 1986 after a 10-year construction programme. In bad weather, the Barrier's 65 enormous gates can be slammed shut on the North Sea, while at other times they remain open to preserve the inlet's valuable saltwater shellfish beds and mudflats.

Delta Park (tel: 0111-655655; www. neeltjejans.nl; Apr–Oct daily 10am–5.30pm, mid-July–Aug until 6pm) on Neeltje Jans, an artificial island in the middle of the Eastern Scheldt, tells the story of Zeeland's 2,000-year struggle with the sea. Models demonstrate the 1953 flood and the operation of the Storm Surge Barrier, and you can go on a boat trip to see the real thing. You can also visit the aquarium and Whale World, see sea lion shows, take a boat trip and splash around in the waterpark. Nearby is the unmanned Visitor Centre for the **Oosterschelde National Park** (daily 10am–5pm, June–Aug until 9pm), which has an exhibition, a film on local sea life and an interactive map of things to do in the area.

Other works protect threatened areas in Zeeland, and yet more lie to the north in the delta area of neighbouring Zuid-Holland province. The sea still presents a threat – albeit a much diminished one – and it's said that no one sleeps soundly in Zeeland when the North Sea rages beyond the defensive walls.

Schouwen and Duiveland islands

It's as well that the sea offers compensations – and Zeeland takes advantage of every one of them. Coming into the province by the coast road from Rotterdam, over the broad back of the Brouwersdam, you arrive at the one-time islands of **Schouwen** and **Duiveland**. On the seafront, 17km (11 miles) of magnificent sands form the main attraction, with beach cafés at strategic points. Behind the beach are 1,100 hectares (2,750 acres) of dunes – hilly, sandy terrain criss-crossed by a network of paths that are great for walking, cycling and horse riding. Campsites have been tucked out of sight behind the dunes, yet between holidaymakers and day-trippers even this amount of beach fills up on sunny summer days.

From **Westenschouwen** ❷ beach you have a fine view of the Storm Surge Barrier, and its serried ranks of giant towers stretching into the distance. You can get an even better view by taking a flight on a glider from nearby Nieuw-Haamstede airfield and

The Eastern Scheldt storm surge barrier (Oosterscheldekering).

asking the pilot to swing out over the water. The small towns of Schouwen are mostly residential. **Slot Haamstede** ❸ is a castle with elements from the 13th century and a well-appointed Ridderzaal (Hall of Knights). Near **Burgh-Haamstede** it is worth a visit. Further east, the north coast of Duiveland is a windsurfer's paradise. The now freshwater **Grevelingenmeer** (Grevelingen Lake) provides a huge expanse, ideal for practising. There is fishing, too, with boat trips leaving from the harbour villages of **Scharendijke** and **Brouwershaven**.

The farmland interior of Duiveland offers motorists – and cyclists even more so – one of Zeeland's delights: exploring side roads that lead either nowhere in particular, or to tiny villages, identifiable only by their church towers, that appear from the haze on the horizon. **Dreischor** ❹, neat and peaceful, its 14th-century church ringed by a canal and a circle of enchanting houses, is foremost among these must-see Zeeland gems.

In **Zierikzee** ❺, founded around 800, Duiveland has one of Holland's most elegant towns, so nearly perfect that you could easily believe beauty to have been its creators' prime requirement. Though the approach to Zierikzee is through unappealing modern suburbs, the road soon brings you to the old town's attractive cobbled streets, rows of stately merchants' houses and snug sailors' cottages dating from the 16th to the 18th centuries, and a medieval harbour, fronted by two towers.

Zierikzee looks like an open-air museum but is a living town, with *gezellig* (cosy and friendly) bars and some fine restaurants. The recently renovated **Stadhuismuseum** (Town Hall Museum; Meelstraat 6–8; Apr–Oct Tue–Sat 11am–5pm, Sun 1–5pm, July–Aug also Mon 1–5pm, Nov–Mar Tue–Sun 1–5pm) has a fascinating collection of objects relating to the town's heyday, including what is said to be the oldest kayak in the world.

Zeeland's least developed 'island Tholen, and neighbouring **St Philipsland**, bordering the adjacent province of Noord-Brabant, are mainly agricultural. Their long coastline

Mussels growing with water-plants on the beach at low tide.

ZEELAND FLEXES ITS MUSSELS

Before starting their journey to consumers' plates, Zeeland mussels rest in beds off Yerseke in the Oosterschelde (Eastern Scheldt) estuary. Whip-like branches sticking out of the shallow water mark the location of each merchant's 'parcel'. During April and May, fishing boats 'plant' mussel-seed: young mussels that will form next year's crop. By the time they have grown to 4 or 5cm (1.5 or 2ins), they have joined together in dense carpets for mutual support against tidal pull. The boats scoop them up and move them to other parcels, called 'wet warehouses', which are freer of sand, for the final two-week growth to maturity. At between 6 and 7cm (2.5 and 3ins), they are ready for harvesting.

At this stage, the mud-encrusted mussels would scarcely be appealing to devotees. The salt tang of the sea merges with danker smells dredged up from the bottom. They spend between 4 and 16 hours in the merchant's treatment works being sluiced by constantly running sea water to remove sand and other impurities. Each mussel filters more than 50 litres (11 gallons) of water a day. A falconer employed by the Mussel Bureau at Bergen op Zoom helps keep seagulls, and their guano, away from the mussel beds. You can find out about the industry at the OosterscheldeMuseum (Kerkplein 1; www.oosterscheldemuseum.nl; Tue–Sat 9.30am–12.30pm, 1–4pm) in Yerseke.

provide plenty of watersports opportunities, and they are quieter and closer to the mainland than Zeeland's main tourist centres. Sport fishing is the main draw on Tholen. Boats leave from **Stavenisse** harbour, and anglers take up position along the shore. A nature reserve near **Sint Maartensdijk** attracts birdwatchers and ramblers.

An island once connected to its neighbours only by ferry, **Noord-Beveland** is now linked by one road to Schouwen-Duiveland via the Oosterschelde Storm Surge Barrier and the 5km (3-mile) -long Zeeland toll bridge, and by two other dam-top roads to its southern companions, Walcheren and Zuid-Beveland. Agriculture, fishing and tourism are the main activities here. The freshwater Veerse Meer (Lake Veere) is an exceptional yachting and windsurfing area, and the Schotsman holiday centre just behind the Veersegat dam recalls nearby Veere's former maritime trading links with Scotland. Like the rest of Zeeland, Noord-Beveland's coastline is dotted with picturesque fishing villages such as Colijnsplaat, and

yachting harbours like Kortgene on the Veerse Meer.

Fruits of the sea

Off **Yerseke** ❻, on the eastern landward coast of **Zuid-Beveland**, lies one of the reasons why a movable barrier rather than a solid dam was built to protect the Eastern Scheldt. Zeeland mussels and oysters are renowned for their quality, and special deliveries rush the pick of the crop from Yerseke's auction house to fancy shops and restaurant tables across Europe. Eating a steaming potful of mussels is an essential Zeeland experience.

During the mussel season, between July and April, a stream of fishing boats from Yerseke lift ton after ton of 'black gold' from offshore beds. Restaurants throughout Zeeland brandish *Zeeuwse Mosselen* signs and a feeding frenzy for this fresh, inexpensive delicacy develops. (The finest are exported to Belgium, where demand is even greater.) A visit to Yerseke's mussel auction is a must.

One of the province's few large towns, **Goes** ❼, on Zuid-Beveland,

Canal scene in Goes.

FACT

In 1944, during operations to clear the approaches to Antwerp harbour, Allied planes bombed Walcheren's dykes, flooding the island and forcing its heavily entrenched German defenders to withdraw. It was the first of many battles in this area that were part of the Anglo-Canadian Operation Infatuate and the wider Battle of the Scheldt.

has added a modern shopping centre to its Zeeland Renaissance-style town and harbour front, but the Tuesday market in the Grote Markt makes for a more colourful shopping experience, as local women dress in traditional Zeeland costume. Old-world charm also lives on in the **Zuid-Beveland Stoom Trein** (South Beveland Steam Train; tel: 011-327 0705; www.destoomtrain.nl; Apr–Dec, times vary), that puffs its leisurely way southwards from Goes through a beautiful landscape of dykes, lakes and woods.

Zeeland's two most important transport arteries, the A58 motorway and the only regular railway line, run through Zuid-Beveland. They connect Goes, Middelburg and the busy port of Vlissingen with the 'mainland'; both are crowded during summer peak times.

Walcheren

Zeeland is a holiday area par excellence, and **Walcheren** is its star performer. Ringed by beaches and dunes, the historic island is a magnet for beach lovers, but even at the busiest times of year there always seem to be wide stretches of sand that no one has occupied.

The North Sea and Westerschelde coasts together form the most obvious attraction, with a constellation of small resort towns that shelter behind the dunes, rather fancifully dubbed the 'Zeeland Riviera'. The principal resort is **Domburg** ❽, where people have come for centuries to take the curative waters, and where, in the early 1900s, an artists' colony developed that counted Mondrian among its number. A 7km (4.5-mile) bike ride away is the quieter resort of **Westkapelle**, with its giant lighthouse, and not much further, the small resort of **Zoutelande**. Hotels, campsites and bed and breakfast lodgings are plentiful.

From the Westerschelde shore, you can watch an endless parade of cargo ships of all sizes streaming through the narrow (and unfortunately polluted) estuary, heading into or out of Antwerp.

On the banks of the Veerse Meer stands picturesque **Veere** ❾, a well-preserved medieval town with Gothic town hall built in the 1470s

Walcheren groynes.

that has a 48-bell carillon in its Renaissance belfry, and a 15th-century fortified harbour tower, the **Campveerse Toren**, now a hotel and restaurant. Veere once held a monopoly on the Scottish wool trade, and beside the harbour, at 25 and 27 Kade, are the two 16th-century **Schotse Huizen**, which were once the offices and warehouses of prosperous Scottish wool merchants. Nearby **Vrouwenpolder** has a tranquil beach on the Veerse Meer, with the adjacent North Sea shut out by the Veerse Gatdam.

Middelburg

Middelburg ⑩, the provincial capital, is a busy yet elegant canalside town of 48,000 inhabitants, whose beautifully ornamented **Stadhuis** (guided tours daily at 3pm via the tourist office) on the Markt (Market Square) is one of the Netherlands' finest town halls. The Gothic façade dates from the 15th century, and the belfry is 55 metres (180ft) tall.

Zeeland's provincial government is housed in the old **Abdij** (abbey) founded in the 12th century, part of the abbey complex that dominates the town centre. Festivals are held in the square throughout the year. Its famous spire, known as **Lange Jan** (Long John) (tel: 011-847 1010; opening times vary), looms 91 metres (300ft) above the town. The view of Middelburg and Walcheren from its upper reaches makes the climb worthwhile.

The ancient Romans had a fleet base in this area, and at the **Zeeuws Museum** (Zeeland Museum; www.zeeuwsmuseum.nl; Tue–Sun 11am–5pm) in the abbey, you can see Roman finds that include an altar and votive offerings to a local sea goddess, Nehallenia. Other rooms display 16th- and 17th-century tapestries depicting naval actions during Holland's war of independence against Spain, Chinese porcelain, furniture, silverware, traditional Zeeland costumes, and more besides.

Visitors from the United States may be interested in the **Roosevelt Study Centre** (tel: 0118-631 590; www.roosevelt.nl; contact in advance about visiting; free). It covers local historical aspects of US presidents Theodore and Franklin D. Roosevelt, whose

The terraces are packed on a hot and sunny day in Middelburg.

ancestors emigrated from Zeeland to America in the 1640s.

Frequently choked beyond its capacity with peak-time summer traffic, Middelburg is the hub of Zeeland. Many of the town's cafés and restaurants merit the prized description *gezellig*, and its cobbled streets reward the casual stroller.

Miniatuur Walcheren (tel: 011-847 1010; www.minimundi.nl; opening times vary) in Molenwater Park is a walk-through depiction of the island, showing scaled-down models of its main buildings and centres seen from a bird's-eye view. Its miniature houses, churches and public buildings are brilliantly executed. Radio-controlled trains and boats, and Lilliputian carillons add to the sense of realism. There is also a small amusement park and indoor play area.

Vlissingen

Vlissingen  (Flushing) is the industrial heart of Zeeland and an important port, with a ferry service across the Westerschelde to Zeeuws Vlaanderen. On a stroll through the old town, you can visit the Oude Kerk (Old Church), dating from 1308 but restored after a fire in 1911, and the muZEEum (Maritime Museum; Nieuwendijk 11; Mon–Fri 10am–5pm, Sat–Sun 1–5pm, Dec–Mar closed Mon), which explores Zeeland's maritime past and present on four themes – water, work, glory and adventure – set in four buildings dating from the 16th to 21st century. The sea-wall walkway offers a pleasant promenade beside the harbour and another view of Antwerp-bound cargo ships. A statue of the famous 17th-century admiral Michiel de Ruyter gazes out across the water.

Zeeuws Vlaanderen

Just as Zeeland seems a place apart from the Netherlands, its southernmost section, **Zeeuws Vlaanderen** (Zeeland Flanders), bordering Belgium, is different from the rest of the province. The area is connected to the rest of Zeeland by car ferries, which operate between Breskens and Vlissingen in the west, and Perkpolder and Kruiningen in the east. Road links run through Belgium's Flemish region, specifically via Antwerp.

The old harbour in Vlissingen, lined with sailing boats and old houses.

At both its western and eastern extremities are nature reserves associated with that inexhaustible Zeeland resource: water. In the east is the **Verdronken Land van Saeftinge** (Drowned Land of Saeftinge), a birdwatcher's paradise comprising mudflats once reclaimed from the Schelde and now mostly taken back by the river. On the North Sea coast is another birdlife sanctuary, **Het Zwin** ⑫, which continues across the border into Belgium.

Sluis ⑬, on the border, is possibly better-known in Belgium than in the Netherlands, because many Belgians hide their 'black' money from the taxman in its banks and patronise the town's numerous porn shops and sex clubs – some cultured souls might even pause to glance at the Stadhuis (Town Hall), which has the only surviving 14th-century belfry in the Netherlands, although it had to be rebuilt after being knocked down in 1944. The Golden Age artist Jacob Van Loo (1614–70) was born here, but, due to the destruction of the city's archives in World War II, little is known about his early life.

Beaches and mussels

There are popular beaches around **Cadzand-Bad** ⑭, from where it is possible to walk through Het Zwin to the nearby Belgian resort **Knokke-Heist**. Other handsome Belgian cities – among them Bruges, Ghent and Antwerp – lie within a short distance of the border.

Along the canal from Terneuzen to Gent, the terrain is mostly industrial, although there is another nature zone nearby at **De Braakman**, a former inlet on the Westerschelde, which is now dammed off to form a lake.

Philippine, a neighbouring village, is the place to go for mussels. It has some of the best mussel restaurants in this part of Zeeland and has become a place of pilgrimage for mussel fanciers. Try De Oude Haven (Waterpoortstraat 3; tel: 011-549 1691; www.deoudehaven.com) or Mosselbank (Havenstraat 9; tel: 011-549 1576; www.mosselbank.nl).

As in most of Zeeland, fishing in Zeeuws Vlaanderen is a primary recreation; you can make sea-fishing trips from **Breskens** and **Terneuzen**.

Stork at Het Zwin.

NOORD-BRABANT

From the carnivals of Den Bosch and
Bergen to the forests of the Biesbosch,
the south caters for many moods.

Main Attractions

Biesbosch National Park
Sint Janskathedraal, Den
   Bosch
Jheronimus Bosch Art
   Center, Den Bosch
Van Abbe Museum,
   Eindhoven
Van Gogh Museum
   Vincentre, Nuenen

Noord-Brabant (North Brabant) is one of the country's largest provinces. A variety of landscapes are contained within its boundaries, including forests, moorland (in De Kempen) and fens (in De Peel). Its northern limits are bounded by the River Maas (Meuse), to the south it borders Belgium and the east adjoins hilly Limburg. Apart from the polderland west of Breda, most of the province lies above sea level.

During the 15th century, the southern provinces were ruled by the Dukes of Burgundy, whose legacy is reflected in the culture and religion of North Brabant. The Catholic influence is still strongly felt. Religious festivals are important events on the calendar, and carnival (see page 233), so much a part of Dutch life today, is celebrated with as much enthusiasm and colour as it was during the southern Golden Age.

own of a thousand perils

ounded in the 9th century in the astern reaches of the River Schelde stuary, **Bergen op Zoom** ❶ developed as an independent, fortified arbour town. Thanks to its powerl defences, it fended off five Spanh sieges between 1581 and 1622, efore yielding to the French in '47. Though its fortifications were molished in 1868 and the shabby

Botermarkt (Butter Market) is no longer full of sailors' wives, Bergen's centre still has pockets of architectural splendour, grand red-brick warehouses and glinting weathervanes in the shapes of mermaids and dolphins.

The Oosterschelde coastline around Bergen op Zoom is a classic Dutch setting: polderland so flat it looks as if it's been ironed, windmills and sea. In the great flood of 1953, this part of Noord-Brabant went under the waves and rowing boats bobbed in Bergen's streets. Now, guarded by the distant

The old town square in Bergen op Zoom.

ramparts of Zeeland's Oosterschelde Storm Surge Barrier (see page 213), shoppers flood the Dutch Renaissance town centre and soak up the atmosphere in the Markiezenhof's illuminated courtyard.

In the **Grote Markt**, the main square, reminders of Bergen's stormy past include an inscription from 1611 on the Stadhuis (Town Hall) that says *Mille pericula supersum* (I overcome a thousand perils), referring to fears of flood, fire and lack of faith in the declared Spanish truce. The first Town Hall was destroyed by fire in 1397, and the builders of this one seemingly lacked confidence in their handiwork's survival. As Bergen op Zoom expanded, so did the Stadhuis, swallowing up the adjoining English Merchant Centre and a burgher's house.

Also in the Grote Markt is a Gothic bell tower topped by an 18th-century pepper-pot lantern turret, the Peperbus, added after much of the church was destroyed by fire in 1747. This is all that remains of the 14th-century Sint Gertruidiskerk (St Gertrude's church), whose motto could just as easily have been 'I fail to overcome a thousand perils'. The church was looted in 1580 and destroyed in 1747 by the French. A replacement burned down in 1972.

At night, the pepper-pot tower, gold weathervane and herringbone brick are illuminated. Around the square, restaurants and open-air cafés serve traditional local delicacies, such as asparagus and oysters.

Northwest of the Grote Markt, in Steenbergsestraat, is the town's finest building, the **Markiezenhof**, former palace of the Marquises of Bergen op Zoom. Although comparable to The Hague's Ridderzaal, the 15th- to 16th-century Markiezenhof is closer in spirit to the architecture of Bruges in Belgium than to any other building in the Netherlands. An imposing gateway leads to an illuminated inner courtyard adorned by a delicate gallery and well. Inside this part of the palace is the **City & Region History Museum** (Tue–Sun 11am–5pm) which displays a mixture of Flemish tapestries and Louis XV furniture, as well as a Fairground Museum.

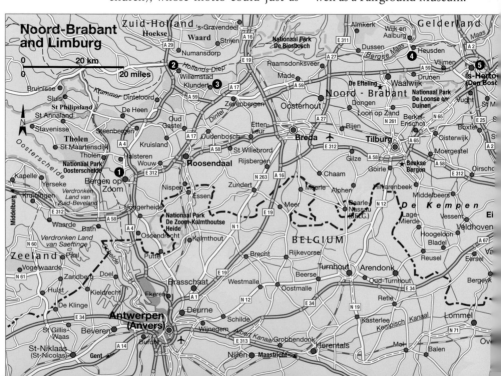

Nearby, visit the **Gevangenpoort** (also known as Lieve Vrouwepoort), Bergen's only remaining medieval gateway. Gothic in style and Flemish in spirit, this turreted stone and red-brick gateway is now a focus of the town's pre-Lenten carnival procession (see page 233). Its prison (Tue–Sun, times vary by season) has been restored and now visitors can learn about its history and former residents.

Northwards to Willemstad

From Bergen op Zoom, the N259 leads north across the polders to **Willemstad ❷**, a handsome village on the Hollands Diep and formerly a fortress town with a strategic importance far beyond its size. Approaching Willemstad, the wide estuary of the **Hollands Diep** comes into view. Cars on the raised road into the town are dwarfed by the slow-moving barges on the Diep. If you are willing to face the wind that blasts the observation tower at the southern end of the **Haringvlietbrug** (Herring River Bridge), overlooking the nearby Volkerak sluice, you'll be rewarded with a view

of marine traffic jams, as barges queue to pass through locks connecting the Rivers Maas and Waal with ports in southwest Holland. An information board modestly points out that Dutch barges handle 70 percent of Western Europe's canal and river traffic.

A narrow bridge leads into Willemstad's star-shaped bastions, a stronghold bounded by canals, moats and the Hollands Diep. In 1583, William the Silent completed the transformation of a fishing village, celebrated for its herring catches, into a fortress town that he named after himself. Built to guard the entrance to the Hollands Diep, Willemstad is one of the best-maintained fortress towns in the country, its perfect geometry shown in 17th-century prints, topographical maps and aerial photographs.

The compact town is centred on the inner harbour, now a marina full of Dutch, Belgian and German boats.

A walk past outdoor cafés, clog shops and a half-hidden disco suggests that Willemstad is only a thin shell concealing a modern bazaar, yet tourism never swamps local life.

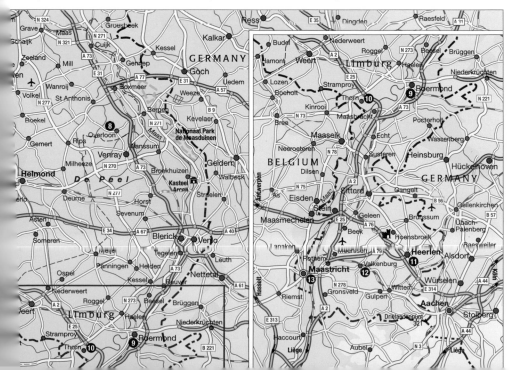

TIP

A relaxing way to explore the Biesbosch National Park is by bike. Dordrecht station is a good place to rent bicycles, and the VVV supplies brochures with suggested cycle routes. It's about a half-hour ride from town to the reserve's northern perimeter. You can also find out about cycling, and other activities, on the Park's website www.np-debiesbosch.nl

Biesbosch's distinctive landscape.

Neat white houses, duck-filled canals and tiny wooden bridges may make Willemstad look unreal, but this is an illusion. The octagonal **Reformed Church**, from 1607, surrounded by a shady cemetery, was one of the Netherlands' first Protestant churches. Enclosed by a small moat, it lies at the end of a leafy arbour. A short walk brings you to the **Oranjemolen**, a cosy 18th-century windmill beside the ramparts and the old outer harbour, beyond which is a wide estuary dotted with barges.

From the ramparts, a long walk leads along the old fortifications and main canals, while a shorter walk traces smaller waterways back to the inner harbour. Behind the inner harbour, perched like anthills on top of the star-shaped bastions, are concrete bunkers from World War II. Nearby is a cemetery for 134 Belgian prisoners-of-war who died in 1940 when their ship struck a mine.

If you are tired and hungry at this point, stop at the **Arsenal**, rebuilt in 1793 by the French and now a restaurant, which is as good a place as

any to recall the time when Willemstad was the main fishing port on the Haringvliet.

The Reed Forest

From Willemstad, an inland route leads past Oudemolen, Klundert, Zevenbergen and Made to Drimmelen, a village that makes a good base for exploring the nearby wetlands in the Biesbosch National Park. The most appealing village on the route is **Klundert ❸**, which has a free-standing, Flemish Renaissance **Stadhuis**, with a well, double staircase and lion statues reflected in its blue-green windows. Facing the Town Hall, the renovated **Prinsenhof** bears the town's blue-and-yellow insignia.

Drimmelen, an unremarkable port on the River Maas, is the gateway to the watery wilderness known as De Biesbosch (Reed Forest). The flat dreary landscape around the village gives no hint of the ecologically rich wetlands beyond.

The **Biesbosch** (http://np-debiesbosch nl) owes its unique character to a great flood on St Elizabeth's Day, 1421

A PRINCELY RESIDENCE

Looking down on harbour is the **Mauritshuis** (Mon 1–5pm, Tue–Fri 9.30am–12.30pm and 1–5pm, Sat times vary), also known as the **Prinsenhof**, a severe, red-brick Dutch Renaissance building from 1623. Originally a hunting lodge for Prince Maurits (1567–1625), it was later the provincial governor's residence, then the Town Hall. It is now mainly used as a conference and events centre, although it is also open for individual visits to see the historic paintings and small exhibition about the house. A mermaid weathervane on the roof once graced the Markiezenhof in Bergen op Zoom and now enjoys a fine view of Willemstad's inner harbour, with its watchtower, warehouses, the old arsenal converted to a hotel, windsurfing school and seafood restaurant.

A storm broke the dykes along the Rivers Waal and Maas, flooding the polderland. The waters reached Geertruidenberg, Drimmelen and Heusden, turned Dordrecht into an urban island and created an inland sea. The *St Elizabeth's Day Panel* in Amsterdam's Rijksmuseum shows houses submerged to their gables, floating churches and marooned sheep. More than 10,000 people drowned and 70 villages were lost underwater.

Gradually, sludge and sand deposited by the Maas and Waal accreted, and the area became overgrown with rushes, reeds and willows. In 1685 and again in 1904 parts of the Biesbosch were reclaimed for farming and for gathering materials for thatching and basket-weaving. The opening of the Haringvlietdam in 1971 changed the ecological balance of the area. Today, the Biesbosch is an ever-changing pattern of water and land, but still home to rare plants and animals – among the latter are beavers, which are being reintroduced. As exhibits at the **Biesbosch Visitor's Centre** (Biesboschweg 4; Tue–Sun 10am–5pm;

free) suggest, you have plenty of opportunity to see what makes the Biesbosch the Netherlands' richest nature reserve. As you explore on foot, by boat or by bike (most tourist facilities are concentrated in a small area on the northern perimeter of the reserve, a few kilometres east of Dordrecht), look out for hawks and heron, swans and spoonbills, cormorants and kingfishers, as well as wild ducks and geese. Squirrels and bats inhabit the willows, and beavers and polecats may be lurking among the marsh marigold and yellow irises.

Easily reached southeast of Klundert, on the route towards Eindhoven, **Breda** is another pretty, historic town; a splendid Gothic cathedral overlooks its Grote Markt and, on the hill above, is the castle in which, in 1660, Charles II of England signed the declaration which restored the English monarchy.

Heusden

After the wild and scenic Biesbosch, civilisation beckons at **Heusden ❹**, an ancient fortified town similar to Willemstad, on the Maas east of

A windmill and wooden drawbridge in the fortress city of Heusden.

Drimmelen. After the Union of Utrecht was formed in 1579, Heusden declared allegiance to the Protestant cause and star-shaped bastions were built around its castle and harbour. Within the safety of the walls, an elegant canal-lined town thrived on boatbuilding, arms-dealing and herring-fishing. Heusden remained a Protestant stronghold and garrison town until the French invasion of 1795. Although shelled in 1940, the town has been restored to its 16th-century glory and, four centuries later, even the local trades remain little changed.

The liveliest spot in town is the former fish market, sandwiched between the butter market and the harbour. Both the **Vismarkt** and **Botermarkt** are framed by assymetrical gabled houses, many of them converted to fish restaurants. At one end of the Vismarkt is an incongruous-looking stone portico, built in 1591, that looks more like a Roman arch than the Custom House (Commiezenhuis) it is. But once you pass through the arch onto a wooden landing stage, the Vismarkt's hustle and bustle is forgotten. It's as if

Carnival is a major event in the city of 's-Hertogenbosch.

you've gone behind the looking-glass to be presented on the other side with an altogether calmer scene: a circular sheet of water, its surface unbroken but for reflections of a feathery tree, a miniature bridge, a raised windmill and a neat lock-keeper's house. The Dutchness of this scene lies in its scaled-down perfection and simulated naturalness.

Heusden, like an emblematic Dutch town, appears to grow organically out of the landscape. Yet the landscape is itself landscaped: the pool is a basin; the river a canal; the river banks ramparts and sea walls. Here, nature is unnatural, right down to the over-domesticated ducks.

Nor does the rest of the town disappoint in its Dutchness, from Gothic **Sint Catherinakerk** (St Catherine's church) to the functional Stadhuis, gabled houses and 17th-century market halls. As if for confirmation, there is yet another windmill, a tumbledown castle and the provincial governor's house, enclosed by courtyards and gardens. The Woonhuis also represents a very Dutch welcome: built

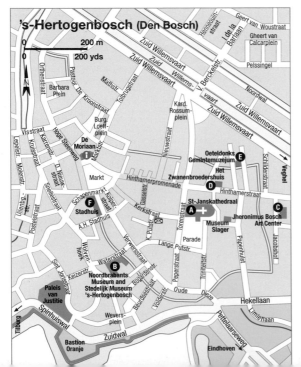

on the site of a medieval arms factory, this ornate 18th-century building remained a family-run armaments business until relatively recently.

For a traditional Dutch farewell, return to one of the fish restaurants around the Vismarkt and be comforted that the herring and hospitality are real.

The Duke's Woods

The Dutch call **'s-Hertogenbosch Den Bosch ❺**, pronounced 'Den Boss'. The full title means 'the Duke's Woods', a reference to the fact that the town grew up on the site of a 12th-century hunting lodge owned by Henry I, Duke of Brabant, who in 1185 gave the town its charter. Den Bosch flourished as a wool town and, after absorption by Burgundy in 1430, became a noted centre of the arts, whose most famous exponent was the painter Hieronymus Bosch (1450–1516). It was governed by Spain until 1629, when William the Silent's son took the town after a long siege.

When the Kingdom of the Netherlands was proclaimed in 1814, Den Bosch and the rest of Noord-Brabant soon joined it, while southern Brabant declared allegiance to Belgium. This division of allegiances has left its mark on Den Bosch, which is moored to the Netherlands politically and economically, though the stronger cultural pull is towards Catholic Flanders and the hearty tastes that characterised the old Burgundian Empire.

In today's Den Bosch, rustic cuisine, locally brewed beer, a noisy carnival and lively cultural scene ensure that Burgundian instincts survive. There are classical concerts and modern dance, and the North Brabant Orchestra in residence at the Schouwburg, near the cathedral. The shape of the old city, a triangle centred on the cathedral and bounded by the Binnendieze, the inner canals, has changed little.

The Netherlands' Gothic masterpiece

A visit to Den Bosch opens with a view of soaring **Sint Janskathedraal ❹** (St John's Cathedral; Apr–Oct daily 8am–5pm, Nov–Mar Mon–Sat 8am–4pm, Sun 9am–5pm; free), the greatest

Sint Janskathedraal at 's-Hertogenbosch.

The Catholic south

Like many other countries, the Netherlands has a north-south divide – with each self-righteous side not missing an opportunity to point out the other's shortcomings.

'The Dutch are half-baked, without fire, melancholy and stale' was the damning judgement of Lepeintre, the 19th-century French traveller to the Calvinistic northern provinces. By contrast, the southern provinces have always revelled in their Burgundian heritage. As the Dutch specialist, William Shetter, puts it: 'Residents of the southern provinces may well feel themselves to be religious, bourgeois and dominant, but they do not easily fit the Dutch stereotype of unemotional, reserved or earnest.'

Instead, these latter-day Burgundians pride themselves on their warmth and generosity and accuse their northern neighbours of meanness. In fact, niggling miserliness *(krenterigheid)* is the

Looking out across the River Mark, with Ulvenhout church in the distance, Brabamt.

defect that southerners find synonymous with the Dutchness of Holland, along with the smugness known as 'Calvinistic fascism'.

The northerners are not slow to respond: southerner jokes feature in the standard cabaret routines of The Hague and Amsterdam. Southerners are mocked for their soft Flemish accents, liberal Catholicism and suspect morals. The term 'southern Lowlands' is something of a misnomer, since Noord-Brabant and Limburg form the High Netherlands, a mainly sandy region lying above sea level.

At the heart of differences are the great rivers forming the most prominent cultural boundary in the Netherlands. The term *'beneden de Moerdijk'* refers to people 'below the rivers', the Moerdijk being the wide river delta south of Rotterdam. The term can also embrace Belgian Flanders, thereby implying a Flemish solidarity which transcends or ignores modern boundaries.

Language differences

The Flemish are often called the only Romance people to speak a Germanic language, and certainly many southern Dutch feel a greater cultural affinity with the Belgian Flemish rather than with 'Hollanders', the northern Dutch. The origins of the southern provinces predate Dutch statehood. In the Middle Ages, Flemish culture was the predominant one in the region and, as a result, Noord-Brabant's medieval towns, such as Den Bosch, have more in common with Bruges and Leuven than with Amsterdam or The Hague.

From the 16th century the southern provinces were conquered by the Princes Maurits and Frederik Hendrik and, with the 1648 Treaty of Münster, became part of the United Provinces. Dutch Brabant and Limburg were allowed to remain Catholic but were otherwise alienated and excluded from power by the rising Dutch Republic. In the 17th century the Protestant Dutch Republic was a forward-looking maritime nation. By contrast, the southern provinces, populated by Flemish-speaking Catholics, looked to the rural hinterland and, alienated from the Dutch state, dwelled on past glories.

There was no equality of wealth until the late 19th century. The reversal of the cultural brain drain from south to north only began with the electronics-led economic boom, and more recently the region has been termed the 'silicon flatlands' thanks to its ability to attract high-tech industries.

Gothic church in the Netherlands and the most Flemish of cathedrals. **Parade**, the town's central square, accords Sint Janskathedraal the space it demands. Enough of its plain, Romanesque bell tower remains to provide a severe counterpoint to this flight of Gothic fantasy. But unadorned red brick loses out to Flamboyant Gothic at its most exuberant. As the house of Hieronymus Bosch overlooks the cathedral, you can imagine that the view of richly carved sculptures and surreal symbols must have wormed its way into the painter's work.

The cathedral was built between 1330 and 1550 and, in keeping with the religious politics of the Netherlands, switched its allegiance frequently. In 1629, it was seized by the Protestants but returned to the Catholics by Napoleon in 1810, a change more in tune with its spirit. You enter the cathedral through its great west door, your first impression being one of space followed by disappointment that a 1980 restoration has left it too neat and sparse, Dutch rather than Flemish.

The grandeur of conception is clear in the vaulted ceiling, yet the eye is drawn to artistic details. After looking at the magnificent organ, choir stalls and carved baptismal fonts, your gaze falls upon aisles decorated with statues of calm women staring at stony-faced men. One small chapel off the left aisle contains dramatic Byzantine icons, including a dark-faced Christ against a rich orange background.

In the north transept there are *grisaille* figures of the Virgin and St John, reputedly by Bosch, which originally decorated the cathedral's doors. Even in this minor work, there is a sense of the charge levelled against Bosch in his lifetime: 'He had the audacity to paint mankind as he is on the inside.' Ultimately declared a heretic, Bosch is not much celebrated in his home town. Most of his works are in Rotterdam's Boijmans Van Beuningen Museum and in the Prado in Madrid, to which Philip II spirited away his favourite Flemish treasures.

Nearby is the flowery, over-restored **Chapel of Our Lady**, which houses a 13th-century statue of the Virgin, traditionally associated with miracles. In

Market Square in historical 's-Hertogenbosch.

adjoining **St Anthony's Chapel**, the cathedral's finest work, the *Altar of the Passion*, is an early 16th-century panel-painting that depicts the life of Christ through a combination of vivid Flemish paintings and carved figures.

Noordbrabants Museum

Outside, in the bustling Parade cafés, a crowd drinks under the stern gaze of a statue of Bosch. The painter also supervises the Markt, site of the Town Hall and De Moriaan, the Duke of Brabant's fabled hunting lodge. Turning your back on Bosch, walk down **Verwersstraat**, to see among its attractive gables a 14th-century bakery, still in use, and, at No. 78, a façade decorated with Delft tiles.

A small alley, **Oud Bogardenstraatje**, leads over a canal to an enclosed gateway, a restored mews and a rear view of the **Noordbrabants Museum** Ⓑ (Tue–Sun 11am–5pm), its gardens dotted with modern sculpture.

This 18th-century patrician building houses a collection reflecting the province's medieval origins and Burgundian traditions. In addition, works by Brueghel and Rubens pay tribute

to the population's Flemish Catholic character. Van Gogh's paintings of Brabant peasants stress the region's rural roots and the painter's attachment to the wooded Meierij area outside town. The popularity of brooding works by Flemish-Belgian Expressionist Constant Permeke underlines the local affinity with Flemish culture, an affection that continues to transcend modern political boundaries.

Also on site is the **Stedelijk Museum 's-Hertogenbosch** (Tue–Sun 11am–5pm), which has a collection of ceramics and jewellery by leading contemporary artists and designers.

Reminders of Hieronymus Bosch

From the museum, narrow Beurdsestraat leads you back to Verwersstraat, and a left turn along Peperstraat returns you to the cathedral. En route, the mayor's gilded residence is indicated by a miniature **statue of Atlas**, his back burdened by the (minor) cares of office.

At the cathedral, turn right into **Hinthamerstraat**, once home to Bosch

The exterior of the Noordbrabants Museum.

HET NOORDBRABANTS MUSEUM

Sadly, the painter's undistinguished gabled house (No.74) has no architectural flights of fancy and is devoid of winged demons and gluttonous monks. The house grounds the imagination with the reminder that Bosch led a comfortable burgher's existence here, even though his works were collected fanatically by Burgundian and Spanish rulers, including Charles V and Philip II. Bosch is still seen as a solitary genius, belonging to no artistic school. The painter's spirit, if it lives at all in his home town, hovers above the cathedral gargoyles or floats into the city's Burgundian restaurants. Up the street, housed in a former church and its outbuildings, is the **Jheronimus Bosch Art Center** **C** (Jeroen Boschplein 2; tel: 073-612 6890; www.jheronimusbosch-artcenter.nl; Apr–Oct Tue–Fri 11am–5.30pm, Sat–Sun noon–5.30pm, Nov–Mar Tue–Sun noon–5pm). After learning about the artist's life and work and taking in the view of the town from the church spire, visitors can enjoy a meal in the brasserie of the charming, six-bedroom Stadshotel eroen next door.

Almost next door to the house of Bosch, **Het Zwanenbroedershuis** **D** Tue, Wed, Thu and Sun from 2pm) houses one of the country's oldest religious societies. Founded in 1318, the Swan Brotherhood is signalled by statues of the medieval stations in life, om lawyer to priest. Bosch belonged to this medieval society which, then now, promoted and popularised church music, religious art and encouraged Christian good works.

In 1629 the Brotherhood opened its doors to Protestants as well as Catholics and has attracted active support om the Dutch royal family ever since. though the Swan Brotherhood's all collection of antiques, books and tuary is rarely visited by foreigners, tch people find comfort in its musty, changing displays. The characteristic reverence shown by Dutch visitors tly explains – even if retrospectively osch's need to rebel. Turn up Zusters Orthenpoort street to check out

the **Oeteldonks Gemintemuzejum** **E** (National Carnival Museum; Tue–Sun 11am–5pm), which has a fascinating collection of costumes, film footage and music from carnivals around the world.

The rest of Hinthamerstraat's devotion to earthly pleasures is exemplified by the number of gabled shops and restaurants in adjoining streets, but older trade is suggested in Korte Waterstraat, a blind alley leading to the original town ramparts, and in the **Binnenhaven**, the Inner Harbour. To reach the Markt from the main train station turn right and walk along Visstraat in the direction of the centre *(centrum)*. Turn right at the end when you reach the Hoogsteenweg. It's worth stopping at the **Stadhuis** **F** (Town Hall; Mon–Fri 9am–5pm) for a closer look at the classical façade and carillon. If you happen to stop by on a Wednesday between 10 and 11am you will see mechanical horsemen trot out to its half-hourly chimes. The brasserie in the 16th-century cellar is also worth a visit.

Some 11km (7 miles) northwest of Den Bosch, medieval **Kasteel Ammersoyen** (Ammersoyen Castle; tel:

Kasteel Ammersoyen.

073-599 5506; Tue–Fri 11am–5pm, Sat–Sun 1–5pm) has been restored as closely as possible to its 14th-century condition, which means not much in the way of life's comforts and conveniences. You can tour the castle's interior apartments as well as the defensive works of the powerfully fortified, square keep, with its four round towers and moat.

South to Eindhoven

From Den Bosch, the motorway south to Eindhoven passes through **De Kempen**, an unspoilt region of woodland, heaths and sand dunes. Unlike coastal dunes that protect the inland plains, the sole function of these sands is to be the green lungs of the Den Bosch–Tilburg–Eindhoven industrial triangle. The landscape runs through deeply wooded river valleys until the trees peter out among dunes and broom-covered heath.

Until the 19th century De Kempen was neglected by inhabitants and visitors. The poet Potgieter poured scorn on the bleak landscape: 'Grey is your sky and stormy your beach. Naked are your dunes and flat your fields… Nature created you with a stepmother's hand.' Yet today's visitors appreciate these sandy expanses and horizons seemingly placed so low that the heath merges with the cloudy sky. The views towards Eindhoven are reminiscent of Van Ruysdael's spacious, forlorn landscapes.

Eindhoven ❻ needs to be placed in this rural perspective if it is not to be dismissed as a soulless metropolis. Often referred to as 'Philips Town', home of the multinational electrical company, the city can afford to be materialistic and monolithic because it has the countryside to keep it sane. De Kempen stretches south and west while the marshy Peel overlaps the Brabant-Limburg border. Now the high-tech centre of the Netherlands, Eindhoven was a mere village until the arrival of the Philips dynasty around 1900. Although no architectural beauty (it was heavily damaged during World War II, and rebuilt in modern style), Eindhoven has a reputation for its strikingly modern sculpture, inspired or funded by the family firm. Just outside the station is an imposing statue of Dr Anton Philips while, on Emmasingel, the original **Philips building** has been preserved complete with low-tech chimney and sculpted bust of G. L. Philips. Outside another Philips building, on Mathildelaan, is *Natuursteen*, Fred Carasso's tribute to nature in the form of a dancing globe-shaped bronze.

By contrast, Mario Negri's statue of an automaton on the central **Piazza** represents the dehumanising nature of city life. As if confirming this idea, it shields a sharply metallic library and clinical shopping centre; the only humour lies in the steel tubing designed to look like a cross-section of a Philips component.

Eindhoven's artistic focus is the **Van Abbemuseum** (10 Bilderdijklaan; www.vanabbemuseum.nl; Tue–Sun 11am–5pm, Thu until 9pm), which houses a unique modern art collection and puts on innovative exhibitions throughout the year. Set beside landscaped gardens on the

The old Philips factory building and modern building in the city centre of Eindhoven.

River Dommel, the museum was established by industrialist H. J. van Abbe. Cubist works by Picasso and Braque complement Surrealist paintings by Chagall and Delvaux, and Expressionist works by Kokoschka, Kandinsky and Permeke. The Dutch De Stijl movement, with Mondrian at the forefront, is well represented, as is the cobra school. Pop Art, conceptual art and modern German art feature prominently.

Van Gogh's Peel

As if to compensate for modern Eindhoven, the surrounding countryside contains much of historical interest, with Kempen farmhouses and, at **Heeze**, a 17th-century castle with period furniture and Gobelin tapestries. A quiet route from Eindhoven leads northeast to **Nuenen** ❼, Van Gogh's home village. In 1883 Van Gogh came to stay in the family rectory at Nuenen. Returning home was an admission of his defeat as a preacher in Belgium and followed a troubled relationship with Sien Hoornik, a prostitute and artist's model in The Hague. In Nuenen Van Gogh made his first studies of peasant life, spending more time in the fields than in his small studio. His sketches of faces and hands were awkward and rough, echoing the timbre of his life.

The culmination of the artist's explorations in Nuenen was the first of his early masterpieces, *De Aardappeleters* (*The Potato Eaters*). Vincent's brother, Theo, was at first shocked by the coarseness of the work but Van Gogh, equating manual labour with honesty, replied: 'These people, eating potatoes in the lamplight, have dug the earth with those very hands they put in the dish.'

Nuenen today is a shrine to Van Gogh; the rectory, with its green shutters and neat hedgerows, remains frozen in time. A monument honours the painter's memory, as does a permanent exhibition in the **Van Gogh Museum Vincentre** (Berg 29; tel: 040-283 9615; www.vangoghvillagenuenen.nl; Tue–Sun 11am–5pm), where you can experience the town through the artist's eyes and follow an outdoor trail of his painting locations. **Sint Clemenskerk**, the solitary, pointed church, is a reminder that the painter's friendship with the verger resulted in the loan of a studio. In 1885 Van Gogh's father died and the painter abandoned the Netherlands for Antwerp, Paris and the radiant Mediterranean light near Arles.

Just east of Nuenen is the mysterious **Peel** marshland. Its most characteristic sections, De Grote Peel and Helena Peel, are peatland nature reserves. For background information, visit the **Museum Klok & Peel** (Clock and Peel Museum; open Tue–Fri 9.30am–5pm, Sat–Mon 1–5pm) in **Asten,** which also has an internationally renowned collection of bells and clocks. This small town is the home of the **Royal Eijsbouts bellfoundry,** the world's largest manufacturer of bells and clocks, which has made bells for Notre Dame Cathedral in Paris and the 2012 London Olympics. For centuries this part of Noord-Brabant was deserted or, in the popular imagination, haunted by spirits, outlaws and vagabonds. In the 1850s, impoverished peat-cutters moved into the area,

Vincentre interior.

using the old defensive canals for transporting peat. As the peat was removed, bogs and lakes gradually formed and, in the process, attracted black-headed gulls and marsh birds. The lakes were not drained and transformed into polders because the soil underlying the peat is sandy and infertile.

Reforestation has turned parts of De Peel into heath and woodland, with an occasional traditional village. The authentic Peel landscape has contracted but not disappeared. East of Eindhoven, **Helena Peel** and **Peel de Veluwe** still lie among bird-filled swamps, crossed by humpback *knuppel* bridges.

Access to the nature reserve is via Moostdijk. Black-headed gulls are visible between March and July and are most vocal in early spring, when they nest among the reeds. To many hikers, rare insects and views over bleak fens encrusted with World War II pillboxes are reason enough to visit the area at any time of year.

Theme and safari parks

If you're travelling with children, they'll be glad to hear that there's more to Noord-Brabant than scenic variations and historic towns. The **De Efteling** theme park (tel: 041-653 7777; www. efteling.co.uk; Apr–Oct daily 10am–6pm, July–Aug until 9pm) at Kaatsheuvel north of Tilburg, is one of the Netherlands' best. From the Fairy Tale Forest, through mystical Arabia of the Thousand and One Nights, and the Flying Pagoda, De Efteling recreates the world of goblins, fakirs, wizards and sprites.

Beekse Bergen Safari Park (tel: 0900-233 5732; www.safariparkbeeksebergen.com; daily 10am–4pm, Feb and Nov until 4.30pm, Mar–June and Sep–Oct until 5pm, July–Aug until 5.30pm) at Hilvarenbeek near Tilburg takes you on a trip through the real world, but the experience is equally exciting. Herds of elephants and giraffes, prides of lions, flocks of brightly coloured birds and many other exotic animals patrol the Noord-Brabant 'savannahs'. All in all there are around 1,250 animals from 150 species. You view most of the animals on drive-through excursions, but there is also a walk-through area where you can see penguins, flamingos and monkeys, among others.

In De Efteling theme park.

Riotous fun

From cross-dressers and old wives to 700 brass bands and a giant prince, Bergen Op Zoom's pre-Lent carnival is a weekend you'll never forget.

Carnivals in Amsterdam pale in comparison to the celebrations held in Bergen op Zoom and Den Bosch during *Kermissen*, a concept embracing most folkloric festivities. Carnival is a heartfelt tradition in the southern Lowlands, and harks back to the 15th century when the southern provinces were ruled by the Dukes of Burgundy. Burgundian rule coincided with the southern Golden Age, a time of opulent Town Halls, noble mansions and artistic excellence. The region acquired a taste for open-air theatricals, feasting and banqueting and, above all, riotous carnivals, which remain an integral part of southern Dutch life today.

Seven weeks before Easter the carnival is at its pre-Lent peak, but preparations begin months before. Bergen op Zoom's 700 brass bands practise in neighbouring towns; the witches' costumes are created; the totemic giants are repainted; the carnival cabaret is rehearsed; a new carnival song is composed in local dialect. A Carnival Prince is also elected as master of ceremonies. In the weeks leading up to the carnival, shops are decorated with folkloric characters and bands perform in local bars and children's clubs. Masked children torment passers-by with off-key renditions of the carnival song, *Wa d'n Kemedie* (What a Comedy).

Traditional events

The traditional Old Wives Ball, held a few days before the grand carnival weekend, is a colourful pub crawl attended by young women (and occasionally men) dressed as old hags, harridans and witches. At midnight, the women and 'transvestites' are unmasked and, if female, are kissed by male revellers hovering in the wings.

During the carnival weekend, restaurants are full of brass bands and cooking plays second fiddle to performing. The weekend is for adult revellers but Monday is Children's Day, a private occasion when local youngsters wear fancy dress and meet the Carnival Prince in the Grote Markt. The Prince, or an imposter with a head for heights, greets the children from his eyrie in the Peperbus, the church tower. Dressed as a giant, the Prince dangles huge arms and legs over the side of the tower and challenges children to hunt him through the town. A mad chase ensues, while truanting parents can be found ensconced in cosy bars.

The carnival procession itself, led by giants, floats and the long-suffering Prince, is a stage-managed occasion designed to appeal to the thousands of visitors. The Bergen op Zoom carnival is a peacock's public display. Community spirit can verge on exhibitionism. At midnight, the celebrations stop and Lenten austerity begins.

On canvas

Jan Steen's *The Fat Kitchen* depicts the Dutch love of carnival, but it's left to a southern painter, Bruegel the Elder, in *Battle of Carnival and Lent*, to suggest the yin and yang of 'fat' carnival and 'skinny' Lent. In this symbolic confrontation between Church and inn, a merry band of guzzlers is pitted against crippled beggars and Calvinist moralists. The victory appears to be with the beer barrels, pancakes and giant-tailed fish – a southern vision of the world.

Made up for a pre Lent party.

LIMBURG

Maastricht, the provincial capital, is one of the Netherlands' oldest towns and renowned for its haute cuisine culture and tradition.

Amsterdam

Maastricht

The Dutch divide Limburg into three zones. North Limburg includes a moorland area west of the River Maas (Meuse), sparsely populated despite the presence of the market towns Weert and Venray. Middle Limburg, centred on industrial Roermond, is flat and has lakes, rivers and canals. The South, by way of contrast, is hilly enough to merit being called 'the Dutch Alps', particularly near the Drielandenpunt, at 321 metres (1,050ft) the Netherlands' highest point. Nearby are Maastricht and Valkenburg, where you find caves, castles and classy cuisine.

History has not always been kind to this province. The tramp of armies criss-crossing the landscape became familiar as threatening waves elsewhere in the Netherlands. Maastricht, provincial capital, was a particularly coveted prize. In the 1970s, coal mines that gave Limburgers hard-won prosperity closed for good, leaving the province without an economic engine. Limburg has been busy reinventing itself, thanks to a development policy that might serve as a model for other European regions faced with dislocating change. Maastricht has converted a strategic position in the European Union's 'golden triangle' into a prime economic asset, and tourists discovering Limburg's scenic and cultural attractions – while wrestling

with myriad dialects that change from village to village. The history and culture of Limburg province and the region along the River Maas is the theme of the **Limburgs Museum** in Venlo (Keulsepoort 5; tel: 077-352 2112; www.limburgsmuseum.nl; Tue–Sun 11am–5pm).

Historic battlefield

Venray, in North Limburg, is a market garden centre – a term that took on special significance in the autumn of 1944 when the Allies launched Operation

Main Attractions

Oorlogs Museum, Overloon
Kasteel Hoensbroek
Gemeentegrot, Valkenburg
Sint Servaasbasiliek, Maastricht
Onze Lieve Vrouwebasiliek, Maastricht
Bonnefantenmuseum, Maastricht

Castle Oud Valkenburg.

Market Garden to open a corridor from the Belgian border through Eindhoven and Nijmegen to Arnhem. Following their failure to capture Arnhem, Allied troops sought to broaden the base of the corridor and cut off German forces west of the Maas. At **Overloon** ❽ (in Noord-Brabant), north of Venray, British and American forces clashed with the Germans in the biggest armoured battle of the war on Dutch soil, with some 300 tanks knocked out. Overloon was destroyed.

A visit to the region's war cemeteries gives you an idea of the extent of American, British, Canadian, Polish and German casualties of the sustained fighting in the southeastern Netherlands. Between Deurne and Venray, the IJsselsteyn cemetery alone has 30,000 German graves. The **Oorlogs Museum** (tel: 047-864 1250; www.oorlogsmuseum.nl; Mon–Fri 10am–5pm, Sat–Sun 11am–5pm) lies on the original battlefield, and a well-marked route leads you past tanks, planes, artillery pieces, minefields, bombs, anti-tank weapons and other detritus of the battle.

Lakes and water gardens

After this harrowing pilgrimage, you can escape to the Maas. Following the river south through Limburg provides plenty of opportunities for leaving the motorway to visit riverside castles, and enjoy watersports or water-gazing. Just off the N271, graceful **Kasteel Arcen** (tel: 077-473 6010; Apr–Oct daily 10am–6pm) is an 18th-century moated chateau and estate set amidst a series of islands interspersed with water gardens. A walk past the chateau leads you to an orangerie, ornamental lake and a vivid rosarium. Oriental gardens, tropical gardens, terraces, waterfalls and pergolas delight garden-loving visitors.

Roermond ❾ is a modern industrial city, though its Prinsenhof (governor's palace), Gothic cathedral and Munsterkerk have been restored since 1945. The city's greatest attraction lies just outside it: the **Maasplassen** are artificial lakes in former sand and gravel pits, whose landscaped shores are popular with sailors and windsurfers. At Maasbracht is what looks like a giant parking lot for barges with names like *Fatima*, *Tulipe* and *Marjan*. Some of the massed boats sport the last word in high-tech appliances, while others are more like river tramps, but a fine smell of shipboard cooking emanates from all.

Between borders

Below Roermond, Limburg narrows to a finger of land squeezed between the Belgian and German borders. Almost on the Belgian border, **Thorn** ❿ is a picturesque but self-conscious village that barely escapes being twee. Cobbled streets lead past former almshouses, converted abbey buildings and whitewashed brick cottages. Its saving grace is a quiet spirituality, in keeping with its earlier incarnation as a religious centre.

The original religious community was centred around the 10th-century **Abdijkerk** (Kerberg 2; Mar noon–5pm, Tue–Sat 9am–5pm, Su

Roermond view.

10am–5pm) run by an abbess and a chapter of noblewomen. The church's Romanesque crypt remains but the rest of the church is Gothic with a Baroque face-lift. An overblown Rubens painting competes for attention with the mummified remains of past canons and canonesses.

South of Thorn, the Maas runs along the Belgian border, and South Limburg's rolling landscape ushers in wilder, less classically Dutch views. A romantic flavour is added by border castles and fortified farms. South of the Susteren lakes, two feudal castles, Wittem and Limbricht, survey a wooded scene. North of Heerlen at Hoensbroek, **Kasteel Hoensbroek** (Klinkertstraat 118; tel: 045-522 7272; www.kasteelhoensbroek.nl; daily 10am–5.30pm), with its 14th-century red-brick towers squatting in a murky green lake, is the finest castle between the Maas and Rhine. Inside, 16th- and 17th-century furnishings reflect the period of Hoensbroek's first major restoration. Views towards distant narrow river valleys and hills beyond shatter another Dutch stereotype of iron-flat landscapes.

Imaginative museum

Skirt industrial Sittard and Geleen in favour of **Heerlen** ⑪, a diffuse yet rewarding town, which at first glance is an overgrown shopping centre. Heerlen, though, has a rich past.

A Roman trading post on the Cologne–Calais road, Heerlen supplied glassware, earthenware and provisions to the legions. The remains of Roman *Coriovallum* were excavated during the 1960s and a small museum built to house the circular Roman baths, furnace room, shops and sports field. The result is the imaginative **Thermenmuseum** (Coriovallumstraat 9; tel: 045-560 5100; www.thermenmuseum.nl; Tue–Fri 10am–5pm, Sat–Sun noon–5pm), a metal hangar painted red, yellow and blue. Inside, a raised steel walkway provides views over the complex below, in which Roman bathers went from the sauna to warm, lukewarm, cold, and full-immersion baths. In one room are the remains of a stone temple, a reconstruction of a potter's workshop and a collection of excavated jewellery, coins and statuettes.

FACT

From the late 19th century until 1975, Heerlen was the centre of the Dutch coal-mining industry. The discovery in 1960 of natural gas in Groningen spelled the end of Heerlen's 'black fairytale'.

White Houses, Thorn.

TIP

For a fine view of the gently rolling countryside around Valkenburg, take a ride on the open cable car that takes you up to the Wilhemina Toren (www.agogovalkenburg.nl), a bar-restaurant on top of the hill above the castle. Also here is a range of activities including minigolf, tubing and a zipline.

Southern Limburg

Visually, southern Limburg is not classic Dutch and, for that reason, attracts many Dutch tourists. Its novelty is an undesigned natural landscape, an irregular patchwork of woods, meadows and hills with forbidding castles and half-timbered farms set at jaunty angles. For many foreigners, the novelty lies more in historic caves and castles rather than in landscape. The 'Dutch Alps' could easily pass for Belgium's Ardennes, Germany's Eifel or England's rolling Dorset countryside. Yet there is enough Dutchness to enjoy in its shallow valleys and freshly whitewashed farms.

Valkenburg , in the wooded Geul valley, is the most popular non-coastal destination among Dutch visitors. The spa-town atmosphere and casino provide stimulation when country walks pall. For a more history-oriented stay in the region, you can spend a weekend at **Kasteel Erenstein** (Kerkrade; tel: 034-775 0454; www.kasteelerenstein.nl) or the farmhouse hotel **Winselerhof** (Landgraaf; tel: 045-546 4343; www.

chateauhotels.nl), each with a gourmet restaurant.

At **Thermae 2000** (www.thermae.nl; daily 9am–11pm), an invigorating spa centre in the hills, treatments include Roman, Turkish and Swedish baths, as well as *Medizinisches Heilwasser*, German health cures. Housed under a glass pyramid, mineral-rich springs are channelled to allow swimmers to glide between exotic water experiences.

Following Grotestraat from the Spaans Leenhof (the tourist office) to the castle provides a snapshot of Valkenburg. At the lower end of the street is the **Streekmuseum** (Local History Museum; Tue–Fri 11am–5pm, Sat–Sun 1–5pm), a cluttered collection redeemed by an elegant marlstone building, decorated with stained-glass windows and a stone falcon. Glimpses of the tumbledown castle overshadow unpromising lines of gift shops and bars. As the Netherlands' only elevated fortress, its jagged ruins, towering over modern clutter, have a dramatic appeal. At the foot of the castle, turn left into Berkelstraat and walk through the medieval **Berkelpoort** gateway

Looking out over the rooftops of Valkenburg.

CAVE ART

The cave's first section is covered with abstract art carved by students of Breda University. Many of these 1960s designs are primitive, even by prehistoric caveman standards. The 15th- and 16th-century works include a sculpture of St George, an impressive lion rampant and a painting of Knight Willem, a local hero. The best modern picture is of the Dutch royal family: different generations of royals attended sittings in this damp site between 1885 and 1950.

The strangest sculptures are by a 19th-century blacksmith who, inspired by the prehistoric world, spent all his time underground, carving dinosaurs. One looks like the Loch Ness monster, while another, a life-size megalosaurus, resembles a demented crocodile.

before visiting the castle. From the De La Ruïne hotel, steep steps lead past a curious sandstone grotto hewn into the rock; during carnival, a dummy of a witch is suspended over the entrance.

Still higher is the **Kasteel Valkenburg** (tel: 043-820 0040; www.kasteel-valkenburg.nl; open hours vary), which offers fine views over the River Geul valley. The 11th-century fortress was built by the feudal lords of Valkenburg ('Falcon Castle'). It attracted Flemish, Spanish and French hunters, and finally succumbed to Louis XIV after a siege. On retrieving control from the French in 1672, William III ordered that the castle be demolished. The remains (restored in 1921) include a tower, chapel and arsenal, and a network of secret tunnels leading to the **Fluweelengrot** caves (guided tours hourly during castle opening times) and former quarries. There are great views from the café.

Caves and grottoes

Return to Berkelstraat and turn left into Munstraat. After passing under Grendelpoort, the second medieval gate, glance back at the statue of the Virgin in a niche, a foretaste of the Lourdes grotto to come. The **Lourdesgrot** on Cauberg was built as a replica of the French shrine and attracts sick pilgrims, particularly on the Feast of the Assumption. Valkenburg's hills are pitted with such caves, among them reconstructions of modern coal mines and Roman catacombs. The most incongruous are the **Gemeentegrot** (Cauberg 4; tel: 043-601 2271; www.gemeentegrot.nl; hourly guided tours daily 11am–4pm), the municipal caves between Grendelpoort and the Lourdes grotto. As with all Dutch caves, they are man-made but exceptional in that they have been quarried since Roman times. Marlstone, a type of limestone, was worked here until recently. Now prohibitively expensive, marlstone's use is restricted to restoration work and statuary.

The caves are vast, covering 110 hectares (275 acres) and 75km (47 miles) of tunnels, of which about 5km (3 miles) are open to the public. Given the constant temperature of 11°C (52°F), it is best to see the caves in cold

The well-known tourist spot of Valkenburg is home to a replica of the Lourdes Cave, including a statue of the Virgin Mary.

weather when it feels warmer inside. Earlier visitors followed this logic and amused themselves during winter by carving and painting the caves' porous marlstone, which is soft underground. Once exposed to the outside air, it hardens rapidly. The oldest known cave sculptures and paintings date from the 15th century, but some of the modern ones are no less intriguing.

While you're waiting for a guided tour by 'train' or on foot, expect to be accosted by an enterprising sculptor who, working on the captive-audience principle, is willing to carve anything on the spot, from family crests for Belgian aristocrats to statuettes of beloved pets for homesick, globe-trotting Canadians.

The caves have played an important role in local history as well as local art. During World War II, 3,000 citizens hid inside, leaving behind their names, messages and, occasionally, paintings. The Germans gained control of the caves and built a secret factory to produce flying bombs. Now mostly ruined, the factory was dismantled by liberating American forces in September 1944.

To Maastricht

From Valkenburg, a short route leads across the plains to **Maastricht** , the provincial capital and most Burgundian city in the Netherlands, a sophisticated, open-minded border town, far removed in spirit from the regimented northern provinces. Aficionados of the south consider Maastricht the country's most user-friendly city, combining quality of life with standard of living in a way northerners haven't quite got the hang of yet. In his satirical novel *In Nederland*, Cees Nooteboom decries the north as 'an orderly human garden' and praises the south as a land of untamed cave-dwellers leading freer lives.

Of all the southern towns, Maastricht has the least trammelled spirit and as one the Netherlands' oldest cities, it has been open to foreign influence from Roman traders, Charlemagne's soldiers and Burgundian merchants. The result of such a cosmopolitan history is no bland internationalism, but a relaxed society confident of its traditions

Panorama of Maastricht from the River Maas.

and its dialect, which, unlike many parts of the Netherlands, Maastricht has retained. So distinctive is it that locals half-jokingly claim not to speak Dutch. Before the euro the city accepted three currencies, reflecting its position in the important economic triangle delineated by Maastricht, Aachen and Liège. Germans cross the border for art exhibitions, Belgian students for the nightlife and northern Dutch for the hilly countryside and a chance to release their Calvinistic inhibitions.

Maastricht started out as a Roman garrison and trading post commanding an important river crossing. From there, all roads led to Cologne, London and Rome. The establishment of a 4th-century bishopric under St Servaas brought the town great prestige and wealth. However, its role as a frontier town resumed in 1204 when the Duke of Brabant shared power with the Prince-Bishop of Liège. For over 200 years, this dual authority was reflected in the city's geography: upstream from St Servaasbrug the Bishop of Liège held sway, while Brabant governed the area downstream from the bridge.

In the 15th century the city was absorbed by the Burgundian Empire and became a great trading centre, matched by a flourishing reputation for *Maasland (Mosan)* art. At its apogee in the early 16th century, Maastricht rivalled Flemish Ghent and Antwerp. Thereafter, its fortunes fluctuated according to the effects of repeated Spanish and French invasions. From the successful 1579 Spanish siege to the last French invasion, in 1794, Maastrichters became used to adapting to foreign tastes.

Rich heritage

Architecturally, foreign influence brought greater diversity than you see in most Dutch cities. The city's Roman remains and rings of medieval fortifications are still in evidence. It has Romanesque arches and murals, French Gothic churches, indigenous *Maasland* Renaissance architecture, onion towers imported from the East, and, from the 17th century, the classical style favoured by northern Dutch Calvinists.

Vrijthof square.

GET YOUR BEARINGS

Maastricht's centre is on the west bank of the Maas and stretches towards the Belgian border. Most visitors arrive in the Wijk district on the east bank and so need to cross the river. Once in the historic heart, you can explore the city's three most appealing districts. The centre, including two major squares, churches and the town hall, is the civic and spiritual core. The Stok quarter, the Roman and medieval district, is bounded by Sint Servaasbrug to the north, the Maas to the east, Onze Lieve Vrouwebasiliek (Basilica of Our Lady) to the south, and Wolvenstraat to the west. The Jeker quarter, south of the Stok quarter, embraces the city's medieval fortifications, mills and almshouses, and follows the course of the River Jeker to the south and Tongersestraat to the northwest.

Under Louis XIV, an aristocratic French community encouraged the creation of Baroque residences. Later in the 18th century, symmetry gave way to frenzied rococo lines. As for German influence, Maastricht's helm roofs are a copy of the Rhineland's. The city's architecture continues to be inspired by the past, particularly in its saddleback roofs. More imaginatively, bold modern statues delight in holding a distorting mirror to the past. At best, as in Mari Andriessen's *Mestreechter Geis* (Spirit of Maastricht), there is both a past memory and the essence of the city today. Maastricht may be a result of dynastic bargaining but its spirit remains intact.

The heart of town

The *Stad aonde Maos* ('the town on the Maas') has two main central squares, the largest of which is the spacious **Vrijthof Ⓐ**. Approached via inward-looking alleys that typify the old centre, this light-filled square seems out of keeping with Maastricht's nature. Its origins are disputed: built over marshes along the River Jeker, the area was originally unsuitable for building and, by medieval times, was used as a military parade ground, execution site and pilgrims' meeting place. Every seven years, the 'Fair of the Holy Relics' attracted pilgrims, craftsmen and traders to the lively square. Something of this chaotic spirit is recaptured in the Vrijthof at carnival time. A food festival, Preuvenmint, takes place here at the end of August.

One side of the square is lined with cafés and in summer, the wide pavements are filled with tables which draw a constant stream of human traffic. On the other side of the square the two magnificent churches of **Sint Servaasbasiliek Ⓑ** and **Sint Janskerk Ⓒ** survey the scene, almost reproachfully. They provide a sombre counterbalance to the carnival spirit and café culture.

Sint Servaasbasiliek (www.sintservaas. nl; Mon–Sat 10am–5pm, Sun 12.30–5pm, July–Aug until 6pm Mon–Sat; Mass in English Thu at 7pm) is one of the oldest churches in the Netherlands and a fitting tribute to its Armenian founder, St Servaas, who

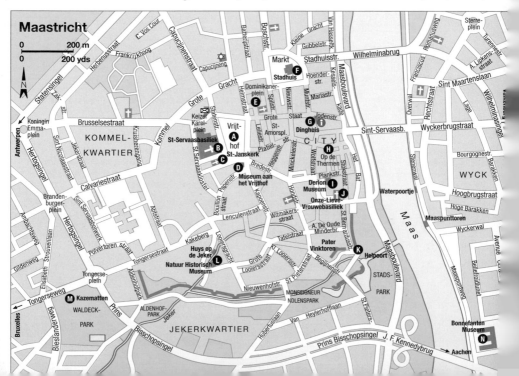

became Maastricht's first bishop and brought the town fame and fortune. The church is said to stand on his burial site and contains his relics. Begun in the 11th century, the Romanesque basilica was enlarged and embellished over the next four centuries. Its front façade has the grim impregnability of a fortified town, but this forbidding impression is a feature of Romanesque *Maasland*, a style prevalent along the Maas. The heavy apse is flanked by square, twin towers beyond which soars the Gothic spire of Sint Janskerk.

Sint Servaasbasiliek hides its lyrical side around the corner, in the **Bergportaal** on the south side of the church (entrance during services). The 13th-century, French High Gothic doorway is a *trompe l'œil* of inner arches. Each section is adorned with sculpted vegetation, mythological animals, biblical scenes and hidden symbolism. Viewed from the sloping steps beside this doorway, Sint Janskerk appears to offer a severe Protestant rebuke to the fanciful aspirations of St Servaas. The interior of St Servaas has been somewhat over-restored. Its 10th-century crypt, Gothic porch, chapels and cloisters are more authentic than the clinical-looking choir. Catholic Maastrichters ruefully say that the restorers must have been Protestants.

Bright, zigzag patterns on the capitals are a preparation for the jewellery-shop appearance of the **Schatkamer** (Treasury) in the former sacristy. This Aladdin's Cave glitters with silver, gold, copper and precious stones. In addition to a 12th-century cross encrusted with amethysts, treasures include a lovely statue of St Anne, a platter depicting St John's head on a plate, ivory reliquaries and illuminated manuscripts. The undisputed masterpieces, however, are a 16th-century silver bust of St Servaas, ornamented with reliefs telling his story (it is carried through the town in Easter processions) and a bejewelled 12th-century chest reliquary that is a high point of *Maasland* art. Craftsmanship shines through the rich decoration so that it is not the profusion of emeralds and sapphires that you admire but the workmanship itself.

The tomb of Sint Servaasbasiliek in the church named for him.

Outside, the faded 15th-century exterior of **Sint Janskerk** (Mon–Sat 11am–4pm), Maastricht's main Protestant church since 1632, awaits you. Surrounded by gabled houses and flowerbeds, the structure is more remarkable for its location and exterior than for its stark interior. Apart from the impressive red Gothic tower (which you can climb for a fee), the Louis XVI pulpit, a smattering of marble tombs and testaments to local notables, the church is a disappointment.

Before leaving the Vrijthof in the direction of Dominikanerplein, have a look at the **Spanish Government House**, 16th-century seat of the provincial government. Its exterior is adorned with Habsburg symbols, including the motto *Plus oultre* (Still further). The building is now home to the **Museum aan het Vrijthof** (www.museumaanhetvrijthof.nl; Tue–Sun 10am–5.30pm), which tells the story of the city and has an attractive courtyard café. **Dominikanerplein** , the adjoining square, is a small, intimate affair, crowded with café tables. A sober Gothic church,

Christmas market in Maastricht.

the Dominikanerkerk, dominates the scene. The austerity and rigour of its exterior is in keeping with the Dominican ethos. The friars were renowned for their scholarship and intellect, and played an unbending role in the Inquisition. The dark interior contains faded murals and the overall impression is sombre. Only at carnival does the church come alive with children's displays of monsters and figures of fun – the Dominicans would not have approved.

The market square

From Dominikanerplein, attractive alleys and shopping streets lead to the Markt, another busy square which vies with the Vrijthof as a city centre. On Wednesday and Friday mornings the Markt wins out because these two market days attract crowds of locals as well as day-trippers from Aachen and Liège. The ever-popular herring stall is rarely without a queue and is as good a place as any to sample the Dutch speciality. Even on other days, the bars in and around the square are crowded.

Centrepiece of the square is the **Stadhuis ⒡** (Mon–Fri 9am–12.30pm and 2–5pm; free), a severe, 17th-century classical town hall by Pieter Post, a pupil of Jacob van Campen. You approach its interior by two flights of stairs, designed so that the two competing city authorities of Brabant and Liège could literally go their own way. The entrance chamber radiates cool gravity, but its exuberant rococo ceiling adds a touch of frivolity. It is here that the Mayor hands over the keys of the city to the Carnival Prince. You may be lucky enough to hear the 43-bell carillon – in typical Maastricht style, the 17th-century council abandoned solemn dirges in favour of spirited folk tunes; happily the practice continues.

The medieval quarter

Grote Staat, the main shopping street, leads from the northern end of Vrijthof to the Stok quarter, the heart of the medieval and Roman city. Grote Staat, like most other streets in this area, is well provided with bars, patiseries and cheese shops. There are frequent opportunities to sample local specialities, including a *Limburgse vlaai* (fruit flan) and *rommedou* cheese. If you can resist the aroma of asparagus omelette and trout, you may succumb to tempting displays of *pralines* and gingerbread delicacies, washed down with a glass or two of local beer, or a bottle of rare Maastricht wine. Napoleon closed most of the region's vineyards, but three small ones still produce 25,000 bottles a year).

At the end of Grote Staat stands the **Dinghuis ⒢**, a narrow Gothic building with a steep saddleback roof. Now the city's friendly and efficient VVV tourist office (May–Oct Mon–Sat 9am–6pm, Sun 11am–5pm, Nov–Apr Mon–Sat 10am–5pm, Sun 11am–5pm), it has barred ground-floor windows, left over from its Napoleonic days as a prison.

The compact Stok quarter is the oldest part of the city, dating back to Roman times. Its northern boundary is the Gothic **Sint Servaasbrug**. Built of grey Namur stone, it is the oldest bridge in the Netherlands (although it was rebuilt after being demolished in World War II). Nearby, Mari Andriessen's *Mestreechter Geis* statue represents the spirit of Maastricht and guards the entrance to the old quarter.

Stok quarter buildings date from medieval times, when it was the central market area. Street names testify to the presence of grain, fish, meat and timber markets, though **Stokstraat** got its name from the nearby stocks and city prison. In the 17th and 18th centuries the area became fashionable, and a number of intricate façades and gable stones remain from the period. No. 26 is one of the finest, a *Maasland* Renaissance masterpiece that owes more to freely interpreted Gothic than to Renaissance symmetry. No. 17 has an ornate rococo façade decorated with scallop shells which was peeled off a town house on Grote Staat: proof that wandering is not restricted to gable stones.

TIP

A good place to catch an English or American movie in its original version (i.e. not dubbed but with Dutch subtitles) in Maastricht is the Cinema Lumière (www.lumiere.nl). In the summer of 2016, it moved to a new home in the boiler house of the old Sphinx factory on the waterfront in the north of the city.

Shopping on Grote Staat in Maastricht.

Off Stokstraat is a handful of medieval squares, including **Op de Thermen** , a chic square with boutiques, a half-timbered medieval tower and a statue of a decapitated *Amazon*. The square lies on top of the Roman baths, whose outline is traced on the pavement.

Around the corner, in Plankstraat, the **Derlon Museum** (Sun noon–4pm; free) houses a small Roman collection unearthed when the Derlon hotel was built. Remains dating from the 2nd century include a wall, gate, well, part of a temple to Jupiter and a section of cobbled Roman road. Tired visitors can view the display from the comfort of the hotel's tearooms.

In the 19th century, the fashionable centre moved to the Markt and Vrijthof, leaving Stokstraat to degenerate into a cholera-infested slum with open drains and brothels. Sensitive 1960s restoration, however, has made the Stok quarter a perfect place for strolling and window-shopping. Designer boutiques rub shoulders with friendly working-class bars, modern statues and old gable stones. Swans, lions,

cherubs, grapes, trees, even a sphi are clues to their previous owne trades and professions.

Romanesque treasure

The **Onze Lieve Vrouwebasiliek** (Basilica of Our Dear Lady; East Oct daily 11am–5pm, Nov–Easter S 1–5pm; church free, fee for treasur surrounded by cafés and restaura on shady Onze Lieve Vrouweple grandly delimits the district's sou western end. On the site of a vanish Roman temple, the fortified Rom esque church is the city's oldest. Bu in the year 1000, it is flanked by t circular turrets, pierced by arrow sl and topped by a squat helm roof. forbidding west front owes more German Rhineland architecture th to Flemish or Dutch styles. Inside, atmosphere is slightly eerie, heig ened by the delicate sculpted capi decorated with scenes from the C Testament and an apse decorated w gauzy Romanesque frescoes. Chris depicted against an azure backdr with stars and angels beyond. T church's struggle for supremacy o

Helpoort is one of the few functioning medieval gates in the old Maastricht city walls.

St Servaas ended in failure: by the 15th century it was banned from displaying relics and selling indulgences. As a result, the basilica has a much smaller collection of treasure.

Student quarter

From the Onze Lieve Vrouweplein, St Bernardusstraat leads south to the **Jeker quarter**, a gently tumbledown district of narrow winding streets, mill streams and ruined fortifications. This area is popular with Maastricht's big student population, so bars and 'alternative' shops are tucked into the side streets. Compared with the Stok quarter, this relatively large area has fewer grand old buildings. It is characterised by its mills and almshouses, and the quiet pathways running through parks and gardens, or along the three tiers of ramparts (a popular jogging route).

Helpoort Ⓚ (Hell's Gate), at the end of St Bernardusstraat, built in 1229, is a sinister steep-roofed gateway marking the city's medieval boundaries. Beside it a lone tower, the **'ekertoren**, marks the former territorial demarcation between Liège and Brabant. Beyond Helpoort, a tranquil walk along the city walls leads to Hekenstraat and the university quarter, passing the main park, a mini zoo and various derelict towers.

The fast-flowing **River Jeker**, on the far side of Helpoort, is flanked by an old tower and a row of neat 17th-century cottages that once formed part of the city's Begijnhof (Beguine's Convent). On the river's opposite bank is the **Anker**, a water-driven paper-mill on the site of the former Pesthuis ('lague House), built to keep plague victims safely out of harm's way – which meant outside the city walls. Instead of tracing the city walls, you an follow atmospheric alleys from elpoort to Lang Grachtje, a filled-in er enclosed by the city walls. This ds to **Grote Looiersstraat**, one the city's loveliest spots. Until the th century, it was filled with tanries but later became a sought-after

residential area. Although the canal is now filled in, gracious 17th- and 18th-century houses remain. Several bear witness to virtuous 17th-century Dutch society: No. 27 was once a Catholic almshouse, and No. 17 a Poor House – an admonitory motto over the door says: 'He who gives to the poor shall suffer no harm'. En route, look out for an informal group of bronze figures sitting on a stone bench. The sculpture is dedicated to Fons Olterdissen, a local storyteller.

Musical city

Grote Looiersstraat leads to **De Bosquetplein** and the university quarter, between the arms of the Jeker. The **Natuurhistorisch Museum** Ⓛ (Natural History Museum; De Bosquetplein 6; http://nhmmaastricht. nl; Mon–Fri 11am–5pm, Sat–Sun 1–5pm) houses a small exhibition on the flora and fauna of the area and has a well-kept garden.

As you walk along the steep Heksenstraat (Witches' Street) and admire the clear views over the river, you will pass a mill and a stone carving of a witch

Performing at Carnaval Maastricht.

on the wall – hence the name. Heksenstraat adjoins the Academy of Music so the air here is often filled with conflicting snatches of classical music and jazz. Also on this stretch of the Jeker is the **Huis op de Jeker**, a perfectly preserved *Maasland* Renaissance house spanning the river. Nearby, the former Grey Sisters Convent is a poetic if dilapidated haunt favoured by romantic couples in search of privacy.

From here, most streets lead back to the centre via Platielstraat and **Sint Amorsplein**, a fashionable square overlooked by a reproving statue of the saint. On the square, the Troubadour Chantant is a lively student café which lives up to its name, with regular performances of singing, dancing, cabaret and even poetic monologues.

Maastricht is a musical city, offering everything from classical music to cabaret, opera to musical puppet shows and, in October, hosts a well-known jazz festival. Churches, including Sint Servaas, hold regular organ recitals, and on Sunday mornings the voices of the Mestreechter

Bonnefantenmuseum.

Staar male choir can be heard rehearsing in the Staargebouw concert hall. In July, the city's most famous resident, the violinist André Rieu, holds a weekend of concerts in the Vrijthof.

Visitors with any energy left can visit the **Kazematten Ⓜ**, the city's old fortifications, or explore the galleried Sint-Pietersberg and Sonneberg caves just outside town. These are similar to the Valkenburg caves, but had a more pronounced military function, used both in 17th-century sieges and during World War II. See www.maastrichtunderground.nl for details of tours.

Italian and Flemish Masters

The stylish, modern **Bonnefantenmuseum Ⓝ** across the river (Avenue Céramique 250; www.bonnefanten.nl; Tue–Sun 11am–5pm) has works by Italian and Flemish Masters, and holds the country's finest collection of *Maasland* art. The Italian collection, covering work between 1300 and 1550 includes some of the greatest Sienese Florentine and Venetian artists, from

Sano di Pietro to Filippo Lippi and Bellini. Domenico di Michelino's *Expulsion from Paradise* approaches the power of Masaccio's Florentine frescoes, while Sano di Pietro's luminous *St Catherine* is the envy of Sienese museum curators.

It is no accident that the Netherlands' ever-growing Italian collection is housed here: national museum policy confirms the view that, as the nation's most Latin city, in spirit and in reality, Maastricht is the rightful home for such Southern European works.

The same logic applies to the museum's collection of Flemish Masters, tactfully known as 'South Netherlandish' painters. Covering the period from 1480 to 1650, these paintings embrace the region of old Flanders, stretching from Bruges and Antwerp to Den Bosch and Maastricht. The collection includes Pieter Brueghel's *Wedding in front of a Farm* and the *Census at Bethlehem*, as well as local landscapes, still lifes and portraits. Although Amsterdam's Rijksmuseum collection is far bigger, Maastricht's pre-17th-century works are comparable with those on display in the capital.

Museum highlights

Pride of the museum is its *Maasland* art collection, paintings from the River Maas area dating between 1270 and 1550. Often known by the French term, *Mosan*, this important school is best represented in Maastricht and over the border in Liège. *Maasland* art is rooted in craftsmanship and expressive detail, and is at its best in silver work and sculpture, especially woodcarvings. Sadly, the frequent incorporation of jewels and precious metals meant that many works were stolen, dismantled or melted down in former times.

Enough precious works of art remain to confirm the theory that 'Maastricht doesn't feel part of the Dutch Golden Age – all that belongs to northerners. Here, the Golden Age came much earlier and had different influences.' Highlights include a 15th-century wooden *Pietà*, a life-size 16th-century *Mary in Sorrow* and a serene Liège School angel that looks graceful enough to fly away at any moment.

Sint Pietersberg caves.

LIFE ON THE WATER

The Dutch have always had an inextricable link with water – whether reclaiming it or enjoying it.

Any visitor to the Netherlands could be forgiven for thinking they had arrived on a carpet of islands. There are boats everywhere, ranging from rowing boats to supertankers (Rotterdam is the largest port in Europe). Because waterways are quite shallow, many boats are flat-bottomed and of narrow build. In appearance they are similar to Britain's Norfolk wherries or Thames barges, but offer a wider variety of sizes and functions. Many of the old tugboats, known as sleepboten, that were once used to tow boats around narrow canals are now used for pleasure purposes instead.

The Netherlands' vintage vessels, however, are by far the most charming. Where deeper navigation is possible, you are almost certain to see tall ships and multi-masted vessels from days gone by with names reflecting their place of origin. Given the universal love of all things maritime, the Netherlands provides probably the best retirement home for these ageing ladies of the sea.

Numerous boat festivals underline the local passion, the most famous of all being Sail Amsterdam, which extends its welcome to the world. Launched in 1975 to celebrate Amsterdam's 700th birthday, it is now repeated every five years (next one in 2020) and has become a truly international maritime event, attracting thousands of boats and millions of visitors. The opening parade includes around 800 traditional Dutch sailing vessels.

The clipper Stad Amsterdam leads the fleet of tall ships du the opening of Sail Amsterdam. The event is held every fiv years and attracts hundreds of thousands of spectators.

Old wooden sailboats moored along Hoorn's banks.

Cheese arriving at the cheese market by boat in Alkmaar.

Houseboats require a lot of ongoing maintenance.

HOME IS WHERE THE BOAT IS

The Dutch have a passion bordering on the religious for all forms of water transport, be it a modern hydrofoil or a graceful old sailing ship of the former Dutch East India Company. Boats rival bicycles as a favoured means of transport, and when people are not cruising the waters in whatever craft they have chosen from the vast range available, many retire to their homes on the water.

Houseboats come in three basic varieties. First is the purpose-built modern and palatial woonarken, or residential 'ark', built on a pontoon or flotation chamber. Prices for these often rival those for freehold property. Second is the old barge that has had its cargo hold converted into living quarters. It remains mobile by using either a sail or motor. Last is the converted smaller vessel that remains moored in one place. Its unwique construction and domestic compromise makes this houseboat the most interesting and amusing for onlookers to observe. You can find out what life is like on board at the Houseboat Museum (Prinsengracht 296 K; tel: 020-427 0750; www.houseboatmuseum.nl; July–Aug daily 10–5, Mar–June and Sep–Oct Tue–Sun 10–5, Nov–Feb Thu–Sun 10–5) in Amsterdam.

A typical houseboat in Amsterdam.

GELDERLAND

From an unmatched Van Gogh collection to an historic battle site, Gelderland province offers visitors plenty to see and do.

O n a fine spring day, when the quiet river and fruit-growing area of Gelderland was look-ng its best, a small river boat moved lowly through the lush still country-ide near the town of **Zaltbommel** . Suddenly the chimes of the town's arillon rang out, holding the boat's assengers transfixed. One visitor, he composer Franz Liszt, found the igh sweet tones particularly seduc-ve, so much so that he asked to be ut on land. He made his way to the wn, met the carillon player and was troduced to his beautiful daughter, gifted pianist. Liszt arranged for the rl to study in Paris and it was there e met the Impressionist painter louard Manet. The couple eventu-ly went back to Zaltbommel to be arried in the historic Town Hall.

Another visitor of note was Karl arx, who, while staying with rela-es, is purported to have worked his monumental *Das Kapital*. en came the Philips brothers, who rked on the design for the first ctric light bulbs, going on to found famous Philips multinational npany in Eindhoven. Zaltbom-l seems to encourage the creative; nay have something to do with pastoral beauty of the surround-countryside and the heavy scent ruit blossom. On the other hand, uld have been, and probably was,

Cycling in Nationaal Park De Hoge Veluwe.

mere coincidence which drew so many famous names to the area.

The Veluwe

The Province of Gelderland is the largest of the Netherlands' 12 prov-inces, and several hundred years ago was an independent duchy. It can be subdivided into three major areas: the Veluwe, the Achterhoek and the river area. The Veluwe is bounded in the north by the former Zuiderzee (now the IJsselmeer) coastline, an area dominated by wild heather, pines,

Map on page 254

Main Attractions
Nationaal Park de Hoge Voluwe
Kröller-Muller Museum
Sint Walburgiskerk Library, Zutphen
Airborne Museum, Arnhem
Paleis Het Loo, Apeldoorn

heathland and sand dunes, and in the south by the Rhine and Arnhem. The main attraction of this popular area is the **Nationaal Park De Hoge Veluwe** ❷ (www.hogeveluwe.nl), one of the country's most beautiful conservation areas. Once royal hunting territory, it still has miles of forests that are rich in wildlife, including deer and boar. A good place to start is the Visitor Centre (Apr–Oct 9.30am–6pm, Nov–Mar 9.30am–5pm), where there is also a museum, **Museonder**, which looks at everything that lived or was found underground. The best way to explore the parkland is on one of the hundreds of white bikes that visitors can borrow free of charge.

At the centre of the Hoge Veluwe Park, near Otterlo is the exceptional **Kröller-Müller Museum** (tel: 031-859 1241; Tue–Sun 10am–5pm; entrance to the park is included in the ticket price), a striking glass-walled structure with light-filled rooms that houses a magnificent collection of 278 of Vincent van Gogh's paintings and drawings (rotated as there is not enough room to show them all at once). The extensive collection also includes works by other modern European masters such as Mondrian, Van der Leck, Seurat, Redon, Braque, Picasso and Gris.

In the grounds of the museum is one of Europe's largest **sculpture gardens** (Tue–Sun 10am–4.30pm). Try to pick a fine day and wander at will through beautifully kept gardens where you will come across

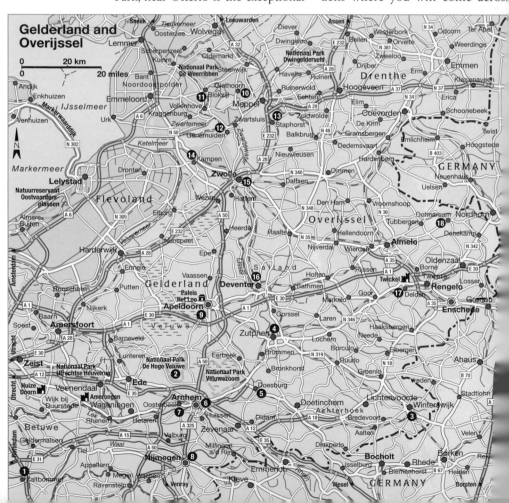

the work of Rodin, Moore, Lupchitz, Tajiri, Volten, Visser, Paolozzi and Marini. Nature and art are in peaceful harmony here. Within the Rietveld-designed pantheon you can enjoy the work of Barbara Hepworth under the open sky, and admire Marta Pan's beautiful white sculpture, *Otterlo*, that floats in a pond. This just perceptively moving piece looks like a strange and silent mating of two swans frozen in time – or, to be more mundane, like a meringue in an *île flottante*.

At the northern end of the park, about 3km (2 miles) from the Visitor Centre, is the **Jachthuis Sint Hubertus**. This Art Deco hunting lodge was built from 1915 to 1920 by Dutch architect Berlage, and dedicated to St Hubert, the patron saint of hunters. It is currently undergoing restoration.

Achterhoek

The second area of Gelderland lies between the River IJssel to the west and the German border to the east. Once covered with marshes, land reclamation over the last few centuries has turned the **Achterhoek** (literally 'back corner') into a fertile expanse of fields and meadows hemmed on all sides by woods. Stately castles, farmhouses, pristine gardens and tiny, unexpected museums all lie along the hundreds of bicycle routes, waiting to be discovered.

In the eastern section of the Achterhoek, around the town of **Winterswijk** ❸, you can still find marshland areas where rare plants and flowers flourish, including certain varieties of orchid. To the north of Winterswijk is another beautiful rural area with woodland streams and masses of wild flowers, perfect for long walks. Here you'll come across the famous 'mosaic floor of the Netherlands', an area where ancient stones have risen to the surface, and where palaeontologists claim to have found dinosaur traces.

The IJssel, which is an offshoot of the Rhine, forms the western border of the Achterhoek. This is a lovely meandering river with green banks and bays which are used for watersports such as windsurfing and swimming.

The Achterhoek in autumn.

The Battle of Arnhem

The subject of 1977 film *A Bridge Too Far*, this daring World War II operation resulted in 16,000 Allied casualties and victory for the Germans.

As September 1944 began, the population of the Nazi-occupied Netherlands waited in expectation. The Allied armies of liberation were poised to the south on the Dutch-Belgian border, and the German army was on the run. It seemed that the four-year nightmare of occupation was about to end. But the Allied offensive from Normandy was beginning to run out of steam. Soldiers were exhausted by three months of continuous fighting, German resistance on the Dutch border stiffened and the advance ground to a halt. Something was needed to break open the front, and the strategy called Operation Market Garden was born.

A daring plan

British Field Marshal Montgomery's plan was simple in essence, but breathtakingly daring.

British paratroops in their aircraft en route to Arnhem.

Some 35,000 parachute and glider-borne troops of the 1st Allied Airborne Army would drop from the sky to capture each of the river, stream and canal bridges along a 100km (60-mile) road running from the Belgian border through the cities of Eindhoven, Nijmegen and Arnhem. Meanwhile, an armoured column would punch a hole in the German front then race along this road, over the captured bridges, and cross the Rhine at Arnhem, gateway to Hitler's Reich.

It was a gamble that could end the war by Christmas. The Airborne Commander, General Browning, thought the operation feasible, but told Montgomery: 'We might be going a bridge too far.' Battle commenced on 17 September. Dutch civilians watched in amazement as thousands of parachutes blossomed in the daylight sky. Troops of the US 101st and 82nd Airborne Divisions quickly secured most of their objectives, but an important canal bridge near Eindhoven was blown up and the vital bridge over the River Waal at Nijmegen was strongly defended by the Germans. The ground assault was held up along what became known as Hell's Highway.

The British had played down Dutch Resistance reports that the German 2nd SS Panzer Corps was in the Arnhem area, and many troops were shot even before hitting the ground. Of those who landed safely, only some 600 managed to fight their way to the Rhine bridge, before running into SS tanks and artillery. This handful of 'Red Devils' held the bridge at Arnhem for four days against overwhelming odds, but eventually they were overcome.

Defeat for the Allies

The Battle of Arnhem ended in defeat for the Allies. Much of Eindhoven, Nijmegen and Arnhem was destroyed. Today, the only evidence of former conflict is in the peaceful military cemeteries that dot Hell's Highway.

The Liberation Museum at Groesbeek outside Nijmegen and the Airborne Museum at Oosterbeek west of Arnhem contain mementoes of the fighting and record the struggle of the soldiers who came from the sky.

Though their numbers lessen with every year that passes, veterans still return to the rebuilt 'bridge too far' in Arnhem, where an occasional solitary figure wearing his red beret with pride can be seen looking down into the muddy water, pondering the past, and remembering.

One of Achterhoek's historic centres is **Zutphen** ❹, a fortified town founded in the 11th century, bounded by magnificent old walls complete with look-out towers. The huge Gothic **Sint Walburgiskerk** (St Walburga's Church; opening times vary) houses the medieval **Librije**. This was one of the first public libraries in Europe and has some wonderful illuminated manuscripts and 16th-century tomes on display. Not far from the church is one of the old city gates, the **Drogenapstoren**, an impressive 15th-century brick tower in the ramparts.

About 19km (12 miles) south of Zutphen is the old town of **Doesburg** ❺, another beautifully restored centre worth a visit if you're passing by.

The river area

The third area of Gelderland lies between the Rhine (called the Neder Rijn on this stretch of its course through the Netherlands) and the Maas. The wide River Waal, another arm of the Rhine, cuts through it, linking the German Ruhr area and the North Sea to form the busiest inland shipping route in Western Europe. This region is also watered by the delightful River Linge, which flows through the fruit and vineyard district of the Betuwe (literally 'Good Land'). The Rhine and the Maas are excellent for watersports. Some of the river meanders, now cut off from the main stream, have been turned into watersports resorts with marinas, beaches and campsites.

A particularly attractive trip can be taken by bike or car from **Zaltbommel**. It runs along the top of the gently stepped dykes and offers wonderful views, with the River Linge on one side and orchards and picturesque houses built into the dykes on the other.

Arnhem

Gelderland has three main cities. **Arnhem** ❻ will always be associated with the Allied paratroopers who landed here September 1944 in a brave attempt to capture the strategic bridge over the Neder Rijn. Most of the Battle of Arnhem actually took place around **Oosterbeek** ❼, about 8km (5 miles)

DRINK

When in Nijmegen, be sure to visit the De Hemel micro-brewery (Franseplaats 1; tel: 024-360 6167; www.brouwerijdehemel.nl; Sat–Sun 1–5pm). When it opened in 1983, it was the first independent brewery to launch in the Netherlands in more than 100 years. As well as a range of beers, they also make liqueurs including jenever.

Arnhem's John Frost Bridge, named in honour of the commander who defended the orginal bridge in the Battle of Arnhem.

GREEN FINGERS

The Dutch, fond as always of gardening, go to De Tuinen Van Appeltern (Waalstraat 2a; tel: 048-754 1732; www.appeltern.nl; Apr–Sep daily 10am–6pm, Mar, Oct and Nov daily 10am–5pm) to get inspiration. It is by far the largest model garden complex in the Netherlands, with more than 100 different types of garden represented. Ranging from simple patios and plant boxes to intricately manicured lawns, tea gardens and gazebos, all conceivable plants and materials available to amateur and professional gardeners alike are on display here.

The visitor's centre has an extensive library and a display of rare species. After you've feasted your eyes on all this, you can relax in the beautiful winter gardens or enjoy some refreshments in the garden café.

west of Arnhem. Here, on the north bank of the Rhine, in the beautifully kept **Oosterbeek War Cemetery**, are the graves of the 1,748 Allied troops who tried to take the Arnhem Bridge.

The cemetery lies in a peaceful green clearing surrounded by trees, and is maintained by the staff of the War Graves Commission. Each year in September a touching memorial service is held, usually attended by about 3,000 people, including ex-servicemen and the widows, children and grandchildren of the dead. A touch of poignancy is added by children from the local schools who place bunches of flowers on each grave during the ceremony.

War museum

The devastating story of the Battle of Arnhem can be traced at the **Airborne Museum** (tel: 026-339 1785; http://airbornemuseum.nl; Apr–Oct Mon–Sat 10am–5pm, Sun noon–5pm, Nov–Mar Mon–Sat 11am–5pm, Sun noon–5pm) in Oosterbeek, located in the former Hotel Hartenstein, which served as the headquarters of the British 1st Airborne Division commander,

Airborne Museum memorial.

General Urquhart during the harrowing days of the battle. Visitors can follow the various stages of the bloody confrontation thanks to large-scale dioramas, spoken commentary and a photographic display.

If you are visiting the original Arnhem Bridge, a detour to the **Nederlands Openluchtmuseum** (Schelmseweg 89; tel: 026-357 6111; www.openairmuseum. nl; Apr–Oct daily 10am–5pm, Nov Sat–Sun 11am–4.30pm; Dec–mid-Jan Mon–Fri 11am–5pm, Sat–Sun 10am–6pm). on the outskirts of the city, is also worthwhile. The open-air museum spans 300 years of Dutch rural history reflected in over 100 different period buildings ranging from a wealthy merchant's house to a primitive paper-mill. It also has one of the more interesting exhibitions on traditional costume. A vintage tram ferries visitors around the complex (wheelchairs are also available).

Nijmegen

Nijmegen ❽ is the oldest city in the Netherlands. Formerly called Novio magus, after the Roman fortress that was built here, it was granted city rights 1,900 years ago under the Roman emperor Trajan. During the early Middle Ages it was controlled by the Franks. Under Charlemagne rule, it was an important administrative centre and the emperor built an imposing **palace** on the Valkhof. It was later destroyed by the Normans, and only scant remains can be seen (in the park east of the main square). Nevertheless, the city centre is rich in grand medieval buildings, relics of the city's former wealth and power. Despite extensive bombing during World War II the **Grote Markt** is well preserved.

Built on seven hills overlooking the River Waal, Nijmegen is an important city of the Catholic south, and many religious institutions are situated here including the main Catholic University with a student faculty of over 19,000.

The **Museum Het Valkhof** (Kelkensbos 59; Tue–Sun 11am–5pm) is largely a celebration of the city's

Roman past. An extensive range of coins, glassware, jewellery and ceramics are on display here. But the museum is not confined to the Roman collection: there are also art galleries dedicated to Pop Art and modern Expressionism, and exhibitions of less contemporary art including etchings, sculptures and silverware.

A royal family home

Apeldoorn ❾ is known as the 'Pen-pushers' Paradise' because of its large population of civil servants; they arrived in the 1960s when many government offices were relocated from Amsterdam and The Hague to Apeldoorn.

The town itself is nothing to write home about, but just outside is one of the loveliest Dutch palaces, **Paleis Het Loo** (tel: 055-577 2400; www.paleishetloo. nl; Tue–Sun 10am–5pm). This beautiful 17th-century palace was first occupied by William III, *Stadhouder* of the Netherlands and King of England and Scotland, who built Het Loo between 1685 and 1692 as a country seat. In the 18th century William III's successors, William IV and V, used it frequently. In

the 19th century William I, II and III all lived here. For the Dutch, Het Loo is especially associated with Queen Wilhelmina, who retired to this country residence after her abdication in 1948 and lived here until her death in 1962.

The palace is now a museum tracing the history of the House of Orange-Nassau and its ties with the Netherlands, which have existed since 1403. The palace itself has benefitted from magnificent restoration work, which entailed peeling off the white plaster façade to reveal the original brickwork, hidden since the 19th century when Louis Napoleon, installed by his brother Napoleon I as King of Holland in 1806, took over Het Loo and 'renovated' it. Mercifully his idea of what constituted good taste proved reversible.

The **gardens**, too, have been restored to their former 17th-century glory, making them the best surviving example of the horticultural trends of William and Mary's reign. The **Royal Stables**, built between 1906 and 1910, now house a collection of carriages, coaches, sledges and vintage cars used by members of the royal household.

Palace Het Loo and gardens, Apeldoorn.

OVERIJSSEL

Although it is a small, overpopulated country, the Netherlands has many provinces where you can get away from it all.

The province of Overijssel (pronounce the 'ij' like 'eye') lies between the German border and the IJsselmeer, and is divided into three regions. The **IJssel Delta** in the west is famous for its flora and fauna and is a popular area for watersports enthusiasts. **Salland**, the central area, is one of the few places in the Netherlands with hills. The third area, **Twente**, is perfect for walking and exploring its many tiny, picturesque villages.

Venice of the North

One of the loveliest (and most visited) villages in the province is **Giethoorn ⑩**, often likened to Venice because of its amazing network of narrow waterways, little footbridges and the punts that are used for transport – but the similarity ends there. It's a green, manicured village with neat Dutch sugar-loaf houses, smooth thatched cottages and the occasional austerely elegant merchant's house. To get a good feel of the place visit the **Museumboerderij' Olde Maat Uus** (Farmhouse Museum; Binnenpad 52; Apr–Oct Mon–Sat 11am–5pm, Sun noon–5pm, Nov–Mar Sun noon–5pm). Built in 1826 it now houses a collection of vintage agricultural implements and other utensils, while in the rear of the building there are seasonal exhibitions and

local crafts and skills are permanently represented.

Patrician houses

If you are an admirer of historic gabled houses but are looking for a quieter alternative to Amsterdam, stop off at **Blokzijl ⑪**, a small fortified town founded in the 15th century by merchants of the county of Holland. During the 17th and 18th centuries the town prospered through shipping and commerce, when the IJsselmeer was the Zuiderzee and deep enough for

Main Attractions
Giethoorn
Kampen
Museum de Fundatie, Zwolle
De Waag, Deventer

Typical houses in Blokzijl.

large vessels to drop anchor. The many restored houses bear witness to Blokzijl's former wealth. On Brouwersgracht is a 17th-century **Dutch Reformed Church** built in the shape of a Greek cross. Like most Reformed churches in the Netherlands, it's a little austere but worth a visit for the splendid pulpit dating from 1663 and the magnificent chandeliers. The **Kaatje bij de Sluis** (Brouwerstraat 20; tel: 0527-291833) restaurant, in a converted 17th-century mansion, is one of the best in the Netherlands.

Smoke-free zone

Genemuiden ⑫, awarded town status in 1245, is one of the few towns in the world with a street where smoking has been illegal for more than a century. The small street is called the **Achterweg**, and smoking is forbidden because of the fire risk to the old wooden buildings with their hay-storage areas. The prohibition, and one of the 'No Smoking' signs, dates from 1899.

Fire is not the only elemental threat to Genemuiden. Like so many places

in the Netherlands, the village is fighting a ceaseless battle against water levels. To appreciate the way they tackle the challenge here, visit the steam-powered pumping station **Stoomgemaal Mastenbroek** (Kamperzeedijk 7; tel: 038-344 6494; open first Sat in June, first and third Sat in July and Aug and first Sat in Oct 10am–4pm; visits outside these times can be arranged by appointment).

Calvinist traditions

Travelling south towards Zwolle, just off the motorway, is the village of **Staphorst** ⑬ notable for its Reformed church and staunchly religious culture which, to the modern observer, may seem oppressive.

Some of the inhabitants still wear traditional village costume, which is relentlessly black for men, but with a little intricately coloured relief for women and children. On Sundays they stay at home reading the Bible or spending time with their families, venturing out of doors only to visit the church. The farmhouses painted bright green and blue add a touch

A Staphorst resident's traditional costume.

of colour to the place, but do ask the villagers before taking photographs of them or their houses. Photography is not allowed in the vicinity of the church on Sundays out of respect for churchgoers.

Towers and spires

Lying on the flood plain of the IJssel, the small town of **Kampen** ⑭ has the Netherlands' finest series of gables and façades and a plethora of towers and gateways, making it a lovely place for a leisurely stroll. It reached its peak as an important trading town in the 16th century, when the most beautiful of the buildings were constructed.

The **Kroonmarkt** is dominated by the graceful 15th-century Gothic **Church of St Nicholas**, and a 14th-century **Town Hall** (Oudestraat 33). This building was partly devastated in 1543 but was rebuilt in the same decade. The most interesting part of the old wing is the medieval 'Magistrate's Hall', notable for its barrel-vaulted roof and splendid carved-stone chimneypiece.

The building now houses the **Stedelijk Museum** (Tue–Sat 10am––5pm, Sun 1–5pm), which has an exhibition on four themes: water, faith, law and the House of Orange. Try some apple pie in the contemporary café before you leave.

Provincial capital

Zwolle ⑮, the economic and cultural centre of West-Overijssel, and capital of Overijssel, is an ancient town of great architectural beauty. Throughout the 15th century it prospered as an important member of the Hanseatic League, an association of medieval towns formed to protect and advance their commercial interests. Most of the inner city's old buildings have been well restored, and there are many beautiful old gateways, some dating from the 15th century. Its bastions and star-shaped moat date from the 17th century. The city also has its supply of pretty canals, and a pleasant way of seeing it is by water-pedal boat.

The **Grote Markt** is dominated by the austere Church of St Michael. Next to it stands the **Hoofdwacht**, a

Relaxing in Zwolle's main square.

beautiful 17th-century gabled building which once overlooked the site of public executions.

To appreciate the history and understand the finer points of the town's evolution, a visit to the **Stedelijk Museum Zwolle** (Melkmarkt 41; open Tue–Sun 11am–5pm) is a must. There are permanent and temporary exhibitions dedicated to the cultural and social history not only of Zwolle, but of the entire province. The museum is housed in an 18th-century mansion, and its permanent exhibition includes several period rooms, a unique 18th-century kitchen, collections of archaeological finds, paintings, silverware, porcelain and textiles. There are also displays encompassing the economic, religious and municipal history and life of Zwolle. The entrance is in the new wing, which focuses on cultural history and contemporary art.

The **Museum de Fundatie** (Blijmarkt 20; www.museumdefundatie.nl; Tue–Sun 11am–5pm), housed in a former courthouse, has an art collection dating from the 17th to 20th century

Playing in Salland area woods.

featuring Dutch and international artists including Van Gogh and Chagall. The museum also has a sculpture garden at **Kasteel het Nijenhuis** (Mar–Oct Tue–Sun 11am–5pm, Nov–Feb Thu–Sun 11am–5pm) in Heino, about half and hour's drive from Zwolle. Ninety works by leading sculptors such as Zadkine and Allen Jones are dotted around the castle's parkland.

One of Zwolle's greatest architectural gems is the **Sassenpoort** (53 Sassenstraat; Sat 1–5pm, also Wed 1–4pm Apr–Oct), a Unesco-listed medieval gatehouse dating back to 1409. It is now used as a visitors' information centre, dedicated to the history of the town, with architectural models and various old photographs on display.

Gothic splendour

About 30km (19 miles) south of Zwolle, in the Salland area of Overijssel, is the delightful old town of **Deventer** ⑯, another riverside town that prospered from the booming Zuiderzee trade. The 15th-century **Lebuïnuskerk** (Groote Poort Mon–Sat 11am–5pm; free), a gran

---

HILL COUNTRY

If you get the yearning to see some hills, head for the Salland area. At Holten railway station you can pick up a map describing a bicycle route of about 26km (16 miles). Known as the *heuvelrug* route (hill-range route), it takes cyclists over the hill range formed in the last Ice Age that now delineates the Salland-Twente border. The scenery, consisting largely of ancient forests and heathlands, is beautiful.

The best place to rent bicycles is from *Jan Stam Fietsverhuur* (Waagweg 7, Holten, tel: 054-836 6802), where you can also buy the aforementioned map. You'll need to present some form of identification and pay a returnable deposit for each bicycle.

Walkers can take the Holterberg route (maps are available from Nijverdal railway station). The leisurely 14km (9-mile) walk begins at the visitor's centre (Sallandse Heuvelrug; Grotestraat 281; tel: 054-861 2711; Apr–Oct daily 10am–5pm, Nov–Mar Tue–Sun 10am–4pm), which is run by forest rangers. Here you can buy a special ticket which allows you to continue your walk through a protected nature reserve. This is one of the few areas in the Netherlands where you can spot the black grouse in its natural habitat. There are a few steep hills, but none is too strenuous, and all footpaths are in excellent condition. The walk ends at Holten railway station.

Gothic building, is the embodiment of Deventer's former wealth and importance and one of the finest ecclesiastical buildings in the eastern Netherlands. Energetic types might want to climb the 46-metre (150ft) tower (May–Oct Sat 1–4pm, daily in school holidays), which has 220 steps – but the views are worth it. Another rather impressive church is the 12th-century two-towered **Bergkerk** on Kerksteeg, dedicated to St Nicholas.

The most interesting sight in town is **De Waag** (Brink 56; Tue–Sat 10am–5pm, Sun 1–5pm), the old weigh house, which dates from the 16th century and has an exhibition on local history. It also houses the tourist office.

About 20 minutes' drive south of the town in Gorssel is **Museum More** (Hoofdstraat 28; www.museummore.nl; Tue–Sun 10am–5pm), which opened in 2015 and is devoted to Dutch Modern Realism. As you'd expect, there is a stylish café for refreshments.

A walk in the woods

In the eastern Overijssel area of Twente, near the German border, you will come across the town of **Delden** ⑰, whose main attraction is **Twickel Castle** – which sounds just like a place in a children's storybook. The castle itself is not open to the public, but the gardens are (tel: 074-376 1020; www.twickel.nl; Apr–Oct Wed–Sun 10am–5pm). The castle is surrounded by a magnificent oak forest, the largest in Western Europe, which is great for walking.

Another very attractive town in the area is **Ootmarsum** ⑱. Most of its 18th-century houses have now been restored, and there is a magnificent 12th-century church. But prettiest of all is the surrounding countryside, with walks through quiet fields past wonderful 16th-century windmills. Watermills are plentiful here too, and four of these are open to the public. Watermolen Singraven (Schiphorstdijk 2, Denekamp; tel: 054-135 2345; guided tours Apr–Oct Sat 1–5pm) dates back to the 15th century and is unique because it has three wheels; visitors can still see the flour mill and saw mill.

Twickel Castle near Delden dates from medieval times.

FLEVOLAND

Amsterdam

The Netherlands' newest province has few historic centres, but it does offer excellent watersports facilities, sandy beaches and green countryside.

Nieuwland Polder Museum, Lelystad
Batavia Werf, Lelystad
Cycling the wetlands
Urk
Fishing

Waterside houses in the Almere region.

Much of this, the flattest province in the Netherlands, is made up of recently reclaimed land ringed by a channel of water, and its modern towns are built on what was formerly the bottom of the Zuiderzee (see page 270). Reclamation of Flevoland began after World War II, but the work wasn't finally completed until 1986 when the newly created polders – Oostelijk Flevoland and Zuidelijk Flevoland – were officially declared the 12th province of the Netherlands.

Ships and planes

Lelystad ❶ is the capital of the new province, named after the engineer who pioneered the Zuiderzee reclamation scheme. The first inhabitants arrived, mainly from Amsterdam, in 1967, and since then the town has grown into a long-range commuting suburb of Amsterdam. Although it has many parks and nearby nature areas, shiny new Lelystad has yet to put down deep community roots. Apart from some interesting housing developments, the main points of interest in the town are its museums. The **Nieuw Land Polder museum** (Oostvaardersdijk 113; tel 032-022 5900; www.nieuwlanderfgoed.nl Tue–Fri 10am–5pm, Sat–Sun 11.30am–5pm), occupying an eye-catching building, has a permanent exhibition centre on land reclamation which transport you through 15 different themes, ranging from the old Zuiderzee culture to current coastal defences. One of its most prized exhibits is the oldest skeleton found in the Netherlands. The museum is very child-friendly and also supplies audioguides in English.

The nearby **Batavia-Werf** (Batavia Wharf; Oostvaardersdijk 01-09; tel 032-026 1409; www.bataviawerf.nl; daily 10am–5pm) is a popular attraction, and for good reason. The traditional ship-building yard initially gained its fame for its authentic working replica of the 17th-century Dutch East India Company merchant ship, the *Batavia*, which visitors are allowed to explore freely. T

wharf is currently building a replica of Admiral de Ruyter's legendary ship, *De Zeven Provinciën (The Seven Provinces)*, a 17th-century 'man-o'-war' constructed with traditional materials and crafts of the period. De Batavia-Werf is a working museum, not only in shipbuilding but also in conservation. In another wing, they are busy preserving the wreck of a 16th-century ship, under the supervision of the Dutch Institute of Shipping and Underwater Archaeology.

The Dutch have a proud aviation history, and for aircraft enthusiasts a visit to **Aviodrome,** at nearby Lelystad Airport (Flying Museum; Pelikaanweg 50; tel: 032-028 9842; www.aviodrome.nl; Tue–Sun 10am–5pm), which has a collection of more than 100 modern and vintage aircraft, is a real treat.

Modern architecture

Almere is the province's fastest-growing new town, but although the ambitious town-planners created a pleasing design, with modern sculpture an integral part of the town's layout, it is not the success people had hoped for. Unless you are interested in 'progressive and radical' architecture – **De Fantasie**, completed in 1983, is a complex of unusually shaped family houses, while **Bouw Rai** is another modern housing area with 225 homes designed by 15 different architects – there's nothing much to recommend it.

Nature trails

Near Almere, the Oostvaardersplassen region, with its 6,000 hectares (15,000 acres) of wetlands – small lakes, reed marshland and woods – is one of Europe's more important nature reserves. Half-wild horses and cattle have been imported to this area, and there is an excellent protected natural bird sanctuary. There are even colonies of cormorants.

The town of **Dronten**, 7km (4 miles) east of Lelystad, is an excellent base for bicycle trips and walks in the surrounding nature areas and is ideal for camping holidays, too. Maps of walking and cycling routes are available from the local VVV (De Rede 80–82; tel: 088-008 0740). The Stadsbosbeheer (State Forest Authority) ranger guides are particularly informative.

Protestant tradition

Urk ❸, formerly a small island, is an especially interesting place to visit. The 1,000-year-old fishing village is a very pretty, traditional place, where the local dialect is still spoken and some older inhabitants still wear the local costume, examples of which are on display in the **Museum Het Oude Raadhuis** (Wijk 2-2; tel: 052-768 3262; Apr–Oct Mon–Fri 10am–5pm, Sat 10am–4pm, Nov–Mar Mon–Sat 10am–4pm).

The community is intensely Protestant, which means that everything stops on Sundays. Nowadays, attitudes are much more relaxed, but once upon a time anyone who dared sail into Urk harbour on a Sunday would have had their boat pelted with stones. Urk remains a hard-working fishing village, but has also become a yachting centre and is an ideal centre for a waterways holiday.

TIP

About 15 minutes' drive west of Urk is Schokland: a long, thin strip of peat land that used to be an island. Now a Unesco World Heritage Site, you can learn about its turbulent watery past at Museum Schokland (Middelburt 3; tel: 052-725 1396; Apr–Oct Tue–Sun 11am–5pm, July–Aug daily 10am–5pm, Nov–Mar Fri–Sun 11am–5pm).

Tourists visiting a local fair in Urk.

THE IJSSELMEER

Land reclamation schemes changed the
face of northern Holland, turning former
fishing and whaling ports into yachting
communities and market towns.

Main Attractions
Zuiderzee Museum
Hoorn
Sailing
Volendam

The IJsselmeer, a large freshwater lake north of Amsterdam, was created in 1932 by the enclosure of the saltwater Zuiderzee (South Sea), which was once open to the North Sea. This feat was achieved with the construction of the *Afsluitdijk*, a huge engineering project that took five years to complete. The Zuiderzee formed during the Middle Ages when flooding slowly turned what was then Lake Flevo into a North Sea inlet. In the 13th century, the Dutch began clawing back lost land by constructing dykes and draining the enclosed areas to form stretches of land known as polders. Large areas of the northern Netherlands have been reclaimed in this way. A polder is a very distinctive form of landscape which stands out clearly on a detailed map. The outline of each drained lake is marked by a canal (called a *ringvaart*), lined with windmills to pump water out. The reclaimed land is marked with a grid pattern of roads and drainage ditches, and the towns built on it are laid out with straight streets.

Fishing to farming

Many old villages around such drained lakes were forced to transform themselves from fishing ports into inland market towns. You may be surprised to find a fishing and whaling museum in landlocked **De Rijp**, but back in the Middle Ages this town was a port on the

western shore of the Beemster lake. In 1612 the lake was drained by engineer Jan Leeghwater (his name means 'Empty Water') to create a large polder, prompting the Italian ambassador, Trevisano, to observe: "It seems incredible, when one tells it, a land dry and ploughed that shortly before was a deep and large lake."

Financially this project was highly successful; Amsterdam merchants eagerly bought up the new land to form country estates, and the remainder became fertile farmland. Encouraged by the profits, Leeghwater drained two

Sailing on the IJsselmeer.

other lakes, creating the Wormer polder in 1622 and the Purmer polder in 1626. The economy of **Purmerend**, which lay between the three lakes, changed dramatically as a result. Like De Rijp, it had been a fishing and whaling town, but in the 17th century it metamorphosed into a landlocked market town surrounded by fertile polders.

Most villages prospered from land reclamation, and many celebrated their success in the 17th century by building imposing new town halls. Leeghwater was kept busy designing those of De Rijp, Graft and Jisp (one of few towns in the area still standing on a lake).

Sealing up the Zuiderzee

The most ambitious land reclamation project of all was the enclosure of the Zuiderzee. The first plans for a dyke were drawn up in 1891 by I.C. Lely (after whom Lelystad new town is named), but it was a long time before work actually got under way. After endless debate, and the devastating floods of 1916, which spurred some action, the 32km (20-mile) long **Afsluitdijk** ❹ was finally completed in 1932, and

the Zuiderzee became the IJsselmeer. The roadway built on top of the dam to connect North Holland to Friesland is now a major artery in the country's road network.

History on the waterfront

A modest, well-preserved town (population 18,000), **Enkhuizen** ❺ was the Netherlands' foremost herring port during the 17th century, hence the three herring motif on its coat of arms. The most attractive spots are around the harbours, in particular at a secluded promontory overlooking the backs of the houses on Bocht. The fishing industry is not quite dead here, and a small fish auction is still held on **Buitenhaven**.

Many of Enkhuizen's most striking buildings, such as the **Munt** (Mint) of 1611 at Westerstraat 22, and the **Weeshuis** (Orphanage) at Westerstraat 111, built five years later, are designed in jaunty Dutch Mannerist style. North of Westerstraat is a peaceful, almost rural area, often overlooked, known as the **Boerenhoek** (Farmers' Quarter), where you still come across large farmhouses built alongside urban canals.

NEW POLDERS

After Afsluitdijk, three new polders were created in the southern part of the lake. The Noordoostpolder between 1937 and 1942, Oostelijk Flevoland between 1950 and 1957, and Zuidelijk Flevoland between 1959 and 1968. While many towns prospered from land reclamation, the creation of the Afsluitdijk and the surrounding polders had enormous repercussions for the many fishing towns around the IJsselmeer. Access to the sea was now blocked and the fishing communities that once thrived on the shores of the Zuiderzee disappeared. A proposed fourth polder, the Markerwaard, was abandoned after objections from Hoorn and other affected towns which did not want to end up landlocked. The dyke that would have enclosed the Markerwaard now carries a road linking Enkhuizen and Lelystad.

The Zuiderzee's fascinating history is vividly presented at the **Zuiderzee Museum** in Enkhuizen (Wierdijk 12–22; www.zuiderzeemuseum.nl; daily 10am–5pm). Though enthusiasts mooted the idea of a Zuiderzee museum back in the 1930s, the **Binnenmuseum** (indoor museum) didn't open until 1950; another 33 years were to elapse before the **Buitenmuseum** (open-air museum; Apr–Oct) joined it. The Binnenmuseum is housed in a Dutch Renaissance waterfront complex from 1625, a local merchant's combined home and warehouse. When the Enkhuizen Chamber of the United East India Company later acquired it, it became known as the **Peperhuis** because of the company's lucrative trade in Indonesian pepper.

A large hall houses an extensive collection of traditional Zuiderzee fishing boats and pleasure craft. It is interesting to see how different styles of boat-building developed in fishing towns only a short distance apart. Local furniture also varied in style from one town to the next. But the greatest diversity seems to be in the costume, as illustrated in the series of furnished rooms depicting different local styles. Terschelling Island, industrial Zaanstad, West-Friesland, Hindeloopen (famous for hand-painted furniture), Marken, Urk, Spakenburg and Volendam are all represented.

Enkhuizen open-air museum

The only way to reach the nearby open-air museum is by boat (the return trip is included in the entrance ticket), either from the pier near the railway station or from a car park at the beginning of the dyke road to Lelystad. The inconvenience of this arrangement is outweighed by the thrill of arriving by boat, though the landing-craft boats built for the museum look out of place alongside traditional brown-sailed boats in Enkhuizen harbour.

The museum, a reconstruction of fishing communities, is made up of around 130 buildings rescued from towns around the Zuiderzee. Some of the houses were shipped intact across the IJsselmeer, and one three-storey wooden cheese warehouse was transported from Landsmeer along Noord-Holland's inland waterways on two barges. The layout of the museum is based on *buurtjes* (quarters) modelled on different towns. The harbour, modelled on Marken's, has several old fishing boats moored at the quayside. There is even a small reconstructed corner of Amsterdam hidden behind the museum shop.

Labels attached to houses provide interesting snippets of information about their former occupants. Large families, such as the couple with nine children who lived in the house from Venhuizen (VH1), often inhabited the tiniest houses. Many of the houses are neatly furnished in period style, with tea trays set out in front rooms as if the occupants might return at any moment. A grocery shop in the Harderwijk quarter sells delicious smoked sausage and boiled sweets, there's a post office from Den Oever, and a

Enkhuizen open-air museum is a former fishing village and an important local tourist attraction.

baker's shop on the main canal sells traditional cakes. Demonstrations of local trades are given in some buildings, such as the painter's shop and the steam laundry.

The museum has four restaurants: the most attractive is the dyke house restaurant, with a gleaming tiled interior from Hindeloopen that overlooks the harbour. There are also several shops including The Cheese Warehouse, which was originally located in a nearby village, and sells the local fenugreek-seasoned cheese.

Ideally, you need a whole day to visit both parts of the museum, and another day to visit the town of Enkuizen itself.

Seafaring towns

A quiet old port 21km (13 miles) northwest of Enkhuizen, **Medemblik ❻** is one of the oldest towns in the Netherlands. Its harbour is a popular mooring spot for visiting yachts, but its main attraction for tourists is **Kasteel Radboud** (Oudevaartsgat 8; May–Sep Mon–Sat 11am–5pm, Sun 2–5pm, Oct–Apr Sun 2–5pm), a heavily restored 13th-century castle overlooking the harbour,

Kasteel Radboud.

named after a Frisian king defeated by the Franks in AD 689.

The summer steam train pulls in at the old railway station (where you'll also find the VVV). The **Stoommachine Museum** (Oosterdijk 4; Mar–Oct Tue–Sun 10am–5pm, mid-July–mid-Aug also Mon 10am–5pm) has an interesting collection of well-preserved old steam engines.

Hoorn ❼, 19km (12 miles) to the south, was one of the Dutch Republic's great seafaring towns. Among many famous mariners born here were Abel Tasman, the first European to reach Tasmania, and Jan Pietersz Coen, founder of the Dutch Indonesian trading post Batavia (now Jakarta). Another Hoorn native, Willem Schouten, named Cape Horn after his home town. Today, the town is effectively a dormitory adjunct of Amsterdam, but many mementoes of its maritime history have survived. The harbour quarter to the south of **Grote Oost** is particularly interesting to explore, with the best view from south of Binnenhaven towards a row of step-gabled merchants' houses on Veermanskade. Three curious 17th-century houses on Slapershaven, named the **Bossuhuizen** after a Spanish admiral, are decorated with colourful friezes depicting a sea battle off Hoorn in 157□

A magnificent Dutch Mannerist building overlooks the **Rode Steen** (main square, literally 'red stone'). Built in 1632 for the College of the States of West-Friesland (Alkmaar, Edam, Enkhuizen, Hoorn, Medemblik, Monnickendam and Purmerend), it houses the **Westfries Museum** (www.westfriesmuseum.info; Tue–Fri 11am–5pm, Sat–Sun 1–5pm; Apr–Oct also open Mon) local history, filled with the confidence of the Dutch Golden Age, and containing furniture, guild group portraits, ship models and period rooms. Opposite, **Waag** is a handsome, Dutch classical weigh house from 1609. Streets north of Rode Steen contain other relics of Hoorn's glorious past. These include the Dutch Renaissance **Statenpoort** from 1613 at Nieuwstraat 23, for

government representatives' lodgings. In Muntstraat opposite is the Hoorn Chamber of the United East India Company, completed in 1682.

There are a couple of other museums in town worth visiting: the **Affiche Museum** (Grote Oost 2-4; www.affiche museum.nl; Tue–Fri 11am–5pm, Sat–Sun noon–5pm), a collection of Dutch posters from the past 100 years, and **Museum van de Twintigste Eeuw** (Museum of the Twentieth Century; Krententuin 24, Oostereiland; Mon–Fri 10am–5pm, Sat–Sun noon–5pm), which is housed in the old prison on an island in the harbour, and looks at daily life during the last century.

Yachting and windsurfing

Monnickendam ❽, 16km (10 miles) northeast of Amsterdam, is an attractive little port with picturesque canals. The harbour's vast collection of pleasure boats of every size and type, from dinghies to ocean-going luxury cruisers, as well as fishing boats and windsurfing facilities, is surprising for such a small place. An enticing smell of smoked eel wafts through narrow lanes by the harbour, where there are several old smokehouses.

From the harbour, boats ply the Gouzee in summer months to **Marken** ❾. Once an isolated and somewhat eccentric fishing community, Marken was 'discovered' by 19th-century French tourists. Now linked to the mainland by a causeway, the island has lost something of its romantic appeal. But the community has held on to its identity and Marken's traditional black-and-green wooden houses on stilts form an attractive scene. **Havenbuurt** (Harbour Quarter), a village whose painted houses cluster around the tiny harbour, and **Kerkbuurt** (Church Quarter) get pretty crowded, but there are quiet corners to explore in the eastern part. The remainder of the island is farmland, and you reach the white lighthouse at its end by taking a brisk walk along the old sea dyke where it's possible to watch old-time IJsselmeer sailing ships, *boters* and

skûtsjes ply the waters offshore. The **De Taanderij** café overlooking the harbour is a convivial place for lunch or coffee.

Artists' haven

A boat service links Marken with the former fishing town of **Volendam** ❿, a few kilometres north of Monnickendam, and unusual in these parts because of its predominantly Catholic population. The populist face of Dutch tourism is on display here. Some local people occasionally wear traditional costume, and you can have your picture taken wearing clogs and short jackets, or long flowery aprons and milkmaid hats. Harbourside fish stalls do brisk business, especially with smoked IJsselmeer *paling* (eel).

The harbour front has been taken over by tourist shops, though a few narrow canals behind the dyke are still worth exploring. During the 19th century, Romantic painters flocked here to paint the fisherfolk in traditional costume. The Spaander Hotel (Haven 15-19; www.hotelspaander.nl) where they stayed still stands; on its café walls are paintings that the owner accepted as payment.

Cycling to Marken's lighthouse.

WILDLIFE AND NATURE RESERVES

The Dutch have acted with characteristic resolve and attention to detail to preserve wild places in their small, densely populated country.

With 16.5 million inhabitants living in 42,000 sq km (16,000 sq miles), the Netherlands has one of the world's highest population densities. Though the entire country could fit inside America's Yellowstone National Park it has its share of protected places: national parks and nature reserves managed by the Staatsbosbeheer (State Forestry Service; www.staatsbosbeheer.nl) and the Vereniging tot Behoud van Natuurmonumenten (Federation for Nature Conservancy). These bodies protect forests, heathland, dunes, marshes, lakes, rivers, an island, and the habitats of rare and endangered wildlife and plants. Despite their modest size, the parks and reserves are eclectic and varied. As with many Dutch landscapes the Biesbosch National Park, near Rotterdam, bears the imprint of flooding. This 'forest of reeds' was once isolated and almost inaccessible, but now its flotilla of marshy islands have been partially stitched together and the flooded area reduced.

Equally memorable are the inland sand dunes of the Loonse en Drunense Duinen near 's-Hertogenbosch (Den Bosch). It seems as if desertification has struck the watery polders (reclaimed land), but only sand-grasses and scrubby trees prevent this granular landscape from blowing away on the wind. In Noord-Brabant and Limburg, the peat moors of Groote Peel National Park is another of those places, formerly wild and inhospitable, that must now be protected if its original character is to survive.

Atmospheric moorland in winter at Veluwezoom National

Free bicycles provide perfect motivation for exploring the heathland, forests and fens of Hoge Veluwe National Park north of Arnhem.

Deer, fox and wild boar are among the few large mammals to survive.

A little owl peers out from within a hollow tree stump in Krimpenerwaard, Zuid-Holland.

ON A WING AND A PRAYER

The absence of any large mammals in the Netherlands makes birdwatching, for species like wood owls, a major draw. Taking a boat trip into the Biesbosch National Park (www.np-debiesbosch.nl) is to drift into a far different world from the open polder land that surrounds it. The ecologically rich wetlands environment south of Rotterdam is a paradise for birds. Kingfishers dart along narrow channels, and coots and hawks flutter overhead. Heron, storks, geese, ducks and cormorants are just some of the other avian species that make their homes in the park. It's worth noting that there are also around 250 beavers here, the park's most famous residents, which were reintroduced to the area in 1988 after dying out in the 1820s.

Although there is plenty of woodland habitat, however, the country's vast amounts of freshwater resources – rivers, lakes, canals – long coastline and wetlands, are especially attractive to waterbirds. Heron are a frequent sight, as are oyster catchers, spoonbills and ducks. The white stork is rare and protected. One of the best areas for observing seabirds is the Wadden Islands.

Schiermonnikoog Island in the Waddenzee earned ...al park status for its tranquillity and sea dunes lined ...oods.

...y boat is the best way to get to grips with the ...h National Park, a swampy area most of which ...nerged during the St Elizabeth Day flood in 1421.

Nature reserves and nationalparks provide badly needed protection for many bird species, such as this kingfisher. Its habitats are endangered by urban sprawl and the intensive agriculture now practised on the polder lands.

Take an active holiday in Drenthe.

DRENTHE

Green and pleasant Drenthe, with its woodlands and rolling hills, is regarded by many Dutch as a home from home.

Vincent van Gogh was perhaps Drenthe's greatest admirer. It was love at first sight for the artist, who spent his short life in pursuit of serenity and found it for a time in Drenthe.

More famous for his paintings of the sunflowers in the fields around Arles, Van Gogh was equally captivated by the peaceful bog and moorland countryside of this province, where he painted some of his best canvases. Once, while visiting Drenthe, he wrote: 'What peace it would give me if I could settle permanently in this region.' Instead of settling, he went to live in France, where he died prematurely in 1890, after a life of unrelenting poverty and misery.

A visit to the province will quickly reveal what appealed to Van Gogh. In an overpopulated, highly industrialised country, Drenthe can still be described as sparsely populated. This very green province in the northeast of the Netherlands, bordered on the east by Germany, was once rather snootily regarded by the Dutch as being no more than a backward 'Farmers' Republic'.

Out of the land

Centuries ago the sheep farmers of Drenthe were very much a part of the rural economy, and the sheep were responsible for creating arable land, thanks to their manure production. The more sheep a farmer had, the more arable land could be used, and consequently the more wool and meat was produced. No wonder sheep used to be referred to as animals with golden hooves. Sheep herds have now dwindled from their thousands, but smaller herds are maintained for conservation reasons in the fen and moorlands. In the small village of Exloo there is a herd of 150 sheep which are taken out of their pen every day from 15 April to 1 November at

Main Attractions

Orvelte
Meppel
Kamp Westerbork

Drenthe Heath sheep in Ruinen.

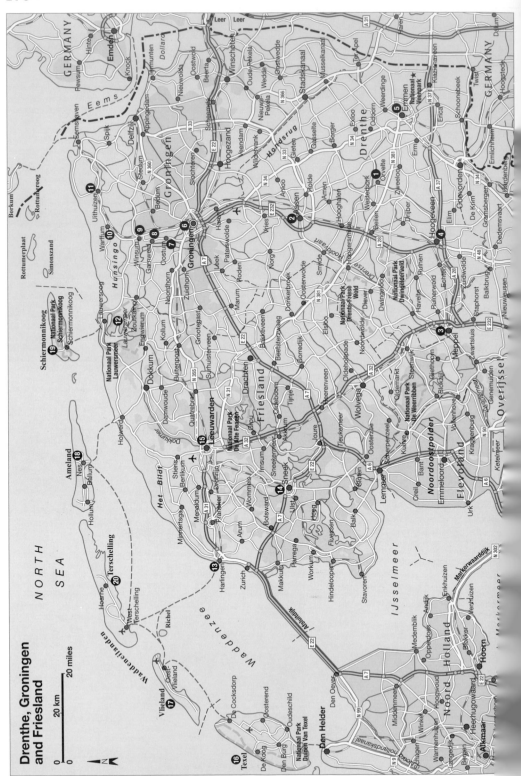

Drenthe, Groningen and Friesland

GERMANY

NORTH SEA

Waddenzee

Waddeneilanden

IJsselmeer

Markermeer

Noord Holland

Overijssel

Flevoland

Noordoostpolder

Friesland

Groningen

Drenthe

Hunsingo

Het Bildt

0 20 km
0 20 miles

Emden
Leer
Winschoten
Stadskanaal
Emmen
Nationaal Beekpark ★
Hoogeveen
Assen
Meppel
Groningen
Delfzijl
Appingedam
Hoogezand
Veendam
Leeuwarden
Drachten
Heerenveen
Wolvega
Sneek
Lemmer
Harlingen
Dokkum
Schiermonnikoog
Ameland
Terschelling
West Terschelling
Vlieland
Texel
Den Helder
Alkmaar
Hoorn
Enkhuizen

Nationaal Park Lauwersmeer
Nationaal Park Schiermonnikoog
Nationaal Park De Alde Feanen
Nationaal Park De Weerribben
Nationaal Park Drents-Friese Wold
Nationaal Park Dwingelderveld
Nationaal Park Duinen Van Texel

1
2
3
4
5
6
7
8
9
10
11
12
13
14
15
16
17
18
19
20

10.30am, and returned at 5pm. Other herds can be seen in the villages of Baloo, Odoorn, Orvelte, Ruinen and Dwingeloo.

Land is at a premium in the Netherlands, which is less than one-third the size of Ireland but with more than three times the population. The Dutch see Drenthe as their historical homeland, as indeed it is, for Drenthe existed before much of the Netherlands was reclaimed from the sea.

The old country

Drenthe was once an area of bog or fenland, and archaeologists have managed to recover a vast number of amazingly well-preserved wooden artefacts and utensils from the peat bogs. The province also has all but one of the Netherlands' *hunebedden*; these prehistoric sepulchral mounds are built of boulders or megaliths and date to the 4th and 3rd centuries BC. During more recent times Drenthe was bartered between various European conquerors. The Romans came first, and the province still has traces of their roadways; then came the Frankish kings and German emperors. Later, when all the southern and northern provinces were confederated in the Republic of Holland, Drenthe had no separate representation; it was seen as being a backwater not worth bothering about.

Local people did not mind much and continued to enjoy the serenity of their cosy rural life. When the area was officially declared a province in 1815, life continued exactly as before. Even today Drenthe has that peaceful, forgotten-world quality that is increasingly difficult to find in more developed northern European countries. Drenthe is the place the Dutch now visit to relax and escape the crowds.

Village life

Many of the rural villages of the province still have their *brinken*, or village green, surrounded by beautiful traditional Dutch cottages, old-fashioned gardens and pristine cobbled streets echoing to the clatter of clogs. Though clearly not Scandinavian, there is something about the

TIP

A good place for cycling in this area is the Drentsche Aa National Park (www.drentscheaa.nl), which covers 10,000 hectares (24,710 acres) northwest of Assen. There is no visitor centre but there are trained hosts in local businesses including the Bicycle Gasselte bike-hire shop at Dorpsstraat 20 in Gasselte (tel: 059-956 4607).

Aalden windmill.

KAMP WESTERBORK

In the middle of Drenthe lies the infamous and haunting **Kamp Westerbork** (Oosthalen 8; tel: 059-359 2600; www.kampwesterbork.nl; Feb–Dec Mon–Fri 10am–5pm, Sat–Sun 1–5pm), a former World War II transit camp for unfortunate victims, mainly Roma gypsies and Dutch and German Jews, who were headed for concentration camps. The story of their everyday life in Kamp Westerbork is told in the remembrance centre. A partially furnished barrack room, a last-minute scribbled greeting thrown out of the train, a large model of the camp and a drawing of children playing combine to form a mental image of Westerbork's past. Personal stories in the exhibition and 1944 film footage help to make this period accessible to children.

villages of Drenthe which conjures up images from Hans Christian Andersen. It's as if there could be inchworms measuring the marigolds, gingerbread houses in the woods and fairies at the bottom of every garden.

Not content with its collection of naturally preserved villages, Drenthe also has a 'show' village called **Orvelte** ❶ (May–Oct Tue–Sun 11am–5pm, daily July–Aug, Nov–Apr Sat–Sun 11am–5pm), dubbed a 'living monument of historically interesting rural architecture.' This is quite unlike those so-called 'native' villages in different parts of the world where the 'natives' arrive in the morning, park their cars, and pretend to be honest-to-goodness villagers during the day while the cameras click. People born in Orvelte go to school, marry and die there. First stop in Orvelte should be the VVV (Dorpstraat 1a; tel: 059-3322 332; Apr–Oct Tue–Sun 10am–5pm, daily July–Aug), where staff will help you plan a route around the vast array of cottage industries.

Look out for birds in Orvelte.

Not all buildings have free entrance. You'll find workshops specialising in flint-knapping, clog- and candle-making, a tin foundry and, of course, a village pub.

Similar in concept are two other museums close by. The **Nationaal Veenpark** (tel: 059-132 4444; Apr–Oct 10am–5pm, July–Aug until 6pm), near the village of Barger Compascuum to the east of Emmen, is a museum-village illustrating life in a mid-19th-century peat colony. Exhibitions explain the process of extracting peat, primarily for use as fuel, but also for the construction of turf-walled cottages. Other attractions include a theme park for children, based upon the characters in the books by Herman Veen. You can then take a trip on a peat barge to the nearby village.

The **Openluchtmuseum Ellert en Brammert** (tel: 059-138 2421; www.ellertenbramert.nl; Apr–Oct daily 9am–6pm) at nearby Schoonoord recalls life at the turn of the 19th century, through its buildings and exhibitions centred on the exploit

of two local friendly giants, Ellert and Brammert. It also has a children's farm.

Exploring the towns

Drenthe has four main towns. The best-known among speed fans would be Drenthe's capital city, **Assen ❷**, where the famous TT Moto GP Superbike race is held annually on the last Sunday in June. But the town also has its antiquities; the most beautiful and historically interesting is the 13th-century convent of the Cistercian order of Maria in Campis. The convent was originally built on bogland in 1245 in an area called Coevorden near Assen. However, the nuns found the area too damp, and the building was moved lock, stock, barrel and bricks to the town. After the Reformation, in 1598, the convent was secularised and taken over by the district council.

Today, in the grounds of the beautiful 13th-century abbey church, you will find the **Drents Museum** (Brink 1; www.drentsmuseum.nl; Tue–Sun 11am–5pm), which has a fine collection of Germanic, Roman and medieval artefacts, as well as several bodies of prehistoric bog people discovered well preserved in their peat graves.

Meppel ❸ is one of the oldest towns in Drenthe, with a 15th-century church and some fine 15th-century houses. Also worth a visit is the c.1840 *Theekoepel* (tea dome) in Wilhelmina Park. In neighbouring Nijeveen is the *Boerkerk* or farmer's church, built in the style of a 15th-century farmhouse. This attractive town of 33,000 inhabitants is an important hub for land and water transport and has some of the area's best watersports facilities.

Hoogeveen ❹ used to be a busy inland harbour in the days when south Drenthe was a land of peat colonies. Today it is an attractive place to shop. On Sunday mornings a drummer parades through the streets calling people to church, a custom dating back 300 years to

the time when the inland waterway was the most important source of income for the town. The inhabitants wanted things to stay that way and so followed the drummer to church every Sunday to enlist heavenly aid.

Emmen ❺ is the largest town in Drenthe. It has a lively market place where you can buy comfortable wooden clogs for walking around the nearby **Noorder Dierenpark** (Hoofdstraat 18; tel: 059-185 0855; daily from 10am), a small zoo where animals roam freely in an open natural landscape. In nearby Erica, **Industrieel Smalspoor Museum** (Griendtsveenstraat 140; tel: 059-130 3061; May–Oct Wed 1–4.30pm, Thu and Sat 10am–4.30pm, Sun 11am–4.30pm) is an industrial narrow-gauge railway museum housing a collection of working and static 1930s diesel locomotives. Admission includes a round trip in one of these curious vehicles, taking in a peat moor and the only remaining turf-shredding factory of its kind in the Netherlands.

In Hoogeveen's Grote Kerk yard.

GRONINGEN

This is where many find the image of the Netherlands they've been looking for – a flat, green landscape dotted with windmills.

Groningen, like its neighbour Friesland, is *terpen* country. These mounds – usually built on top of what was once a kind of communal rubbish heap – were used by the earliest inhabitants, the so-called 'marsh Dutch', to raise their buildings above the floodplain.

Boating, biking or driving through the northern countryside, typically as flat as a billiard table and just as green, you can still see many remaining *terpen* that serve to elevate medieval churches and sometimes even whole villages. Eventually the northerners turned to dykes, in preference to mounds, building row after row of some of the biggest in the world as they painstakingly reclaimed the land from the sea – a process that is still going on and which can be witnessed today, especially in northern Groningen.

Amsterdam of the north

Groningen ❻ is the name of the capital as well as of the province. The city (population 193,000) is a busy commercial centre that regards itself as the Amsterdam of the north. Not much remains of the old city, which was pretty well destroyed during the Allied liberation in 1945. Groningen's attraction lies more in its atmosphere than in its appearance. One of the dominant aspects of Groningen is

its youthful population and vibrant intellectual scene. The university is prestigious, and an estimated 29,000 students live in the city, along with an equal number of other young people below the age of 30. It also attracts many artists.

Aside from the university, the main industry is producing sugar from beet. The locals, with the typical northern Dutch wryness of humour, like to say Groningen's sugar production makes it 'the sweetest town in Europe' – unless

Main Attractions
Groninger Museum
Groningen Almshouses
Winsum 'Canoe Village'
Menkemaborg

Groningen University's main building.

the wind from the factory is blowing the wrong way.

Groningen gets few foreign tourists, other than passing Scandinavians and Germans. Locals ruefully admit that many of those tourists are en route to Amsterdam, often to buy drugs, and the drugs trade has now come to Groningen itself – another reason the city is called the Amsterdam of the north. But even for those not interested in drugs, Groningen's history and its lively pub scene are worth a visit.

The city centre, nearly 2km (1 mile) across, is encircled by a canal with further bisecting canals. One of the main landmarks is the **Martinikerk** (tel: 050-311 1277; www.martinkerk.nl; opening times vary), the imposing Gothic church that dominates the **Grote Markt**, one of the city's two main squares. The 97-metre (318ft) spire, familiarly known as 'The Old Grey Man', was destroyed and rebuilt several times; there are fabulous views from the top. The interior is decorated with some beautiful 16th-century wall paintings. There are two series of frescoes: one portrays the story of Christmas, the other depicts the Easter story.

Like most Dutch towns, Groningen was made for strolling, and there are plenty of interesting sights in almost every corner of the city. This was an important trade centre and a rich town in the Golden Age, hence the various museums dedicated to shipping and the history of tobacco. The **Groninger Museum** (Museumeiland 1; tel: 050-366 6555; www.groningermuseum.nl; Tue–Sun 10am–5pm), housed in splendid contemporary pavilions opposite the railway station, boasts one of Europe's finest collections of oriental ceramics, as well as a fine display of local paintings, including several works by Jan Wiegers and other members of the well-developed Groningen School of Expressionism. Interesting temporary exhibitions are mounted in the east pavilion throughout the year.

There are several other museums in the city worth visiting including the **Noordelijk Scheepvaartmuseum**

Modern design at the Groningen Museum.

ALMSHOUSES

Keep an eye out for the many surviving *gasthuizen* and *hofjes*, almshouses built around pretty little courtyards providing accommodation for travellers, the elderly and the poor. You can peer in through the gates, but visitors should get permission before entering the courtyards to look around. Good examples can be found on Munnekeholm, Kerkstraat, Nieuwe Kerkhof and Visserstraat. One of the locals' favourites is the **Pepergasthuis**, on Peperstraat, dating from the 15th century. It has been renovated but still provides low-rent homes for the poor and elderly. Look out for Oude Kijk in 't Jatstraat (Old 'Look Down the Street' Street), named after the evil-eyed statue that has been staring down for centuries from high up on a building wall.

(Maritime Museum; Brugstraat 24; www.noordelijkscheepvaartmuseum.nl; Tue–Sat 10am–5pm, Sun 1–5pm), which looks at the northern Dutch shipping and shipbuilding industry from the Middle Ages to the present day, and the **Nederlands Stripmuseum** (Dutch Comic Strip Museum; Westerhaven 71; www.stripmuseum.nl; Tue–Fri 12.30–5pm, Sat–Sun 10am–5pm, also open Mon July–Aug), where visitors can find out how comic strips are created.

Alongside the 'official' events and curricula of the university, Groningen's cultural scene centres on the bars, pubs and 'brown' cafés. They are ubiquitous, especially around the central squares and on Peperstraat and Poelestraat. Pubs are generally open most of the day, and seem to serve as much coffee as alcohol. People set themselves up at the big wooden tables with newspapers, books, notepads and sketchbooks, sip their coffee at leisure and wait for friends to arrive so that the conversation can begin.

A good example is **Café Mulder** (Grote Kromme Elleboog 22). Like many other pubs in this artistic outpost, Café Mulder is decorated with local paintings, and it is not unusual to find the artist relaxing beneath one. In fact, one of the best ways to get into conversation with the locals – and Groningers love to talk – is to ask them about the paintings. Likely as not, they'll have an anecdote about the painter, the subject (some, like the fat blonde lady with the huge breasts, are as well known in Groningen as the artists) and how the painting came to hang where it does.

The whole town has a comfortable, vaguely beatnik feel to it and, while it may not have a great deal to recommend it architecturally, it's certainly a lively place and ideal for those on a budget.

Hiking, biking and boating

The villages north of Groningen can be explored easily by car, but the quiet, flat roads and picturesque canals are a magnet for many Dutch, especially southerners, with the time and energy to spend a few days

Evening along the Drentsche Aa river.

cycling, hiking or boating. Indeed, most of the week-long or fortnight holidays taken by the Dutch involve some combination of all three – whether making their way by bike or canoe between campsites, or travelling on a houseboat or covered pontoon and making daily jaunts away from the canal into the countryside.

Several attractive villages, including **Oostum** ❼, lie barely 3km (2 miles) from central Groningen and are easily reached by bicycle, boat (which can be rented in Groningen) or on foot by lunchtime. Nearly every village has a little café that serves passable food in what looks like, and often is, someone's sitting room. An especially popular stop for tea, coffee or a meal is the quaint little village of **Garnwerd** ❽, just 11km (7 miles) from central Groningen.

If canoeing appeals, **Winsum** ❾, the 'canoe village', is an ideal starting point. Canoes can be rented, and the locals are eager to give their recommendations on where to go and what to see. **Warffum** ❿ is a mecca for folk dancers, especially around the annual folk dancing festival in June.

Feudal grandeur

Groningen has a number of grand old manor houses. The most interesting of these is **Menkemaborg** (www.menkemaborg.nl; Mar–Sep Tue–Sun 10am–5pm, also Mon July and Aug, Oct–Dec Tue–Sun 10am–4pm), in the village of **Uithuizen** ⓫, about 25km (16 miles) north of the city. This fortified manor house dates back to the 15th century, was rebuilt in the late 17th century and has since been restored and refurbished to the casual, functional elegance of the 18th century.

Six rooms are open to the public, including the ladies' drawing room (walls covered in damask silk), the state apartment (a pipe organ in a fake cabinet), the library (several good paintings and an ornate desk) and – always the most interesting in any restored landmark home – the kitchen, with its big black pots and huge open fireplace, flanked by all manner of antique cooking tools and utensils.

Lakeland

The mudflats on Groningen's northern coast lack the attraction of Friesland's natural sand beaches and coves, but the **Lauwersmeer** ⓬ worth a visit. This huge freshwater lake about 35km (22 miles) northwest of Groningen, cut off from the sea by the Lauwersoog dam, another popular area for boating, fishing, windsurfing, cycling, and bathing from its man-made beach.

Lauwersoog, the port on the lake, is the place to catch the ferry for the 50-minute journey to Schiermonnikoog (see page 298), the westest and most isolated of the Frisian Islands. Naturalists should not miss the seal sanctuary, Zeehondencrèche (www.zeehondencreche.nl; daily 10am–5pm) located at **Pieterburen** not away.

Canoes ready for launching in Garnwerd.

FRIESLAND

**Little-known Friesland will repay intrepid visitors
with a wealth of natural beauty, unassuming locals
and a stunning natural environment.**

L
ike their neighbours in Groningen, the other northernmost
province of the Netherlands, the
Frisians enjoy a lifestyle that is far
removed in every way – except miles
of course – from the sophistication
and bustle of the southern parts of
the Netherlands. This northern section of the country is where many of
the Dutch go for their holidays, and
it offers an attractive array of outdoor
and cultural activities for holidaymakers, especially those with families.

Friesland was one of the earliest
areas of human settlement in the Netherlands, and Iron Age remains have
been found dating back to around 400
BC. Over the centuries the Frisians
have won and lost battles with many
different invaders. The Romans had a
fairly typical experience. They found
the Frisians much tougher to beat in
battle than they had anticipated and,
even after the Frisians were subdued,
they refused to pay the taxes demanded
by the Romans. In the end, even the
Romans left Friesland alone; it just
wasn't worth the trouble involved.

Distinct from the rest

The overriding characteristic of the
Frisians is provincial chauvinism; they
make it clear that they are a distinct
people from the rest of the Dutch –
the 'Scotland' of the Netherlands, some
call it. Their own language, Frisian, is

spoken regularly by about half the
province's 646,000 residents and used
in many schools. Frisian is an odd language, with the same Germanic roots
as Dutch but more similar to English.
Many Frisians speak Frisian at home
and Dutch at work or out in the shops,
but the language most heard on the
streets is 'town Frisian', a corruption
of both languages where the speaker
might switch from Frisian to Dutch
between sentences or even from word
to word, depending on which language offers a more vivid expression.

Main Attractions

Voorstraat, Harlingen
Mudwalking
Watersports
Eisinga Planetarium
Leeuwarden
The Wadden Islands

A day at the beach on the Waddenzee.

Friesland has its own flag. It features four diagonal blue bands and three diagonal white bands on which seven red water lilies appear, representing the seven 'free Frisian coastal countries' in the Middle Ages. It was first used in 1927 and is now the home jersey design for SC Heerenveen football team.

Frisians are proud that they are apparently descended from a different race from the rest of the Dutch. Instead of developing from people who emigrated from Central Europe, their ethnic heritage is Scandinavian or possibly Celtic. Hitler was particularly keen on recruiting people from Friesland into his bureaucracy and army because the Frisians, with their height, strong features and blond hair, matched his concept of Aryan genetic supremacy.

Within the Netherlands, Frisians are sometimes the butt of jokes because of their supposed backwardness, rural ways and lack of modern sophistication. The people of neighbouring Groningen, perhaps to compensate for their own sense of inferiority at being so far – by Dutch standards – from the urban south, are particularly fond of telling Frisian jokes.

It is easy to see why the jokes paint the northerners as country bumpkins, as hillbillies without hills. They don't speak as quickly or use the same city slang as southerners. The north has more than its share of windmills that still work, including at least one that

Demonstrating an old Dutch folk dance.

is actually used as a mill, to m flour. And while 2 million pairs wooden shoes manufactured in Netherlands each year are sold tourists, most of the remaining lion are sold to people in Friesl (and Groningen) who wear then everyday shoes, particularly in wet. These aren't, of course, the sharp-pointed clodhoppers sold at souvenir shops; instead, they are l and strong, made out of poplar, ally painted black, with some lea trim – and they last for years. Visi seldom notice that the man ric by on a bike or the woman shopp with her children is wearing woo shoes unless it's pointed out.

Frisian independence

One thing visitors, even other Du are careful not to joke about is issue of Frisian independence. Th is a strong, long-time movemen the province to declare independe and secede from the rest of the N erlands, and it would be unwis mock the movement in the prese of its most ardent supporters, mos

whom refuse to speak anything except Frisian but nonetheless understand both Dutch and English perfectly.

Most Frisians, of course, realise that secession is a political and economic unreality and have no interest in its actual realisation, but that, perhaps, helps them lend their casual support to the notion of Frisian independence. Perhaps even more than other Dutch, the northerners love sports. Cycling, camping, canoeing, sailing and hiking are all typical weekend pursuits. In winter even the smallest villages have a field especially flooded so that the locals can skate with each other after work. In summer, many communities enjoy that strange form of pole-vaulting peculiar to the Dutch – the vaulters plant their pole in the middle of a canal and leap to the other side, with the possibility of a hilarious mid-canal landing.

In the coldest winters, when the canals all freeze solid (it happens, on average, once every five or six years), Friesland stages the **Elfstedentocht**, or '11-cities race', so named because skaters must traverse a 200km (125-mile) loop of frozen canals between the 11 cities (towns, really) of the province. Twenty thousand people or more, some wearing the traditional wooden skates still popular in the north, may be gathered at the early-morning starting line for this punishing race. But only a fraction of them will finish it hours later, in darkness, sore and tired and sometimes frostbitten. When Crown Prince (now King) Willem-Alexander skated under an assumed name in 1985 and managed to finish the race (though well behind the winner), his public popularity soared. The last race took place in January 1997.

First port of call

The ancient fishing village of **Harlingen** ⓑ, on the Waddenzee (variously translated as 'mud sea' or 'salt flat sea'), is the first stop for many who enter Friesland after driving up from Amsterdam across the *Afsluitdijk*, the 32km (20-mile) -long, 90-metre/yards wide dyke built to enclose the Zuiderzee, now the IJsselmeer. With a population of 16,000, nearly all of central Harlingen – the part along the docks – is a national conservation

Admiring modern clogs.

area because of the exquisitely gabled 16th-, 17th- and 18th-century homes and buildings, including a number of old United East India Company warehouses. In the dock area is the obligatory statute of the little Dutch boy who allegedly stuck his finger in the dyke to save the sea wall from collapsing. In the interests of civic pride and tourism, many Dutch seafront communities today claim the legendary boy as their own little hero.

Leading away from the harbour, the main street, **Voorstraat**, has many pleasant shops. At No. 56 is the **Hannema Huis** (tel: 051-741 3658; Tue–Fri 11am–5pm, Sat–Sun 1.30–5pm), the city's history museum, which has audioguides in English. The street is especially attractive on Saturday market days, when colourful stalls and booths are run by people in local costume. **Harlingen** is still a working seaport, and in strolling along the harbour you can watch a variety of boats coming and going, or look over the dockside to the fishing trawlers and small shipping steamers that carry cargoes to Germany and other Dutch

Mudwalking.

ports. Harlingen harbour is also the place to catch ferries that run up to four times a day in season to two of the most popular Wadden Islands, Vlieland and Terschelling.

Stavoren

Having mentioned Harlingen, it would be unfair to leave out **Stavoren**, on the IJsselmeer shore. This legendary harbour, famous for its long history, dates back to 500 BC. Stavoren was once the seat of ancient kings, and thanks to its location became a major trading port with shipping and cargoes from France, England and Scandinavia. This easily explains the wealth which the city obviously enjoyed centuries ago, still visible in some of the rich buildings. Alas, Stavoren's merchant days are all but gone, but the harbour, like that in Harlingen, plays host to many clippers and cutters of a bygone era.

The ships that always draw the most attention, however, are the antique sailboats, many of them a century or more old. Many of them were designed specifically for sailing the peculiar waters of the Waddenzee, the

WALKING ON MUD

The first organised walk on the seabed was held in 1963. Since then, hundreds of thousands of people – always led by registered guides – have joined walks from the mainland to one of the outlying inhabited Wadden Islands a few miles away, or to one of the larger uninhabited salt flats. Some mudwalkers compare it to mountain climbing, given the amount of exertion required to make your way through the mud.

The walks are particularly popular among birdwatchers because of the many species, some quite rare outside Friesland, that feed on the exposed seabed. Besides the bird life, the Waddenzee serves as something of a nursery for many different types of fish that are spawned in the North Sea and then seek out the slightly warmer waters of the shallow Waddenzee until they mature and head back out to the North Sea.

Wadlopen trips, usually undertaken only in the summer months, became very popular in the late 1960s and early 1970s, but Friesland officials have since severely restricted the number of walks for two reasons: to reduce the number of drownings among mudwalkers who set off on their own and to avoid damaging the delicate Waddenzee environment. Because of these restrictions, and the limited number of groups licensed to sponsor *wadlopen* outings, interested visitors should make arrangements in advance at a local VVV.

shallow and often wild corner of the North Sea that stretches from Friesland to Germany and Denmark. The Waddenzee is no more than 1 metre (3ft) deep in many places, and rarely more than 3 metres (10ft) deep in any one place, even at high tide. Consequently, when the tides go out, the salt flats and mud that gave the sea its name are revealed. The Fries, who seem to be able to make a sport out of almost any activity, subsequently invented *wadlopen*, or 'mudwalking'.

The depth of the Waddenzee, or rather the lack of depth, makes navigation tricky, even for the antique sailboats with their remarkably shallow draft. The boats are all but flat-bottomed and, instead of keels, they have large wooden 'swords' amidships to both port and starboard; the swords are lowered and raised by means of back-breaking cranks on the deck.

Sailboating

Antique sailboats are especially popular among Dutch and German school organisations or groups of families that hire them, along with a captain and mate, for a week or a weekend. With full galley facilities on board and berths for up to three dozen, the ships ply the Waddenzee, hopping from island to island, beach to beach, all the way to Germany, mooring in tiny island villages, or simply dropping anchor on an inviting sandbar. One of the attractions of such a trip is that, while the captain and mate can sail their boats themselves in any weather, the passengers are encouraged to learn and to take up as much of the running of the boat as they want. Various operators offer sailing packages on antique vessels; the VVV offices in Friesland can give you details.

Watersports capital

There are many small villages in Friesland, and visitors who wander by bicycle, canal boat or on foot are rarely disappointed. For those interested in watersports, **Sneek** ⓮ (pronounced 'snake') is a must; this town

is the watersports capital of Friesland, a province whose numerous seaports and lakes make it the watersports playground of the Netherlands. The main attraction is the **Fries Scheepvaart Museum** (Maritime Museum; Kleinzand 16; Mon–Sat 10am–5pm, Sun noon–5pm), which also covers the history of the town. Some non-boating places are appealing, too. **Franeker**, 10km (6 miles) inland from Harlingen, was an influential university and market centre in the Middle Ages. It is little more than a pleasant small town today, though its elaborately decorated 1594 Dutch Renaissance Town Hall and several museums still draw many tourists.

Friesland's planetarium

Across from Franeker's Town Hall, one of the most popular museums – a home-made planetarium – is truly unique. **Eisinga Planetarium** (Eise Eisingastraat 3; tel: 0517-393 070; www.planetarium-friesland.nl; Tue–Sat 10am–5pm, Sun 1–5pm, also Mon 1–5 Apr–Oct) was built by Eise Eisinga, a wool-comber and amateur scientist, in the sitting room of his family home

Traditional Frisian sailing ships at sunset.

between 1774 and 1781, in an attempt to quell local fears that a collision among the planets would lead to the Earth's destruction. To help convince the local burghers that devastation was not imminent, Eisinga made sure to put Franeker at the centre of the universe. Now the oldest planetarium in the world, Eisinga invited local people into his house to show them how the solar system worked – even though Uranus, Neptune and Pluto are missing because they hadn't yet been discovered.

In over 200 years, the timing of the planetarium's movements – hours, days, weeks, months, seasons and years – has been readjusted only once, and was off by just two degrees. Visitors can explore the whole house, not just the sitting room but also the attic, which houses the mechanism made of oak hoops and 10,000 hand-forged nails that Eisinga used to create his model on a scale of 1 millimetre to 1 million kilometres.

It is an inspiration to anyone who has ever tinkered in a workshop, and fascinating to everyone else. The house features other globes, telescopes, sundials, maps, models and timepieces, and is refurbished to show how a tradesman in 18th-century Friesland might have lived. There are also changing exhibitions related to the stars and the planets.

Last resort

A few more miles inland is **Leeuwarden** ⑮ (population 95,000), the capital of Friesland. The city, which will be European Capital of Culture in 2018, is pleasant enough and the people are charmingly self-deprecating, despite their pride in their province and its independent history. People will say, for example, that yes, of course, Leeuwarden gets tourists – when it's raining and all the people sailing from Harlingen or biking or camping elsewhere in Friesland head for the town to dry out.

In truth, there are several museums, a number of decent restaurants and an active pub scene. For example, in Oude Doelesteeg, a small alley off the main shopping street, Nieuwestad, are several different inviting bars and brown cafés, ranging from one that draws a billiards crowd to another that pulses with heavy-metal rock music.

The VVV office adjacent to Leeuwarden station offers a free brochure recommending a walk through town depicting buildings and provides interesting background on Leeuwarden. Of particular interest is the childhood home of Mata Hari (Margaretha Geertruida Zelle), the renowned dancer, supposed temptress and purported World War I spy who was born in Leeuwarden in 1876. She has been adopted as a heroine of modern tourism despite a shadowy career that ended when she was shot by the French in 1917. Her former home is at Over de Kelders 33 and there is a statue of her on a nearby bridge.

On a historical note

Also noteworthy in Leeuwarden numerous other small statues scattered on various corners, and and at least

Shopping in Leeuwarden.

four museums worth seeing: the **Fries Museum** (Wilhelminaplein 92; tel: 058-255 5500; www.friesmuseum.nl; Tue–Sun 11am–5pm), which displays antiquities and costumes, provides a comprehensive history of Friesland and has a room devoted to Mata Hari; and the **Verzetsmuseum** (Resistance Museum; Ruiterskwartier 92; tel: 058-255 5500; www.friesverzetsmuseum.nl; Tue–Sun 11am–5pm), comprising a series of walk-through exhibits dedicated to the Dutch role in World War II. For a small fee, visitors get an audioguide that relates the hardships of Friesland under German occupation, when there were 30,000 deaths and a famine in the final winter of the war that forced people to eat anything they could find, including tulip bulbs, to survive. The **Keramiekmuseum Princessehof** (Grote Kerkstraat 11; tel: 058-294 8958; princessehof.nl; Tue Sun 11am–5pm) has the largest collection of Chinese porcelain in the Netherlands, including Ming, and also a fine collection of Dutch Art Nouveau and Art Deco. Kids will love the engaging **Natuurmuseum Fryslân** (Nature Museum; Shoemaker Perk 2; www.

natuurmuseumfryslan.nl; daily 10am–5pm), which looks at the area's flora and fauna.

The Wadden Islands

The Wadden Islands, dividing the Waddenzee from the North Sea, are a natural wonder treasured by people looking for a certain kind of holiday: somewhere definitely out of the way, a bit harder to get to, with plenty of outdoor activities. The islands represent the remains of an arching natural dyke that lay between the North Sea and a huge ancient marshland. That marshland is now the Waddenzee, flooded by a gradual raising of the sea level that took place when the Ice Age glaciers melted. Because of their unique physical history, and the shallowness of the Waddenzee, all the islands are renowned as havens for feeding and migratory birds – and consequently for birdwatchers.

The largest and southernmost island, **Texel** ⑯, is the most accessible because it is reached by a short ferry ride, not from Friesland but from Den Helder, on the western side of the IJsselmeer. Texel is the most developed island, and is consequently quite crowded in

Playing in the dunes on Texel.

Riding a bike in the Vlieland dunes..

summer, especially with cars, which are either rare or banned from the islands of Vlieland and Schiermonnikoog. There are several museums including the **Schipbreuk en Juttersmuseum Flora** (Shipwreck and Beachcoming Museum; daily 10am–5pm), and the **Walvisvaardershuisje** (Whaler's Cottage; May–Oct Mon 2–5pm). Also worth visiting is the **Ecomare** (Ruijslaan 92; tel: 022-231 7741; www.ecomare.nl; daily 9.30am–5pm) seal sanctuary. Here you can also find out about the Dunes of Texel National Park (www.npduinenvantexel.nl) and the various outdoor activities on offer.

Apart from the seven villages and more than 300 species of birds, Texel's most famous inhabitants would have to be the sheep, which outnumber the human population. Wool products are almost as diverse as the many shops on the island, and for the omnivore, Texel lamb is famous for its slightly sweet yet delicately briny flavour.

On your bike

The next island, **Vlieland** ⓱, is accessible by ferry (90 minutes, depending on the weather), and limited high-speed catamaran service (45 minutes) from Harlingen, the busy little port where chartered antique sailboats and commercial ships nestle up to the foot of the historic town centre. Vlieland (population 1,200) offers the visitor an acquaintance with nature that Texel has difficulty in matching. Motorised transport is limited to inhabitants only, so you are compelled to hire a bicycle from Oost Vlieland, the island's only village, with shops, restaurants and two small 'supermarkets' (West Vlieland was consumed by the sea centuries ago).

Cycle rentals are cheap, and plenty of friendly shops cater to all needs, especially families with young children and the physically challenged. The island is criss-crossed by a labyrinth of excellent cycle paths traversing dunes, fragrant woods alongside cranberry fields, and moorlands where wild fowl, birds of prey, migratory birds and rabbits are plentiful. Vlieland's two claims to fame are 96 species of bird and the longest nudist

beach in Europe. Amateur botanists may enjoy a broad spectrum of flora and fauna, including rare orchids.

The wreck of the Lutine

The western side of the island is one expansive stretch of sand, some 8km (5 miles) long, with a few vegetative dunes known as the Vliehors. It is used for part of the year as a firing range. Fortunately, the Dutch military are very committed to conservation; just don't walk across their terrain when red flags are hoisted, as you might run the risk of being preserved in situ. Like all the islands, Vlieland has had its share of shipwrecks, and has arguably the most famous of all: the British warship HMS Lutine, which foundered in 1799 while transporting a cargo of gold bullion. In 1999, newly minted coins commemorated the bicentennial of this sad incident and a Lutine walk was created with gold-coloured slabs commemorating other wrecks. The *Lutine*'s bell hangs in Lloyd's of London (where it used to be rung to announce the loss of a ship), but in return Lloyd's donated a memorial plaque.

For a complete insight into the treasures of this island, natural or otherwise, a visit to the **Informatiecentrum De Noordwester** (Dorpstraat 50; tel: 0562-451 700; www.denoordwester.nl; opening times vary) is a must. Apart from its impressive collection of beach-combed finds, the ground floor exhibits anything and everything pertaining to Vlieland. Seasonal exhibitions feature local painters.

Other attractions include **Tromp's Huys**, or Admiral Tromp's house (Dorpstraat 99; Sep–June Tue–Thu and Sat 2–5pm, Fri 10am–1pm, July–Aug Tue–Fri 10am–5pm, Sat 2–5pm, Sun 2–4pm). The less energetic can board the **Vliehors Express**, a sort of luxurious army truck that makes a trip around the beaches to the Post House and Vliehors (further information from the VVV office opposite the ferry terminal).

Ameland and Schiermonnikoog

The two northernmost islands, Ameland (population 3,000) and Schiermonnikoog (population 1,000), are too quiet for all but the most world-weary, privacy-seeking Dutch. **Ameland** ⑱ is the busier of the two, boasting three villages, Hollum, Ballum and Nes, where a number of distinctive skippers' houses from the 17th and 18th centuries can be seen.

Hollum's **Cultuur-Historisch-museum Sorgdrager** (Herenweg 1; opening times vary) focuses on cultural history, and, in common with the other islands, exhibits memorabilia concerning the whaling industry that once existed on Ameland and the neighbouring islands. On a happier note, the **Reddingsmuseum Abraham Fock** (Oranjeweg 18), dedicated to the history of lifeboats and sea rescue and presented via photographs and numerous artefacts.

The **Natuurcentrum** (Nature Centre; Strandweg 38; tel: 519-542 737; opening times vary), is to be found in Nes. It aims to make the visitor aware

Ameland beach pole.

of the region's natural history and includes an impressive sea aquarium. Ameland's ferry departs from Holwerd, a village about 40km (25 miles) up the Frisian coast from Harlingen.

Nature reserve

Schiermonnikoog ⓳, the most isolated island, is accessible only from the tiny port of Lauwersoog in northern Groningen. Lauwersoog harbour gives the traveller a foretaste of the isolation: the only things to be seen are its small fishing fleet and a row of sluices, while a simple restaurant takes 90 percent of its clientele from those leaving or arriving on the island. Travellers who find no contradiction in the words 'bleak' and 'beauty' should find it worth the effort.

Upon arrival a bus takes passengers to the only village, Schiermonnikoog. If you have arranged to stay at the island's oldest hotel, you will be picked up in a vintage charabanc, or bus. **Hotel van der Werf** is worth a visit if only to view numerous photographs depicting the social history of the island. Stepping into its lounge and dining room, with its rich

The fishing fleet at Lauwersoog.

wood-panelled walls and traditionally attired staff, is like stepping back in time. Not surprisingly it's a favourite haunt of authors and literary figures.

By the statue of Schiere Monnik in the village are two upstanding whale jaws brought in by the famous ship, the *Willem Barentsz*. Predictably, the entire island (like Vlieland) is designated as a nature reserve, hence the no car policy (you can get around on horseback, by bicycle or on foot).

Whatever mode of transport is employed, it would be sinful not to climb up the observation point known as the **Wasserman**, which offers a phenomenal panoramic view; the stirring North Sea on one side contrasted by the almost mill-pond quality of the Waddenzee.

The visitor's centre, the Oude Centrale (Torensteek 20; tel: 0519-531 641; www.np-schiermonnikoog.nl) is recommended. All the information about the island's flora and fauna – which include 50 percent of Europe's native species – can be found here. Rare plants include some varieties of orchid otherwise extinct in the wild.

ELEVEN CITIES TOUR

Since not everyone can skate the 11-cities race (see page 291) or put up with freezing temperatures, no matter how much hot chocolate is on offer, the Beleef Friesland organisation (tel: 058-233 0740; www.visitfryslan.nl) has put together numerous packages enabling visitors to see the 11 cities by alternative means of transport, be it bicycle, in-line skates, walking, horse or car. Cycle tours take from four to seven days, horseback tours at least five days, walking eight days and roller skating seven days.

The 11 cities tour starts in Leeuwarden and is then followed by Sneek, Ijlst, Sloten, Stavoren, Hindeloopen, Workum, Bolsward, Harlingen, Franeker and Dokkum, with the last leg returning to Leeuwarden. Other packages, varying from one to three days, are available for those who are of a shopping persuasion, and there are trips for culture vultures and restaurant lovers too.

Depending on the length of your stay in the Netherlands, these comprehensive arrangements make for a pleasant holiday in their own right, and are reasonably priced. There's plenty of scope to tailor tours to individual requirements. And don't forget the *Frysk Paspoart*. Costing only €5, it contains vouchers valid for reductions in museums and other attractions in the 11 cities. So, grab a hot chocolate, and happy non-ice skating.

An entertaining alternative way of seeing the island is to reserve a seat on the **Balgexpress**, a sort of portable cabin on wheels which is tractor-drawn and transports its passengers around the beaches and, on occasion, in and out of the sea. Don't worry, it's perfectly safe – and, like the island itself, unforgettable.

Terschelling island

The second-largest of the five main Wadden islands, **Terschelling** ⑳ (population 3,000) offers a good compromise between crowds and desolation. Terschelling was important as a port in the 16th to 18th centuries and was a centre for the Dutch whaling industry. The harbour of the main town, **West-Terschelling**, is guarded by a 16th-century Brandaris lighthouse, the largest in the Netherlands. The town itself is known for its little 17th-century gabled houses. There is a small cultural museum on Commandeurstraat and there are a number of unpretentious family restaurants both in West-Terschelling and in nearby villages. Cranberries and the fruit's by-products, from wine to tarts, are local specialities.

A landscape in flux

Terschelling offers exhilarating cycling on paved or dirt-packed paths, through spectacular scenery ranging from grassy dunes to mature forests whose tall trees block out the sun, emit a sweet scent and obligingly scatter pine cones for children to collect (bikes with child seats can be hired on the harbour front).

The vast North Sea beaches of Terschelling are backed by dunes that are constantly being formed and re-formed by the wind and currents. Considerable areas have been planted with grass, and breakwaters have been constructed to hold the dunes in place, keeping them from shifting eastward under the constant battering of wind and waves from the west.

Terschelling, like the other Wadden Islands, is in effect a vast laboratory of wind, sea and land. And for anyone who travels as far north as Friesland, it would surely be a crime against the ethics of good travelling not to take a ferry out to one of these beautifully wild and, for the most part, undiscovered Dutch islands.

A small village on the island of Terschelling.

TRAVEL TIPS
THE NETHERLANDS

TRANSPORT

GETTING THERE AND GETTING AROUND

GETTING THERE

By air

Most visitors, whether from America or other parts of Europe, fly into Schiphol airport, 9km (5 miles) southwest of Amsterdam. The airport has connections to around 300 cities. With its expanded terminals, casino, business centre, VIP centre, six hotels and a children's play area – along with its reputation for efficiency and easy access to all parts of the Netherlands – Schiphol remains one of the world's most popular international airports.

For flights from the UK, the following airlines provide service to Amsterdam (plus a few flights to Rotterdam, Eindhoven and Maastricht) on schedules that range from hourly to daily, from airports all round the UK. Note that this is only a selection of carriers: airlines come and go.

British Airways
Tel: 0844-493 0787
www.britishairways.com
Cityjet
Tel: 0871-405 2020
www.cityjet.com
easyJet
Tel: 0330-365 5000
www.easyjet.co.uk
Flybe
Tel: 0371-700 2000
www.flybe.com
KLM Royal Dutch Airlines
Tel: 0207-660 0293
www.klm.com

From Ireland, **Aer Lingus** (tel: 1890-800 600; www.aerlingus. com) flies from Dublin and Cork to Amsterdam, while Ryanair (tel: 1520-

444 004; www.ryanair.com) flies from Dublin to Amsterdam and Eindhoven.

Regular flights link Schiphol with all major European airports, and there are several flights a day from the US and Canada.

By train

There are good rail connections to all parts of the Netherlands from Brussels, Paris, Antwerp, Cologne, Hanover and London, and the North Sea ports.

The Eurostar train goes direct from London (St Pancras) to Brussels in 1 hour 50 minutes, from where a connecting train will take you to Rotterdam (1 hour 15 minutes), The Hague (2 hours) and Amsterdam (1 hour 50 minutes). Tel: 03432-186186; www.eurostar.com. A direct service from London St Pancras to Rotterdam and Amsterdam is due to start in December 2016.

Day and night rail/fast ferry services operate from any Greater Anglia station including London (Liverpool Street) to any station in the Netherlands via Hoek van Holland (Hook of Holland) – total journey time is around 10 hours to Rotterdam, 11 hours to Amsterdam. See www. stenaline.co.uk/ferry-to-holland/rail-and-sail for details.

By sea

For crossings from Britain direct to the Netherlands, try the following:
Stena Line (tel: 08447-707070; www.stenaline.com) operates two sailings a day from Harwich to Hoek van Holland (Hook of Holland), taking 7 hours 15 minutes.
P&O Ferries (tel: 0800-130 0030; www.poferries.com) has a

daily overnight sailing from Hull to Rotterdam, taking 10 hours.
DFDS Seaways (tel: 0871-522 9955; www.dfdsseaways.com) has a daily overnight sailing from Newcastle to Ijmuiden near Amsterdam, taking 15 hours.

By car

To drive in the Netherlands, you must carry a current driving licence (an international licence is not necessary), vehicle registration document, Green Card insurance policy and a warning triangle for use in the event of an accident or breakdown. The Netherlands has an excellent network of roads and signposting is good. But once you're in the cities, a car is often more of a hindrance than a help. In most large cities, you are required to buy parking tickets at specially posted vending machines along the streets, marked with a 'P'. Amsterdam and other Dutch cities are notorious for high fines, parking clamps and a very enthusiastic parking-enforcement team.

From the UK, Eurotunnel (tel: 08843-35 35 35; www.eurotunnel. com) provides a 35-minute drive-on train service between Folkestone and Calais, France, from where there is a straightforward toll-free motorway connection through Belgium.

All the companies mentioned in the By sea section above offer a car ferry service. Advance bookings are advisable in summer. From Hoek van Holland to Amsterdam, travel time is roughly 2 hours 30 minutes. If you don't mind a longer drive on the Continent you can take the shorter cross-Channel ferry route from Dover to Calais.

GETTING AROUND

Public transport

Exploring the Netherlands is made easy by the excellent public transport system. All towns of any size have a railway station, which usually also acts as the main terminus for the bus, coach, tram and metro services. Bicycles can also be hired at most railway stations.

Tickets

Tickets are sold in the form of the *OV-chipkaart*, an electronic form of payment, which can be used on buses, trams, metro and the train between stations anywhere in Holland. The easiest place to buy the cards is at a railway station from an NS machine, though they are also sold at many newsagents, supermarkets and tobacconists – look out for the pink logo.

The most suitable card for a short stay is the 'anonymous' card. They cost around €7.50 and then you have to load it with money (€10, €20 or €50), which is deducted per trip. Load at least €20 for a train trip; you will need to activate your card for use on trains. You must show your card to the electronic sensors when you get on and off the bus, train or tram; a green light indicates that your card has been read. For the metro, you put your card on the reader at the barrier before you get on the train. There are also 'disposable' or 'single-use' cards, which are suitable for single or return bus, tram or metro journeys in one city. For further information see www.ns.nl/en/travellers/ov-chipkaart.

If you just plan to stay in Amsterdam, there is the Amsterdam Travel Ticket, which includes a return train ticket to the airport and is valid for 1–3 days.

By air

Schiphol (www.schipol.nl), near **Amsterdam**, is the Netherlands' principal airport. Amsterdam Schiphol railway station is located below the arrivals hall. Trains leave for the principal Dutch cities every 15 minutes or so between 5.44am and 0.13am, and every 60 minutes or so during the remaining period.

Rotterdam (www.rotterdamthehagueairport.nl) has a small airport served by flights to 40 destinations, located 15 minutes from the city centre. A regular local bus service (No. 33) runs between the airport and metro station Meijersplein from where you can get a train into the city centre.

Eindhoven, **Groningen** and **Maastricht** all have airports, linked to the city centre by regular buses or taxi.

By train

Netherlands Railways (Nederlandse Spoorwegen; www.ns.nl/en) has a national inter-city network of express trains linking major cities. There is a fast direct train link every 15 minutes between Schiphol airport and Amsterdam. There is also an hourly night service between Utrecht, Amsterdam, Schiphol, The Hague, Rotterdam and vice versa. 'Stop' trains provide connections to smaller places. Most stations are located centrally. There are at least half-hourly services on most lines and anything from four to eight an hour on busier routes. It is not possible to reserve seats on national train services.

Tickets and passes

Train tickets and travel passes can be purchased at any railway station in the Netherlands, at the domestic *(Binnenland)* office or from the yellow ticket machines in the stations. Although instructions are in Dutch, the machines are not difficult to use, plus there is a surcharge of up to €1 if you buy a single or return ticket at the ticket window rather than the machine. A return ticket is cheaper than two singles and valid for one day. First and second class one-day travel passes are also available *(NS Dagkaart)*, providing one day's unlimited train travel anywhere in the Netherlands and must be bought with an *OV-chipkaart*.

A Group Travel pass *(NS Groepsretour)* offers substantial savings for four to 10 people. For children between the ages of 4 and 11 accompanied by an adult, there is a Railrunner option for €2.50 per child, which is valid for one day's unlimited travel throughout the Netherlands. Any fare-paying adult above the age of 18 can take up to three children on Railrunners. Children under four travel free.

Interrail (www.interrail.eu): This pass is only available to citizens of the EU. It entitles you to 3–8 days of unlimited travel within a one-month period. A three-day pass for the Benelux countries (Netherlands, Belgium, Luxembourg) costs around €87 and eight days is €176. There are reductions for travellers under the age of 26 and also for families.

Eurail (www.eurail.com): This rail pass is only available to non-European residents. It entitles you to 4–10 days of unlimited rail travel within a two-month period. A 3-day pass for the Benelux countries costs around €157, and eight days will cost €292. There are reductions for travellers under the age of 26 and families.

Information

For further information about public transport information and tickets:
Nationwide
Tel: 030-751 5155 or 0900-9292 (70 cents per minute). For information on international trains see www.ns international.nl/en or tel: 030-230 0023. More information on train travel in the Netherlands may be found on the following web page: www.ns.nl/en/travellers/blinded-pages/holland-by-train.html
Amsterdam GVB tickets and info
Stationsplein, Centraal Station
Tel: 0900-8011 (70 cents per minute). Open Mon–Fri 7am–9pm, Sat–Sun 8am–9pm.
http://en.gvb.nl
Netherlands Railways
www.ns.nl/en
Train planner, train travel times, ticket offers, and how to book tickets.

An IJveer ferry boat on the IJ canal behind Amsterdam Central Station.

Biking is by far the best way to get around Amsterdam.

Train taxis

The NS Zonetaxi is a form of transport where you share a taxi with others at a reduced rate. Train taxis take you to and from over 130 stations in the Netherlands. The fixed price is around €6 per taxi (carrying up to four people) for 2km (1.25 miles), then €3 per 2km (maximum 30km/18.5 miles). You must register online at www.nszonetaxi.nl/registreren (one off) and then you can book taxis up to 30 minutes in advance via the Trip Planner Xtra app, or tel: 0900-679 8294 (€1 per call).

Taxis

Taxis will not stop if hailed in the street. It is customary in the Netherlands to book a taxi by phone, although they can always be found at taxi ranks near hotels, stations and busy road junctions. Make sure that you use an authorised taxi. Always ask the driver upfront how much the fare to your destination will be. The taxi meter price includes service charge. A fare starts around €7.50 then increases by about €2 per kilometre. Uber taxis are available in major Dutch cities.

Driving

Highway code

Stay on the right and overtake on the left. All road users should allow free passage to police cars, fire engines and ambulances that are using their sound and light signals. A tram may not be held up on its course. Seatbelts must be worn in the front and rear seats of vehicles.

Vehicle hire

Car hire

Avis, Budget, Hertz and all the other well-known global car-hire firms have offices at Schiphol airport, in central Amsterdam and around the Netherlands. There are a variety of price comparison websites to find the best prices.

Otherwise, for local operators – who are invariably cheaper and more flexible than the major firms – search online for **Autoverhuur** ('car hire' in Dutch)

The national motorists' organisation, with breakdown service, is ANWB (www.anwb.nl). To contact them call their advice line, tel: 088-269 2222; or for the 24-hour emergency line, tel: 088-269 2888. The ANWB may also have reciprocal arrangements with visitors' national motoring organisations.

Camper van hire

Several local firms rent out camper vans in the Netherlands. As good a place to start your pre-trip investigations as any is BW Campers:

Braitman and Woudenberg
Mastwijkerdijk 128, 3147 BT
Montfoort
Tel: 020-622 1168
www.bwcampers.com

Speed limits

Within a built-up zone the maximum speed is 50kph (30mph). In residential areas, indicated by signs of a white house on a blue background, vehicles may only be driven at walking pace. Outside the built-up area the speed limit is 80kph (50mph). A speed limit of 130kph (80mph) applies on motorways and a limit of 100kph (62mph) on most major roads. Lower limits are sometimes indicated, too.

Fuel

Petrol stations on national highways are open 24 hours. Most major petrol stations sell LPG (liquid petroleum gas for cars).

National highways

A1 Amsterdam–Hoevelaken–Apeldoorn–Holten–Borne
A2 Amsterdam–'s-Hertogenbosch/Eindhoven–Maastricht–Eijsden
A4 Amsterdam–Burgerveen–Leiderdorp–Den Haag
A5 Amsterdam–Haarlem
A6 Muiderberg–Flevopolder–N.E. Polder–Emmeloord
A7 Amsterdam–Hoorn/Lambertschaag–Den Oever–Zurich–Joure–Drachten–Groningen–Hoogezand
A8 Amsterdam–Westzaan
A9 Alkmaar–Haarlem–Schiphol–Ouderkerk
A12 Den Haag–Utrecht–Arnhem–Bergh (German border)
A13 Den Haag–Rotterdam
A16 Rotterdam–Breda–Hazeldonk (Belgian border)

Cycling

Bicycles are ubiquitous. The 18 million bicycles in the Netherlands are used extensively by people of all ages for commuting, shopping, walking the dog, transporting young children, towing windsurf boards and sometimes even to move house (using an old-fashioned *bakfiets* – baker's bicycle).

Even on the coldest winter days, you will see hardy cyclists. The Dutch favour old-fashioned heavy-framed bicycles for town use, without gears or hand-brakes (you stop by backpedalling).

By hiring a bicycle, you join in the life of the nation. The Dutch railway service, NS, offers a bike-rental system from about 100 stations called *OV-fiets* (tel: 030-751 5155; www.ov-fiets.nl). The cost is €3.15 per 24 hours and after 72-hours' rental it goes up to €5 per 24 hours. You will need to reserve in advance by phone, pay a deposit and carry a valid ID to collect the bike. Bikes can be taken on trains for a charge of around €6, except weekdays during the morning and evening rush hours. Parents with young children can also hire a small seat, which is fixed on the back of the bicycle. Most railway stations provide secure lock-ups for bicycles.

Within Amsterdam, bicycle hire locations include:

Damstraat Rent-a-bike
Damstraat 20-22
Tel: 020-625 5029
www.rentabike.nl

MacBike
Stationsplein 5 (Centraal Station)/
Weteringschans 2 (Leidesplein)/
Waterlooplein 199
www.macbike.nl
Open daily 9am–5.45pm

Otherwise, VVV offices can supply a list of hire companies. There is usually a deposit of around €50 and rental costs are about €10 a day.

To find out more about cycling in the Netherlands visit www.holland. com/uk/tourism/theme-1/cycling.htm.

Safety

Be warned: the Netherlands may be Europe's cycling heartland, but it is also a nation where theft is all too common, especially in the larger cities. Always lock your bike and, wherever possible, secure it to an immovable object. When cycling in Amsterdam, keep in mind that anarchy reigns. Taxis are allowed to drive on tram tracks, daring cyclists go through red lights and every rider must be on the defensive at all times.

Cycle routes

A network of almost 32,000km (19,800 miles) of cycle paths has been created in the Netherlands, complete with separate traffic lights for bikes at road intersections. For information visit www.hollandcyclingroutes. com. Though cycling is safer than

Package tours

Numerous companies offer two- to seven-day packages, principally to Amsterdam. These often (but not always) work out cheaper than fixing your own travel and accommodation. To qualify for the air packages, you have to spend a Saturday night away. The packages range from all-inclusive (meals, excursions, welcome parties included) to basic travel and accommodation.

in many other countries, it is worth familiarising yourself with the bicycle and the rules of the road before setting off into the traffic. Bear in mind that cars entering a road from your right usually have priority.

The best maps to use are the ANWB 1:100,000 series, on which cycle lanes *(fietspaden)* are indicated by a dotted black line. Cycle routes are well signposted, and signs at important junctions are often numbered so you can pinpoint your location on the map. In planning a route through the country try to avoid large cities and busy intersections. Cycling across the flat Dutch polders or along long straight canals or roads can be bleak, especially in bad weather. Though the Netherlands is dotted with attractive campsites, hotels are often difficult to find, particularly in rural areas. It is also worth bearing in mind that restaurants outside the big cities tend to close early in the evening.

River routes

By far the most attractive routes in the north of the country are those that follow the rivers. The Lek (which changes its name to the Neder Rijn east of Wijk bij Duurstede) provides an attractive route between Rotterdam and Arnhem, passing through pleasant river towns such as Schoonhoven, Culemborg, Wijk bij Duurstede and Rhenen. There are hardly any bridges across the Lek; numerous small ferries link the two banks.

Nationaal Park De Hoge Veluwe

From Arnhem, the most interesting cycling country is to the north through the rolling hills and moors of the Nationaal Park De Hoge Veluwe. A unique feature of this park is the free white bicycles which can be used anywhere within the park boundaries (a similar scheme foundered in Amsterdam when all the white bicycles were immediately stolen and repainted). Beyond the park, you can continue through moorland to Zwolle, north of which is an extensive area of lakes stretching to the attractive Frisian town of Sneek.

The IJsselmeer

It may seem tempting to head west across the IJsselmeer by the 32km (20-mile) Afsluitdijk, but this tends to be an ordeal, particularly in high winds. A far better way to cross the IJsselmeer is by the small ferries that ply between Stavoren and Enkhuizen in the summer.

Between the towns

In the densely populated Randstad, safe cycle routes are often difficult to find. To cycle from Rotterdam to The Hague, the best route is to follow the River Schie to Delft, then the Vliet to the outskirts of The Hague. The meandering Oude Rijn is a good route to take from Leiden to Utrecht, keeping always to the quiet side of the river. Cycling from Leiden to Amsterdam, you can follow a string of lakes north to Uithoorn, then enter the city by the beautiful Amstel route.

To cycle from Amsterdam to Utrecht, follow the Amstel to Ouderkerk, turn down the Holendrecht to reach Abcoude, then take the Angstel to Loenersloot. Here, you cross the Amsterdam-Rijnkanaal to reach the River Vecht, which then flows into the heart of Utrecht.

Among the dunes

The dunes offer an alternative route along the west coast, linking Hoek van Holland, The Hague and Haarlem. Once across the Noordzee Kanaal at IJmuiden, you can continue along the coast north to Den Helder, where the ferry departs for the island of Texel.

Water transport

A popular way to get to know cities such as Amsterdam, Haarlem, Utrecht, Leiden and Delft is by taking a canal tour. Numerous companies operate these tours, and tickets can be booked in advance from the local VVV office. Tours take an hour or more. Candle-lit dinner cruises are also available. Fuller information is given in the Excursions section.

The city's Hop-on, Hop-off Citysightseeing service (tel: 020-530 1090; www.lovers.nl) stops at seven major sites at 25-minute intervals – well worth considering if you intend doing a lot of sightseeing. Tickets can be bought for 24 or 48 hours from Stationsplein 15, next to the tourist office. Boats leave Centraal Station daily from 9.15am to 6.15pm.There is also a canal bus (tel: 020-217 0500; www.canalbus.nl/en/canal-bus) offering a regular service through the canals between the Rijksmuseum and Centraal Station. Modern glass-topped launches will pick you up at various points of the city and take you through some of the loveliest parts of Amsterdam. Day tickets with unlimited use are available. Be prepared to queue in summer. There are three routes and 16 stops and the 24- or 48-hour tickets can be combined with museum entry.

A – Z

A HANDY SUMMARY
OF PRACTICAL INFORMATION

A

Accommodation

Reservations

Wherever you plan to stay, it is wise to book in advance during the summer and holiday seasons and (in the case of North Holland) during the bulb season (April–May). This is especially true of Amsterdam, where the central hotels are usually booked up during June, July and August. Having said that, it is worth telephoning hotels if you visit Amsterdam at short notice, to check for cancellations.

You can book directly with the hotel – invariably the person who answers the phone will speak English – but these days most people book online. It's a good idea to compare prices on a price comparison website such as www.trivago.com, www.travelsupermarket.com or www.kayak.com, but often a hotel will give the best rates on its own website so check this too. The website of the Netherlands Board of Tourism, www.holland.com, has details of all the kinds of accommodation available in the country. Alternatively, you can book in person by going to VVV offices in major towns. Amsterdam VVV offers an online reservations system on their website, www.iamsterdam.com/en/visiting/plan-your-trip/where-to-stay. You will be expected to pay for accommodation on the spot, plus a small booking charge.

Choosing a hotel

All hotels are graded on a variety of criteria, in line with the European HOTREC (www.hotelstars.eu) classification system. Most local tourist offices will have booklets listing the hotels in their town and area, along with their star rating and facilities, which include information for guests with disabilities. This information will also be available on their website. As a general rule, the quality of accommodation in the Netherlands is high – but you do get what you pay for. Prices vary according to the season; winter prices are commonly 30–50 percent lower than the published rates. But you need to ask for a discount – it will not be offered automatically.

Bed and breakfast

VVV tourist offices in major towns keep lists of *pensions* (rooms in private houses) where you can stay the night inexpensively. Although these days many Bed and Breakfasts rival the smartest boutique hotels (with prices to match), others offer quirky accommodation, such as in a lighthouse or a log cabin. Whatever you decide, you'll be guaranteed a delicious breakfast and a host or hostess who is keen to tell you what you can do in the area.

Youth hostels

There are 23 official Youth Hostels in the Netherlands, including three in Amsterdam (the Stadsdoelen on Kloveniersburgwal, a central canal, the Zeeburg to the east and one in Vondelpark). If you do not already belong to the IYHA, membership can usually be taken out on the spot. Most offer dormitory accommodation but some have private rooms. For full details, contact Stayokay Hostels (tel: 020-551 3133; www.stayokay.com).

In several cities, especially in Amsterdam, you will find numerous so-called 'youth hostels', and you may well be approached at the station by touts looking for likely customers. Some of these hostels are well-run establishments offering clean, basic accommodation – though you should expect to have to share rooms and bathrooms.

Camping

Dutch campsites are numerous and well equipped. Some sites offer *trekkershutten* – cabin accommodation, with basic furniture – for up to four people, for around $25 a night. Some offer accommodation in yurts or teepees. The Netherlands Board of Tourism has details on their website www.holland.com.

Admission charges

Museum admission prices vary but count on paying around €17 to get into the Van Gogh Museum or Rijksmuseum in Amsterdam. Prices are lower in provincial museums. Admission to museums is normally free for young people under the age of 18 and holders of a *Museumkaart* (see page 315). But it's always advisable to read the Visitor Information on a museum website to find out if any special deals are available. For example, the Mauritshuis in The Hague offers a combined ticket with the Prince William V Gallery.

Arts

Museums

There are over 600 museums in the Netherlands and you can find out more about them at www.holland.com/global/tourism//interests/

The Dutch National Opera & Ballet in Amsterdam

elegant century-old Koninklijk Theater Carré' on the Amstel in Amsterdam.

Ballet

The Amsterdam-based Dutch National Ballet (Amstel 3; tel: 020-625 5455; www.operaballet.nl) performs traditional, classical and romantic ballets. The Netherlands Dance Theatre (Schedeldoekshaven 60; tel: 070-88 00 333; www.ndt.nl) in The Hague specialises in modern dance. The Scapino Ballet (www.scapinoballet. nl) performs narrative ballets mainly for young people around the country. Many internationally respected dance companies visit the Netherlands throughout the year.

Cinema

The Netherlands not only shows foreign films in the original language with Dutch subtitles, but is also acquiring an international reputation for its own home-produced films. The Rotterdam Film Festival (www. iffr.com; Jan/Feb) and the Utrecht Film Festival in September provide a chance to see the past year's production of Dutch films. In late November the International Documentary Film Festival (www.idfl. nl) takes place in Amsterdam.

museums.htm. The entry price varies; some are free. A Museum Card (Museumkaart) gives free admission to all of them. Most museums are open Tue–Sun 10am–5pm.

Performing arts

Amsterdam, The Hague and Rotterdam take pride in their cultural centres: The Nationale Opera & Ballet (previously Muziektheater), the Anton Philipzaal and De Doelen, respectively. The national opera, ballet and theatre companies are all based in Amsterdam, while The Hague and Rotterdam have their own resident orchestras and dance companies.

In Amsterdam, over the last weekend in August, theatre, dance and music companies from all over the country perform extracts from their year's forthcoming programme in the streets of the city (the Uitmarkt). In June, an ambitious month-long arts programme called Holland Festival takes place in cultural centres in Amsterdam, featuring international artists. Most performances are in Dutch, but during the Holland Festival foreign companies also perform in different languages. For details contact: Holland Festival, Piet Heinkade 5, 1019 RP Amsterdam (tel: 020-523 77787; www.hollandfestival. nl). Amsterdam is putting on more English-speaking events for international guests year-round, and the VVV publishes brochures promoting these Amsterdam Arts adventures in summer and winter months. See Festivals for details of other special events in the arts.

Music

The Netherlands has several symphony orchestras of international repute. The Amsterdam Concertgebouw Orchestra achieved world-wide fame under the baton of Bernard Haitink, and in recent years under the able direction of Riccardo Chailly. The Netherlands Radio Philharmonic Orchestra is in residence at the Beurs van Berlage, Amsterdam's former Stock Exchange. The Rotterdam Philharmonic and the Residentie Orchestra of The Hague are also well known. Small ensembles, including the 18th-Century Orchestra, the Amsterdam Baroque Orchestra and the Schonberg Ensemble are very successful. André Rieu is the Netherlands' best known classical musician; his Johann Strauss Orchestra is a wildly successful touring company.

There is a wide range of jazz and improvised music: Willem Breuker, Louis Andriessen and Misha Mengelberg are among the leading names with an international reputation. The leading venue for jazz is Bimhuis (tel: 020-788 2150; www. bimhuis.nl) at Piet Hein Kade 3 in Amsterdam.

Opera and musicals

The main opera company is the Dutch National Opera (Amstel 3; tel: 020-625 5455; www.operaballet.nl), which stages about 10 productions a year, mainly in Amsterdam and The Hague. Visiting companies often perform at the RAI congress centre. In recent years, The Netherlands Opera has achieved international prestige under the inspired direction of Pierre Audi.

Several companies tour the country with Dutch productions and adaptations from foreign musicals, which are presented mainly at the

B

Budgeting for your trip

The Netherlands is not the most expensive European country: you will find that accommodation costs in particular can be a drain on your budget – especially in the centre of Amsterdam – but this is often outweighed by reasonably priced restaurants and good-value public transport.

Expect to pay €3–4 for a beer, €5–6 for a glass of wine, €10 for a main course in a café and up to €30 in a smart restaurant. Budget hotel rooms are around €60 per night, €80 for an average hotel and over €100 for the luxury end of the market. Prices will be higher in Amsterdam.

The cost of a taxi from Schipol into the centre of Amsterdam is €40–50. Prices for public transport are around €2.20 for a one-way ticket, but it's advisable to get an OV-chipkaart (see page 303). Day tickets are available and cost around €7.50 for 24 hours.

It's not difficult to stick to as little as €50 a day per person if you cycle everywhere, picnic on supermarket-bought food and sleep under canvas. You should reckon on a more realistic budget of around €100 a day per person for two decent meals, public transport to get around, the odd admission fee and a modest hotel. Add on roughly another 20–30 percent if you're staying in Amsterdam.

C

Children

Children are treated with respect and affection in the Netherlands. The notion that they should be seen and not heard is alien, and children are involved in adult life from an early age – one reason why Dutch children can seem unusually well behaved and mature.

Children are welcome in restaurants and cafés, many of which serve a *kindermenu* (children's menu). It is easy to hire bicycles fitted with children's seats for getting about town or for excursions into the country.

Ask at the VVV for details of special activities for children. Several cities now have *kinderboerderijen*, or children's farms; in Amsterdam, for example, there are city farms within the zoo complex and at the Amstelpark (located near the Rai Exhibition Centre in the southern suburbs; daily 10am–4pm). Top children's attractions include Artis Royal Zoo, Planetarium, Geographic and Zoological Museums, the NEMO Science Center, Madame Tussaud's and the Tropenmuseum Junior in Amsterdam; the Zuiderzee Museum in Enkhuizen; Burger's Zoo in Arnhem; the Omniversum Space Museum and the Madurodam miniature town in The Hague; the Zoo and the Maritiem Museum in Rotterdam; Utrecht's Railway Museum (Nederlands Spoorwegmuseum); and De Efteling amusement park in Tilburg. A good place to go for general information is www.holland.com/uk/tourism/theme-1/kids-attractions.htm.

This is, of course, far from being an exhaustive list; in fact the towns of the Netherlands, with their harbours, bridges, canals, parks and windmills, naturally appeal to children.

Climate

The Netherlands has a mild, maritime climate with much the same temperatures as the UK, but it is wetter and marginally cooler in winter. Summers are generally warm but you can expect rain at any time

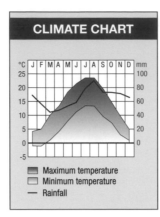

CLIMATE CHART

Maximum temperature
Minimum temperature
— Rainfall

of year. Spring is the driest time of the year and a favourite time for tulip enthusiasts. The advantages of a visit in winter are the cut-price package deals and the fact that museums and galleries are pleasantly uncrowded.

What to wear

Whatever time of year you visit, it's always a good idea to take an umbrella and a waterproof jacket. In winter, bring warm clothes. And if you plan to do a lot of sightseeing, walking shoes are the order of the day.

Crime and safety

Amsterdam and Rotterdam are major European centres for drugs, and much criminal activity here is drug-related. Nonetheless, crime in the Netherlands has fallen in recent years and continues to do so. As a visitor, you are unlikely to be affected directly by the drugs trade, but you should take sensible precautions against becoming a victim of petty crime – just as in any major city. Keep a careful watch on wallets, bags and other valuables, especially on public transport. Leave large amounts of cash and jewellery in a safe at your hotel.

The Dutch police ('*politie*') wear navy trousers, white shirts with navy epaulettes and flat, peaked hats. They drive white cars with blue and orange diagonal stripes.

Customs regulations

Personal possessions are not liable to duty and tax provided you are staying for less than six months and you intend to take them out again. There is no restriction on the amount of currency that you can bring into the Netherlands, although non-EU residents must declare

if they are carrying more than €10,000. Among prohibited goods are meat and milk from non-EU countries, protected species, weapons and narcotic drugs.

Residents of EU countries are likely to be asked questions if they are carrying more than:
Tobacco products: 800 cigarettes; 400 cigarillos (max. 3g each); 200 cigars; 1kg smoking tobacco;
Alcoholic beverages: 10 litres of spirits over 22 percent; 20 litres of alcoholic beverages less than 22 percent; 90 litres of wine (though no more than 60 litres of sparkling wine); 110 litres of beer.
Visitors from outside of the EU can bring into the country:
Alcohol and alcoholic beverages
Over 17 years olds can bring (in personal luggage) the following quantities:
1 litre of alcohol that does not exceed 22 percent volume of alcohol, or undenatured ethyl alcohol 80 percent volume and over; 2 litres of alcohol that does not exceeds 22 percent volume of alcohol; 4 litres of still wine; 16 litres of beer. Passengers can combine the first two types of alcohol as long the alcohol volume does not exceed 100 percent.
Duty-free
Duty-free allowances vary according to where you bought the goods. Duty-free shopping is not available to travellers within the European Union. Despite this, travellers departing from Schiphol airport to destinations in and out of the EU may still take advantage of reduced prices on all goods except alcoholic beverages and tobacco. Visitors from non-EU countries can claim a refund on purchases they have made while in the country (see page 315).

Pets

Dogs and cats entering the EU or moving within it are required to have an EU pet passport (for EU residents), a microchip ID, and a vaccination against rabies. Owners will need to have a certificate of proof from a vet that the animal meets the requirements of entry. If you are coming from a non-EU country, the animal will need to have a certificate of health from a vet.

D

Disabled travellers

Many train stations have lifts, which are marked clearly at arrival points. Many older hotels have very steep staircases and no lifts; check before booking whether your hotel has wheelchair access and a lift. Most of the 4- and 5-star hotel chains have wheelchair access and lifts. Many towns and cities have cobbles, which can be difficult for manoeuvring a wheelchair. The Dutch national organisation for disabled people is ANGO (tel: 033-465 4343; www.ango.nl).

You can find information useful for disabled travellers in Amsterdam at www.iamsterdam.com/en/visiting/plan-your-trip/practical-info/disabled-travellers and you can find information about travelling by train at www.ns.nl/en/travellers/service/travelling-with-functional-disabilities/travelling-with-functional-disabilities

E

Eating out

What to eat

When it comes to dining out in the Netherlands, you can choose from the simplest fare in an *eetcafé* or the more costly, formal environs of a top level restaurant. In between, you can select from one of the many ethnic restaurants, which are especially predominant in larger cities like Amsterdam, Utrecht, Rotterdam, Maastricht and The Hague.

Eetcafés are a kind of informal local eatery, offering a daily changing menu with a choice of fish, meat or vegetarian main course. They are popular because they are reasonably priced; but don't arrive too late or the menu will be sold out.

Broodjes, filled sandwiches with cheese, meat or fish are the fare when it comes to lunch, and generally you need to consume a couple of them to fill you up. Soups and salads also predominate on café menus.

Culinary influences from the US and elsewhere in Europe show up on menus all over the country in the form of bagels, focaccia, *insalata caprese* (mozzarella and tomato salad) and club sandwiches, and salad bars are a common sight in restaurants.

Home cooking

When it comes to Dutch cooking, you will find restaurants that serve traditional *hutspot*, featuring red cabbage, sauerkaut or endive. Vegetarians should be cautioned that these hearty stews are usually

cooked with sausage chunks and bits of bacon. This also goes for the winter soups like *erwten* (green pea) or *bruinenbonen* (brown bean). If you want a late-night snack, most bars/cafés serve *tostis*, a basic grilled cheese sandwich, often topped off with ham. Pancakes are a very Dutch tradition, plate-sized versions which you can eat with a sweet topping of fruits or liqueurs, or savoury fillings of ham, mushrooms, cheese or tomato ragout. *Poffertjes* are mini-pancakes topped with powdered sugar. For snacking on the run, stop at one of the seafood trailers located in prime locations around the city and on beaches in spring and summer. If you prefer not to eat raw herring, you can get a *broodje* filled with smoked salmon, local shrimp, eel or mackerel.

Cheap eats and haute cuisine

Pizzerias are abundant in the Netherlands and serve a variety of plate-sized pizzas, salads and pastas. Chinese restaurants are also ubiquitous, and many are combined with an Indonesian kitchen. The upscale restaurants favour French cuisine, but in recent years, there has been an influence of so-called 'fusion' East-meets-West cooking, with chefs creating their own unique flavours.

Cafés

Every Dutch town has a choice of cafés, invariably serving good coffee – often with apple tart or spicy biscuits. A typical brown café is an intimate, semi-bohemian bar with nicotine-stained walls (hence the name), rugs on tables, sawdust on the floor and newspapers to peruse. These are usually frequented by the locals as well as tourists, and are places where you can often get good quality food at reasonable prices or linger over a drink and a book on a rainy afternoon.

Cafés displaying a green-and-white placard sell soft drugs as well as coffee.

Electricity

In the Netherlands the standard voltage is 230 V and the standard frequency is 50 Hz.

Embassies and consulates

Australia
Carnegielaan 4, The Hague
Tel: 070-310 8200
http://netherlands.embassy.gov.au

Canada
Sophialaan 7, The Hague
Tel: 070-311 1600
www.canada.nl
Ireland
Scheveningseweg 112, The Hague
Tel: 070-363 0993
www.embassyofireland.nl
New Zealand
Eisenhowerlaan 77N, The Hague
Tel: 070-346 9324
www.nzembassy.com/netherlands
South Africa
Wassenaarseweg 40, The Hague
Tel: 070-392 4501
www.zuidafrika.nl
UK
Embassy: Lange Voorhout 10, The Hague
Tel: 070-427 0427
www.gov.uk/government/world/organisations/british-embassy-the-hague
Consulate: Koningslaan 44, Amsterdam
Tel: 020-676 4343
www.gov.uk/government/world/organisations/british-embassy-the-hague
US
Embassy: Lange Voorhout 102, The Hague
Tel: 070-310 2209
http://thehague.usembassy.gov/
Consulate: Museumplein 19, Amsterdam
Tel: 020-575 5309
http://amsterdam.usconsulate.gov/

Netherlands abroad

Australia
Embassy: 102 Empire Circuit, Yarralumla ACT 2600
Tel: 02-6220 9400, http://australia.nlembassy.org
Consulate: Level 23, Westfield Tower 2, 101 Grafton Street, Bondi Junction NSW 2022, Sydney
Tel: 02-9387 6644
Canada
Embassy: Constitution Square Building, 350 Albert Street, Suite 2020, Ottawa, ON K1R 1A4
Tel: 1-877-388 2443
http://canada.nlembassy.org
Consulate: Cadillac Fairview Building, 1 Dundas Street West, Suite 2106, Toronto, ON M5G 1Z3
Tel: 1-416-598 2520
Consulate: Suite 883, Three Bentall Centre, PO Box 10098, 606 Durrard Street, Vancouver BC 1, V7X 1C4
Tel: 1-604-684 6448
Ireland
160 Merrion Road, Dublin 4
Tel: 01-269 3444
http://ireland.nlembassy.org
New Zealand
20 Ballance Street, Wellington 6011

Tel: 04-471 6390
http://newzealand.nlembassy.org
South Africa
210 Florence Ribeiro, New
Muckleneuk, Pretoria 0181
Tel: 12-425 4500
www.dutchembassy.co.za
UK
38 Hyde Park Gate, London, SW7 5DP
Tel: 0207-590 3200
http://unitedkingdom.nlembassy.org
US
Embassy: 4200 Linnean Avenue NW,
Washington DC 20008
Tel: 202-244 5300
www.the-netherlands.org
There are consulates in New York,
Chicago, Miami and San Francisco.

Emergencies

The only emergency number in the
Netherlands is 112. Calls can be
answered in English.

Etiquette

The Netherlands has a reputation
for tolerance. Foreigners, including
minorities, are always welcome and,
as a visitor, you are likely to find Dutch
people pleasant, polite and civilised.
They may not be very demonstrative
or vivacious, but they are rarely
inhospitable or unfriendly. Most speak
excellent English, and will not expect
you to speak Dutch (a language which,
although very similar to English, is
quite hard to pronounce correctly).

You may be surprised at the
leniency towards drugs and
prostitution, especially in cities
like Amsterdam. There has been a
crackdown on hard drugs, but you can
still buy soft drugs in many city cafés.

Tradtional costume at a festival.

Many locals argue that the drugs
problem is no worse than in other
major cities – just more open.

F

Festivals and events

January
Amsterdam: Amsterdam Fashion
Week (www.fashionweek.nl). Jumping
Amsterdam (www.jumpingamsterdam.
nl) showjumping competition.
Rotterdam: International Film
Festival (www.iffr.com).

February
Big pre-Lenten carnivals take place
all over the country, especially
in the southern provinces of
Noord-Brabant and Limburg,
but with parades in Amsterdam
and The Hague as well. Forget
about Rio; temperatures are low
here in February, so don't expect
scanty costumes. Floats are wittily
decorated, and there is always lots
of beer.
Rotterdam: February The ABN Amro
World Tennis Tournament (www.
abnamrott.nl) brings world-class stars
to Rotterdam.

March
Amsterdam: early March, the
Antiquarian Book Fair. Good Friday,
the dramatic and emotional St
Matthew's Passion is performed by
the Concertgebouw Orchestra.
Lisse: late March is when the world-
famous tulip park, De Keukenhof
(www.keukenhof.nl), opens for the bulb
season, which ends in late May.

Maastricht: the European Fine Art
Foundation (www.tefaf.com) brings
hundreds of fine art dealers together
and attracts thousands of visitors for
the art fair REFAF Maastricht.

April
King's Day, the king's official birthday
on 27 April, sees every city and
village in the Netherlands in the
grip of festivities. Nowhere does it
quite like Amsterdam though, with
bands playing music at all the major
intersections, and a boat parade,
market and firework display.
Alkmaar: mid-April–mid-September,
the traditional cheese market opens
with porters wearing their historic
guild uniforms. There are usually
demonstrations of old crafts during
the colourful market that is held
every Friday.
Amsterdam: World Press Photo (www.
worldpressphoto.org).

May
The second weekend in May is
National Windmill Day, when 950 of
the country's icons open their doors
to the public.
Amsterdam: every Sunday, May–
October: antique markets on the
Waterlooplein.
The Hague: the beautiful Japanese
Gardens at Clingendael Park are
open. **Scheveningen:** the colourful
Vlaggetjesdag at Scheveningen
harbour marks the opening of the
herring season. All the fishing boats
are decorated with flags, there is a
traditional market and, of course, lots
of fish to eat.

June
This is Holland Festival month, with
various events taking place around
the country.
Amsterdam: international rowing
competition, the Bosbaan; June–
September, the summer-long Open-
Air Theatre season takes place
in Vondelpark, where it has been
happening since the 1960s.
Assen: the big, noisy, International
Netherlands Motorcycling TT Grand
Prix. Big bikes, the latest in fashion
leathers, and lots of fun; bring your
own earplugs.
The Hague: Parkpop (www.parkpop.
nl) music festival.
Rotterdam: Poetry International
(www.poetryinternationalweb.net)
draws poets and poetry lovers from
around the world. CHIO (www.chio.nl)
international equestrian competition.
Scheveningen: in early June,
there's an Air Show with stunt flying
demonstrations.

Terschelling: Oerol (www.oerol.nl) outdoor performance festival. Texel: Ronde Om Texel (www.roundtexel.com), the largest catamaran race in the world.

July

Amsterdam: Science Park Chess Tournament (www.amsterdamchess.com), with many well-known Masters. Nijmegen: Vierdaagse (www.4daagse.nl), the world's largest walking event takes place over four days. **Scheveningen**: street parades, with jazz and Dixieland concerts, take place along the main boulevard. **Rotterdam**: the Summer Carnival Street Parade wends it way through the city streets. North Sea Jazz Festival (www.northseajazz.nl).

August

Amsterdam: Uitmarkt, when previews of the next year's artistic events are performed in the city streets and squares. Every five years, Sail Amsterdam plays host to thousands of seafaring vessels (next one 2020). Grachtenfestival (Canal festival) of classical music. Amsterdam Gay Pride Festival.
Flevoland: Lowlands (www.lowlands.nl), three-day music and arts festival.
Groningen: Noorderzon (www.noorderzon.nl), 11-day performing arts festival.
Leersum: a colourful Flower Parade.
Scheveningen: major fireworks display for the International Firework Festival.
Yerseke: this is the month to eat mussels, and the fishing village of Yerseke, in Zeeland, is the place to eat them, especially on Mussel Day, the first of the new season.

September

Taking place countrywide (second weekend) is European Heritage Day (www.openmonumentdag.nl), when listed buildings around the country are opened to the public.
Amsterdam: HISWA Boat Show (www.hiswatewater.nl.
Aalsmeer to Amsterdam: a stream of flowers and music all the way from Aalsmeer to Amsterdam make up the Bloemencorso.
Delft: Old Art and Antiques Fair.
The Hague: third Tuesday in September: the State Opening of Parliament by the king. Colourful parade along Lange Voorhout to the Binnenhof (Parliament Square), with the king riding in the traditional Golden Coach.
Rotterdam: Wereld Havendagen, harbour celebrations.

Scheveningen: International Kite Festival.
Utrecht: Gaudeamus Music Week (www.muziekweek.nl) celebrates young music pioneers. Nederlands Film Festival celebrates Dutch cinema.

October

Amsterdam: Amsterdam Dance Event (www.amsterdam-dance-event.nl), five-day electronic music festival.
Leiden: Leidens Ontzet celebrates the end of the Spanish siege in 1574.

November

Amsterdam: International Documentary Film Festival (www.idfa.nl).
Countrywide: 17 November (or nearest weekend): this is the time for children, when St Nicholas arrives in the country from his home in Spain. At all major harbours a traditional steamboat pulls in, complete with St Nicholas, riding on his white stallion and accompanied by his Moorish assistant known as Black Pete.

December

Amsterdam: New Year's Eve celebrations. The whole city turns into one big party.
Gouda: mid-December: beautiful scenes in this old town, where the historical town square is lit by candles. The lighting of the Christmas tree, accompanied by singing and a carillon concert, is a major crowd-puller.

G

Gay and lesbian travellers

The Netherlands is very 'gay friendly', particularly Amsterdam, Rotterdam, The Hague and Utrecht. You can get a general overiew here: www.holland.com/us/tourism/article/outside-amsterdam-gay-guide.htm. The gay scene in Amsterdam is one of the best in Europe and is centred around Reguliersdwarsstraat, Amstel and Kerkstraat with the more 'anything goes' establishments along Warmoesstraat and Zeedijk. The annual Amsterdam Gay Pride event on the first weekend of August attracts around 500,000 revellers. There is also a party, Roze Wester, at the Homomonument (see page 141) on King's Day. Useful websites are www.gayamsterdam.nl, www.amsterdam4gays.com and www.pinkpoint.org. Café Montmartre (Halvemansteeg 17) is regarded by many as the best bar in town. The age of consent in the Netherlands is 16.

H

Health and medical care

No health certificates or vaccinations are required for European Union citizens.

EU citizens who have obtained an EHIC (European Health Insurance Card; tel: 0300-330 1350; www.ehic.org.uk) before departure are entitled to free treatment by a doctor and free prescribed medicines. This insurance is not comprehensive and won't cover you, for example, for holiday cancellation or the cost of repatriation. If you want full cover, you should take out separate medical insurance.

Medical services

The standard of medical and dental services in the Netherlands is very high, and most major cities have an emergency doctor and dental service; enquire at your hotel or consult the introductory pages to local telephone directories. Most doctors speak English. To be put in touch with an emergency doctor out of hours in Amsterdam call 088-003 0600. Pharmacies (Apotheek) take it in turns to open for 24 hours; in Amsterdam call 020-592 3315 for information. Sint Lucas Andreas Apotheek at Jan Tooropstraat 164, Amsterdam West, tel: 020-510 8826, is open 24 hours.

I

Internet

Most hotels will have internet access, although not all provide it for free. Most cities have cafés that provide free WiFi. You can find out more at www.openwifispots.com/country_free_wifi_wireless_hotspot-Netherlands_NL.aspx

L

Left luggage

Most hotels offer a left luggage service for free. There will also be left luggage facilities at most railway stations for a fee. You can find out more at www.ns.nl/en/travellers/about-your-trip/travelling-by-train/facilities-at-the-station

Lost property

You should report loss or theft of valuables to the local police

TRANSPORT

A – Z

LANGUAGE

immediately, as most insurance policies insist on a police report. Loss of passport should be reported immediately to the police and your embassy or consulate.

Most large cities have a police lost property office and there is usually a separate office for items lost on public transport.

M

Maps

The VVV issues a useful road map of the Netherlands, updated each year. For anyone who requires more detailed maps for walking or cycling, the ANWB 1:100,000 series is sold in many VVV offices and bookshops.

Most VVV offices sell or give away street plans of towns and cities in their locality; when using them it helps if you remember that *straat* means street, *plein* means square and *gracht* means canal.

Media

Newspapers and magazines

The main national newspapers are *NRC Handelsblad*, the most respected paper, the left-wing *De Volkskrant*, and *De Telegraaf*, on the political right. British and Irish newspapers arrive on the day they are published and are widely available, as are the *Wall Street Journal Europe*, *International New York Times* and *USA Today*, plus news magazines like *Time*, *Newsweek*, *Business Week* and *The Economist*. There is a local English-language newspaper, The Holland Times (www.thehollandtimes.nl), which is published monthly.

In Amsterdam, A-mag is a listings magazine published six times a year and is available from the tourist office for €3.50, although many hotels offer it to their guests for free. Subbacultcha (www.subbacultcha.nl) specialises in music and publishes a monthly magazine with gig listings. The Xpat Journal (www.xpat.nl) is a quarterly magazine for expats. A useful English-language listings website in Amsterdam is www.amsterdo.com.

Television and radio

On cable TV you can watch Britain's BBC1 and BBC2, plus Sky, CNN and various other international networks. English-language films are frequently shown on Dutch TV channels,

un-dubbed. On the radio, you can tune into the BBC World Service. There is also an English-language radio station in Amsterdam, English Breakfast Radio (www.englishbreakfast.nl), at 106.8FM.

Money matters

The unit of currency in the Netherlands (and in most other countries of the European Union) is the euro (€). There are 100 cents in a euro. Euro coins are 1 cent, 2 cents, 5 cents, 10 cents, 20 cents, €1 and €2. Banknotes come in the following denominations: €5, €10, €20, €50, €100, €200 and €500.

Changing money

GWK (Grenswisselkantoren NV) is a national financial institution where you can exchange any currency and also use credit cards and travellers' cheques. There are GWK offices located at main railway stations, city centres and airports in the Netherlands and at the country's borders. They open Monday–Saturday 8am–8pm, Sunday 10am–5pm and sometimes in the evening at main stations and airports.

Currency exchange is also available at post offices (at a good rate) and banks. There can be a considerable difference in commission charged between the various institutions and at the different times of night or day. Many banks with outside dispensers accept recognised bank cards for money exchange. GWK and other currency-exchange outlets also accept major credit cards.

Credit cards

Credit cards are accepted at most hotels, restaurants, shops, car-rental companies and airlines. American Express, Diners Club, Eurocard, Visa, MasterCard and JCB card are all recognised, plus many more (but not all cards are accepted everywhere). It's usually more cost effective to use a credit card which doesn't charge for transactions to make your purchases, rather than taking travellers' cheques.

Service and tips

When dining out, bear in mind that 15 percent service charge and Value Added Tax (BTW) are invariably included in bills, both for restaurants and bars, and there is no compulsion to tip in addition, although an additional 10 percent is generally expected at finer restaurants. At simple cafés and bars, just leaving

the remaining change from your bill is quite acceptable.

Taxi meters also include the service charge, though it is customary to give an extra tip of €1 or so.

N

Nightlife

Amsterdam

After dark in Amsterdam, entertainment focuses on three main areas: Leidseplein, for lively discos and nightclubs; Rembrandtplein for clubs, cabarets and strip shows pandering to older tastes; and the red light district, notorious for scantily dressed females sitting in windows and notice-boards saying 'room to hire'.

Strip shows, porn videos and sex shops centre on the main canals of Oudezijds Voorburgwal and Oudezijds Achterburgwal. The smaller, sleazier streets leading off these two canals are best avoided, and you are advised never to take photographs.

On an entirely different note, you could spend the evening on a candle-lit canal cruiser, with wine and cheese or full dinner provided. On-board theatre is sometimes provided as an added attraction.

In any case, try out one of the numerous brown cafés, a classic grand café with a reading table and more of a modern ambience, or, alternatively, one of the new-wave bars, with cool, whitewashed and mirrored walls, an abundance of greenery and a long list of cocktails. Some cafés and bars have live music, often jazz or blues. They usually post notices in the windows announcing events.

The Hague

Look for the free listings magazine *Den Haag Day by Day* at hotels and the VVV.

Most people start off the evening at one of the bars and cafés in the Plein before heading to the Grote Markt, the centre of the city's nightlife. Paard Van Troje at Prinsengracht 12 is the leading venue for live music. In summer, locals go to Zwarte Pad on the Scheveningen coast for beach parties and seaside drinking and dining. Holland Casino (Kurhausweg 1; tel: 070-306 7777) in Scheveningen, which has a bar and restaurant, is open daily from 11.30am to 3am.

Rotterdam

Look for the local listings magazine *Rotterdam This Month*, free from hotels and the VVV. The hippest spot in town is Witte de Withstraat: try NRC at No. 63, which used to house a newspaper but is now a café-bar with DJs at the weekend. Villa Thalia (Kruiskade 31) was once a cinema but is now the place to go for dinner with a cabaret. Popular with the gay crowd is Strano (Van Oldenbarneveltstraat 154; www.cafestrano.nl), for cocktails and clubbing. One of the city's best live music venues is Rotown (Nieuwe Binnenweg 19) near the Museumkwartier. Beer fans should head to Melief Bender (Oude Binnenweg 134b), the city's oldest café, which has a good selection of Belgian and Dutch beers. The place to go for jazz is Dizzy ('s Gravendijkwal 127) while Maassilio (Maasshaven ZZ1) is one of the country's leading dance-music clubs.

Utrecht

Look for the free English-language directory in *'n out Utrecht*, 'a guide to eating, drinking, going out and sleeping'. Utrecht has a lively scene around the Oude Gracht, where cafés and restaurants line the lower level of the tree-lined canals. You can dine on Indian, Italian and other international food, or enjoy a Dutch pancake.

O

Opening hours

Normal shopping hours are 9am–6pm. In recent years, food stores have extended their hours on Saturday to 7pm or 10pm, with some grocery chains such as Albert Heijn remaining open on Sundays from noon–6pm. Most shops close at 5pm on Saturdays, though some have extended to 6pm, and, in larger cities, many department stores and speciality shops are now open on Sundays. Shops open late (until 9pm) one day a week in big cities: Thursday in Amsterdam and The Hague; Friday in Rotterdam and Delft.

All shops close for one half-day on Monday morning and all of them display their opening times in the door or window.

Banks are open Monday–Friday 9am–4pm, with some larger branches open to 5pm.

P

Photography

Under no circumstances should you take photographs of the prostitutes in Amsterdam's Red Light District (or in any other city) or you might find yourself face-to-face with one of their 'minders'. You should also be wary about taking photos of government buildings, given the current national security levels. Most museums will usually have a sign telling visitors whether photography is permitted or not.

Postal services

Post offices are usually found in tobacconists, supermarkets, bookshops and some newsstands and stationery shops. The main post office in Amsterdam is at Singel 250 SOUS and is open Monday–Friday 7.30am–6.30pm and Saturday 9am–5pm. A stamp to send a 20g letter abroad costs €1.15. Dutch post boxes are red or orange and there are two openings: the one on the right is for Amsterdam (if you are in the city) and the one on the left is for everywhere else.

Public holidays

Banks and most shops close on the following days:
1 January New Year's Day
Good Friday, Easter Sunday and Monday
27 April King's Day
5 May Liberation Day
Ascension Day
Whit, or Pentecost, Monday
25 December Christmas Day
26 December Boxing Day

R

Religious services

A survey by Statistics Netherlands in 2013 found that 26 per cent of the Dutch population identified as Roman Catholic, 16 percent as Protestant, 5 percent as Muslim and 6 percent as 'other'. Ethnic and religious tensions certainly do exist. Approximately 56 per cent of the population has no religion. Many towns and cities have Roman Catholic, Protestant and Jewish services in English and a good website for information is www.expatica.com/nl/out-and-about/ places/Religious-services-in-English-in-the-Netherlands_101528.html.

S

Shopping

Amsterdam

Bargains are a rarity but browsing is fun, particularly in the markets and the small specialist shops. For general shopping the main streets are Kalverstraat and Nieuwendijk, for exclusive boutiques try P.C. Hooftstraat, and for the more offbeat shops, head to the Jordaan northwest of centre, where many local artists live. Two shopping malls are worth a visit: Magna Plaza opposite the Royal Palace and Kalvertoren on Kalverstraat. Most cities have branches of pocket-friendly Hema (www.hemashop.com) department store and Albert Heijn supermarkets.

The VVV Tourist Office produces brochures on shopping for antiques and diamonds. These give maps, route descriptions, places of interest and a list of addresses and shop specialities.

Antiques

Nieuwe Spiegelstraat (starting opposite the Rijksmuseum) is lined with small and immaculate antique shops. Look out for Old Dutch tiles, copper and brass, glass, pewter, snuff boxes, clocks and dolls. Respected dealers include Frides Lameris, Ines Stodel, Frans Leidelmeijer and Jaap Polak. In markets, beware of imitation antique copper and brass, made in Tunisia.

Art and prints

The major museums and art galleries, particularly the Stedelijk and Rijksmuseum, have excellent reproductions of paintings in their collections. There are numerous commercial galleries selling original oil paintings, watercolours, drawings, engravings and sculpture. For old prints and engravings, try Antiekcentrum de Looier, Elandsgracht 109, www.antiekcentrumamsterdam.nl.

Books

The city has an exceptionally large choice of books, both new and second-hand. For English-language books and newspapers go to the three-storey American Book Center (www.abc.nl) at Spui 1,2,5. Oudemanhuispoort Book Market is a treasure-trove of second-hand books, mainly in Dutch. Boekie Woekie, at Berenstraat 16, is the place to go for art books and Stadsboekwinkel, at Vijzelstraat 32, specialises in local history.

Clothes

The major department stores are around Kalverstraat and Nieuwendijk, but the biggest and most prestigious is De Bijenkorf, 1 Dam. For designer labels, try P.C. Hooftstraat, Rokin, Van Baerlestraat and Leidsestraat. For quirky boutiques, the Jordaan or the 'nine streets' side streets between the canals are the places to go. Also try Magna Plaza shopping mall opposite the Royal Palace or the Kalvertoren mall on Kalverstraat.

Jewellery

Jewellery shops all over town have eye-catching displays of modern and traditional pieces, some original and designed on the spot. Note: the fact that Amsterdam is a major diamond-cutting centre doesn't mean you'll get them cheap. For modern jewellery designs, visit Hans Appenzeller at Grimburgwal 1 or Anneke Schat at Spiegelgracht 20.

Porcelain

Cheap imitations of the familiar blue Delftware are sold all over town. The genuine article, always with a capital 'D', is sold at Royal Delft's official retail branch, De Porceleyne Fles, Muntplein 12 (daily 10am–5.30pm). For a huge range of antique tiles, try Eduard Kramer, Prinsengracht 807.

Markets

Amsterdam's street markets are a source of amusement and interest.
Flower market: Singel. Monday–Friday 9am–6pm, Saturday 9am–5pm. Probably Amsterdam's most famous market, housed in boats and bright with colours and perfumes even in the depths of winter. Prices are reasonable and quality is excellent.
Flea market: Waterlooplein. Monday–Saturday 10am–5pm. Lively and fun.
Farm produce: Noordermarkt or Oudemanhuispoort. Saturday 10am–4pm.
Book markets: Oudemanhuispoort. Monday–Saturday 10am–4pm. Unusual books and prints. Far more interesting is the extensive antiquarian book market, held every Friday 10am–6pm at Spui and during the summer one Sunday each month at Dam Square or next to the Muzeiktheater.

Stamp market: Nieuwezijds Voorburgwal. Wednesday and Saturday 1–4pm. Stamps and coins.
Open-air antiques market: Nieuwmarkt. Daily 9am–5pm May–September.
Antiques, curiosities and junk: 'De Looier', 109 Elandsgracht. Saturday–Thursday 11am–5pm. Indoor market.
Flea and textile market: Noordermarkt/Westerstraat. Monday 9am–1pm. An interesting mix of people and junk. Have a cup of coffee and a piece of apple cake at Winkel Café on the corner – some say it is the best in the city.
Art market: Thorbeckeplein. April–October Sunday 10.30am–6pm. Artists sell their own drawings and paintings – some of the work is very good.
General markets: Albert Cuypstraat: Monday–Saturday 9.30am–5pm; Westerstraat: Monday 9am–1pm.

Dordrecht

Dordrecht's open-air market, which operates every Friday and Saturday on Statenplein, and its three-day Christmas market in December with around 200 stalls, are generally regarded as the best markets in the country.

The Hague

The main shopping street is Grote Marktstraat. Here you will find the department store De Bijenkorf, notable for its fine architecture and interiors. Behind is a network of covered arcades lined with small and characterful shops. For art, antiques and cafés, go to Noordeinde. Stanley & Livingstone at Schoolstraat 21 is the place to go for travel books.

Rotterdam

In Rotterdam the better shops are concentrated around Lijnbaan and Binnenweigplein. Antiques, art and crafts can be found in the market on Mariniersweg, in the old port, on Tuesday and Saturday 9am–5pm and also in the museum quarter on side streets. Witte de Withstraat is where the hipsters head. The spectacular new Markthall at Jan Scharpstraat 298 is the place to go for food shopping.

Smoking

Smoking is banned in public places, on public transport and in hotels, bars, restaurants and cafés. Cannabis, but not tobacco, can be smoked in 'coffee shops'.

Student travellers

ISIC cards offer students many discounts in the Netherlands. You can find out more at www.isicnederland.nl/en/benefits-in-the-netherlands/

T

Telephones

Telephone boxes are green and take phonecards, which can be bought in denominations of €5, €10 and €20 (PKN or Telfort) from post offices, tobacco shops, VVVs and GWKs.

The main mobile networks are Ben, KPN, T-Mobile, Telfort, Tele2 and Vodafone. Phones work on the GSM system, which is compatible with the UK and Australia but not with many North American phones. It's best to check with your network provider before you leave the country. You can buy a pay-as-you go phone in the Netherlands for as little as €15 in the chain store Phone House or a SIM card with a Dutch number for €4 if you have an unlocked phone. You could also consider making calls via an internet service such as Skype.
Dialling codes when calling the Netherlands from abroad:
31 + 20 (Amsterdam), 70 (The Hague), 10 (Rotterdam)
Dialling codes when calling from the Netherlands:
First dial 00 then the country code then the number (minus 0):
Australia: 61
Canada: 1
Ireland: 353
New Zealand: 64
South Africa: 27
UK: 44
US: 1

Time zone

Netherlands: GMT +1 hour
Australia: GMT +10 hours (Sydney)
Canada: GMT -5 hours (Ottawa)
Ireland: GMT
New Zealand: GMT +12 hours (Auckland)
South Africa: GMT +2 hours (Cape Town)
UK: GMT
US: GMT -5 hours (New York)

Ticket offices

Amsterdam ticket offices
For most of Amsterdam's 12,000 annual concerts, theatre, ballet and opera performances, seats can be booked in advance at one of the VVV

information offices at Stationsplein 10. Open daily 9am–6pm. There is also a Visitor Centre at Schiphol Airport, open daily from 7am to 10pm.

There is a ticket office, Tours and Tickets, at Damrak 26 to book sightseeing tours, open from 7.30am to 10pm.

For free admission

The **Museum Card** (Museumkaart) allows free entry to more than 400 museums in the Netherlands. The card costs €54.95 for adults and €27.50 for under 18s. It is valid for one calendar year.

The card can be obtained at VVV tourist offices and many museums as well as at www.museumjaarkaart. nl. Special exhibitions with a separate admission charge may not be covered by the card.

Tourist information

Tourist information offices (Vereniging voor Vreemdelingenverkeer – or VVV for short) are clearly marked and usually located just outside the railway station in every main town and city. Here the multilingual staff will answer all your questions, provide maps and brochures, handle your accommodation bookings and reserve tickets for the theatre. But there is a charge for most of them. It is useful to carry passport-sized photographs for various identity cards you may purchase.

The Netherlands Board of Tourism website is www.holland.com. Offices can be found in:

UK: 2nd Floor, Portland House, Bressenden Place, London, SW1E 5RS.

US: 215 Park Avenue South, Suite 2005, New York, NY 10003.

The main tourist offices are:

VVV Amsterdam Tourist Office
Stationsplein 10 (white building across the road to the left outside Centraal Station); open daily 9am–6pm.
Tel: 020-702 6000; www.iamsterdam. com
There is also an office at Schiphol airport, in arrival hall 2 (open daily 7am–10pm).

Arnhem
Stationsplein 13
Tel: 900-112 2344
www.vvvarnhemnijmegen.nl

Assen
Markstraat 8
Tel: 059-224 3788
www.vvvassen.nl

Den Bosch
Markt 77
Tel: 073-612 7170
www.vvvdenbosch.nl

Eindhoven
Stationsplein 17
Tel: 900-112 2363
www.thisiseindhoven.nl

Groningen
Grote Markt 29
Tel: 050-313 9741
www.toerisme.groningen.nl

Leeuwarden
Sophialaan 4
Tel: 058-235 7550
www.vvvleeuwarden.nl

Lelystad
De Promesse 4
Tel: 088-008 0729
www.vvvlelystad.nl

Maastricht
Kleine Straat 1
Tel: 043-325 2121
www.vvvmaastricht.nl

Rotterdam
Coolsingel 195–197, open daily 9.30am–6pm.
Tel: 010-790 0185
www.rotterdam.info

The Hague
Spui 68, open Mon noon–8pm, Tue–Fri 10am–8pm, Sat–Sun 10am–5pm.
Tel: 070-361 8860
www.denhaag.com

Utrecht
Domplein 9.
Tel: 900-128 732
www.visit-utrecht.com

Regional tourist board websites:
Brabant www.visitbrabant.nl
Drenthe www.magischdrenthe.nl
Flevoland www.ookflevoland.nl
Friesland www.vlsltfryslan.nl
Limburg www.visitlimburg.nl
Zeeland www.vvvzeeland.nl

Tour operators and travel agents

If you're looking for a city break, compare prices at www.travel supermarket.com.

Boat Bike Tours
Tel: 029-931 3071
www.boatbiketours.com
Cycling and cruising holidays

CWGC
www.cwgc.org
Lists companies offering battlefield tours.

Dutch Bike Tours
Tel: 024-324 4712
www.dutchbiketours.com
Self-guided cycling holidays.

Ffestiniog Travel
Tel: 01766-772957
www.ffestiniogtravel.com
Tramways and steam train tours.

Great Rail
Tel: 0800-140 4444
www.greatrail.com

Escorted holidays by train.

HF Holidays
Tel: 0345-4708558
www.hfholidays.co.uk
Cycling and barging holidays.

Inntravel
Tel: 01653-617001
www.inntravel.co.uk
Cycling holidays.

Kirker Holidays
Tel: 0207-593 1899.
www.kirkerholidays.com
Upmarket cultural breaks.

Lindbergh Tour and Travel
Damrak 26, Amsterdam
Tel: 020-622 2766
www.lindbergh.nl
Day trips throughout the country.

Shearings
Tel: 0844-824 6351
www.shearings.com
Escorted holidays by coach.

Travel Editions
Tel: 0207-251 0045
www.traveleditions.co.uk
Escorted art and history tours.

V

Value added tax

Tourists from non-European Union countries are entitled to claim back the 21 percent local value added tax (BTW) on any goods purchased with a value of over €50 in the same store on the same day. Upon purchasing the item the shopkeeper has to fill in a Tax Free Form. When leaving the Netherlands the form is handed to Dutch customs, who will then stamp it (you will need to have your receipts and purchases with you). You can then get your refund at the Global Blue desk or the Premier Tax Free desk, depending on which company has issued your form.

Visas and passports

Visitors from the European Union, the US, Canada, Australia, New Zealand and most other European and Commonwealth countries require only a passport for stays of less than 90 days. Citizens of most other countries must obtain a visa in advance from a Dutch Embassy or Consulate.

W

Weights and measures

The Netherlands follows the metric system:
1 kg = 2 lbs 7 oz
1 km = 0.6 miles

LANGUAGE

UNDERSTANDING THE LANGUAGE

DUTCH PRONUNCIATION

Eavesdropping on any Dutch conversation, you could be forgiven for thinking that Dutch people constantly need to clear their throat! This Germanic language regularly uses a guttural consonant similar to the 'ch' in the Scottish word 'loch'. In Dutch terms this is known as the 'soft g', although the 'hard g' sounds almost the same – if you look at Dutch words that begin with a 'g', then you can make a reasonable assumption that the word starts with that infamous 'ch'". If you wish to greet someone with a *goedemorgen* (good morning); pronouncing the first or second 'g' without the 'ch' sound will identify you as German. Don't worry about being wrongly identified though; any attempt you may make at speaking Dutch will be received as a compliment by this multi-lingual people.

To this end, here are a few tips on Dutch pronunciation:

Consonants

As a rule, the 'hard consonants' such as t, k, s and p are pronounced almost the same as in English, but sometimes a little softer. For example, the Dutch would refer to little as 'liddle'.
j is pronounced as a *y (ja* meaning yes is pronounced *ya)*
v is pronounced as f *(vis* meaning fish is pronounced *fiss)*
je is pronounced as *yer*
tje is pronounced as *ch (botje* meaning little bone is pronounced *botchyer)*

Vowels

ee is pronounced as *ay (nee* meaning no is pronounced *nay)*
oo is pronounced as *o (hoop* meaning hope is also pronounced as *hope)*
ij is pronounced as *eay (ijs* meaning ice cream is pronounced *ace)*
a is pronounced as *u (bank* also meaning bank is pronounced as *bunk).*

DUTCH WORDS AND PHRASES

How much is it? *Hoeveel is het?/ Hoeveel kost dit?*
What is your name? *Wat is uw naam?*
My name is... *Mijn naam is .../Ik heet ...*
Do you speak English? *Spreekt u Engels?*
I am English/American *Ik ben Engelsman/Amerikaan*
I don't understand *Ik begrijp het niet*
Please speak more slowly *Kunt u langzamer praten, alstublieft*
Can you help me? *Kunt u mij helpen?*
I'm looking for... *Ik zoek...*
Where is...? *Waar is...?*
I'm sorry *Excuseer/Pardon*
I don't know *Ik weet het niet*
No problem *Geen probleem*
Have a good day! *Prettige dag nog!*
That's it *Precies*
Here it is *Het is hier*
There it is *Het is daar*
Let's go *Kom/We zijn weg*
See you tomorrow *Tot morgen*
See you soon *Tot straks!*
please *alstublieft*
At what time? *Hoe laat?*
When? *Wanneer?*
What time is it? *Hoe laat is het?*

yes *ja*
no *neen*
please *alstublieft*
thank you *dank u*
(very much) *(wel)*
you're welcome *graag gedaan*
excuse me *excuseer/pardon*
hello *hallo*
goodbye *tot ziens*
good evening *Goeden avond*
here *hier*
there *daar*
today *vandaag*
yesterday *gisteren*
tomorrow *morgen*
now *nu*
later *later*
right away *direct/onmiddellijk*
this morning *vanmorgen*
this afternoon *deze namiddag*
this evening *vanavond*

ON THE ROAD

Where is the spare wheel? *Waar is het reservewiel?*
Where is the nearest garage? *Waar is de dichtstbijzijnde garage?*
Our car has broken down *Onze auto is in panne*
I want to have my car repaired *Ik wil mijn auto laten herstellen*
the road to... *de straat naar...*
left *links*
right *rechts*
straight on *rechtstreeks*
far/near *ver/nabij*
opposite *tegenover*
beside *naast*
car park *de parking*
over there *daar*
at the end *aan het eind*
on foot *te voet*
by car *met de auto*
town map *het stadplan*
road map *de (wegen)kaart*

street *de straat*
square *het plein*
give way *geef voorrang*
dead end *doodlopende straat*
no parking *verboden te parkeren*
motorway *de autosnelweg*
toll *de tol*
speed limit *de snelheids-beperking*
petrol *de benzine*
unleaded *loodvrij*
diesel *de diesel*
water/oil *water/olie*
puncture *een lekke band*
wipers *ruitewissers*

SHOPPING

Where is the nearest bank/post office? *Waar is de dichtstbijzijnde bank/het dichtstbijzijnde postkantoor?*
I'd like to buy... *Ik zou graag ... kopen*
How much is it? *Hoeveel is het?/ Hoeveel kost het?*
Do you take credit cards? *Neemt u crediet kaarten?*
Have you got? *Hebt u...?*
I'll take it *Ik neem het*
I'll take this one/that one *Ik neem dit/deze*
What size is it? *Welke maat is het?*
Anything else? *Iets anders?*
size *de maat*
cheap *goedkoop*
expensive *duur*
enough *genoeg*
too much *te veel*
a piece *een stuk*
each *per stuk*
bill *de rekening*
chemist *de apotheek*
bakery *de bakkerij*
bookshop *de boekhandel*
delicatessen *delicatessen*
department store *het warenhuis*
fishmonger *de viswinkel*
grocery *de kruidenier*
tobacconist *de tabakwinkel*
market *de markt*
supermarket *de supermarkt*
junk shop *brocante/antiquiteiten*

SIGHTSEEING

town *de stad*
old town *de oude stad*
abbey *de abdij*
cathedral *de kathedraal*
church *de kerk*
keep *de slottoren*
mansion *het herenhuis*
hospital *het ziekenhuis*
town hall *het stadhuis*
nave *het schip*
stained glass *het glasraam*
staircase *de trap*

tower *de toren*
walk *de tour*
country house/castle *het kasteel*
museum *het museum*
art gallery *de galerie*
exhibition *de tentoonstelling*
tourist information office *het bureau voor toerisme (VVV)*
free *gratis*
open *open*
closed *gesloten*
every day *elke dag*
all year *het hele jaar*
all day *de hele dag*
swimming pool *het zwembad*
to book *reserveren/boeken*

DINING OUT

breakfast *het ontbijt*
lunch *lunch/middageten*
dinner *diner/avondeten*
meal *de maaltijd*
first course *het voorgerecht/entrée*
main course *het hoofdgerecht*
drink included *drank inbegrepen*
wine list *de wijnkaart*
the bill *de rekening*
fork *het vork*
knife *het mes*
spoon *de lepel*
plate *het bord*
glass *het glas*
napkin *het servet*
I am a vegetarian *Ik ben vegetarier*
I am on a diet *Ik volg een dieet*
What do you recommend? *Wat beveelt u aan?*
I'd like to order *Ik wil bestellen*
That is not what I ordered *Dit is niet wat ik besteld heb*
Is service included? *Is de dienst inbegrepen?*

MENU DECODER

Breakfast and snacks

boter **butter**
boterham **bread with butter**
brood **bread**
broodjes **rolls**
eieren **eggs**
...met spek **bacon and eggs**
...met ham **ham and eggs**
spiegeleieren **fried eggs**
roerei **scrambled eggs**
zacht gekooktei **soft-boiled eggs**
honing **honey**
confitur **jam**
pannekoek **pancake**
peper **pepper**
stokbrood **long thin loaf**
joghurt **yoghurt**
zout **salt**
suiker **sugar**

Vlees/Meat

biefstuk **steak**
brochette **kebab**
carbonnade **casserole of beef, beer and onions**
eend **duck**
eendenborst **breast of duck**
escargot/slak **snail**
gebraad **roast**
gegrild **grilled**
gegrild vlees **grilled meat**
gehakt **minced meat**
gevuld **stuffed**
goedgebakken **well done**
ham **ham**
kalfslever **calf's liver**
kalfsvlees **veal**
kalkoen **turkey**
kikkerbillen **frog's legs**
kip **chicken**
konijn **rabbit**
kuiken **young chicken**
lams vlees **lamb**
lamskotelet **lamb chop**
lendestuk **sirloin**
lendebiefstuk **cut of sirloin steak**
lever **liver**
niertjes **kidneys**
spek **small pieces of bacon, often added to salads**
stoofpot **casserole of beef and vegetables**
tong **tongue**
varkens vlees **pork**

Vis/Fish

ansjovis **anchovies**
calamars/inktvis **squid**
daurade **sea bream**
forel **trout**
garnaal **shrimp**
griet **brill**
haring **herring**
heilbot **halibut**
kabeljauw **cod**
koolvis **hake**
kreeft **lobster**
langoestine **large prawn**
limande **lemon sole**
lotte **monkfish**
mosselen **mussels**
oester **oyster**
paling **eel**
rogge **skate**
schaaldier **shellfish**
sint-jakobsschelp **scallops**
toniin **tuna**
zeebaars **sea bass**
zeevruchten **seafood**
zalm **salmon**

Groenten/Vegetables

aardappel **potato**
ajuin/ui **onion**

TRANSPORT

A – Z

LANGUAGE

artisjok **artichoke**
asperge **asparagus**
aubergine **eggplant**
augurk **gherkin**
avocado **avocado**
biet **turnip**
bloemkool **cauliflower**
boon **dried bean**
champignon **mushroom**
cantharel (dooierzwam) **wild mushroom**
chips **potato crisps**
courgette **zucchini**
erwten **peas**
frieten **chips, French fries**
gemengde sla **mixed-leaf salad**
groene bonen **green beans**
groene sla **green salad**
komkommer **cucumber**
kool **cabbage**
linzen **lentils**
look **garlic**
mais **corn**
noot/walnoot **nut, walnut**
paprika **bell pepper**
peterselie **parsley**
pijnpitten **pine nut**
prei **leek**
radijs **radish**
rauw **raw**
rijst **rice**
selder **celery**
spinazie **spinach**
tomaat **tomato**
witloof **chicory**
witte peen **parsnip**

Vruchter/Fruit

aardbei **strawberry**
ananas **pineapple**
appel **apple**
citroen **lemon**
druiven **grapes**
framboos **raspberry**
grapefruit **grapefruit**
kers **cherry**
limoen **lime**
mango **mango**
meloen **melon**
perzik **peach**
peer **pear**
pruim **prune**
vijg **fig**

Puddings

gebak/taart **cake**
geitenkaas **goat's cheese**
kaas **cheese**
slagroom **whipped cream**

Dranken/Drinks

beer *bier*
bottled *een fles*
on tap *van het vat*

coffee *koffie*
with milk or cream *met melk of room*
decaffeinated *decafeine*
black/espresso *zwart/espresso*
American filtered *filterkoffie*
cold *koud*
fizzy lemonade *limonade*
lemon juice *citroensap*
orange juice *sinaasappelsap*
fresh *vers*
full (e.g. full-cream milk) *volle melk*
hot chocolate *warme chocolademelk*
house wine *huiswijn*
milk *melk*
mineral water *mineraalwater*
fizzy *spuitwater/Spa rood*
non-fizzy *plat water/Spa blauw*
pitcher *karaf*
of water/wine *water/wijn*
red *rood*
rose *rosé*
sparkling wine *schuimwijn*
sweet *zacht*
tea *thee*
herb infusion *kruidenthee*
camomile *kamille*
white *wit*
with ice *met ijs*

USEFUL PHRASES

Help! *Help!*
Call a doctor *Bel een dokter*
Call an ambulance *Bel een ziekenwagen*
Call the police *Bel de politie*
Call the fire brigade *Bel de brandweer*
Where is the nearest telephone? *Waar is de dichtstbijzijnde telefoon?*
Where is the nearest hospital? *Waar is het dichtstbijzijnde ziekenhuis?*
I am sick *Ik ben ziek*
I have lost my passport/purse *Ik ben mijn paspoort/portemonnee kwijt/verloren*
How do I make an outside call? *Hoe krijg ik een buitenlijn?*
I want to make an international (local) call *Ik wil naar het buitenland bellen*
What is the dialling code? *Wat is het zonenummer/landnummer?*
I'd like an alarm call for 8 o'clock tomorrow morning *Ik wil om 8 uur gewekt worden*
Who's calling? *Met wie spreek ik?*
Hold on, please *Blijf aan de lijn, alstublieft*
The line is busy *De lijn is in gesprek*
I have dialled the wrong number *Ik heb een verkeerd nummer gedraaid*

NUMBERS

0 *nul*
1 *één*
2 *twee*
3 *drie*
4 *vier*
5 *vijf*
6 *zes*
7 *zeven*
8 *acht*
9 *negen*
10 *tien*
11 *elf*
12 *twaalf*
13 *dertien*
14 *veertien*
15 *vijfteen*
16 *zestien*
17 *zeventien*
18 *achttien*
19 *negentien*
20 *twintig*
30 *dertig*
40 *veertig*
50 *vijftig*
60 *zestig*
70 *zeventig*
80 *tachtig*
90 *negentig*
100 *honderd*
200 *tweehonderd*
500 *vijfhonderd*
1,000 *duizend*

MONTHS AND SEASONS

January *Januari*
February *Februari*
March *Maart*
April *April*
May *Mei*
June *Juni*
July *Juli*
August *Augustus*
September *September*
October *Oktober*
November *November*
December *December*
Spring *de lente*
Summer *de zomer*
Autumn *de herfst*
Winter *de winter*

DAYS OF THE WEEK

Monday *Maandag*
Tuesday *Dinsdag*
Wednesday *Woensdag*
Thursday *Donderdag*
Friday *Vrijdag*
Saturday *Zaterdag*
Sunday *Zondag*

FURTHER READING

GENERAL AND FICTION

Why the Dutch Are Different: A Journey into the Hidden Heart of the Netherlands by Ben Coates. What makes the Dutch Dutch? Why are the Dutch the world's tallest people? The author explores his adopted homeland.

Girl With a Pearl Earring by Tracy Chevalier. Novel (and film) based on Vermeer's life in 17th-century Delft.

Dutch Painting by R.H. Fuchs. A condensed though comprehensive overview of Dutch painting from the Middle Ages to the present.

A Street in Arnhem by Robert Kershaw. Compelling docudrama about the Battle of Arnhem from the perspective of the Dutch inhabitants and British and German soldiers in one street.

Amsterdam – A Brief Life in the City by Geert Mak. Part history, part travel guide, Mak's book traces the city's progress from a little town of merchants and fishermen into a thriving metropolis.

Tulip Fever by Deborah Moggach. Atmospheric novel about a love triangle featuring art and tulips in 17th-century Amsterdam.

The Light of Amsterdam by David Park. Engrossing novel about three sets of lives that become intertwined on a weekend break to Amsterdam.

The Dutch Revolt by Geoffrey Parker. A brilliant picture of the character of the Dutch in their revolt against the Spanish overlords during the Eighty Years War (1568–1648).

The Tulip by Anna Pavord. Not just a horticultural examination of an extraordinary flower, but also a fantastic piece of sociological and historical research, revealing the tulip's turbulent past.

Dutch Art and Architecture 1600–1800 by Jakob Rosenberg. A standard work, first published in 1966 and rewritten by popular demand, with new insights. especially into the works of Hals and Rembrandt. Richly illustrated but in monochrome.

A Bridge too Far by Cornelius Ryan. Operation Market Garden, the Allied invasion of Nazi-occupied Holland in September 1944, led to the bloody and abortive battle to capture the strategic bridge over the Rhine at Arnhem. Ryan's meticulous account brings into clear focus both the heroism and the tragedy of those desperate weeks.

The Embarrassment of Riches by Simon Schama. An academic but very readable insight into culture and society during Holland's Golden Age.

Rembrandt's Eyes by Simon Schama. A fitting tribute to the artist who could turn the most formal portrait into what Schama terms 'a statement of intimacy'. Schama recreates not only the socio-political circumstances of Rembrandt's world but also its sights, sounds and smells.

Amsterdam: A History of the World's Most Liberal City by Russell Shorto. Focuses on the Golden Age and from World War II to the present day.

The Low Sky: Understanding the Dutch by Han Vander Horst. This thoughtful book investigates below the surface, into modern Holland's dilemmas and taboos.

The Undutchables by Colin White and Laurie Boucke. An irreverent, often accurate, though cliché-ridden, observation of the Dutch and their habits.

The Van Gogh File by Ken Wilkie. A journalist and Van Gogh enthusiast travels in the footsteps of Van Gogh through Holland, Belgium, England and France. Along the way, Wilkie discovers a genuine drawing by Van Gogh and uncovers intriguing insights into the artist's life.

Send Us Your Thoughts

We do our best to ensure the information in our books is as accurate and up-to-date as possible. The books are updated on a regular basis using local contacts, who painstakingly add, amend and correct as required. However, some details (such as telephone numbers and opening times) are liable to change, and we are ultimately reliant on our readers to put us in the picture.

We welcome your feedback, especially your experience of using the book "on the road". Maybe we recommended a hotel that you liked (or another that you didn't), or you came across a great bar or new attraction we missed.

We will acknowledge all contributions, and we'll offer an Insight Guide to the best letters received.

Please write to us at:
Insight Guides
PO Box 7910
London SE1 1WE
Or email us at:
hello@insightguides.com

OTHER INSIGHT GUIDES

Insight Guides comprehensively cover other Western European countries and regions include *Western Europe*, *Germany*, *Scandinavia*, *France*, *Great Britain* and *Italy*.

Insight Explore Guides advise on the best and most rewarding things to see, including up to 20 tailor-made itineraries exploring the main attractions. Western Europe titles include *Amsterdam*, *Bruges*, *Copenhagen*, *Berlin*, *Paris* and *London*.

Insight Fleximaps combine clear detailed cartography with essential travel information. The laminated finish makes the maps durable, waterproof and easy to fold. Titles in the region include: *Amsterdam*, *Bruges*, *Brussels*, *Paris* and *Berlin*.

CREDITS

Photo Credits

Alamy 10BL, 97
Allard Bovenberg/AFF/AFHí 6BL
FLPA 275TR
Getty Images 8M, 10TR, 18, 23,
26/27, 28, 31, 32, 33, 34, 35, 36,
37, 38, 39, 40, 41, 42, 44, 45, 46,
47, 48, 49, 50, 51, 52, 53, 54, 55,
56, 57, 58, 59, 60, 61, 63, 66, 67,
68, 69, 70, 71, 72, 73, 74, 75, 76,
80, 82, 84, 93, 108, 154BL, 155BL,
155ML, 155BR, 207, 219, 224,
228, 232, 233, 252/253T, 252BR,
253TR, 256, 258
Greg Gladman/Apa Publications
8BL, 10TL, 11ML, 101, 110R, 110L,
111R, 112, 134, 135, 136, 139,
140, 146, 153, 155MR
iStock 6MR, 7TR, 11BR, 109, 113,
274/275T, 274BL, 275ML, 319

NBTC 1, 6ML, 6BR, 7MR, 7ML, 7BR,
7TL, 8BR, 9BL, 9TR, 9BR, 11TR,
86/87T, 86BR, 86BL, 87ML, 87BR,
87BL, 87TR, 90, 94, 95, 96R, 96L,
98, 99, 100, 102, 103, 104, 105,
106, 107, 111L, 114, 115R, 115L,
142, 151, 152, 154/155T, 154BR,
155TR, 169, 170, 171, 177, 183,
197, 203, 204, 208, 209, 231, 237,
247, 249, 262, 264, 274BR, 275BL
Public domain 88, 89, 91, 92, 176,
195
Shutterstock 4/5, 7ML, 12/13,
14/15, 16/17, 19B, 19T, 20, 21,
22, 24, 25, 29, 30, 43, 62, 64/65,
77, 78, 79, 81, 83, 85, 116/117,
118/119, 120/121, 122, 123T,
123B, 128, 129, 130, 131, 132,
133, 137, 138, 141, 143, 144, 145,

147, 148, 149, 150, 156, 157, 159,
160, 162, 163, 164, 165, 166, 167,
172, 173, 175, 178, 179, 180, 181,
182, 184, 185, 187, 188, 189, 190,
191, 193, 194, 196, 198, 199, 201,
202, 205, 206, 211, 212, 213, 214,
215, 216, 217, 218, 222, 223, 225,
226, 227, 229, 230, 234, 235, 236,
238, 239, 240, 241, 243, 244, 245,
246, 248, 252BL, 253ML,
252/253B, 252, 253, 255, 257,
259, 260, 261, 263, 265, 266, 267,
268, 269, 271, 272, 273, 275BR,
276, 277, 279, 280, 281, 282, 283,
284, 285, 286, 287, 288, 289, 290,
291, 292, 293, 294, 295, 296, 297,
298, 299, 300, 302, 303, 304, 306,
307, 310, 316

Cover Credits

Front cover: Windmill with tulip field
Shutterstock
Back cover: Begijnhof *Shutterstock*
Front flap: (from top) Heusden,
Shutterstock; Van Gogh poster
Shutterstock; clogs *Shutterstock*;

cyclists in Veluwezoom *Shutterstock*
Back flap: Cycling in the woods
Shutterstock

Insight Guide Credits

Distribution
UK, Ireland and Europe
Apa Publications (UK) Ltd;
sales@insightguides.com
United States and Canada
Ingram Publisher Services;
ips@ingramcontent.com
Australia and New Zealand
Woodslane; info@woodslane.com.au
Southeast Asia
Apa Publications (SN) Pte;
singaporeoffice@insightguides.com
Hong Kong, Taiwan and China
Apa Publications (HK) Ltd;
hongkongoffice@insightguides.com
Worldwide
Apa Publications (UK) Ltd;
sales@insightguides.com
Special Sales, Content Licensing and CoPublishing
Insight Guides can be purchased in bulk quantities at discounted prices. We can create special editions, personalised jackets and corporate imprints tailored to your needs.
sales@insightguides.com
www.insightguides.biz

Printing
CTPS-China

All Rights Reserved

Every effort has been made to provide accurate information in this publication, but changes are inevitable. The publisher cannot be responsible for any resulting loss, inconvenience or injury. We would appreciate it if readers would call our attention to any errors or outdated information. We also welcome your suggestions; please contact us at:
hello@insightguides.com

www.insightguides.com

Editor: Sarah Clark
Author: Victoria Trott
Head of Production: Rebeka Davies
Pictures: Tom Smyth & Dickie Cooke
Cartography: Gar Bowes Design, updated by Carte

Legend

City maps

	Freeway/Highway/Motorway
	Divided Highway
	Main Roads
	Minor Roads
	Pedestrian Roads
	Steps
	Footpath
	Railway
	Funicular Railway
	Cable Car
	Tunnel
	City Wall
	Important Building
	Built Up Area
	Other Land
	Transport Hub
	Park
	Pedestrian Area
	Bus Station
	Tourist Information
	Main Post Office
	Cathedral/Church
	Mosque
	Synagogue
	Statue/Monument
	Beach
	Airport

Regional maps

	Freeway/Highway/Motorway (with junction)
	Freeway/Highway/Motorway (under construction)
	Divided Highway
	Main Road
	Secondary Road
	Minor Road
	Track
	Footpath
	International Boundary
	State/Province Boundary
	National Park/Reserve
	Marine Park
	Ferry Route
	Marshland/Swamp
	Glacier Salt Lake
	Airport/Airfield
	Ancient Site
	Border Control
	Cable Car
	Castle/Castle Ruins
	Cave
	Chateau/Stately Home
	Church/Church Ruins
	Crater
	Lighthouse
	Mountain Peak
	Place of Interest
	Viewpoint

Contributors

This comprehensively updated major new edition of *Insight Guides: The Netherlands* was revised by travel writer **Victoria Trott**, who has previously worked on several other Western European titles for Insight Guides. It was commissioned and edited by **Sarah Clark**.

This book builds on the earlier work of **Joan Gannij**, **Frank Balleny**, **George McDonald**, **Derek Blyth**, **Michael Gray**, **Lisa Gerard-Sharp**, **Tim Harper** and **Joan Corcoran-Lonis**.

Thanks go to **Penny Phenix**, who proofread and indexed this edition.

About Insight Guides

Insight Guides have more than 40 years' experience of publishing high-quality, visual travel guides. We produce 400 full-colour titles, in both print and digital form, covering more than 200 destinations across the globe, in a variety of formats to meet your different needs.

Insight Guides are written by local authors, whose expertise is evident in the extensive historical and cultural background features.

Each destination is carefully researched by regional experts to ensure our guides provide the very latest information. All the reviews in **Insight Guides** are independent; we strive to maintain an impartial view. Our reviews are carefully selected to guide you to the best places to eat, go out and shop, so you can be confident that when we say a place is special, we really mean it.

INDEX

Main references are in bold type

Amsterdam

Nieuwpoortstr.

Haarlemmerweg

Haarlemmervaart

Haarlemmerweg

Westergasfabriek

Realengracht

Nwe Teertuinen

Prinseneiland

Bickersgracht

Grote Bickersstr.

Jan Jonkerpl.

Haarlemmer Houttuinen

Nassau plein

Haarlemmer plein

BEGRAAF-PLAATS VREDENHOF

Sportpark V. Hogendorpstraat

Sporthal

Groothandelsmarkt

FREDERIK HENDRIK-PLANTSOEN

Noordermarkt

Noorderkerk

Hofje De St

Zon's Hofje

Claes Claesz Anslo Hofje

Raep Hofje

Tulip Museum

Anne Frank Huis

Westerkerk

Rozen-Theater

Suiker-Hof

Felix Meritis

Amst Hi

OUD-WEST

Da Costapl.

Kinder-Boerderij

Stadsdeel. Oud-west

Bellamy-plein

Kwakers-plein

De Looier

Hoofdbureau Van Politie

Openbare Bibliotheek

Paleis van Justitie

De Melkweg

Bellevue

De La Mar Theater

Paris

Max Euwepl.

De Balie

Amphitheater

Helmers-plein

Overtoom

Vondel-Kerk

Zeven Landen

Filmmuseum

Rijksmuseum

Van Gogh Museum

Stedelijk Museum

Museum-plein

Concertgebouw